COSMÈ TURA OF FERRARA

COSMÈ TURA

OF FERRARA

Style, Politics and the Renaissance City, 1450–1495

STEPHEN J. CAMPBELL

YALE UNIVERSITY PRESS

New Haven and London

Publication of this book has been aided by a grant from
the Millard Meiss Publication Fund
of the College Art Association of America

Designed by Gillian Malpass

Printed in Singapore

Library of Congress Cataloging-in-Publication Data

Campbell, Stephen J. (Stephen John), 1963–
Cosmè Tura of Ferrara: style, politics, and the renaissance city, 1450–1495/Stephen J. Campbell.
p.   cm.
Includes bibliographical references and index.
ISBN 0–300–07219–8 (cloth: alk. paper)
1. Tura, Cosmè, ca. 1430–1495 – Criticism and interpretation.   I. Title.
ND623.T97C36   1998
759.5 – dc21   97-46071
                                                                     CIP

A catalogue record for this book is available from
The British Library

Frontispiece: Tura, *Virgin Annunciate*. London, National Gallery.
Detail of plate 78.

This book is dedicated to
IAN *and* MARCELLA CAMPBELL
and to
JOHN PAUL CLARK

CONTENTS

facing page   Tura, *St Anthony of Padua*. Detail of plate 50.

facing page   Tura, *Pietà*. Detail of plate 8.

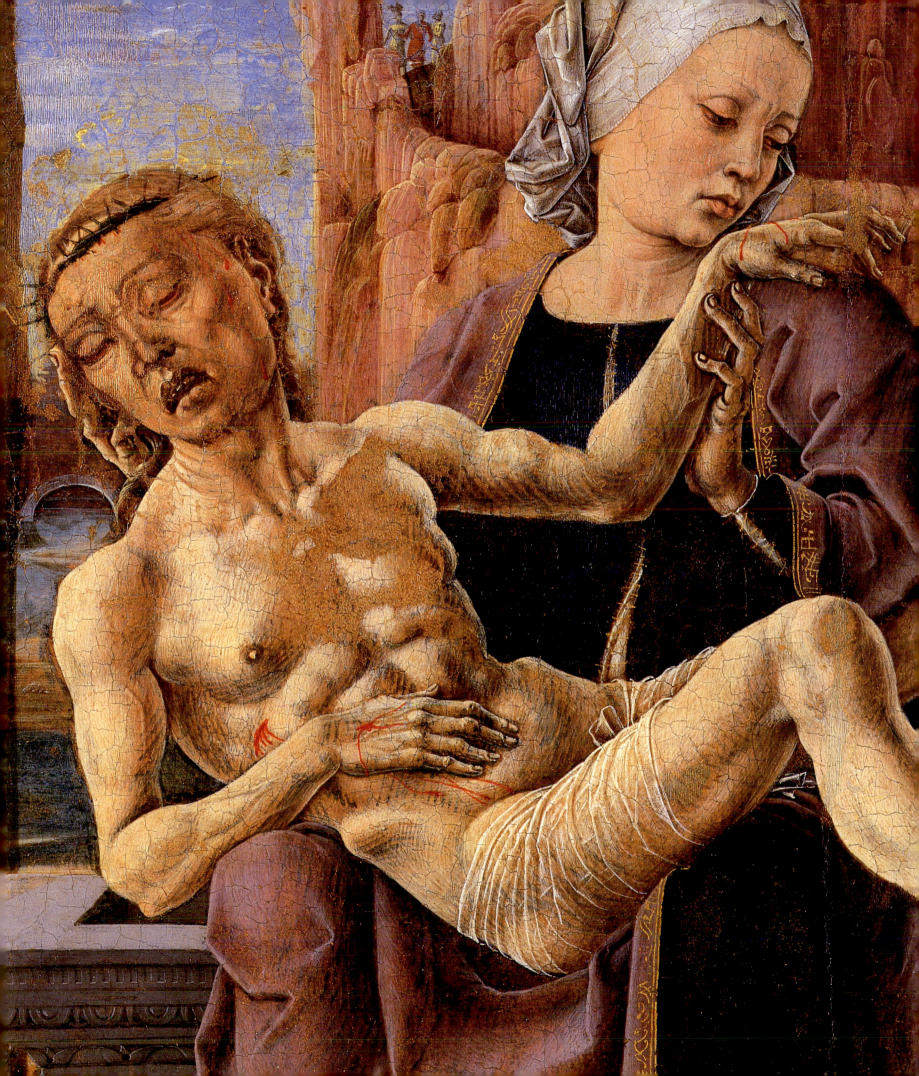

ACKNOWLEDGEMENTS

MORE THAN TEN YEARS AGO, when seeking advice regarding the viability of the Ferrarese *quattrocento* as a research project, I was told that the subject had 'received as much attention as it has deserved'. I remained convinced that there was room for a book on Ferrara, and its greatest fifteenth-century painter, which might address the question that must occur to anyone who ever gives more than a passing glance to a work by Tura or his contemporaries: why does Ferrarese painting look as it does? As it turned out, it would be my good fortune to be pondering this question at a time when Ferrarese studies were undergoing a significant re-invigoration, and not just within the field of art history. A number of significant exhibitions, conferences and publications have made the past decade a lively one for scholarship in Ferrarese literature, politics, religion, court and city culture, not to mention – within art history – the ongoing technical examination of Ferrarese painting. The quincentennial of Tura's death passed unmarked in 1995, but the omission will be made good to some extent in 1998 in Ferrara, with a joint commemoration of the deaths of Tura and Ercole de' Roberti.

My doctoral dissertation, completed in 1993, was informed by many of these developments, and this book has sought to keep pace with them. New data on Tura's distinctive technique – his use of oil medium and his practice as a draughtsman – is still emerging. One of the aims of this book is to illustrate the visible results of the recent cleaning of his works together in one volume. The publication of high-quality colour illustrations would not have been possible without a Millard Meiss Publication Grant from the College Art Association, and a subvention from the office of the Vice Provost for Research at The University of Michigan. From 1994 to 1995 I held a Theodore Rousseau Post-Doctoral Fellowship from The Metropolitan Museum of Art, New York, which facilitated new research and writing and enabled me to establish the basic form of this book. Encouragement in developing the text came from my adviser, Charles Dempsey, Carl Strehlke of The Philadelphia Museum of Art, and Keith Christiansen at The Metropolitan Museum of Art, New York. Other scholars who provided intellectual support and valuable information include Giovanni Agosti, Andrea Bacchi, Patricia Fortini Brown, Elizabeth Cropper, Jill Dunkerton, Caroline Elam, Diane Owen Hughes, Herbert Kessler, Kristen Lippincott, Mary Pardo, Pat Simons, Thomas Tuohy and Richard Stemp. In undertaking research in Ferrara, I could not have managed without the generosity of Don. Enrico Peverada of the Archivio Diocesano. Special thanks are due also to Paolo Bianchi and Gian Antonio Fabbri of the Cassa di Risparmio di Ferrara; I would like to thank also the staff of the State Archives in Ferrara and Modena and of the Biblioteca Comunale Ariostaea, Ferrara, and I doubt that this book could have been written without the resources of the Kunsthistorisches Institut in Florence.

In the process of writing and editing, support and criticism was provided by friends and colleagues in Baltimore, Florence and Ann Arbor; these include Alison Cornish, Giancarlo Fiorenza, Luca Gatti, David Gillerman, Maria Gough, Maria Fabricius Hansen, Morten Steen Hansen, Florian Härb, Megan Holmes, Stanko Kokole, Paolo Squatriti, and Jacob Wamberg. Andrew Kelly helped with the translations from Latin. For assistance in obtaining photographs I am particularly grateful to Corinna Giudici, Marvin Eisenberg, Lelia Raley, and Erich Schlier. A final but heartfelt word of appreciation must go to Gillian Malpass of Yale University Press, for her enthusiasm, patience and encouragement, as well as to Ruth Thackeray, a diligent and sympathetic copy-editor.

Ann Arbor, September 1997.

facing page   Tura, *Lamentation over the Dead Christ*. Detail of plate 85.

1 Letter of Cosmè Tura to Ercole d'Este, 9 January 1490. Modena, Archivio di Stato, Archivi per materie, *Arti belli, pittori*, Busta 16/4.

THE PAINTER, SOCIAL IDENTITY
AND CULTURAL POLITICS

Truly, Illustrious Prince and my Most Excellent Lord, my industry does not support me. I do not know how I shall be able to live and survive in this manner since I do not have the occupation or resources to sustain myself along with my household, apart from what I have earned from my daily labour and skill in painting. I find myself gravely ill with a sickness from which I cannot recover without considerable time and expense, as perhaps Your Excellency knows. I tell you this having six years ago made an altarpiece at my own expense in gold, colours and painting for Francesco Nasello, secretary to Your Excellency, which is in the church of San Niccolò in Ferrara, and from which sixty ducats is owing to me; and having similarly painted for the most Reverend and Illustrious Monsignor of Adria a *Saint Anthony of Padua* and certain other things for which remains a debt to me of twenty-five ducats. I cannot receive satisfaction, which is certainly neither honest nor fair, all the more so because they are powerful and very well have the means to settle and I am poor and helpless and cannot afford to lose the rewards of my labour. For this reason I have humble recourse to you and I implore you, as that one who has graciously deigned to give me satisfaction for the works I did for him, to deign in whatever honourable and appropriate way you see fit to have the aforementioned instructed to give me full satisfaction without more words and delays. This truly settles the claim of payment.[1] And so even if they do not wish to do so for the sake of honour, may Your Excellency subject them to such an order that they will requite me for the sake of obligation. To whose grace I now recommend myself humbly.

Ferrara, 9 January 1490
Your excellency's most faithful servant,
Cosmus Pictor

READERS OF THIS BOOK will probably be familiar with the painter Cosmè Tura from the fragments of his work preserved in several European and North American collections. Viewers tend to have strong reactions to Tura's painting; while most literature on the artist is written in a spirit of admiration or fascination, some more spontaneous reactions reveal a sense of shock, even repulsion.[2] Tura's art seems calculated to produce extreme responses, and to make extraordinary bids to claim the viewer's attention: rich and jewel-like colours in frequently unorthodox tonalities, the reduction of all texture, whether of cloth, flesh or stone, to a gleaming hardness, a constant proposing and undermining of symmetry in the arrangement of form and colour, incongruous and irreverent detail, and above all an incisive, wiry outline which becomes particularly assertive in the rendering of drapery. These qualities have become still more evident following an international campaign of cleaning and restoration since the 1980s, much of it completed by 1995, the 500th anniversary of the artist's death.[3]

The curiosity which Tura's painting seems designed to arouse might direct one to seek out more information, and anyone who does so (as I once did, several years before beginning this book) will find that Tura has been far from neglected in the specialist literature. What will not be found, however, is any systematic or convincing attempt to consider the most fundamental question provoked by this body of work. To put it bluntly, why did Tura paint as he did? Why would an artist working in northern Italy in the second half of the fifteenth century have adopted such a blatantly attention-seeking strategy (which is presumably what still leads scholars to study Tura in the first place)? But such questions have been deemed somehow improper, or impossible, in the scholarly tradition which has dealt with Tura. Style is what engages us, but style is usually seen as symptomatic of nothing other than the artist's uniqueness, his eccentricity, or his absorbtion of more powerful artistic influences. Scholarship frustratingly reproduces the museum's more justifiable isolation of the object from history; in all the diligent and responsible scholarship on Tura, in fact, there has been very little attempt to conceive Tura as a historical figure. By this I do not mean that what is lacking is a properly biographical consideration of the artist, or an adequate assessment of Tura's 'greatness' or 'importance'.

Tura's work generates curiosity, which now partly results from our being induced to imagine historical and cultural difference, to reflect on the experience – perhaps – of a fifteenth-century beholder before the same image. Yet what is the historical status of this curiosity, its significance for these same earlier beholders? If Tura's style can be characterised as curious or attention-seeking, what would this tell us about those who first encountered his paintings, and their various expectations as Christian worshippers, as clergy or courtiers, as subjects of a signorial state, as patrons and evaluators of artistic skill? What might it tell us about an otherwise obscure individual working as a painter in a major Italian city of the late fifteenth century, especially when we juxtapose such an assessment of style with the kinds of historical information which can be gleaned from documents such as the letter cited above?

The one surviving document purportedly in Tura's own words, both as a report on a predicament and as a rhetorical performance, raises a new set of issues for the consideration of this artist. In the winter of 1490, he may indeed have experienced the rigours of age (he was about sixty) and illness, and felt the want of his 85 ducats – his salary while working for the court in 1470 had been 60 ducats per year – yet the protests of poverty should be set against the fact that between October 1489 and November 1490 Tura was able to invest about 240 ducats in various commercial enterprises.[4] What the letter evokes most clearly is the conditions under which a painter in Ferrara was expected to work for the members of a noble and ecclesiastical élite. Tura makes his appeal on the basis of a differential in social power. Two defaulting clients are referred to, the Duke of Ferrara's secretary and the duke's nephew, the Bishop of Adria; in such cases, the letter suggests, disputes between patrons and clients could not be resolved by legal recourse or by anything resembling a professional organisation for painters (none appears to have existed in Ferrara); the only recourse was a principle of justice which lay beyond the courts and tribunals in the will and authority of a prince. It is furthermore noteworthy that in presenting the prince with his abject picture of the 'starving artist', Tura dramatises the disjunction between material circumstance and a sense of social entitlement; there is a contrived impression of education, refinement and self-importance – an elegant epistolary hand (plate 1), a use of a Latin phrase and a portentous Latinising of his name: COSMUS PICTOR. The effect of this self-presentation is unaltered by the possibility that Tura may have drawn here on the services of a scribe; Tura is emphatically not speaking as a member of a class of uneducated mechanicals, despite the indications, as we shall see, that this may have been a common perception of painters in Ferrara.

The documents on Tura, and the works themselves, constantly direct us towards considerations of the status and social definition of the parties involved, towards the identity of groups rather than individuals; the paintings often imply a relation or encounter between different groups in Ferrarese society. It is as such, I hope, that the interest of Tura as 'historical figure' will emerge in succeeding chapters.

The title of this book, with its inclusion of an artist's name, suggests that what follows will be a comprehensive study of a historical individual, assessing his life, his works and his place in the history of art. There have been several attempts to write such a book about Cosmè Tura, beginning with Ferrarese scholars of the eighteenth century. The first 'life' of Tura (c.1706) contains no reliable biographical information, but a eulogy of paintings which were in many cases already undergoing the ravages of war, neglect and dispersal among collectors.[5] Subsequent writers then began to publish miscellanies of documents relating to the painter's commissions and other professional transactions, very few of which, however, could be related with any certainty to an increasingly fragmented corpus of paintings.[6] Twentieth-century monographs on Tura have relied largely on the early eye-witness descriptions of works *in situ* and on documentary compilations. But modern accounts have relied also on powerful models of stylistic transmission and cultural authority which have long shaped the history of early modern Italy, and which often seem to outweigh any appeal to documentary and visual evidence.

The format of the monograph in art history has tended, understandably, to prioritise certain concerns: those of biography, of chronology, of attribution and reconstruction. In the case of Tura, the dearth of materials for addressing these matters has repeatedly led to a sense of impasse. As a monographic subject Tura has largely been a romantic creation, regarding whom lacunae in the historical record have been filled by attributions of personal eccentricity, spirituality and provincial naivety inferred on the basis of his style. Roberto Longhi's description of Tura's absorption in 'medieval' tendencies,[7] which holds sway in recent scholarship, was hardly a significant advance on Bernard Berenson's earlier characterisation of the artist as 'the man mad about tactile values', tactility being the 'only principle he seemed to have grasped' from the progressive art of his time. Berenson epitomised an entire tradition of nineteenth-century scholarship when he presented Tura as having 'no conspicuous mental training and lacking, like all provincials, the intelligent criticism of serious rivals, he was never driven out of his narrow formula into a more intellectual pursuit of his art . . . like all born artists who lack an adequate intellectual purpose [he] ended in the grotesque'.[8] Berenson laid the grounds for the dominant twentieth-century conception of Tura – as wilfully individualistic or expressionist – by using such terms as 'maniacal ferocity' to describe him. Subsequent writing on Tura presents the artist in remarkably inconsistent ways, ranging from such stylistic labels as late Gothic ornamental disorder or proto-Mannerist sophistication to Netherlandish realism, anti-realist 'courtly' stylisation, or a more direct brutalism and violence. Tura is regarded on the one hand as a hybrid of diverse 'influences' from Florence, Padua and the Netherlands, and on the other as an expression of a provincial and even isolationist 'courtly' taste.[9] What all of this critical tradition is avowing, albeit indirectly and with generally negative preconceptions, is the non-Florentine character of Ferrarese art (i.e. in terms of the 'Florentine style' as it has been constructed in art history). The work of artists such as Andrea Mantegna and Piero della Francesca, who – like Tura – worked at the court centres of northern Italy, is generally viewed as manifesting a paradigmatic response to the progressive artistic culture of Florence or its alleged spokesman, Leon Battista Alberti. A rigorous spatial construction, proportionality, the idealisation of human figures derived from the Antique, are all qualities which have made these artists central to conceptions of a normative and rational Renaissance style. Cosmè Tura, by contrast, is conceived as a frontier artist, a prime example of what even sympathetic critics such as Roberto Longhi, Federico Zeri and Eugenio Battisti have characterised as 'rinascimento oscuro' or 'pseudo-Renaissance'.[10] Yet perhaps the 'pseudo-Renaissance' really at issue here is the Renaissance as it has been conceived by a tradition of scholarship which not only forces Florentine art into the anachronistic mould of the 'classical', but also imposes an artificial dichotomy between the art of Florence and that of other centres – Siena, Venice, Ferrara.[11] In so doing, a mode of 'symbolic domination', which began with the Florentines' promotion of their native artists at other centres and was continued in Vasari's *Vite*, is reproduced in modern scholarship.[12] The most retarding effects of the Florence-centred norm have been a tendency to generalise on the expectations of fifteenth-century patrons and beholders from those of the Florentine mercantile class. Mathematical perspective and clearly ordered narrative composition are seen to manifest the rationality of this group, their preoccupation with quantitative thought and concrete reality, their civic spirit. Images in a 'court' culture (a designation itself in need of examination) are seen by contrast as irrational, conservative and escapist.[13] The projection of these values has seriously constrained our understanding of how images might operate within Renaissance urban culture – how painting and sculpture, for instance, might respond to both popular traditions and more 'learned' discourse about representation and visual experience. A substantial amount of fifteenth-century writing polemically addressed what an image is, and what an image does; the best-known example is Alberti's treatise *De pictura* of 1435. The emergence of the idea of painting possessing a *scientia*, or theoretical foundation, was fundamental to the professionalisation of painters in the fifteenth century, and not just in Florence. Yet do we have to understand artistic self-consciousness regarding pictorial representation only within the terms of the literary people, like Alberti? Could artistic practice itself be seen to reflect critically, rather than passively, on those aspects of representation, of knowledge, artifice and truth, which appear in the discourses on verbal and visual fiction in the Renaissance? Was first-hand access to Alberti's text even necessary in order for painters to explore, in their practice, a body of concerns which may have been shared or commonly discussed?

Rather than always adopting the rationalist model of 'painting as window' or 'representation of things seen', might painters have been engaging other models of visual representation? For instance, it has recently been suggested that within Florence itself artists could be seen to comment on the processes of visual understanding and the figuring of knowledge through a pointed subversion of the art's descriptive and illusionistic claims.[14]

This is not to say that images ceased to serve more traditional functions – as devotional objects, memorials, markers of material status. But is it desirable to reduce the work of images in culture only to the predictable requirements which can be inferred from contracts and account books? A broader notion of the 'work' of images in *quattrocento* culture is advocated by Michael Baxandall, who demonstrates how techniques of visual discrimination developed in diverse social practices actively informed the ways in which a *quattrocento* public looked at pictures; their 'cognitive style' derived from activities such as gauging, watching sermons and plays, dance, the preachers' appeal to the visual imagination.[15] Yet the implication of Baxandall's powerful demonstration should not be that early beholders necessarily experienced the fit between 'painting and experience' in a comfortable, familiar or plenary sense, or that there was a utopian, Ruskinian reciprocity between art and life. I do not believe that features of Tura's art which I have characterised as curious or alienating to modern beholders were always necessarily more intelligible to an original audience, in that they spoke directly to social experience; the sense of difference and defamiliarisation, of a challenge or resistance to the viewer, may rather be thought of as a calculated effect, playing upon a lingering cultural mistrust of appearance and representation.

While a *catalogue raisonné* on Tura might yet be compiled, the present book results from the conviction that works by this artist can sustain a different, but no less productive kind of historical account. Such an account must of necessity begin by confronting certain long-standing assumptions which not only inform previous discussion of Tura's style, his audience and 'courtly' orientation, but which have also become fundamental to the study of the image and its social role in early Renaissance Italy in general, and which cannot be addressed, at least with sufficient breadth, within the normal parameters of a catalogue. Preconceptions about Tura's wilful eccentricity, for instance, raise the broader problem of artistic identity and its role in the meaning of the work; how does an artist's style construct artistic persona, and what would this have signified for contemporary beholders? If, as I have proposed, Tura's style solicits an audience, what do we make of the fact that this audience is going to present a spectrum of considerable difference in class, education, understanding of art, attitude to religious and secular authority? Can we conceive of the image as engaging the disparate concerns of an urban public which is fragmented and heterogeneous by its very nature? Particular themes and motifs, certain treatments by the artist of standard subjects, may be present because of their over-determined significance in the society of the time, possessing widely different implications for different viewers: Hebrew inscriptions, discussed in chapter IV, would be an example of an ideologically loaded visual sign – it would have engaged a spectrum of readings ranging from an affirmation of the Law to a defamation of the perceived occult character of Judaism and the impoverishment of the word.

A fundamental question regarding meaning in fifteenth-century painting is of the heuristic value of forms of knowledge presumed to be beyond the reach of most artists, in particular Christian theology and humanist literary culture. There is no reason to suppose that Tura enjoyed educational opportunities substantially different from most other artists and craftsmen of the time; yet, as will be seen, his works constantly allude – with a pronounced degree of consistency and self-consciousness – to more prestigious (if sometimes controversial) contemporary spheres of knowledge. Themes of theological and literary erudition are constantly engaged in his work: the areas of difference and of common ground, the relative expressive capacities, of word and image, and of painting and writing. Tura is unlikely to have initiated such concerns or to have commanded the discourse in question, but it can be argued that, as a socially ambitious artist, he understood current discussions of the word-image *paragone* as having implications for his own work. Different visual formulations of the word-image relation are encountered in Tura's Roverella altarpiece, in the Muses of Belfiore, the Ferrara Cathedral organ-shutters, and in aspects of his style treated in chapter I.

My focus on questions of meaning, of audience and of artistic identity is the result of an attempt to re-evaluate Tura in terms of broader cultural tendencies, and to resist a prevailing scholarly characterisation of his work as the product of a bizarre and even disturbed individual. The individuality read into Tura's work by previous scholars has primarily served as a means by which to exclude or contain a figure who is deeply troubling for their taxonomies of style. Eberhard Ruhmer and Federico Zeri see the ornamental elaboration of outline in Tura's painting as a form of personal handwriting or signature, an idiosyncrasy which places him outside the classical tradition of the true Renaissance: Ruhmer remarks on 'the charming little irregularities expressing something individual and discreetly personal – the expression of the temperament, the mood of the painter, of his own particular attitude towards the traditional subject as he interpreted it'.[16]

I have sought instead to investigate whether Tura's 'calligraphic' style might not be so much personal or private, but rather the result of calculation, and furthermore whether it might not have an intersubjective or social character which addressed the expectations of particular audiences. In other words, to the very extent that Tura emerges as different or unique, he is significant as a manifestation of larger cultural tendencies. His style, handling of complex subject-matter and – insofar as we know – his social behaviour are all indicative of the shaping of identity by the conditions of life in an early Renaissance city.

The 'identity' of Tura that is of most interest, and about which we are best equipped to draw conclusions, is a social identity – a conception of selfhood regarded not as a given, but

as an emerging process, a continual labour of self-production which acquires a particular urgency in the life and career of an artist, whose commodity is his style. Terms used in the fifteenth century to designate artistic style, such as *aria* and *maniera*, were also associated with forms of social behaviour and deportment which had particular significance regarding one's place in society.[17] This urgency becomes even more acute when an individual works between a court and a broader urban environment, as Tura did. Court employment may not have been especially remunerative, but it brought a certain honour or prestige which would have been useful for soliciting other ambitious patrons.[18] An artist here is bound to give visual form to the self-image of a patron, as are all artists in *quattrocento* Italy; he is also, however, bound to demonstrate his fitness for the task, his own status as a cultural property of the rich and powerful – and 'style', in the sense of formalised virtuosity and novelty,[19] is the instrument of this demonstration.

I have chosen the anachronistic term 'identity' more for its cultural than natural connotations, and to qualify the term 'individuality' with all its accumulated historical baggage.[20] The concept of 'social identity' polemically confronted with that of 'heroic' or 'enlightened' Renaissance individuality now claims a large place in Renaissance scholarship.[21] A related discussion I have found to be particularly suggestive in the field of Renaissance literary studies is Stephen Greenblatt's emphasis on individual careers from the point of view of 'self-fashioning' – the psychological mechanisms of adaptation to circumstances of dependency or constraint, the instrumentalising of writers (or artists) by sovereigns, and the shaping of authorial voice.[22] The historian Natalie Zemon-Davis, among others, has provided an important articulation of the relation between 'social identity' constituted in interactions within and between groups, and the scope for 'individual identity', the shaping of behaviour and expression by personal history.[23] Among social historians, Ronald Weissmann has argued persuasively for the study of Renaissance society which moves beyond the atomism of individual careers and biographies or from anachronistic models of class stratification to focus on

> that very social fluidity (which, alas, is often confused with individualism) that makes the study of corporate groups and ideal types so problematic . . . I suggest that a more appropriate unit of analysis for studying Renaissance society is neither the individual nor the group, but rather the *social relationship* that links individuals to each other and to groups.[24]

Potentially this is a desirable model for considering the working conditions of artists, their status and network of contacts across traditional hierarchies. It could also be used productively to inflect the account of an artist's career in terms of the 'self-fashioning' model. In the case of Tura, there are obvious practical obstacles and methodological limitations to both modes of investigation, namely, problems of documentation, special difficulties regarding the discussion of paintings as texts, and complications in dealing with fifteenth-century court society.

In Tura's case there is unfortunately very little detail available to elucidate what Richard Trexler has called 'the social behaviour of dependent individuals'.[25] We have slender information on Tura as a public figure, and apart from tantalising glimpses, still less about his private life. We know that he was the son of a shoemaker. This fact appears to have led Longhi to associate Tura with the hypothetical band of social pariahs ('quella brigata di disparati vagabondi, di sarti, di barbieri, di calzolai e di contadini') who flocked to Padua to be trained in the academy of Francesco Squarcione.[26] Yet what did it mean to be a shoemaker in fifteenth-century Ferrara? The evidence suggests that the Arte dei Calegari (Guild of Shoemakers) was one of the leading corporations of the city. In fact, it was one of the few guilds that the Este princes allowed to exist following their suppression of the major commercial organisations in the late thirteenth century.[27] Its headquarters was on the city's main piazza, flanking the cathedral and facing the site of Ercole d'Este's Palazzo del Corte, in an opulent building with a loggia and frescoes of chivalric scenes (*paladini*) on its main façade.[28] It is thus by no means self-evident that coming from the household of a shoemaker necessarily implies low social standing; such a connection may, in fact, have been enabling.

Such a form of display is one example of the social fluidity or ambiguity for which Weissmann argues further investigation. Recent scholarship has provided some other tantalising examples. The communal government of Ferrara, in partnership with the diocese, was urgently concerned to forestall the blurring of social rank, and the erasure of visible distinctions between Christians and Jews, clergy and laity.[29] At various times, sumptuary legislation was imposed to regulate these differences at the level of luxury display, especially of clothing. Yet since the nobility was exempted from these strictures, those prosecuted for sumptuary violations frequently pursued inventive strategies to argue that they were *nobile*. In the light of this contestability of noble status, it is interesting that Tura often fashioned himself as *nobile*, as discussed further in chapter 1. Tura appears to have crossed boundaries in yet another way: although living as a private citizen with children, other dependants, real estate and money to invest, he had taken holy orders in 1460.

Tura's identity is finally a product in a very literal sense; the historical maker of works of art recedes behind the persona generated in and through the labour of a court dependant. My emphasis shifts from Tura the individual to something which is being constructed as a type – the 'Cosmo nostro' of various court commentators. Tura's staging of an individualising *effect* in his style can be seen as the enactment of a type – the *pictor nobilissimus*. Yet this self-imaging by the artist is called into being by social constraints, by circumstances of clientage and dependence, rather than in defiance of them; his clients will be seen to have had a stake in its production. My focus is primarily on Tura's images as instruments by which certain members of his public negotiated their world, engaged in their own performances of identity, confronting or exploiting social divisions and tensions. Artistic persona is, as we shall see, sometimes a Trojan horse for other agendas.

Some of the most interesting recent art-historical scholarship

on the early Renaissance has shared the concerns of historians of marriage, the family, death and commemoration, and the religious culture of the laity. Scholarship on Florentine art has benefited, above all, from the sharing of these concerns across various disciplines, reflecting the fact that the most influential historical models have tended to be grounded on Florentine materials.[30] Those who study the artistic production of urban centres other than Florence are not as well served as Florence has been by pre-existing traditions of cultural history. Ferrara was a city which would not have been dissimilar to Florence in terms of the everyday milieu and experience of the majority of its inhabitants. As a state, at the level of symbolic and real authority, however, there were crucial differences; the question of how these differences might have affected the character of everyday life remains to be investigated. In Ferrara the signs (heraldic, sumptuary, ritualistic) of traditional hierarchy, proscribed in Florence, were actively maintained; yet the social boundaries marked by these signs were, as we shall see, no longer perceived as intractable. Furthermore, although the identity of the state cohered to a large extent around the ruling dynasty, princely power in Ferrara was dispersed and compromised by other forms of authority. The presence of a court within a *comune*, itself theoretically subject to the Papacy, results in a shaping of social hierarchy and group identity which differs from the oligarchic Republic of Florence. In Ferrara in the late thirteenth century, a style of monarchial, autocratic rule had been imposed on the structures of a communal republic (that is, government by committees of citizens who qualified by class and income, effectually representing the interests of dominant economic corporations).[31] The new lords of Ferrara, the Este, gradually moved from a policy of active curtailment or repression of these older institutions in the late thirteenth century, to a carefully managed coexistence by the early fifteenth, by which time these civic bodies, as well as guilds, had been allowed to regain some of their jurisdictional rights. The Este maintained the posture of upholding the authority of communal institutions.[32] Ferrarese society therefore presents an interesting social spectrum of a princely court with a feudal nobility (whose boundaries were permeable in the fifteenth century), a large mercantile and professional class active in urban government, a community of luxury craft-producers working for the nobles and the upwardly mobile, and finally the *popolo*, a volatile and far from passive group with an occasional propensity for violent demonstrations against either the Este or the *comune*, sometimes against one in the name of the other.[33] Ferrara was also home to a flourishing enclave of Italian Jews, largely active as bankers and pawnbrokers, while some had court appointments. Furthermore, both Este rule and communal authority were impeded by a circumstance which dominates the city's political history in the fifteenth century – the fact that the Pope was the true ancient overlord of Ferrara; the resident secular clergy and its hierarchy were custodians of this right, and more immediately, of the ancient feudal authority of the Archbishop of Ravenna.

The court of Ferrara in the fifteenth century was a network of patronage and favour centred on the prince, who maintained support largely through disposal of land and offices; it did not yet comprise the all-encompassing state bureaucracy and far-reaching authority of absolutist regimes.[34] Sovereignty had not yet left its mark in all actions of the state or in more minute public and private relations; princely power was more engaged in testing its limits, sharing and compromising authority when expedient, above all in demonstrating its legitimacy. Nevertheless, at least at the level of princely ceremony and iconography, there are signs of an aspiration, at least in symbolic terms, to a more total monarchial and even spiritual authority. This tendency, characteristic of the period of Tura's career (c. 1450–95), is manifest in an increasing distance and formality in the conduct of the ruler. Visual spectacle, as we shall see in chapters II and III, acquired great importance in this reshaping of princely rule, and provides an important context for the consideration of Ferrarese painting.[35]

It will be stressed in what follows that the study of most of Tura's surviving work leads us away from the court and to consider the presence of other communities and interest groups in the Este state. Nevertheless the court was Tura's principal employer for much of his career, less for works of painting than as a designer of decorative arts. Tura was a beneficiary of princely largesse and recognition, and he profited socially and materially from this. His participation in court life would have additionally brought him into contact with a class of literary professionals with a particular interest in the status and usefulness of painting. A characteristic of fifteenth-century North Italian courts in this period is the promotion of what might be called a 'cultural policy'. The qualities of ideal rulership are Justice and Liberality; how can these be best be given rhetorical and persuasive form, presented in literary or visual terms as a spectacle? Which forms of representation – poetry, ceremony, painting – can best express the 'magnificence' of a prince, that is, the liberality which Aristotle and contemporary writers had made into a defining quality of the virtuous ruler?[36] Among literary professionals dependent on court patronage, and aristocratic courtiers with a humanist education, the various possibilities sometimes assumed polemical form. Fifteenth-century court society was the site of noteworthy experiments in the imaging of power, with the production of the prince as a cultured individual whose civilising merits entitled him to rule. Magnificence was not self-indulgent, nor was it shallow spectacle; the financial responsibilities and ritual protocols associated with magnificence put those who cultivated it under considerable pressure. At the level of the image or spectacle, magnificence necessitated both constant calculation, resourcefulness, attention to detail and strategic ambiguity, together with an observance of tradition.[37] Even the courtly pastime of hunting, depicted repeatedly in the frescoes of Palazzo Schifanoia and elsewhere, was an act of representation and imitation in itself, a ritual form with a time-honoured tradition. Pope Pius II censured Borso d'Este for pursuing it with excessive zeal when more weighty matters were pressing; yet Borso probably did so less from any escapist impulse than from the obligation to express princely privilege, martial prowess, and the emulation of venerable Este ancestors portrayed as hunters in Este palaces.[38] As I argue in chapters I and II, this reliance on spectacle has particular implications for contemporary evaluations of painting.[39] In accordance with quattrocento princes' perceived need to foster the talents of accomplished artists, figures like Pisanello, Mantegna, Piero and Leonardo became highly prized cultural property. At the height of Pisanello's success as courtier-artist in the mid-fifteenth century, certain humanists addressed themselves to affirming or correcting the princely evaluation of art. Meanwhile, as prime beneficiaries of the prince's cultural patronage and as the custodians of his image for posterity, the humanists claimed rights of arbitration regarding the proper use of the visual arts, their advantages and limits in the cultural formation and self-imaging of rulers. Alberti's De pictura of 1435, ostensibly addressed to artists but dedicated to a prince, gives an important place to litterati – poets and orators – in the production of works of art.[40]

One of the rights of arbitration claimed by humanists working for princes was the determination of which human arts, or what forms of knowledge, could be considered 'liberal' or suitable for the ideal (and aristocratic) pedagogical subject. Their claims for the dignity of classical literature sometimes led to a disavowal of the value of modern vernacular poetry, of the pursuit of Hebrew studies, and of the practice as distinct from the appreciation of painting. The first chapter shows how painting, despite protests from some humanists, participates in the conversion of literary culture and erudition to another form of display, the fetishising of the luxury object in book production for the court. The second chapter deals in particular with the pronouncements of Guarino of Verona on the usefulness and limitations of painting. His perception of limitations is shown to be implicitly challenged by other authors who found in painting a fertile vehicle for their own self-imaging, in so far as its effects exceed the scope of their own literary propaganda. Taken together, chapters I and II examine the contingent and varying nature of the humanist approval of painting, which is investigated as a problem in the fashioning and promotion of an identity by humanists such as Angelo Decembrio, Guarino and Lodovico Carbone.

Yet the range of Tura's production is expressive of more than his clientship with the court, and therefore in the remaining chapters I switch my focus to the image in more public urban contexts, in which it becomes available to different kinds of looking, and is produced for different patrons and spectators. Chapter III places Tura's 'homeless' images of saints within the cult of saints and beati in Ferrara, identifying them as sites of negotiation between popular beliefs and the regulating force of ecclesiastical authority. Chapters IV and V shift the emphasis to outsiders in the state, to the competing representations of marginal and anomalous princely subjects (the Jews) to suspect forms of knowledge (astrology). Both court and clerical interests competed in assigning the Jews particular identities which they were compelled to perform. When Tura produces for the family of the Bishop of Ferrara a work which 'speaks' both to the Jews and of the Jews, the signification of identities becomes particularly complex. Raised here are not only issues of ethnicity and its figuration, but of competing definitions of the state and the supreme authority within it, together with the interpretation of some particularly extravagant gestures of artistic virtuosity.

Church and court compete in enacting the figurative identity of the state. As the court resorts to more secularising and antiquarian forms, such as monumental public sculpture, to represent princely sovereignty, the church re-appropriates the image of the city's patron saint, St George. In doing so the clergy exploits his antiquity as an embodied symbol of Ferrara, his characteristics of nobility and militancy, his legendary authority over sovereigns.

The range of Tura's work, in terms of its original functions and destinations, means that he provides a valid case-study for determining what might be called the 'place of the image' in fifteenth-century urban culture. Each chapter provides not only an account of a different body of work by Tura, but also involves consideration of distinct communities within Ferrarese society – painters, nobles, humanists, clergy, Christian laity, Jews. I trace the different stakes each group had in the circulation of the image, and how each may have encountered something in Tura's imagery which spoke to them about themselves. Conceiving Ferrarese society in terms of Weissmann's fluid heterogeneity, the image can be seen as a site of negotiation or mediation between more than one of these communities, addressing issues of particular conflict or tension.

Tura's paintings engage questions of cultural politics in one further sense, in that some of the major projects can be seen to reflect on the validity or legitimacy of various kinds of knowledge which had become controversial, and had been challenged or defended by different authorities: pagan poetry, astrology, Hebrew antiquarianism, the *scientia* of painting itself. The status of these bodies of knowledge, given visible form, is ambiguous, as it probably was in the experience of many beholders of the image. At stake in the figuring of identity were certain bodies of knowledge which had become controversial, even politicised. The ambiguity of painting afforded particular advantages for the imaging of such spheres of expertise; it is for this reason that they appear in Tura's painting under the sign of curiosity.

The effect of much of Tura's imagery is frequently anomalous, somehow beyond the apparent decorum of the subject depicted. Certain marginal elements are sometimes disturbingly and subversively redolent of a manipulative intelligence at work beyond the painting. However, such motifs do not have the form of a signature or of a constantly recognisable autograph effect. Its force, therefore, is very different from the *manufactured* identity of Tura's calligraphic line. Something or someone distinct is appearing in an imagery of *curiosity*, of sexual, pagan and irreverent marginalia, the effect of which sometimes seems to cancel the claims of representation itself, configuring what the beholder sees as a snare of seductive illusions. In the case of a secular mythological cycle, such as the Muses of Belfiore discussed in chapter II, these *curiosa* can be seen to correspond to qualities of painting which were particularly appreciated by part of Tura's audience, and cannot therefore be seen to have any strongly authorial effect; in religious painting, however, the situation is different. Such imagery opposes itself to 'official' pronouncements, such as those of clerics, on the proper offices of painting, and an authorial persona emerges which appears to distinguish itself from limits or boundaries.

I

THE 'DAEDALIAN HAND':
STYLE, VIRTUOSITY AND ARTISTIC PERSONA

FOR THOSE WHOSE POSITION AT COURT was not secured through noble birth, success depended on strategies of self-presentation. The relative fluidity of court rank brought with it a strong measure of competition and mutual suspicion within and between various interest groups. One of these groups with which this and the following chapters will be concerned is the humanists – professional classical scholars and rhetoricians, teachers and occasional propagandists for the regime. Even beyond court service, humanism in the fifteenth century had a defensive and competitive character. Although once idealised by modern scholars, especially in the more celebratory accounts of the Ferrarese court, humanists have more recently been taken to task for careerism, their identification with authoritarian values, and for the notorious rapidity with which they could turn scholarly polemic into personal attack;[1] much of their literary activity is itself geared towards defaming rivals and opponents, or in making denigrating pronouncements about a host of other professions – preachers, scribes, scholastic philosophers, actors – and painters. These attacks reveal a great deal, however, about the effects of dependency in a society held together by ties of patronage. One of the observable effects is a defensive concern by the humanists with their own self-definition, an anxiety not to be ranked with other dependants of the rich and powerful whose skills were similarly out for hire.

The cultural importance of Renaissance Ferrara for modern scholars has often rested on its community of humanist philologists, pedagogues, orators and poets; these included one of the most esteemed Latin scholars and teachers of the century, Guarino of Verona, while many other leading figures were intermittently resident there.[2] Some of these were in the employ of the *comune*, as public teachers or as university faculty; others, like Guarino, were principally dependants of the Este court, which itself took over responsibility for university salaries in the reign of Borso d'Este, turning it into a further outlet for Este patronage. One of the results was that Ferrara became a centre of vigorous humanist controversy and polemic; if these contro-

versies are regarded in terms of strategies of self-definition, much of consequence emerges not only for the study of humanism, but for the study of art and artists in court society.

At the Ferrarese court, humanists would have encountered Cosmè Tura along with other painters such as Baldassare d'Este and Angelo da Siena. As an 'interest group' at court, artists could aspire to a very different status from that which could be attained by humanists. It was a rare artist who could be considered indispensable or irreplaceable in the manner of Guarino. The Este did not have a regularly salaried position (let alone dignifying 'title') of court artist, although this has often been assumed to be the case with regard to Tura and the younger painter Ercole de' Roberti. The term 'court artist' is perhaps best applied to designate an artist who is given an official position in the prince's household, rather than an artist who merely works for the court on a regular basis, alongside others.[3] Tura's position may have corresponded more to the latter circumstance, lacking the position of conspicuous singularity accorded to Mantegna at Mantua. His situation, however, was probably more advantageous than that of the many artists who competed for princely patronage, often without remuneration, at another court centre, Sforza Milan.[4] However unofficial and provisional Tura's employment may have been, it was at least constant from the 1450s to the 1470s, although it is not possible to determine how his salary of 15 lire per month paid during his work on Borso's chapel relates to the more regular terms of his employment. Tura was chiefly in demand for his draughtsmanship, producing numerous designs for tapestries and occasional drawings for precious metalwork – one set of these drawings was sent to Lodovico Sforza in 1485.[5] Although relatively few works of painting by Tura appear in the court records, these tended to be prestige commissions, where quality of execution was important, rather than cheap and repetitive wall decoration.[6] The latter was the domain of artists designated 'depintori della corte', Trullo and Gherardo da Vicenza.[7] It is clear, none the less, that Tura worked to a considerable extent for clients beyond the court, including clergy, urban nobility, guilds and middle-class patrons.[8] The main advantage of court employment for a painter like Tura was that it could make him famous and draw the attention of prestigious patrons; the Sforza of Milan were clearly interested in his skills, and when Ferrarese humanists did not mention Tura by name, their references to painting probably allude to him. Tura's appearance in notarial records as 'praestantissimum pictorem omnium nostri temporis' ('the most outstanding painter of our time') should thus be taken as more than a mere formula.[9]

This chapter will be very much concerned with the context for such seemingly formulaic statements. It will take the view that early humanist commentary on art and artists frequently employed rhetorical formulae, not mechanically and unreflectively, but pointedly and deliberately in the service of political and professional agendas. I will propose that humanist commentary influenced the visual character of painting in Ferrara in the later fifteenth century, and that this influence is manifest in the social ambition and artistic practice of the most eminent painter of the city, Cosmè Tura. Subsequent to the researches of Michael Baxandall in the 1960s, the Ferrarese provenance of much early poetic and rhetorical commentary on painting has been accorded little significance, least of all with regard to the emergence of a distinctive local artistic tradition.[10] Recent studies of the artist in court society, however, have shown how the interrelation of art, power and intellectual culture might have informed the perception of the artist, his own self-perception and self-presentation through his work.[11]

It is true that in the wake of Alberti's pioneering treatise on painting of 1435, remarks on painting by Ferrarese humanists have an apparently derivative and predictable character. Lodovico Carbone's comments on the nobility of art in his *Oratio pro nipote Galeotti Assassini* from 1460 is one example.[12] Baxandall showed a certain enthusiasm for Angelo Decembrio's *De politia litteraria*, mainly for its reflections of Alberti, but made no secret of the fact that he considers it a boring text, 'a long and badly written book that repels attention in several ways'.[13] These works, however, can be found interesting less from the point of view of original statements about painting, than from their ideological framing of the question of art and its value. Particular historical circumstances led these authors to consider the relation between princely regimes and the kinds of cultural activity which such regimes had been promoting. Although both are concerned with the promotion of literary culture at court, they differ substantially in their appreciation of artistic activity and its status. While their pronouncements certainly reflect a familiar debate about the claims of painting and sculpture to be liberal arts, they can also be read as being more specific and more political in their address.

A sense of this specific historic dimension can lead us to make deductions about the perception of art and artists by the audience who encountered the work of painters like Cosmè Tura. From establishing this, my concern here will be to show how this perception influenced the formation of a status and an identity associated with the capacity of a painter employed at court, and how this identity might be produced in artistic performance

– how it might lead, in other words, to the formation of a style. Hence in this account the 'institutional' factor, the court environment, takes precedence over any personally expressive or individualist dimension to Tura's style, an aspect which has been overplayed in scholarship on the artist.[14] However, one of my chief concerns will be to show how and why this style, although adopted by several Ferrarese painters, nevertheless produces a powerfully individualising effect.

Carbone's remarks on *pictura* affirm its liberal over its manual status: 'pictura scilicet, quae nullo modo cum mechanicis artibus conumeranda, sed liberalibus potius disciplinis omnium doctorum iudicio coniungenda est'. The ancients, he says, regarded painting as a form of poetry, and painting is what he himself takes most delight in after his books:

> For painting was called mute poetry by the ancients, and our Horace wrote that painters and poets were of equal powers, because both can confer immortality on men. Indeed, in my opinion there was never anyone of noble and elevated mind who did not take pleasure in painting. I might name and set before you many princes who devoted themselves to painting and carving, especially Augustus and Nero, who were extraordinarily and unbelievably pleased by painting. I declare that the best images which ever came into my hands were those made at the time of Octavian or Nero. The merits of the princes are reflected in the talents of their subjects . . . Indeed my study is full of numerous paintings, seals, portraits, and panels. Never do I see that image of Leonello which Pisanello fashioned without tears coming to my eyes; thus is his most humane bearing still available to be imitated. That of yourself, O renowned Duke, which Lodovico Castellani made, I hold to be the queen among all others, and it can be seen with its venerable dignity and noble majesty to have incited me to virtue, to wisdom, to eloquence and to every kind of refinement.[15]

Carbone's rhetorical purpose is to link the works of art produced under a prince's rule with the prince's own virtuous qualities. Works of art are not only expressions of princely magnificence but the products of the noble minds in his service; the prince might be judged according to the *ingenium* of the artists he supports. Nothing very extraordinary here, but the orator's observations on art and nobility can be shown to have a significant political dimension with a certain bearing on the very claim of Borso d'Este to be a ruling prince.

The *Oratio* is a panegyric on the not particularly distinguished nephew of the high-ranking courtier Galeotto dell'Assassino which turns into a celebration of more illustrious members of the family. In the reign of Borso's father Niccolò III, Galeotto was working as a goldsmith; however, his family fortunes rose dramatically when his sister Stella became Niccolò's mistress and the mother of both Leonello and Borso, future rulers of Ferrara. Galeotto was elevated to the position of *camerlengo* and appears to have operated as a kind of artistic impresario with responsibility for overseeing the major court commissions. It was he who directed the team of miniaturists who worked on Borso's famous illuminated Bible (Modena, Biblioteca Estense), the most sumptuous illustrated book produced in the *quattrocento*.[16]

Thus for Carbone the praise of *pictura* and *imagines* has direct bearing on more crucial contemporary issues – the nobility of artistic practice had to be affirmed in order to vindicate the nobility of the family of Duke Borso's mother. This in turn can be related to a broader preoccupation with the issue of nobility during the reign in question, which centred on the problem of Borso's illegitimacy and the insecurity of his claim to the succession after the death of Leonello d'Este in 1450. Although Borso had been acclaimed by the *popolo*, the civil government and the leading nobility, it was known that there were several contenders with stronger claims, including Borso's legitimate half-brother Ercole and the son of his predecessor Leonello. Borso sought to counterbalance the potential weakness of his position by restructuring the Ferrarese nobility, creating a strong circle of newly ennobled supporters who were dependent on his patronage for their entitlements and distinction.[17] The resulting social mobility transformed the aristocracy. Several old families dwindled in importance; others fell under the displeasure of the prince and had their properties confiscated and redistributed to Borso's favoured *zentilhomini moderni*.[18] Borso's calculated and highly publicised cultivation of princely liberality enabled those to whom he had granted land, money or urban property to claim socially elevated status on the basis of wealth and personal merit rather than noble blood, and hence to qualify for high-ranking civic and court positions. Controversy arose as the urban new rich laid claim to noble status and its prerogatives of display, such as immunity from sumptuary restrictions.[19] Humanist defences of the nobility of virtue against the claims of old wealth and lineage found a sympathetic audience. The *Disputatio de nobilitate* by the Pistoian Buonaccorso de Montemagno, which features a lively debate between proponents of the claims of virtue and birthright, was probably known in Ferrara even before the 1470s, when Carlo di San Giorgio made a vernacular translation for the Duchess Eleonora d'Aragona, wife of Ercole I.[20] In Ferrara, as in Florence, *nobiltà* could designate not merely a generalised merit or virtue found in individuals irrespective of birth, but could provide a moral basis for social élitism; Carbone's oration merely extends such polemics into the debate regarding the definition of the liberal arts. The process of opening the ranks of court society continued under Ercole I, when court and civic offices were literally put up for sale every year.[21]

Such social mobility was also manifest in the cultural sphere, chiefly with regard to the status of artists and scribes. As we shall see, the very definition of a scribe as one who merely transcribes a text rather than editing, translating and commenting upon it provided occasion for controversy. More than one scribe working for the court professed humanistic interests, writing histories, Latin and vernacular compositions and translations.[22] The phenomenon was not exclusively Ferrarese, but as will become apparent, certain of those in Ferrara who enjoyed the benefits of this transformation of status were the most prompt to criticise the very liberalisation of a cultural status quo which had enabled their own rise.

The *volgare*, including writing in the Ferrarese dialect, was prominent in the literary production of these scribe-authors. The vernacular romance tradition with its popular roots absorbed some of the ethical values of the humanists, but provided ideals of merit and models of speech and behaviour which were more accessible than the classical curriculum to many entering the prince's service.[23] Translation from the classics became an important form of court-sponsored literary production, a circumstance which has caused modern scholars unjustly to characterise Borso's reign in terms of a prevailing anti-intellectualism or even anti-humanism.[24] The literary activities of Leonello's circle of humanists continued under Borso's sponsorship. Carbone, a pupil of Guarino and professor of rhetoric and *humanae litterae* at the University of Ferrara, was himself one of the great success stories of Borso's reign, rising from humble mercantile origins to a condition of great luxury, and receiving noble titles from the Pope and the Emperor.[25] In a Latin dialogue of the 1470s he pays a compliment to one of his contemporaries at the court, 'Cosmos noster, pictor nobilissimus', that is, the court painter Cosmè Tura.[26] Although a painter clearly lacked the resources for advancement available to a humanist or a scribe, there are a number of interesting parallels between the fortunes at court of Tura and Carbone. Carbone was the son of a small merchant, Tura of a shoemaker. Almost the same age, both took minor religious orders, Tura receiving his clerical tonsure in 1460. Since neither afterwards appears to have practised a religious calling it is possible that this was a career move, undertaken in order to acquire benefices; Este retainers frequently took minor orders in order to achieve lucrative benefices through princely patronage.[27] With their court connections, Carbone could play a leading role in academic and court life, while Tura was able to monopolise major commissions for the cathedral, for the clergy and prominent Ferrarese families.

By the year of Borso's death (1471) Tura had acquired considerable wealth. In a will drawn up that year he made a bequest to the poor of Venice, also proposing to erect and decorate a church dedicated to Sts Cosmas and Damian on a site granted him by the duke.[28] This intention, although never carried out, was a bold assertion of status, aligning Tura with two of the most socially ambitious and self-publicising artists of the *quattrocento*, his counterpart Andrea Mantegna at the court of Mantua and the Sienese painter-sculptor Vecchietta, both of whom had themselves commemorated in this way.[29]

Tura's monthly salary of 15 *lire marchesine* during 1469 to 1472, while he was working on the decoration of Borso's chapel at Belriguardo, may seem modest when compared with Mantegna's 38 lire from the Gonzaga court, but corresponds to twice what Carbone was earning in 1457 from his academic position.[30] As with Carbone, the artist's means were enlarged by privileges such as the provision of a house at the prince's expense.[31]

The patronage of artists by Borso was more than a matter of ordering and paying for work; in one documented case it can be seen to have a distinctive ritual aspect which suggests a kind of feudal clientage. Angelo da Siena had been initially employed by Leonello, Borso's predecessor, on the paintings for the prince's *studio*; when Borso took him into his service in 1455 an arrangement was made whereby in return for a grant towards a house in the city, Angelo was to present every year on a certain day a painting of 'a most beautiful rose or lily or other flower as Master Angelo wishes'.[32] Such a ritual recalls the formalised friendship between Leonello d'Este and Pisanello, a relationship between unequal partners where in return for the prince's protection the artist would pay unsolicited tribute, as in the wedding presents – an image of Julius Caesar and one of the Virgin – which Pisanello sent to Leonello in 1435.[33] We have no comparable information about any formal clientage of Tura, if indeed there was any such event, but by the 1480s Tura was a prominent and established citizen with aristocratic pretensions; he is distinguished in various notarial acts as 'nobilem et praestantem virum Cosimum pictorem', 'egregius, et nobilis pictor', a practitioner of the 'ingeniosam artem picture', 'praestantissimum pictorem omnium nostri temporis'.[34] A ducal proclamation of 1487 refers to the 'praestans pictor Cosme del Tura'.[35] The record of his death in April 1495 refers to him as 'el Nobile et Excellente homo Mo. Cosimo dal Tura Pictor Excellentissimo'.[36] This attribution of fame and nobility is exceptional in the records of Ferrarese painters.[37]

One other circumstance needs to be mentioned regarding this figuratively noble status of painting at the Este court. Galeotto dell'Assassino was not the only artist among Borso's relations. One of Tura's painter-colleagues at court was Baldassare d'Este, who is thought to have been another illegitimate son of Niccolò III. Baldassare, referred to as 'nobil pittore e famigliare di Sua Eccellenza', held a number of official and military posts; in the reign of Ercole d'Este he is said to have signed his works with the *diamante*, the duke's own device.[38] Another artist held a role which could be loosely described as that of 'court favourite'. Like the pre-eminent favourite Teofilo Calcagnini, Petrecino da Firenze began his career as a *ragazzo del nostro signore* or page, but is recorded as working on a set of playing-cards with colours and gold leaf in 1457, and from his hand we have high-quality portrait medals of Borso d'Este and members of his court. Petrecino retired to the monastery of San Giorgio in 1460, with copious privileges and benefits from the duke.[39]

To summarise thus far, I propose that Carbone's humanist celebration of art may have reflected a pressing ideological need to idealise art as a more than manual discipline. This followed from the involvement of relations and intimates of the duke in a profession which could still be perceived as basely menial or *ignobilis*, thereby implicating art in the problem of re-defining nobility. The attitude to art manifest in Carbone's oration, the feudal clientage of Angelo da Siena, parallels in the careers of court artists and men of letters, references to Tura as 'nobilissimus', also reflect a loosening of social and professional hierarchies under Borso which enabled advancement at court by members of the lower professions and those without family connections. This did not revolutionise the situation of artists in general; it did not mean that artists would necessarily have affected gentlemanly status in everyday life, or that they would cease to be regarded as craftsmen. The attitude emerges from a courtly competitiveness concerning the merits of those who surround the prince, reinforced by humanist ideas of art as an intellectual virtue which reflects honourably on the patron as much as the practitioner: in Carbone's words, 'quales enim principes talia subditorum ingenia' ('the merits of the princes are reflected in the talents of the subjects'). Such idealism accompanies the enlargement of the status, the material circumstances of artists in advantageous positions like Tura, but Francesco del Cossa's letter to Borso of 1470 stands as testimony to the sometimes perfunctory treatment of even highly qualified artists contracted for occasional tasks.[40] Tura as a historical personality is less retrievable because less important than the way in which his work responds to notions about *ingenium* in the service of the prince, and in which through its stylistic features it perpetuates this mythology by creating a fictitious identity or persona.

The question to be considered now is how Tura lays claim to a certain status through his work – or, how can the work of the hand present itself as dignified and worthy of the attention of noble minds? I will be arguing, against the grain of much Tura scholarship, that Tura's style is neither a passive reflection of an élitist, sophisticated court taste or an eccentric Gothic distortion of a more progressive tendency whose centre is elsewhere – Florence or Padua. Tura's style should be seen as something calculated as such, a response to a consumer demand. I define style here in the sense for which I believe it was most meaningful for the fifteenth century – as a set of gestures or signs through which an artist *performs* his distinctiveness and virtuosity. Quality and individuality become interdependent, to the extent that individuality becomes a conventionalised version of quality. As the evaluator of Mantegna's work in the Eremitani Chapel implied in 1457, individual hands can be recognised in a work – but especially when the hand is that of a superior painter.[41] This implies a recognition of distinguishable artistic identity, but one based on quality or superior performance, the possession of certain properties which distinguish the master artist from the common herd. In documents of commission or payment this quality might be referred to as 'ingegno', or 'difficultà', or 'magistero', a term which is used in connection with leading painters at Ferrara; contracts sometimes specify that a work be completed 'ornate et artificiose', which also suggests a demand for manifest skill.[42] For rank-and-file artists, however, especially for those working in collaboration or in subordination to a master, individualising tendencies are viewed pejoratively in the assessment of quality.[43] Hence the indifference encountered by Francesco del Cossa when he sought extra remuneration for his superior technique, and for giving evidence of 'study' (perhaps his stylistic emulation of Piero della Francesca) in the Hall of the Months in Palazzo Schifanoia. On the other hand, an obviously competent painter such as the September Master may have provided just what was required, in that he carried out his portion of the work in the distinctive manner of Cosmè Tura, the chief painter and probable overseer of the work (plate 3). Differences between 'celebrity artists', on the other hand, were recognised and even encouraged at the Este court – on one famous occasion Pisanello and Jacopo Bellini were encouraged to compete with each other for the portrayal of Leonello d'Este.[44]

3 September Master, *September: The Triumph of Vulcan*. Ferrara, Palazzo Schifanoia, Hall of the Months.

In another artistic competition, sculptors presented different projects for an equestrian monument to Niccolò III; the judge in this case was Leon Battista Alberti.[45]

The conception of the painter as an authorial figure possessing *ingenium*, and of pictorial composition as analogous to literary invention, is central to the most powerful fifteenth-century claim for painting's dignity and status as a liberal art. This was Alberti's *De pictura*, which was studied and circulated at the court of Ferrara; a copy survives with annotations by Lodovico Carbone himself.[46] Alberti places painting among the liberal disciplines requiring *ingenium*, the individual creative faculty possessed most characteristically by the poet.[47] *Ingenium* for Alberti is manifest in demonstrations of quality, in the painter's evident mastery of proportion, perspective, the movements and expressions of figures according to nature, and other aspects of the *scientia* of painting. Painting, however, is defined as the representation of things seen, a conception underscored by analogies with the window and the mirror. Whatever the artist portrays it must appear persuasively natural, ruled by the prin-

ciples of plausibility and decorum, 'elegant and pleasing and appropriate to the subject'.[48] What Alberti strongly opposes, however, is the artist who seeks to advertise *ingenium* through gestures and movements which defy plausibility, resulting in figures which are 'impossible and unsightly' ('impossibile factu, tum indecentissimum visu'). While painting should be richly varied and copious in visual interest, a certain threshold must not be crossed. This is the point where painting looks too much like the work of craftsmen, where the artifice that enables painting becomes visible as such. Alberti denounces the use of gold, the emphasis on outline, the portrayal of figures in frenzied or theatrical poses.

The *Annunciation* on the organ-shutters for Ferrara Cathedral, painted by 1469, features a series of grisaille figures which recall directly Alberti's prescriptions for the seven movements in painting and the principles of weight shift, together with his directions for correlating movement and the expression of emotions, and his recommendation of a variety of nude and partly draped figures (plates 107 and 108): 'There should be some bodies that

13

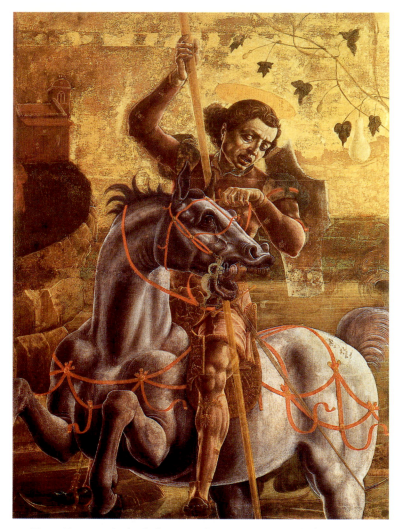

4 Tura, Ferrara Cathedral organ-shutters. Exterior, left-hand panel: *St George and the Princess*. Detail of plate 106.

5 Tura, St Maurelius altarpiece. *Execution of St Maurelius*. Detail of plate 76.

face towards us and others going away, to the right and the left. Of these some parts should be shown towards the spectators and others should be turned away; some should be raised upwards and others directed downwards.'[49] The lower left-hand figure on the panel with the Virgin recalls the following prescription: 'I have also seen that, if we stretch our hand upwards as far as possible, all the other parts of that side follow that movement right down to the foot, so that with the movement of that arm even the heel of the foot is lifted from the ground.'[50] Tura's evocation of Alberti suggests that he is laying claim to the *ingenium* and the *scientia* of Alberti's learned artist. Yet Tura is clearly pursuing other effects, which Alberti's principles do not endorse. There are elements which could be considered excessive or wilfully artificial, especially the manner in which the drawing tends away from its descriptive function and takes on an independent, decorative life of its own, especially in the broken, hard-edged forms of the draperies. Such a feature may be seen to violate Alberti's strictures against making outlines visible, in making *circumscriptio* subordinate to relief: 'I believe', he wrote, 'one should take care

that circumscription is done with the finest possible, almost invisible lines . . . Circumscription is simply the recording of the outlines, and if it is done with a very visible line, they will look in the painting, not like the edges of surfaces, but like cracks [*rimulae*].'[51]

Tura's work is characterised above all by an assertive mode of drawing. His many passages of decorative linear elaboration are sometimes made more visually compelling by being rendered in red. These include the red bridle of the horse in the Ferrara Cathedral *St George* (on the outer face of the organ-shutters, plate 4), which aligns itself strikingly with the pictorial surface, and the extravagant calligraphic flourish of the banner in the *Execution of St Maurelius* (plate 5). The well-turned line was fundamental to his professional role, in that the greater part of his work for the court consisted of the supply of drawings for the use of other craftsmen. Drawings were probably also supplied to other painters, such as those who were paid by the square foot for the frescoes in the Hall of the Months, a circumstance which indicates that the *invenzioni* were not theirs.[52] This output of

6 Tura, *Sts Peter and John the Baptist*. Infra-red reflectogram showing underdrawing. Philadelphia Museum of Art, Johnson Collection (see plate 45).

designs with a distinctive virtuoso flourish assured a kind of stylistic monopoly by Tura at the court; many contemporary panel paintings and manuscript illuminations suggest the extent to which it had become a 'house' style. One of the most remarkable and singular features of Tura's panel-painting technique is his practice of making extremely detailed drawings directly on the panel. Sometimes the underdrawing is apparent where the paint layer is transparent, but recent campaigns of infra-red reflectography have rendered it more strikingly visible (plate 6).[53] Tura here was emulating the practice of Netherlandish artists

such as Roger van der Weyden whose works were collected by the Este, and whose oil technique Tura was among the first Italian artists to exploit. Yet just as his use of oil medium shows a preference for stronger, more lustrous and more artificial colour, so in his use of underdrawing does the artifice of linear pattern maintain a more assertive presence than is ever the case with the transalpine painters.

There are various ways in which this calligraphic quality can be associated with the production of an artistic persona. It is conceivable that Tura's style, which is not without parallel in

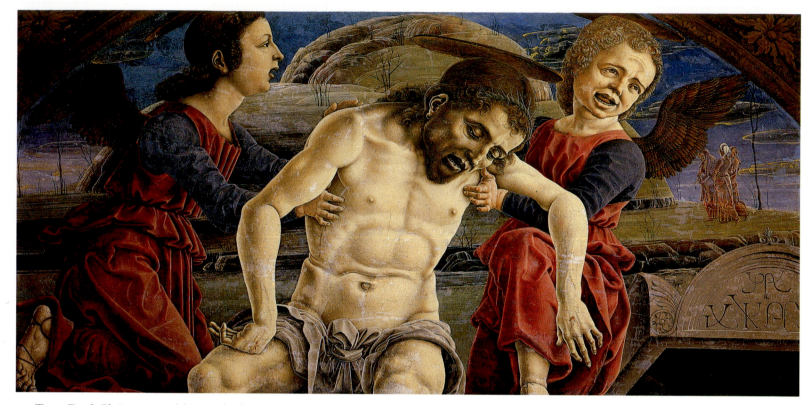

7   Tura, *Dead Christ supported by Angels* (fragment). Vienna, Kunsthistorisches Museum. On canvas, transferred from panel (44.5 × 86.7 cm).

quattrocento Sienese painting, bears some relation to his celebrated predecessor as court painter, Angelo da Siena. Visiting Ferrara in 1449 the famous antiquarian merchant traveller Ciriaco d'Ancona wrote a description of two lost paintings of Muses by Angelo and was prompted to refer to the artist as 'Angelus Parasius'.[54] Was it something about the appearance of these works which prompted Ciriaco to invoke the name of Parrhasius? Ciriaco the antiquarian was probably aware of what, according to Pliny in particular, was the distinguishing quality of this ancient painter. The following passage from Pliny's *Historia naturalis* stresses the greater importance of contour over relief, a priority which Alberti reversed in *De pictura*: 'by the verdict of artists [Parrhasius] won the palm in the rendering of outline, which is the highest subtlety in painting. To render mass and relief is no doubt a great achievement, yet many have succeeded in doing this. But an artist is rarely successful is finding a contour which shall enclose the internal forms of the figure.'[55]

The line features in the mythology of ancient painters in another famous case, which has particularly to do with the identifiability of artists: the hand of Apelles was recognisable from a single fine line drawn by him, which nobody else could have executed so skilfully. The line in this case would have the status of a signature, an assertion of distinctness, but this recognisability is, significantly, based on the assessment of the quality or virtuosity of the line rather than on any individual autograph character.[56]

Another distinctive feature of Tura's painting is his tendency to associate 'calligraphic' drawing with writing itself. Tura's works

are dense with inscriptions; these range from a Roman epigraphic type in his paintings of the *Virgin and Child* in Venice and London, while in the latter, which comes from the Roverella altarpiece of the mid-1470s, a Hebrew inscription is prominently displayed. There also appears, in other works, a kind of cryptic epigraphy, strange markings inscribed in stone just where we would expect inscriptions to occur. One of these occurs in the *Dead Christ supported by Angels* (plate 7); its appearance on a sarcophagus suggests that it is a name in ciphered form. The painting can be seen as producing, but masking and even burying an identity; a persona is invoked, whose name or relation to an actual historical person is not revealed.[57] On other occasions the writing on the sarcophagus assumes a far more pictorial, decorative form, as in the *Pietà* (plate 8), where a series of raised scroll-like forms occasionally assume shapes suggestive of the Latin alphabet. The inscription or pseudo-inscription on the throne of the *St James* (plate 51) is closer to generic Kufic or decorative oriental script.[58] While some of these quasi-inscriptions may have had legible meaning for certain members of Tura's audience, their deliberately cryptic nature turns attention away from any content to their formal or pictorial character, to their status as a kind of pure calligraphy ambiguously hovering between writing and patterning. The Washington *Virgin and Child* (plate 9) provides the most dramatic example of writing removed from the sphere of legibility and being exploited as the basis of linear pattern. Here the forms on the 'sarcophagus' are derived from the flourishes and embellishments of Gothic miniscule, which had a wide currency in the IHS monogram of St

8   Tura, *Pietà*. Venice, Museo Correr. On panel (45 × 31 cm).

Bernardino of Siena (which itself appears in Tura's Venice *Virgin and Child*, plate 11). The pseudo-inscription in the Washington picture is composed of the same flat, bent, metallic strips, and these calligraphic ornaments, demonstrations of masterly penmanship, are picked up explicitly in the broken, intricate folds of the Madonna's mantle.

★   ★   ★

A letter by Guarino to Giovanni Lamola shows a characteristic humanist tendency to play on the equivocal significance of the word *scriptura*:

> In the first place, because it was said that the book is 'judiciously and elegantly written', I did not only mean the nature of the poetry, but also the work of the scribe, insofar as the well-formed and beautiful appearance of the letters, and the correct and antique mode of writing known as 'orthography', is appreciated by the eyes in reading. For this was then the intention of that statement as it was written, however one might care to recall it or slyly to bring it up again now: 'What shall we then consider our Panormita to have done, and shall anyone be born equal in grave and worthy substance to his vigorous genius, when he plays so elegantly with matters so wretched and so redolent of debauched habits?'[59]

The passage provides one of several possible approaches to the analogy between painting and writing which appears to inform Tura's work. Guarino here exploits the dual reference of *scriptor* to 'manual' and 'authorial' spheres of operation, in a rather disingenuous retraction of a letter defending a volume of scandalous Latin poetry. Another possible approach is the association of writing with physiognomic differences or 'signature' effects. Tura might be seen to be drawing quite deliberately on the kind of observation we find in Filarete's *Trattato* comparing the differences between painters to those between scribes:

> One is known from what one builds, and like one who writes or one who paints is identified by his hand; one who paints is known by his manner of rendering forms, and so the style of each is recognisable to all. And this is another matter, that everyone, no matter how greatly he may vary [in his own work], is known by the products of his hand . . . I have also seen scribes to differ in their forming of letters. Where this subtlety, property and comparison comes from, we will leave for the aforementioned intellectuals to decide.[60]

The relation between painting and writing, or between artists and scribes, also becomes an issue in one of the most important literary products of fifteenth-century Ferrarese humanism, Angelo Decembrio's *De politia litteraria*.[61] The relation here is formulated in decidedly negative terms, and this is in keeping with the dominant agenda of the work. Although it has been seen as a nostalgic account of exemplary learned conversations during the 'Golden Age' of Leonello d'Este, Decembrio's text reads as a mythologising of the previous reign in order to criticise the cultural milieu under Borso d'Este, to whom the work was dedi-

cated in 1465.[62] The conversations in *De politia litteraria* implicitly strike at several features of court culture under Leonello's successor – the reduction of nobility to a form of display or masquerade, the decline in 'polite' standards of Latin style, the encouragement of the vernacular, the licence of scribes and the privileging of beautiful appearance over philological rigour in the production of books. The historical Leonello who wrote Petrarchan poetry and, in emulation of the court of Burgundy, established a tapestry workshop in Ferrara, is transformed by Decembrio into an antiquarian purist who excludes Dante and Petrarch from his library and who mocks the art of tapestry as 'transalpinae gentis vanitate'.[63]

The 'Dialogue on Art' published by Baxandall belongs to the later phase of composition of Decembrio's text and can be read as a response to tendencies in artistic patronage during the reign of Borso. With Tura's painting in mind, it is interesting to read what Decembrio, speaking in the person of Leonello, has to say about the painting of his time. The speaker clearly judges painting according to a selective reading of Alberti, understanding the prescriptions on decorum in *De pictura* in terms of a curtailment of manifest artifice, and of individualising tendencies, on the part of the painter. Leonello is made in the dialogue to denounce the rivalry of modern painters such as Pisanello and Jacopo Bellini, whom he contrasts with the artists of antiquity: 'Artists would show their work to each other and then correct it, whereas nowadays, as we know, they are consumed by rivalry with one another.'[64] The ancients did not engage in competitive individualism, or in the satisfaction of tastes and fashions. Instead, they devoted themselves to the eternal truth of nature which stands outside period fashions (*temporum novitate*), seeking to render the correct and invariable proportions and movements of the human figure. The body was represented nude and independent of the temporal variation of fashion. More interestingly, the speaker goes on to remark that the painters of his own time (like Tura?) are more concerned with 'colours, edges and outlines' than with the *scientia* of painting. In making themselves agreeable to the ignorant multitude through such crowd-pleasing ornamental effects they make errors in the description of nature, and their ineptitude resembles that of scribes and copyists: 'sunt et inter nos quoque et apud librarios ac scriptores eos errores'. Failure to standardise and rationalise the hand is a failure to manifest pictorial *scientia*. Giving a specific instance of this failure, 'Leonello' cites the tapestry-makers of northern Europe, who pander to the extravagances of princes and the stupidity of the crowd by overemphasising 'colorum magis opulentia telaque levitate quam picturae ratione'.[65]

A glance at Tura's *Pietà* (plate 8) reveals a number of the characteristics that Decembrio may have singled out for criticism. This is perhaps the most transalpine of Tura's paintings, in its subject, its style and its possible imitation of the glazes and jewel-like colours of Flemish oil technique. The monkey in the tree strikes an intrusive note of *levitate* (plate 117), and Tura's handling of human proportions has a calculatedly shocking effect. Line enforces hard-edged pattern and suppresses the distinctive textures of flesh, stone and fabric. The emphatic and surface-

9   Tura, *Virgin and Child*. Washington, D.C., National Gallery of Art. On panel (53 × 37.5 cm).

10 Tura, *Virgin and Child*, with original frame. Venice, Accademia. On panel (119 × 59 cm, including frame).

affirming drawing seems to undermine the normal relation of parts of the body, and the dead Christ is drawn out into a single, nervous, tapering arabesque. Every variation in the silhouette has been relentlessly emphasised and distinguished, with a priority on novelty and anomaly, most glaringly in the disjunction of the large head with the brittle, tapering legs.

As noted above, for Decembrio edges and outline are related to presumptuous individualism and to the waywardness of professional scribes. His 'Leonello' is moreover disturbed by the fact that Alberti attributes the poet's *ingenium* to the painter; he finally denies that painters have this faculty, just as he has implied that neither is it possessed by scribes: 'poetarum ingenia: quae ad

mentem plurimum spectant: longe pictorum opera superare'.[66] The comment brings about a rejoinder from Guarino, who insists that poets and painters have equal claim to *ingenium* and, more remarkably, that among the ancients the activities of both were referred to as *scriptura*.[67]

Why should Decembrio have equated the perversity of painters with the bad practices of scribes? The term 'scribe' appears to have been a recurrent epithet of abuse among the humanists, deployed as a constant, jarring reminder of the humbler origins of several ambitious literary professionals, such as Decembrio himself. For instance, George of Trebizond was referred to by a Guarino partisan as a 'graeculus' and 'former scribe'.[68] Angelo's censure of scribes is particularly ironic (and even pathetic) in that he had himself worked as a scribe for his brother Pier Candido Decembrio, from whom he later became estranged after his association with Guarino.[69]

The answer might lie in the ambiguity of *scriptura* in the speech ascribed to Guarino. *Scriptura* can refer both to what is written – the text as authorial pronouncement – and to the material substance of writing itself. Decembrio in his dialogue is heavily preoccupied by this distinction: between *scriptor* as author – one who can lay claim to *ingenium*, to an inventive faculty, and the *scriptor* as copyist – a mechanical, reproductive, basely commercial function. Artists for Decembrio would belong within this latter group. The polemic here, I would suggest, is ultimately against scribes who would usurp this distinction, pass themselves off as the *auctores* they were not, and this is identified with a corresponding presumption on the part of painters, the notion that they could lay claim to the poet's *ingenium*.

At stake here is a notion of textuality which may be seen as defining the innovative character of humanism as distinct from previous scholarly traditions. Mary Carruthers has proposed that in the Middle Ages a written text was considered provisional, imperfect and in need of revision. The physical writing down of a text is always a secretarial, scribal function, whether the activity is performed by the author or by a copyist: 'The author produces a *res* or *dictamen*; that which is a *liber scriptus* is in a formal hand on parchment, and the product of a scribe.'[70] Beginning more or less with Petrarch, one can observe a number of changes. First, the separate activities of composing and writing are conceived to a greater extent as professional distinctions. Second, the idea of the text as always open to revision and transformation in the hands of other author-copyists is replaced by the text as a static and closed object, with the 'archaeological' notion of restoring the text to an originary purity. Scribes, almost by definition, are considered mere labourers who require constant supervision if they are not to pervert what they are transcribing, and who can subvert the transmission of the authentic copy by over-indulgence in the manual artifice of their trade. Thus we find humanists from the time of Petrarch devising strategies to normalise the hand, extolling the advantages of a new, chaste and reformed script, purged of personal idiosyncracies.[71] Petrarch wrote to Boccaccio in 1366 of his collected letters, written,

11 Tura, *Virgin and Child, with the IHS monogram of St Bernardino*. Venice, Accademia. On panel (61 × 41 cm).

not however with the voluptuous and unrestrained writing, which is that of the scribes or I should say of the painters of our times, which caresses the eyes from a distance, but from close up it fatigues and disturbs them, and could not be called 'readable writing' as the prince of grammaticians would say. It is written instead in a clear and chaste style which pours itself beyond the eyes and which you will say lacks nothing of orthography or of grammatical method.[72]

The 'dialogue on painting' relates also to humanist debates on the distinction of liberal from mechanical arts. Whereas the work of the artist might still be open to accusations of being mechanical, writing did have a more prestigious status as an attribute of the liberally educated, the free-born rather than the servile. In the Aristotelian systematisation of the arts, writing is included as a part of grammar.[73] In humanist pedagogical theory we encounter drawing appearing among the disciplines constituting a liberal education, but only under the aegis of writing. 'Nowadays', wrote Pier Paolo Vergerio at the court of Padua around 1400, 'drawing does not in practice pass as a liberal art except so far as it pertains to the writing [scriptura] of characters – writing being the same thing as painting and drawing – for it has otherwise remained in practice the province of painters. But as Aristotle says, among the Greeks activity of this kind was not only advantageous but also highly respected.'[74]

While writing could maintain its prestigious status as a sign of authority, learning and literacy, the terms scriptura and scriptor could elide or conceal the supposed split between the manual function of the scribe and the intellectual one of the author.[75] Scribes at the Este court often used the term scriptor when they signed their names on manuscripts, even though a more precise term – librarius – existed to designate the function of copyist. As has been mentioned, several went on to develop humanist authorial pursuits of their own. Carlo di San Giorgio was involved in every stage of book production, as author, scribe and illuminator; the scribe Jacopo Landi also made forays into Latin composition.[76]

A Latin poem by Guarino of 1460 compares the fame and skills of the 'librario politissimo' Landi with those of two painters, one of them the miniaturist Guglielmo Magri (known as Giraldi), the other called 'Cosmo'. This may have been Tura; he was certainly the most famous painter called 'Cosmo' in Ferrara by 1460.

GUARINO OF VERONA TO JACOPO LANDI THE MOST ELEGANT OF SCRIBES
That I may lay off from the praise of shining ancient minds, and pronounce the fate of Daedalian hands: As much glory comes to you, Landi, from your pen, as to Cosmo and Macro, the painters of our age.[77]

Even if Tura is not referred to here, the important point is that a scribe is being compared to two painters. Guarino's poem is yet another example of a North Italian paragone of painters and writers which would culminate in Leonardo da Vinci's well-known exploitation of the dual aspect of writing in making his

claim for the dignity of painting: 'You have set painting among the manual arts . . . if you call it mechanical because it is by manual work that the hands represent what the imagination creates, your writers are setting down by pen by manual work what originates in the mind.'[78] The paragone may have had additional force in Ferrara because of the expanded competencies of many of the personnel involved in the production of books. Throughout the fifteenth century a host of scribes working for the Este were also active as miniaturists.[79] There was no practical reason why one trained in calligraphy should not have been able to execute decorated initials and historiated capitals; in fact, the areas of potentially overlapping competencies between scribes and miniaturists led to attempts at strict territorial demarcation in other cities.[80]

The work of these scribes was extremely diverse: by no means did they produce a uniform bookhand based on the Florentine model of humanist littera antica. Scribes such as Carlo di San Giorgio appear to have devised distinctive hands for use on particular projects, including a variation of the humanist hand adulterated with Gothic features.[81] Transcribing a text could become the occasion for demonstrations of calligraphic virtuosity by the scribe himself; the most famous, even notorious exemplar of this practice beyond the Este court was Felice Feliciano, who in the 1460s and 1470s was pursuing an erratic itinerary from one North Italian town to another.[82] An example of the priority placed by the court on demonstrations of fine writing is illustrated by a payment from 1455 to one Domenico Gatto da Bagnacavallo 'per havere exemplato arte scripture'; the scribe was rewarded for his virtuosity rather than for delivering a commissioned copy.[83]

The work of the scribe and miniaturist is intimately related to the production of identity in that the physical appearance of books was central to an author's ceremonial self-presentation at the Este court.[84] In the dedication page of Giovanni Bianchini's Tabulae astrologiae, made for a member of the court in the 1450s, the decoration of the book encapsulates the theme of the author's courtly identity. The lavish combination of a florid Gothic bookhand with an illumination in the manner of Tura continues the process of 'presenting' the author, conferring on him and his work the capacity to attract and to please a patron, which is the theme of the presentation miniature. This is, in fact, a double-patronage scenario, where Borso d'Este, the author's protector and employer, presents Bianchini to the Emperor Frederick III (plate 12).[85]

It is this state of affairs that Decembrio also finds repugnant. He manifests a Petrarchan prejudice against the work of scribes, considering them ignorant, wayward and careless in their transmission of valuable texts. De politia litteraria (Book V, section 60) contains a dialogue on the evaluation of books and modern authors which has been studied by Jon Pearson Perry. In part this is a polemic against the commodification of decorated books and fine writing encouraged at the court of Borso d'Este. The dialogue is Decembrio's account of the reception of the playwright and popular entertainer Ugolino Pisano by Leonello and his circle in 1437. Ugolino, who hoped to extend his popular

12 Master of the Borso d'Este Missal, frontispiece to the *Tabulae astrologiae* of Giovanni Bianchini: Borso d'Este presents Bianchini and his work to the Emperor Frederick III. Ferrara, Biblioteca Comunale Ariostea. Manuscript on parchment (34.2 × 24.5 cm).

success into élite circles by presenting Leonello with a copy of his latest comedy, is portrayed by Decembrio as a deranged figure eventually ridiculed for his presumption by Leonello's supercilious little group of 'generis nobilitate et equestrii ordine praestantes'. His downfall results from his theatrical manner of self-presentation (Decembrio refers to him as 'laureatus larvatus', the masked or phony laureate); he is dressed incongrously in sumptuous, princely style, and this signifies his crowd-pleasing vulgarity and theatrical shallowness. Although sprinkled with learned classical allusions, his speech in the prince's presence rapidly degenerates into coarse, scatological witticisms, and his play, while in elegant script, is an unseemly low-life farce about cookery's claim to be a liberal art. Central to Decembrio's attack is the point where Ugolino truly damns himself, by maintaining that the physical appearance of a book is as important as its content. In the person of Ugolino Pisano the author and the scribe are an indivisible entity; the scribe is essential to the

author's self-fashioning, his generation of a public mask. The point is made all the more forcibly in the text by a confusion of words which scandalises Ugolino's interlocutors:

'Which kind of handwriting do you regard as the most fitting?'
'It is certainly the one that you behold there in this little book, in which I undertook the greatest pains to have the writer copy it in the loveliest hand.'
'Come now,' Tito [Strozzi] replies, 'Shame on you for your vulgar, corrupt way of speaking! Do you call him thus by the name writer [*scriptor*] when you meant to say copyist [*librarius*]?'[86]

This distinction was a matter of the utmost concern to Decembrio, who also wrote a tract called *De scriptore et librario deque eorum variis officiis* ('Of the writer and the copyist and of their different responsibilities').[87]

Ugolino is finally dismissed with the following rebuff:

One book will be superior to another in worth as much as a poet larvate differs from a poet laureate; or as if you were to weigh in the scales here the works of Plato and Aristotle, written on paper and cheaply bound, and there those of a certain Scotus, written on 'the lovely stuff' as the saying goes. To which do you think we ought to be more inclined?[88]

Tura pursued a form of self-fashioning comparable to Ugolino's, as (to a less self-conscious degree) did other Ferrarese artists working in a similar style. The painter's appropriation of calligraphic skill is an emulation of the prestige of writing, something of which professional writers were also able to take advantage.[89] Writing offers a model for the production of a certain kind of identity. As is stated most explicitly by Filarete, it is associated with the autograph and the distinguishability of hands in painting. However, this is an identity which for scribes and painters is assumed and performed through training rather than natural endowment. If a scribe lays claim to an identity through his style, it is on the basis of his skilled penmanship; a scribe has no autograph hand expressive of himself alone. Although his pen is mainly at the service of the visual production of the author, the scribe can occasionally recoup this visual identity as an advertisement for himself. Surviving written samples by Felice Feliciano show not only his command of various types of writing, including a Roman epigraphical majuscule, but also a multi-coloured assortment of figures, intricate patterns and flourishes, labyrinths, knot motifs and figure drawings which demonstrate the full extent of his skill with the pen (plate 13).

Felice's demonstrations of brilliant calligraphy anticipate certain kinds of invention produced by Leonardo at the Milanese court; as noted above, Guarino's poem to Jacopo Landi refers to the scribe in connection with Daedalus, the famous deviser of labyrinths. Felice's own signature is a calligraphic demonstration of this kind. His name is presented in enciphered form, concealed within the Latin words *Felix Augusta*, and this places his

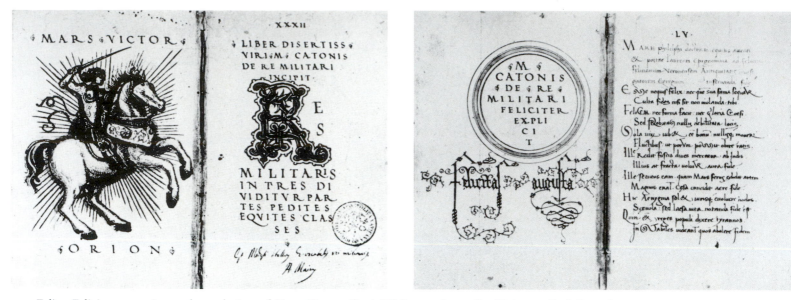

13   Felice Feliciano, opening and conclusion of Cato, *De re militari*. Biblioteca Apostolica Vaticana, Cod. Reg. Lat. 1388.

identifiability as much in the form of the words and in the quality of their execution as in their sense. The fabulous red banner in Tura's *Execution of St Maurelius*, a labyrinthine fantasy claiming much of the visual interest in this little scene showing the martyrdom of Ferrara's patron saint, might be identified as a similar kind of virtuoso demonstration (plate 5). The unusual tondo form of this and other narrative scenes by Tura may itself reflect the modes of pictorial framing characteristic of book production.

There are other kinds of evidence for the social significance of such demonstrations of calligraphic virtuosity. The foregrounding of skilful penmanship has a direct bearing on the expansion of writing practices in the secular sphere – chancelleries, court bureaucracies, secular libraries – and an increase in professional openings for those trained in the various forms of writing in demand. Although definitely an eccentric and extreme case, the pattern of Felice Feliciano's career, in which the profession of scribe expanded opportunistically into a host of other occupations such as illustration, archaeology, composing romance fiction, printing and even alchemy, could be seen as paradigmatic.[90] There are concrete remnants of professional advertisements by other scribes who wandered from court to court, from city to city, from one bibliographical project to another. These are advertisements in the most literal sense – sample books which demonstrate the scribe's command of various hands and examples of book decoration – and these occur throughout Europe in the fifteenth century.[91] They 'sell' the craft of the scribe as the key to the world of learning and to jobs in high places, especially the court.[92] In early sixteenth-century Germany, the language of penmanship disseminated by the manuals and writing-masters finds a striking correlative in the three-dimensional flourishes of the great limewood sculptors.[93] The social prestige of calligraphy increased with the rise of printing. In the early decades of the following century printed

treatises and handbooks on fine writing were among the earliest manifestations of a literature which purported to teach its readers the principles of excelling in an art in accordance with its practice at court.[94]

In conclusion, the calligraphic element in Tura's style, manifest in intricate contour, complex linear patterns and calligraphic marks, are to be seen as the self-conscious production of a style, the invention of an identity through devices associated with manual virtuosity. The practice of the scribe shares with that of the painter a manipulation of the individualising mark in the service of creating a professional persona. Writing serves as the model for the painter because of its connotations of social prestige and its association with an 'authorial' effect. The irony of Tura's style, which first appears extravagantly personal and distinctive, is that it ultimately presents the repeatability of the mark, the trace of the hand, along with its individuality. Even though in Tura's work we seem to encounter the strident presence of the individual, this presence is something which is itself being painted or written as much as it is the agent of the writing. The same pursuit of the individual effect is taken up by several of Tura's followers and later fifteenth-century Emilian painters – frequently by transforming themselves into Tura: Lorenzo Costa, Ercole de' Roberti, the Master of the Schifanoia *September*, Marco Zoppo, Jacopo Filippo d'Argenta, Antonio Cicognara, Antonio da Crevalcore. Some of their works have posed problems of attribution as a result, particularly in the case of miniaturists.[95] Portraiture presents an interesting case of Tura curtailing his calligraphic manner in the interests of description; in the New York *Portrait of a Man* (plate 14), the calligraphic interest is confined to the waves of golden hair. The same can be said of the one miniature which has convincingly been attributed to Tura, the portrait of the Duchess Eleonora d'Aragona (plate 15), which denotes the dedication of a court poet's poem on rulership. But there is irony in the fact that the most Tura-

14   Tura, *Portrait of a Man* (fragment). New York, Metropolitan Museum of Art. On panel (30.2 × 21.6 cm).

A LA ILLVSTRISS·ETEX
CEL·M·M·LEONOADRA
GON·DVD·FERRADEL
MOD·DREGERE·EDRE
GNRE·ANT·CRNZAN

exotic inscription – of the artist working as a scribe or a cipherer – goes along with a pointed witholding of the artist's historical identity. Lorenzo Costa's *St Sebastian* (plate 17), signed by the artist in Hebrew characters, was identified none the less as the work of Tura by Berenson, an ironic effect probably intended by the artist who affirmed yet veiled his authorship.[97] The mysterious Antonio da Crevalcore, one of the latest and strangest practitioners of a manner closely related to Tura's, signed at least one of his works with a regular written signature. The recently discovered *St Peter* and *St Paul* (plates 18 and 19) are the most developed example of this style's self-reflexive aspect, its tendency towards visual wit and paradox.[98] The artist again seems to associate his pictorial mastery with the work of the scribe; one of the most visually compelling elements in the *St Paul* is the still-life of inkwell and pens accompanying the opened codex turned towards the picture surface. The irony here is that this writing stands again as a mask, a concealment of the artist; his identity is not presented in the writing in the painting, which

16 Tura or follower, *Portrait of a Man*. Washington, D.C., National Gallery of Art. On panel (36 × 27 cm).

15 Tura or follower, *Eleonora d'Aragona*. Frontispiece to Antonio da Cornazzano, *De modo regere et regnare*. New York, Pierpont Morgan Library, MS M 731, fol. 2*v*. Manuscript on parchment (24 × 16 cm).

like of Ferrarese portraits, the Washington *Portrait of a Man* (plate 16), is probably not by him. Although the forms of the face have his distinctive angular quality, Joseph Manca has pointed out that the smooth and opaque paint surface, and the lack of linear hatching, is unusual in Tura's oeuvre.[96] As we shall see in relation to his paintings of saints and and in his devotional images, Tura's devices of stylisation were not deployed indiscriminately, but placed in the service of the work's meaning and function.

Two further examples of other artists using Tura's manner show the extent to which it was regarded as a kind of masking or assumed persona. In a few cases the display of writing or

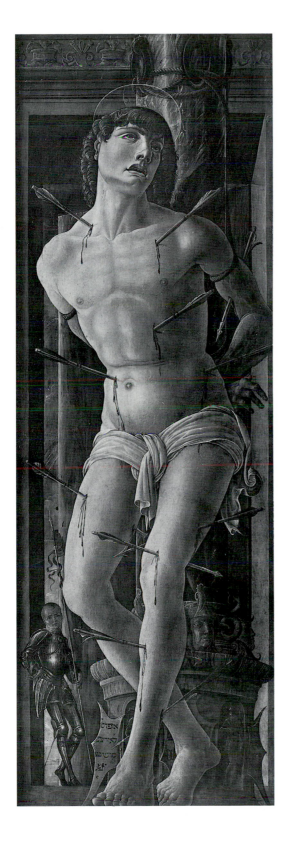

17 Lorenzo Costa, *St Sebastian*. Dresden, Gemäldegalerie.

18 Antonio da Crevalcore, *St Peter*. Rome, Fondazione Memmo.

19 Antonio da Crevalcore, *St Paul*. Rome, Fondazione Memmo.

has the status rather of represented handwriting, the writing of an Other. In the pendant painting of *St Peter*, the artist's identity is disclosed, but distanced from the painting's indexical, manual register. The sign of authorship is buried in the painting, among the ruins and on the sepulchre, in the severed inscription which forms an anagram of his name.

'NON VANIS AUT LASCIVIS': PAINTING, POETRY AND THE *STUDIO* OF BELFIORE

THE PRINCELY *STUDIO*

ONE OF THE MOST DISTINCTIVE CULTURAL FORMS associated with the princely courts of the fifteenth century was the *studio* or *studiolo* – a small and magnificently decorated space ostensibly devoted to the prince's pursuit of cultivated leisure. The symbolic force of the private study in figuring the 'contemplative life' was not itself new; what distinguished the princely *studio* was its redirection of humanist ideals of privacy (*otium*) towards the political ends of display, a circumstance also manifest, as we have seen, in the production of manuscripts for the court.[1] In essence the *studio* was a backdrop against which the prince could stage the appearance of industrious solitude, thereby affirming the humanist ideology of personal culture as an entitlement to rule. The *studio* could be seen as expressing a union between ideals of private cultivation, as described by Pliny or Cicero, and the more ostentatious gestures of princely magnificence.[2]

The first princely *studio* of the *quattrocento* to be known for its decoration was created at the palace of Belfiore outside Ferrara for the Marquis Leonello d'Este in the 1440s; this was the latest and most innovative of a series of novel artistic experiments devised at his court, through which Leonello sought to express his emulation of ancient rulers.[3] Specially singled out for praise by contemporary poets and orators who referred to the *studio* was a series of paintings of the nine Muses by Cosmè Tura, Angelo da Siena and other artists. The enthusiastic response of these early commentators testifies to the pioneering status of these paintings; they can now be recognised as the earliest pictorial cycle of the Renaissance to depend indisputably on the mythological and philological interests of the humanists. They are the forerunner of a succession of mythological works which are today mostly better preserved and better known: the reliefs of the Tempio Malatestiano, the Temple of the Muses in Urbino and the mythologies of Mantegna and Costa for Isabella d'Este.

Different personal and political concerns were bound up with the cycle of the Muses from the beginning. The initiative was primarily that of Leonello d'Este, though there is no trace of his conception of the cycle, in whatever form he expressed it; there is, however, a letter of 5 November 1447 in which his friend and former teacher, the humanist Guarino of Verona, instructed the prince on how the Muses should be represented. It is largely in terms of this intervention by Guarino that the Belfiore cycle has been viewed in modern scholarship. The letter has been the basis for the association of six dispersed panel paintings which are now identified as survivors of the original decoration, and for Michael Baxandall and Anna Eörsi the programme has been the key to interpretation of the images and the understanding of the rationale for the commission.[4]

Although the paintings are manifestly dependent on Guarino's instructions, they are far from being straightforward pictorial re-creations of the text. By contrast, a series of reliefs of the Muses executed by Agostino di Duccio in the 1450s for the Tempio Malatestiano in Rimini manifests a far more scrupulous attempt to follow Guarino's specifications regarding the attributes, attitudes and other particularities of the figures. The Ferrara cycle was not completed until more than a decade after the death of Leonello in 1450, during the reign of his brother Borso whose cultural policies and tastes as patron may have placed a different set of demands on artists. The paintings that survive are composite products which, as recent scholarship has revealed, have been subjected to a substantial process of revision and alteration. There has been little attempt so far to see the divergences from Guarino's programme in the first phase of execution, under Leonello, or the reworking of the painting by later artists, under Borso, as having a coherence and purpose which might require interpretation. My concern here will be to describe these disjunctions as marking the traces of other interests. They are testimony to the pressure of other initiatives, which the explanation of the paintings entirely in terms of Guarino's programme would not allow us to specify. I also want to restore to the paintings their status as products identified with a hand or a persona, that of 'Cosmos noster', whose style is emblematic of certain values for his audience.

The role of the artist and the status of painting may have emerged as a particular concern for humanists at this time because the Belfiore commission appears to have brought about a difference in the treatment and perception of the principal painters involved. Leonello employed Angelo da Siena, to whom Ciriaco d'Ancona referred as Angelo Parrasio in a celebratory description of two Muses in 1449 and who is mentioned by Guarino alongside Gentile da Fabriano and Pisanello, the greatest painters of the century, in 1452.[5] Borso, as we saw in the previous chapter, ceremonially invested Angelo with a house in return for an annual feudal tribute. In 1460, following Angelo's death, Cosmè Tura is referred to in the accounts of the Camera Ducale as 'depintore dello studio', although he had probably become involved under Angelo at a much earlier stage.[6] By 1461 his reputation was sufficiently established that Gian Galeazzo Sforza sent an artist protégé to Ferrara to study under Tura.[7] While one of the paintings for Belfiore, the *Thalia* now in Budapest, bears the proud signature of another artist – 'Ex Michaele Panonio' (Michele Pannonio) – it is only the names of the official painters Angelo and Cosmè which are preserved in the literary and archival records of the *studio*.

The anomalies and disjunctions between Guarino's programme and the paintings may be explained as no more than typical idiosyncrasies of the artists themselves. Odd or disquieting aspects of other works by Tura, such as the Roverella altarpiece, have been frequently dealt with in this way. Since my discussion of the paintings is largely centred on their relation to a beholder, I am less interested in establishing the division of labour between artist and humanist adviser than in considering the artist as a persona staged by the work of art, in and through the totality of its effects. The problem can be confronted by considering again what Tura's audience or audiences may have expected from works of art. Since the theme of the Muses has a direct bearing on the concerns of the humanists at court, it will be necessary to consider this literary intelligentsia's responses to art and its conception of the relation between images and letters. A certain reading between the lines of the humanists' most frequently articulated prejudices will, however, be necessary, since its characterisations of painting often occur in the form of negative comparisons with poetry or history. I will argue for a theory of the image which cannot be documented by taking literally humanist comparisons and analogies between painting and poetry; the more productive ground is precisely those areas of poetic performance which fall outside rational and moralising humanist characterisations of the art. It is largely within their own practice that painting and poetry speak to and corroborate each other, rather than at the level of theoretical statements about poetry which characterise their subject by

establishing its superiority to its rivals – and painting most frequently appears as a rival.

I will be considering the Muses as a metaphor for cultural practices which coexisted and influenced each other at the court – humanist pedagogy and classical scholarship, the revival of particular kinds of Latin verse, the painting and viewing of pictures, the cultivation of a private or public self-image by two Ferrarese princes. The Muses could stand for all of these, because of the multivalent traditions and values they had come to personify by the fifteenth century. These cultural practices were also controversial, and their reference to the Muses reflect the strongly gendered terms in which matters such as classical antiquity, poetry and painting were discussed. There was above all an ambivalence about the Muses as feminine symbols which provided a means of addressing broader ambivalences regarding humanist culture, the nature of artifice and the ethics of display. The Muses had an equivocal status which occasionally reached the level of articulate debate, regarding the precise qualities which they could be said to designate. Were they the learned foundations of poetry, the wisdom which speaks within it, or were they part of its seductive, rhetorical effect, on the level of ornament and style? One might say that this instability becomes particularly charged in relation to painting, above all because of fundamentally sensual nature of painting – does the painting of a Muse redeem the art of painting as an elevated or noble pursuit, or does 'she' cooperate in the most specious tricks of the painter's artifice? In the move from the intellectual, verbal construction of the Muse to her visual depiction, a tension is set up between woman as object of beholding, of sensual attraction, even idolatrous worship, and woman as abstract sign, an allegorical vessel within which solemn moral and scholarly preoccupations can be made sensible, if not sensual. The humanists characterised their pursuit of *scientia* in highly eroticised and gendered terms. This is John Argyropoulos, writing in 1458 on the mind's image of Science 'in the guise and appearance of a maiden': 'Her comeliness, which can be perceived in the mind, cannot in any way be described in words. O what loves would she then arouse, what ardours, what desires, indeed, if I may say so, what lusts, to approach, to embrace, to cherish her, if she were seen by the mind as she really is.'[8] Was it possible that painters, classed by humanists as base mechanicals incapable of such lofty thoughts, could give visible form to this desire?

What, in any case, did the cultivated leisure supposedly conducted in the *studio* consist of? In the case of the princely *studio*, what kind of knowledge was symbolised by the room and its decorations? The comments of two rival humanists encountered in the previous chapter are not on the surface incompatible, but the shades of difference they register point to a broader divergence of values, above all with regard to the status of antiquity and ancient knowledge, especially poetry. Decembrio's *De politia litteraria* begins with a dialogue on the furnishings, apparatus and activities appropriate to the private humanist library, again involving the participation of Leonello d'Este. Typically, the kinds of activity envisioned as taking place there are of a rather sober nature: reading from a library of select Greek and Latin authors, a little music and astrology, the contemplation of certain appropriate and decent pictures, such as 'the Caesars, or the Gods, or the ancient heroes' or, even better, 'St Jerome writing in his hermitage'.[9] The maligned poet Ugolino Pisano, on the other hand, comments in passing on the function of a private study in the context of a discussion of the decorum of reading:

> Juvenal, Persius, Martial, Propertius, Tibullus, Catullus, the *Priapeia* of Virgil, Ovid's *Ars amatoria* and *Remedia amoris* should not be read in public but left to the private study of those wanting to see them. Thus knowledge may be gained and no inexperienced youth will be contaminated by reading them.[10]

What kind of knowledge is being referred to here? Why was it considered to be contaminating? This knowledge at any rate seems bound up with a problematic relation to antiquity, a relation conceived in terms of dangerous curiosity; the function of the *studio* as it appears here is to contain that dangerous relation by consigning it to privacy. As we shall see, however, the Belfiore *studio* seems also to have been designed to make that relation visible in all its ambivalence, and to exhibit it as a privilege of the *studio*'s occupant.

THE PROGRAMME AND THE PAINTINGS

Guarino's letter of 5 November 1447 begins with a compliment to Leonello for his admirable and magnificent idea of painting the Muses.[11] The idea is worthy of a prince, writes Guarino, since it is free of vain and lascivious *figmentis*. But the issue is more complicated than Leonello realises, he adds, since there is a debate about the number of the Muses and about their specific characteristics. The Muses are defined as 'notiones . . . et intelligentias' which correspond to the human desire for knowledge and the investigation of knowledge in its various forms. As μωσθαι means to investigate, so Μουσαι are 'women who investigate'. However, the quasi-Platonic conception of the Muses as ideas suggests that for Guarino, as well as symbolising a human faculty, the Muses are sources rather than effects of human labours – the divine origin of poetry.

Clio, who presides over history, fame and antiquity, should hold a trumpet and a book, and be dressed in garments embroidered with various colours and figures, in the manner of old-fashioned silk cloth. Thalia's name signifies germination; thus she developed the planting of fields, and should be represented holding small cuttings in a dress decorated with flowers and leaves. Erato presides over matrimony and the duties of love, and so will be shown joining and placing a ring on the hands of a boy and a girl. Euterpe invented pipes and gives direction to the leader of a choir; Melpomene, discoverer of vocal melody, holds a book of musical notes; Terpsichore devised ritual dances and movements of the feet and is thus to be shown as a director of a group of dancing boys and girls. Polyhymnia, who controls the cultivation of fields, wears hitched skirts and carries bowls of seeds and clusters of grapes and wheat; Urania, the Muse of astronomy, should hold an astrolabe and contemplate the heavens. Finally Calliope, the Muse of poetry and knowledge imparted by teaching (*doctrinae*), who provides the other arts with a voice, should have three faces corresponding to the universal range of poetry – divine, heroic and human.

Among the many features of Guarino's letter that might require comment or interpretation I wish to give particular attention to four points: first, the implied importance among all the arts of Calliope and poetry; second, the displacement (or possible absorption by Calliope) of the more familiar significances of Thalia, Melpomene, Polyhymnia and Erato – respectively, comedy, tragedy, mime and erotic lyric poetry; third, the assertion that the idea of painting the Muses does not proceed from wanton or trivial delusions ('non vanis aut lascivis referta figmentis'); and fourth, the prominence given to agriculture. But before addressing these issues, it will be necessary to introduce the paintings and consider their relation to Guarino's letter.

The humanist commentators on the *studio* – Ciriaco d'Ancona, Basinio da Parma, Lodovico Carbone – refer to only one or two paintings, those of Clio and Melpomene, neither of which survives. In a letter of 1449 Ciriaco records a visit to the *studio* of Leonello, which he found 'beautifully and marvellously adorned with the divine images of the Muses, with sacred attributes and exceptional and remarkable ornaments'.[12] There were at that time to be seen two works in progress by 'Angelus Parasius': Clio is described in accordance with Guarino's description, and Ciriaco records the *epigramma* which Guarino had provided for this Muse as being inscribed beneath the figure.[13] Melpomene, however, was not depicted with a musical score but playing a cithara and singing what seemed to be a sacred hymn while looking towards Olympus.[14] Ciriaco considers Angelo the equal of 'Roger of Bruges', and he lavishes much praise on the gems, flowers and rich cloths with which the Muses were adorned, for through these, he says, 'I am led even more to admire the painter's genius' ('vehementius equidem pictoris ingenium admirari cogor').

A panel in the Szépművészeti Múzeum in Budapest is now recognised as *The Muse Thalia* from the Belfiore series (plate 21). The painting, signed by Michele Pannonio and bearing both Guarino's Latin verse and a Greek version, shows a woman crowned with ears of corn and seated on a richly jewelled throne, holding a rose and a vine branch in her hands which she appears to offer to the observer. The forms of her body swell beneath her tightly fitting dress, which is becoming unlaced beneath the right breast, and which is raised and gathered at her right knee. Above her head four putti bear branches heavy with peaches and the throne is flanked by two jewelled vases containing lilies, an Este emblem.[15] Between the cartouches bearing the Latin and Greek versions of Guarino's epigram (the Latin runs 'Plantandi leges per me novere coloni': 'Through me the country folk know the rules of planting') appears the *paraduro*, an *impresa* of Borso d'Este showing a rustic fence used in drainage and irrigation. As a result the panel has

The meaning of Thalia's rose, however, might be considered to assume different connotations when placed alongside the figure (formerly in the Strozzi-Sacrati collection and now in the Ferrara Pinacoteca Nazionale), which Anna Eörsi convincingly identified as *The Muse Erato* (plate 22). The two-tier structure of the sides of the throne even suggests a massive 'E'. Erato, who again coolly engages the gaze of the observer, holds a long stem of red roses in her right hand; with her left, she unlaces the bodice of her close-fitting black dress. Her green and white mantle has fallen from her shoulders and she shakes her

21 Michele Pannonio, *The Muse Thalia*. Budapest, Szépművészeti Múzeum.

22 Angelo da Siena (?) and a collaborator of Tura, *The Muse Erato*. Ferrara, Pinacoteca Nazionale.

been dated within the 1450s, probably in the interval between Angelo's death and Tura's appointment as court painter (1456–9).[16]

There appears to be a specific and emphatic address to a viewer here, with the figure's extended, strangely foreshortened arms, and with the extraordinary narrow-eyed gaze and facial expression, of a type favoured in court art under Borso and occuring in the miniatures of Taddeo Crivelli. The eye is also engaged by the level of visual play within the painting – the subtle disturbance of symmetry in the forms of the vases, the cartouches, the poses and gestures of the putti. Nothing here appears very much at odds with Guarino's characterisation of Thalia.

23 Agostino di Duccio, *The Muse Erato*. Rimini, 'Tempio Malatestiano' (San Francesco), Chapel of the Liberal Arts.

Boccaccio, the most important authority on mythology for the period, had written on the rose as a symbol of desire, the ephemerality of pleasure, and its aftermath.[18] The panel has been assigned to Angelo da Siena, with a substantial later reworking in oil of the green mantle and the foot by Tura or one of his collaborators.[19]

The Muse Terpsichore (Milan, Museo Poldi-Pezzoli; plate 24) is again the work of multiple hands, with Tura's intervening in the rendering of the drapery of the Muse and in the dancing putti, to whom he gave a more sinuous and elastic contour and hence a greater sense of abandoned and vigorous movement (plate 34).[20] At a later point, probably after the passing of Ferrara from Este control into the hands of the Papacy at the end of the sixteenth century, the figure was converted into a *Charity*. It may even have been one of the Four Seasons, along with the *Thalia*, the London panel and an unidentified fourth, which could be seen in the Tribunal of the Inquisition at San Domenico in Ferrara until 1783 before acquisition by private collectors.[21]

Despite its survival in another guise, the figure is still recognisable from Guarino's specifications, but again the contrast is noteworthy with the solution devised by Agostino di Duccio (plate 25). Here Terpsichore is a solemn, commanding figure, soberly draped and bearing a wand. She is encircled by dancing boys and girls as specified by Guarino. The Belfiore Muse is a more voluptuous being, richly attired in corporeally expressive garments and watching over the unruly behaviour of three naked, leaping children, of male or indeterminate sex. Exhibitionistic little boys appear in *ekphrases* by Manuel Chrysoloras and Guarino himself, where 'teneriorum aetatis lasciviam' ('wantonness of childhood') is a source of humour or visual delight,[22] but it is hard to reconcile these leaping, grinning and shouting figures with the instruction in movements for divine worship which Guarino assigned to Terpsichore and expressed in the proposed inscription for the figure: 'Ipsa choris aptat saltus ad sacra deorum' ('She arranges the choric dance for sacrifices to the gods'). Naked male children appear throughout the fifteenth and sixteenth centuries in artistic contexts related to marriage, fertility or 'profane love'.[23] Could Tura's particular rendering of the putti again indicate the transposition of the Muse into levels of meaning not apparently allowed for by Guarino's programme?

An anonymous artist influenced by Piero della Francesca (in Ferrara around 1450) painted the standing female figure identified from Guarino's letter as Polyhymnia (Berlin, Gemäldegalerie; plate 26). A preliminary technical examination has tentatively found in favour of its association with the London, Milan, Budapest and Strozzi panels,[24] but the fact that the figure is standing rather then enthroned might be seen as a major breach of uniformity. The landscape manifests a more convincing link with the other Muses, as does the possibility that the same hand can possibly be identified in the *Urania* panel. Apart from a few details (the hitched skirts, the bowls of seed, also disregarded in the corresponding figure of Polyhymnia in Rimini), the connection with Guarino's letter is persuasive, but more substantial technical evidence is wanting for its relation to the other

stockinged foot free of its sandal. In pointed contrast with these gestures of loosening and unbinding is the artfully braided and fastened hair, which we are probably also intended to imagine as soon to be unfastened.

How do such details relate to Guarino's *epigramma* 'Connubia et rectos mortalibus addit amores' ('She gave to mortals matrimony and honest loves') and his direction that Erato preside in a priestly capacity over a marriage, as she was represented in the more faithful visualisation of Guarino's programme by Agostino di Duccio at San Francesco in Rimini (plate 23)? If this Erato still presides over marriage or 'rectos amores' she embodies a more earthly or (literally) epithalamic conception of matrimony; the motif of undressing suggests Lucian's description of the painting of the *Marriage of Alexander and Roxana*. Perhaps here, however, Erato is being restored to the role in which she appears in Ovid and other poets, as the patroness of erotic poetry. Red roses might have had a rather charged significance in a court society where the most popular reading-matter was the vernacular romances of chivalry, and the erotic connotations of the red rose were also maintained in humanist Latin poetry.[17]

24   Tura and collaborator, *The Muse Terpsichore*. Milan, Museo Poldi-Pezzoli. On panel (117.5 × 81 cm).

The most problematic member of this group of images, in terms of Guarino's letter, is also the best known and most admired – Tura's masterly Muse, long known as *Venus*, *Springtime* or *Allegorical Figure* (London, National Gallery; plate 28). On a throne ornamented with monstrous golden dolphins, shells, pearls and rubies, a sumptuously attired figure bearing a branch of ripe cherries averts her gaze and assumes a posture of studied indifference. The mantle on her shoulders falls into an intricate but rigorously controlled cluster of glistening folds around her legs, a particularly strident instance of Tura's three-dimensional, labyrinthine calligraphy. The affinities with the other panels are strongest in the case of *Thalia*, with the incorporation of figurative elements in the architecture of a canopied throne, together with the intense, swelling corporeality of the figure. There are

26 Ferrarese, *c.*1450, *The Muse Polyhymnia*. Berlin, Staatliche Museum, Gemäldegalerie.

25 Agostino di Duccio, *The Muse Terpsichore*. Rimini, 'Tempio Malatestiano' (San Francesco), Chapel of the Liberal Arts.

panels – and hence its presence in the *studio* by around 1460 – to be secured. It is noteworthy that the figure lacks the modifications by Tura which would have given it some uniformity with the other figures.

With the *Urania* (Ferrara, Pinacoteca Nazionale; plate 27) the connections with the series are more persuasive. The Muse of astronomy adopts an elegant, diagonally balanced pose in order to contemplate the heavens, while with her left hand she holds an astrolabe. Given special prominence here on the back of the throne are the unicorn and the *steccato* (stockade), both devices of Borso d'Este. The association of the unicorn, which signified the chastity of Borso, and the celestial domain symbolised by Urania, must have been recognisable to contemporary viewers from other associations of the unicorn with the duke's 'divinity'.[25]

27 (?) Angelo da Siena and a collaborator of Tura, *The Muse Urania*. Ferrara, Pinacoteca Nazionale.

also similarities with *Erato*, above all in the 'epithalamic' aspect – but with the London Muse the bodice is already unlaced, the hair is unbound, and the sandals and stockings have already been discarded. Anna Eörsi sees this figure as a second version of *Erato*, conceivably painted for an entirely different set of Muses.[26] It is also the most heavily repainted of all the panels we are considering. Beneath the painted surface another enthroned female figure is concealed, with differences in posture, drapery and in the elements of the throne.[27]

The possibility has been raised that Tura's image, together with his repainting of the Strozzi and Poldi-Pezzoli panels, dates from

substantially later; in 1481 Tura is documented as making alterations to a group of four oil paintings of women and for the execution in oil of three nude figures of women, all for the new *studio* of Duke Ercole d'Este in the Palazzo del Corte.[28] Should this ever prove to be the case, the interpretation proposed in this chapter regarding the paintings and humanist self-imaging does not change. The paintings are all sufficiently close to Guarino's programme to indicate how the text was understood, resisted or transformed by humanists and artists either around 1450 or as late as 1481. Before resuming the discussion of the paintings as a realisation of Guarino's directions, I will show that there are in any case reasonable grounds for an earlier dating of this painting.

DATING TURA'S ALTERATIONS

The most complete of the records of Tura's work on the 1481 project refers to a payment for 'the painting in oil of three nude figures of women and the alteration of four panels painted in oil with four female figures'.[29] It has been suggested that the London panel, together with the *Terpsichore*, *Urania* and *Erato* – all of them wholly or partly repainted – formed part of this later cycle of unknown theme, possibly including three individual panels with nude figures. The inclusion of nude figures, and the possibility that the later series consisted of only seven panels, suggests that this later series did not represent the nine Muses (who are almost never shown nude), but Virtues or Liberal Arts.[30] The *Terpsichore* could have been adapted as a *Charity* for a Virtues cycle (as indeed happened to the figure at some point in its history) and the *Urania* could have been reclassified as *Astronomy* for a Liberal Arts series. Yet even if all the surviving panels were re-used, their identities were not so radically altered that it is no longer meaningful to consider them in relation to Guarino's programme; on the contrary, figures such as the *Thalia* and *Erato* make most sense in relation to his conception of the Muses.

It is not possible to be conclusive on this point, but there are enough grounds to be cautious about assigning the surviving panels under discussion to the 1481 *studiolo*. The *Thalia* still bears the inscription identifying her as a Muse, and the panel bears no signs of repainting. Tura's alterations to the London panel suggest an intention to bring the figure into a uniformity of conception and design with the *Thalia*, *Urania* and *Erato*, works which stylistically and iconographically pertain to the 1450s. The *Urania* seems to me to belong to the reign of Borso rather than Ercole d'Este; the device of the unicorn (without the palm tree) appears occasionally on coinage from the reign of Ercole, but it was more extensively and prominently employed in Borso's personal imagery – for example, in his great illuminated Bible (Modena, Biblioteca Estense), in the *March* fresco in Palazzo Schifanoia and for his triumphal entry into Reggio in 1453, when two 'unicorns' drew a chariot bearing a palm tree. Also, a gilt statue of a unicorn adorned the courtyard of Borso's palace at the Carthusian monastery of San Cristoforo; and a description of a Roman

28   Tura, *The Muse Calliope*. London, National Gallery. On panel (115.7 × 71.3 cm).

29   Taddeo Crivelli, *Justice*, from a page of Leviticus in Borso d'Este's Bible. Modena, Biblioteca Estense, MS V. G. 12=Lat. 422, I, f.56r.

banquet held in 1473 in honour of Eleonora d'Aragona, mentions that one of the dishes was adorned 'with the date palm and the unicorn from the device of Duke Borso'.[31] In terms of design if not artistic hand, as well as provenance, the Strozzi *Erato* forms a pair with the *Urania*. If we discount any connection of the *Urania* with Ercole's *studio* it seems reasonable that the *Erato* must also be excluded. By 1481 the Strozzi figures must also have seemed somewhat naive or archaic; it would be surprising if any repainting carried out at that time were confined to the drapery of the figures.

Regarding the London figure, finally, there is important evidence that it is the work of the younger Tura and that the repainting took place much earlier, during the continuation of the *studio* decoration under Borso d'Este.[32] A miniature in Borso d'Este's Bible, executed by Taddeo Crivelli around 1456–7, reflects elements from both the *Thalia* and the London Muse.[33] This is the figure of *Justice* (plate 29) who, like the London Muse, is swathed in a cloak, holds her arms in a similar posture and maintains a comparably aloof demeanour; her throne is similarly composed of a shell and sea-monsters, around which putti besport themselves with peaches (as in the *Thalia*) and cherries, which are also held by the London Muse.

THE IDENTIFICATION OF THE LONDON *ALLEGORICAL FIGURE*

If the London Muse can be accepted as part of the Belfiore cycle, her identity still poses a problem. In addition to Erato, she has been identified recently as Calliope, but on the basis of a rather vague association of cherries with justice, which falls remotely within the offices of Calliope.[34] The overpainted image discovered through technical examination shows a female figure without conspicuous attributes seated on a throne, the back of

which consisted of a series of closely packed columns or tubes. The conservators identify this as an organ, which prompts them to suggest an identification of the original figure with Euterpe, the 'discoverer of pipes' in Guarino's letter. Such a radical repainting of the figure, suppressing any vestige of this attribute, would make nonsense of Guarino's proposed inscription, 'Tibia concentus hac praemonstrante figurat' ('The flute produces harmony according to her precepts'); it makes more sense to assume, therefore, that with the repainting of the Muse, if she was Euterpe, her identity was changed.

The identification of the figure with Calliope can, however, be strengthened: since pipe-organs are not readily usable as pieces of furniture for sitting on, it might be more plausible to regard the parallel rods in the overpainted image as a bundle of timber, arranged like a rustic fence around the back of the throne.[35] While in keeping with the pastoral or even 'agricultural' theme in the imagery of the Belfiore Muses, the timber throne-back might be a play on the Guarino inscription for the image of Calliope: 'Materiam vati et vocem concedo sonantem' ('I grant to poets their raw material and resounding voice'). *Materia* occurs with some frequency in ancient Latin to refer to wood or timber;[36] this enables an allusion, highly appropriate for painting, to the notion of poets as makers or fashioners as distinct from mimics or imitators, a principle which Tura carries into the virtuoso craftsmanship of the sea-monsters, creatures of poetic fable and artistic ingenuity.[37] The associated notions of making poetry and art are suggested again by an element of the painting which is almost always disregarded or uninterpreted – the cave in the right background showing a smith hammering metal in what appears to be a forge. The inclusion of this element by Tura further helps to dispel doubt that the figure should be seen as a Muse (rather than as a Virtue, or Sibyl, or as Venus[38]) since the presence of the smith is charged with references to the invention of music, which literally means 'the art of the Muses'.

The story of Tubalcain could be intended here; in the fourth chapter of Genesis, Tubalcain is the instructor of artificers in metal, and in a later Ferrarese painting by Dosso Dossi (Florence, Horne Foundation) he is also presented as the inventor of music. A reference could also be intended to the discovery of harmony among the blacksmiths by Pythagoras; harmony was constantly associated with the Muses throughout antiquity and the Middle Ages.[39] In the harmonic bell-like tones which we can imagine as ringing from the forge, we might also find a pictorial metaphor for the 'vocem sonantem' with which, as we could once have read below the image, Calliope equips the poets. Finally, the fantastic throne may itself represent the copious

30 X-radiograph of Tura's *Calliope* (see plate 28).

31 Florentine, 1470s. *The 'prisci vates' Linus and Musaeus*, from the *Florentine Picture Chronicle*. London, British Museum, Department of Prints and Drawings, 1970.3, fol. 32*v*. Pen and ink on parchment.

inventiveness and boundless novelty of the poetic faculty: in the *Florentine Picture Chronicle*, executed in the circle of Maso Finiguerra in the 1470s, the *prisci vates* Linus and Musaeus deliver their songs from similar marvellous thrones composed of acanthus, huge scrolls and naked putti (plate 31).

The monster-dolphins and other 'marine' imagery of the throne, together with the sensuality of the London Muse may also recall an ancient belief which identified the Muses with Sirens. In ancient Greek cosmology both Sirens and Muses were movers of the celestial spheres, and there are a number of poetic substitutions of Sirens for Muses as goddesses of song and of rhetoric.[40] Some authorities even regarded Calliope or Melpomene as the mother of the Sirens.[41] In the Christian tradition this association assumed a negative character, and the invocation of the Muses was always afterwards potentially beset by controversy.[42] In the case of two authorities important for the early Renaissance, the Sirens displace the Muses as figures for pagan poetry. St Basil advised students of the pagan authors to be always ready to stop their ears when they came upon immoral stories of the pagan gods or the lies of the orators, just as Odysseus did when he sailed past the lair of the Sirens.[43] Basil's ironic mis-citation of the episode in Homer (Odysseus did not of course stop his own ears, only those of his men) illustrates the ambivalence and potential duplicity of subsequent Christian attempts to rehabilitate the pagan authors. Among poets connected with the Ferrarese circle of around 1450, Pontano is notable for chosing as his Muse the Siren of Naples, and he dedicated his *Liber Parthenopeus* to her.

Boethius' condemnation of the Muses proved most problematic for later students of antique literature; his *Consolation of Philosophy* begins with the Lady Philosophy driving out the *sirenes* and *scenicas meretriculas* (theatrical whores) who had been dictating tragic elegies to the distressed poet. Boethius' denunciation was to resound throughout the fifteenth century, in the anti-poetic polemics of Giovanni Dominici and Ermolao Barbaro the Elder. In their defences of poetry Albertino Mussato, Petrarch and Boccaccio produced alternative readings of the *Consolation* in order to prove that Philosophy had not banished all of the Muses, but only those of licentious and theatrical as opposed to moral and philosophical poetry; in Mussato the two kinds of poetry are personified by Melpomene and Urania.[44] By the second half of the *quattrocento*, however, there are occasional allusions to the Siren Muse, both by poets with connections to Ferrara and in conjunction with a much less defensive attitude towards the reading or imitation of the pagan authors. Before we can consider this transformation of the Muse in the *quattrocento*, I want to situate Guarino's letter on the Muses more clearly in relation to those debates about poetry in which the Muses had appeared as controversial.

GUARINO AND THE DEFENCE OF POETRY

Although poetry appears to receive only a minor emphasis in Guarino's letter, any discussion of the Muses by a teacher of the *studia humanitatis* writing at this time cannot fail to evoke what had been their most important significance for several generations of humanists since Albertino Mussato – the Muses as goddesses of literature, or as poetry itself.[45] Since antiquity the Muses had designated all intellectual pursuits, but particularly the forms of knowledge which became available to the poet who called on them for inspiration. By the fifteenth century, Virgil's second *Georgic* and Hesiod's *Theogony* and *Works and Days* were regarded as testimony of the encyclopedic knowledge which fell to those who placed themselves under the divine tutelage of the Muses. This knowledge was conceived as a form of inspired cognition and utterance, and its identification with the Muses had assumed a polemical importance with Mussato, Petrarch, Boccaccio and Coluccio Salutati, who were seeking to redeem poetry from the charges levelled against it by Boethius' Lady Philosophy. Far from being opposed to theology or philosophy, they argued, poetry was the originary form of theology – Aristotle himself had stated

that poets were the first to teach knowledge of the gods. Poets, according to Boccaccio, drew on fable (*fabula*) for their subject-matter, and employed artificially wrought modes of speaking which differed from the ordinary, but true poetry concealed religious and philosophical truth under a veil of fiction and was to be distinguished from vulgar story-tellers and devisers of fireside tales:

> This poetry, which ignorant triflers cast aside, is a sort of fervid and exquisite invention, with fervid expression, in speech or writing, of that which the mind has invented. It proceeds from the bosom of God, and few, I find, are the souls in whom this gift is born; indeed so wonderful a gift is it that true poets have always been the rarest of men. This fervor of poesy is sublime in its effects: it impels the soul to a longing for utterance; it brings forth strange and unheard-of creations of the mind; it arranges these meditations in a fixed order, adorns the whole composition with unusual interweaving of words and thoughts; and thus it veils truth in a fair and fitting garment of fiction.[46]

In his later years Salutati resorted frequently to the defence of poetry against both secular and clerical opponents.[47] With Salutati, the accent falls specifically on the educational value of poetry. When the Dominican Giovanni Dominici attacked the teaching of the poets as both useless and potentially corrupting, evoking Boethius' banishment of the Muses, Salutati responded with an account of poetry's central position among all of the Liberal Arts, insisting on its necessity for the social preparation of the individual. As well as their moral value, their reconcilability with Christian doctrine and their usefulness as a preparation for reading scripture, the poets also teach eloquence, which Salutati claimed to be one of the prime goals of education.[48] Borrowing from *De genealogia deorum* and from *Lezione* VII of Boccaccio's *Comento sopra il Dante*, Salutati wrote in 1405–6 a long exegesis of the Muses in his unfinished account of the poetic fables of the ancients, the *De laboribus Herculis*. In the eighth chapter of the first book Salutati discusses the cosmological account of the Muses, citing Martianus Capella and the *Platonici* on the harmony of the spheres, thus enabling him to associate the art of poetry with a divine or celestial origin.[49] As Guarino does later, Salutati treats the number of the Muses as a matter for debate, but the nine-fold division of the cosmos is an argument for their being nine. He follows Boccaccio in providing a specifically pedagogical account of the significance of the Muses, and Fulgentius is cited with approval on the etymological interpretation of the Muses as the process of learning. In view of Guarino's later exegesis, Salutati's explication of Thalia is of particular interest, in that he associates her with 'putting forth shoots' ('germina ponentem').[50] Clio, Urania and Calliope correspond to the meanings generally assigned these Muses – fame, knowledge of the heavens (although in a more theological than astronomical sense), the possession of eloquence ('optime vocis melos'). The remaining Muses, however, are given meanings quite different from their usual associations with genres of poetry or with dance, a feature we also noted with Guarino.[51]

In his next chapter, entitled 'Excusitatio diversitatis allegoriarum', Salutati considers whether Fulgentius perverted the significance of the Muses as it had been ordained by so many ancient authors.[52] But then, since Fulgentius' explanation rings true and seems worthy of approval, it might not be considered inappropriate for those who value learning to choose between the more ancient meaning and finding something new, 'in which, if I am not mistaken, all will benefit, because if we reveal something undiscovered by others, scholars can make progress in the clarity of a better explanation'.[53]

Interpreting the past was thus a poetic as well as a philological enterprise; it involved invention as well as interpretation and following authorities. The example of Salutati shows that Guarino's concerns were shared by the broader community of humanists; the Muses were associated with the humanist investment in pedagogy, and their interpretation has a polemical aspect in that it occurs in the context of a broader defence of poetical myth and the literature of antiquity. Salutati may also have provided a precedent for Guarino's assertion of many possible meanings, and the licence to discover more; this could have enabled Guarino's account of the Muses to be more than a philological compilation and to have the status of an autonomous poetic invention, to be admired (in Albertian terms) as an autonomous literary performance in addition to providing directions to a painter.

Furthermore, in his defence of poetry Salutati stressed the social usefulness of the study of literature which Guarino, in his invention on the Muses, might be seen to be elaborating. In Guarino's characterisation of the Muses as a subject 'neither lascivious nor pointless' he may be seen to be taking Salutati's side against the polemic of Dominici who had attacked the study of poetic *figmenta* on precisely these grounds.[54] Guarino could not have been unconscious of the Boethian attack against the Muses as goddesses of poetry, but the licence to find new meanings enables him to veil strategically their less defensible poetical connotations. His identification of Thalia, Melpomene, Polyhymnia and Erato with agriculture, marriage and vocal melody are a displacement of the more familiar jurisdictions of these Muses – comedy, tragedy, mime and erotic poetry, and it was probably a similar caution that led Guarino to associate the art of dance, presided over by Terpsichore, with sacred worship, a connection put in doubt by the painting. These are the very sensual Muses of the theatre who, in Boccaccio's reading of Boethius, Philosophia had branded as harlots. The theatrical Muse who 'frequented theatres and street corners, exhibiting herself for a fee in low compositions, destitute of a single commendable grace' now required a philological rehabilitation at Guarino's hands (an example of what Stephanie Jed has called 'chaste thinking').[55] The most popular commentary on Boethius in the *quattrocento*, that by the pseudo-Thomas Aquinas, glossed 'scenicas meretriculas' by identifying poets with prostitutes, their craft consisting in stirring up the base passions of their public in pursuit of their own material gain,[56] while Salutati's polemic against Carlo Malatesta's reported destruction of the 'idolatrous' statue of Virgil in Mantua dealt with the charge that poets were mere imitators and hence no better than mimes and actors ('histriones') whose only concern is to please the vulgar masses and to flatter princes.[57]

Guarino's own teaching of grammar was heavily dependent on poets of the stage such as Terence. He maintained a patriotic devotion to the Veronese lyric poet Catullus, sprinkling his letters with lines whose original context would have appalled the bishops and preachers to whom they were sometimes addressed. While erotic poetry was, he claimed, officially banished from the classroom,[58] it was in Guarino's own circle and among his students that the Renaissance interest in Catullus could be said to begin in the 1450s and 1460s, and some of his most distinguished pupils and acquaintances became renowned revivalists of the Latin elegy.[59] In addition to the censure of Boethius, Guarino may have been trying to hold at bay a particularly sensuous conception of the Muses, the 'musa iocosa' or 'musa proterva' ('wanton Muse') invoked by Ovid in his *De remedia amoris* (361–2). As we shall see later, the wanton Muse had returned with a particular vehemence in contemporary imitations of Martial and the Latin elegists, especially as practised by poets connected with Guarino.

Poetry could be said to retain a priority, albeit discreetly, in the compound figure of Guarino's Calliope, who conceals in her ungainly tripartite nature the troublingly secular or profane aspects of poetry. Calliope provides the other arts with a voice, a claim by Guarino which reflects the principal humanist rationale for the study of poetry – it enables the acquisition of eloquence. But the claim could have another meaning germane to Guarino's view of poetry's place in education. Poetry may not only provide the other arts with a voice, but the poetic voice could itself be the very means by which the arts themselves come into being and become forms of knowledge, an assumption which also justified the classroom study of poetry.[60] The second part of Guarino's course of study was devoted to grammar, subdivided into the mastery of language and syntax and the study of mythology, history and geography. The poets were read, along with orators and historians, and subjected to a detailed commentary in order that the students would retain disconnected bits of factual information concerning Latin usage, the names and locutions of cities, rivers and mountains, the identity of historical and mythical personages, together with kinds of meaning 'beyond the plain and obvious' as Guarino's pupil Janus Pannonius expressed it – the hidden allegorical sense of poets such as Virgil.[61]

There is another context suggested by Guarino's programme which implies a conception of poetry as universal knowledge. It has been pointed out that a source where Guarino could have found an agricultural characterisation of both Thalia and Polyhymnia was the *scholion* on Hesiod's *Works and Days* written by the Byzantine John Tzetzes around 1135.[62] The understanding of Hesiod this implied may have been specially suggestive for Guarino. Hesiod was one of the most ancient and venerable figures in the literature and a type of the *poeta theologus*: in his two longer poems the Muses appear as presiding goddesses of didactic poetry and the civilising process itself, for they implant not only the principles of husbandry in the poet of *Works and Days* (Tzetzes merely makes their respective contributions more specific) but also the knowledge of law and religion in the untutored shepherd who speaks in the *Theogony*.

Anna Eörsi, and more recently Jaynie Anderson, have related the agricultural characterisation of the Muses to an iconography of 'Good Government', and especially to the agricultural enterprises of the Este.[63] This is not implausible – secular imagery conceived by humanists, such as the Belfiore and Schifanoia cycles, may have been designed to provided unlimited topoi on princely providence; modern historians have been rather sceptical about the effectiveness or even existence of these policies.[64]

The specific reference of the agricultural theme may be accepted, reinforcing the allusions to sexuality and fertility implied by the unlaced dresses of the Muses. Such a detail combines with the description of luxurious materials and cosmetic artifice to give the Muses an alluring and worldly character. The dress with drawstrings has recently been identified as a pregnancy garment; such a garment is also worn by Piero della Francesca's *Madonna del Parto*, but the solemnity and aloofness of the Virgin reinforces a striking difference in accent of the Belfiore Muses.[65] It is perhaps not meaningful to draw firm distinctions between the iconography of fertility and a more general figuration of sexuality at this time, but the attention of recent students of iconography has focused rather narrowly on one end of the spectrum. Fifteenth-century observers may have been less likely to reduce the 'fertility' of the Muses to such a narrow level of referentiality.[66] If pregnancy is denoted by the unlaced dress, this was not incompatible with a frankly erotic appeal. The association of fertility and eroticism can be illustrated from a not much later appearance of the motif from the Ferrara of Borso d'Este, in the *April* fresco at Palazzo Schifanoia, where the unlaced dress is associated with the graphically intimate behaviour of an amorous couple in the Garden of Venus (plate 32).

Guarino's programme also suggests that for him the agricultural enterprise of the prince would not have been a prime concern. Guarino's purpose is more archaeological than panegyrical, arising from his concerns as a scholar and educator. The return to Hesiod authorises a conception of poetry as moral, didactic and 'useful' rather than trivial, sensual or merely entertaining, and suitable for a prince whose wise government results from his absorption of the lessons of classical literature.

There is hence more of an element of polemic in Guarino's letter than has yet been acknowledged. The project of decorating the prince's studio with the images of the Muses provided Guarino with an important opportunity to establish a self-image of his socially beneficial status as the excavator and elucidator of ancient learning. This self-image, founded on a conception of education, was already identified with the Muses by Guarino. Back in 1419 he had written to the *podestà* of Bologna Gian Niccolo Salerno, the product of a humanist education who had successfully put down a popular uprising in the city:

32 Francesco del Cossa, *April* (detail). Ferrara, Palazzo Schifanoia, Hall of the Months.

You therefore owe no small thanks to the Muses with whom you have been on intimate terms since boyhood, and by whom you were brought up. They taught you how to carry out your tasks in society. Hence you are living proof that the Muses rule not only musical instruments but also public affairs.[67]

In 1442 Girolamo Castello addressed a poem to Guarino through the personae of Herodotus and Hesiod, requesting that the ancient historian and poet take themselves to the house of Guarino and seek from him a volume of Plato. The poem is suggestive regarding Guarino's interest in Hesiod – it was included in a manuscript belonging to him which also included a life of Hesiod and a translation of the *Works and Days*. The poem begins with a description of the house and school of Guarino as 'the Council of Phoebus and the Muses'.[68] Guarino was further identified with Apollo and associated with the return of the Muses by his pupil Janus Pannonius in the panegyric on his teacher composed in the 1450s.[69] One of the most striking revelations of the degree to which the Muses may have constituted something like an allegorical self-image for Guarino is a letter composed within a few weeks of the letter to Leonello we have been discussing, and addressed to Carlo Marsuppini, the chancellor of the Republic of Florence.

In late 1447 King Alfonso of Aragon was at war with Florence and had pitched camp near Pisa. In his entourage was Guarino's son Girolamo who, on attempting to leave the camp and return to Naples, had been captured by the Florentines. In his letter Guarino laments the fact that in a city in which he himself had once encountered only friendship and renown his son should now suffer ignominy and hostility; however much the city had been a generous nurse to the father, it is now an abusive stepmother to the son 'and he whom I would raise to be the delight and sustenance of my old age, and *thus fashion my image in the shrine of the Muses*, in my mind I see him confined in torment' (my emphasis).[70] The painted retreat of the Muses discussed the previous month with Leonello has now evolved into an image of Guarino's posterity – the bearer of his likeness and his memorial.

Guarino's Muse-cult, predicated on the usefulness of the *studia humanitatis* for a life of civic engagement or political responsibility, would, however, receive particular prominence through Leonello; the prince was the most noble product of his 'Council of the Muses', and by surrounding himself with their image continued to place himself under their tutelage.[71] Returning again to the letter on the Muses and its polemical element, one might wonder why, a half-century after the last published attack on the literature of the pagans, it maintains such a defensive attitude towards the Muses, and why it was still necessary to obfuscate their identification with poetry. Did Guarino have some insecurity about the durability of the pedagogical and literary ideals he stood for? A cursory survey of Guarino's correspondence from the year 1447 indicates not only an equally aggrandising and self-publicising seizure of opportunities to broadcast the virtues of his scholarship and teaching, but also some of the urgencies that may have led him to do this.[72] All of these letters devote considerable space to the validity of training in letters and in eloquence to the *vita activa* and to their service in the cause of religion. In addressing the Bishop of Ferrara Guarino offers a Latin translation of Cyril of Alexandria as proof that his studies had 'borne fruit not meriting disdain'. Nicholas V is praised as the product of training in many disciplines with the metaphor of Zeuxis and the virgins of Crotona; he is congratulated especially because as the highest prince of the church he is specially positioned to turn precept into action. King Alfonso is praised not only because he encourages literary pursuits but because he himself seeks personal cultivation in literature. The value of letters is ultimately proven, Guarino tells the king, because it is they, more than mute, unlettered, untransportable images and statues, which can keep the fame of great men alive throughout the world and through history.[73]

A letter to Uguccione Abate concerns a sermon delivered in Ferrara on 7 May 1447 by the Minorite preacher and follower of Bernardino of Siena, Fra Alberto da Sarteano. Like Bernardino, Alberto had been a student of Guarino's many years before, and from the enthusiastic references to him in Guarino's letters, the humanist appears to have viewed him as a model product of a literary education, the embodiment of a reconciliation between the cultivation of liberal studies and a militant Christian orthodoxy. The friar had preached on the hierarchy of theology over the secular disciplines:

> You would wish to have heard, O worthy man, what kind and what great quantity of fruits of learning this [Alberto] brought together within the rising stream of his discourse, what aids to virtue, to fame, to merit, to glory he placed before the eyes, and how much of the avoidance of idleness and folly. [You would have heard] of the order and precedence he established in the hierarchy of disciplines, so that some might be maidservants, some courtiers, and some princes, after which comes the knowledge of sacred letters, the queen and mother of them all, to whom the office is given to be the overseer of the others, and of whom the prophet gives testimony, 'teach me knowledge and goodness'. From hearing these things I call this man not a fountain flowing with the milk of eloquence, but a river, indeed 'a river now of milk and now of nectar'. There was no lack of ancient and venerable examples and proofs, of Gentiles, Hebrews and Christians, kings and princes, of examples from the prophets and sibyls, so that everyone was engulfed with such a plenitude of poets, orators, historians and doctors and it seemed that, as an unheard of and marvellous testimony, his discourse would burst its banks like the Po and overflow.[74]

In the hierarchy of disciplines Guarino does not specify what place might be occupied by literature; the extravagant portrayal of Alberto as every inch a product of the cultivation of literary eloquence suggests a role that is anything but subordinate and which is not clearly reconcilable with a 'gradu disciplinarum'. As with Calliope in Guarino's systematisation of the secular disciplines, the part tends to engulf and comprehend the whole. In voicing approval of Alberto's sermon, Guarino is celebrating a harmony between his own secular intellectual values and the friar's theology which, as he knew from his own experience, could not be taken for granted. An episode of thirteen years previously had brought the teacher into confrontation and submission to chastisement by his own pupil, on precisely an issue of intellectual freedom and artistic licence.

The younger Guarino's belief in the reconcilability of the pagan and Christian worlds had led him to some rather audacious formulations in which the extremes of Christian piety and Catullan licentiousness tended to merge. In an introduction to a course on Augustine's *City of God* taught at Verona in 1424, Guarino celebrated the eloquence of the bishop-saint of his native city, St Zeno:

> So that I might pass over Augustine, Jerome and the other

most learned fathers of the church, lest I speak for too long, take note of the most erudite and famous Zeno, Bishop of Verona. For was not his writing evocative of and wonderfully fashioned not only after Virgil and the other serious poets, but also after the elegance of style and aptness of speaking of the comic, lascivious, satirical and wanton writers?[75]

In 1425 Antonio Beccadelli's *Hermaphroditus*, a book of poems in imitation of Catullus, Martial and the more hedonistic Latin authors began to circulate among an avid audience of humanists who applauded its wit and the unsurpassed elegance of its style. More than any other composition by a modern author, the *Hermaphroditus* seemed to fulfil the dream of a *renovatio* of the poetry of the Ancients, in the form of an imitation which modelled itself specifically on their *licentia*, *procacitas* and *facetia*.[76]

A letter by Guarino commending the book and rationalising the unseemly nature of its subject-matter by an appeal to the licence of poets, began to circulate as a kind of preface to Beccadelli's text. Certain humanists, however, and many members of the clergy, were scandalised by the *Hermaphroditus* with its portrayal of brothel activities, depraved friars, its obsessive naming of genitalia and its celebrations of pederasty. Foremost among those to denounce the book were Alberto da Sarteano, Fra Roberto da Lecce and Bernardino of Siena, together with Beccadelli's enemies Antonio da Rho and Lorenzo Valla. In 1431 the book was denounced by Eugenius IV and burned by the public executioner in Bologna, Ferrara and Milan. Alberto demanded a retraction from Guarino which the humanist promised but failed to deliver until subjected to further pressure. Finally, on 1 January 1435, the retraction was dispatched, 'lest', wrote Guarino, 'I bring discredit on my Muses'.[77] The tone of the retraction is somewhat equivocal; most of the letter is taken up with the insistence that the portrayal of vice can be useful for the teaching of virtue, and with an elaboration of Catullus' dictum that poets should not be identified with the immoral personae they sometimes assume in their works.[78] The very arguments regarding Beccadelli were used again by Guarino in 1450 when, as we shall see, he was forced to defend the poetic content of his pedagogical curriculum; at this stage, the defence of poetry explicitly encompasses both ancients and moderns. With Alberto's reappearance in Ferrara in 1447, the study of ancient letters may again have seemed momentarily under threat. In writing the letter on Alberto's sermon, Guarino may have been seeking to assure the world (since these letters were not intended as strictly private communications), and perhaps even assure himself, that a concordat between militant clericalism and the wisdom and eloquence of the pagans was possible.

It was probably in the spirit of such a belief that he undertook his own systematisation of the arts later that year in drawing up a programme for a cycle of pagan deities in which there is no immediately noticeable hierarchy or apparent subordination to Christian schematisations of knowledge, but where poetry can only rule in a disguised form. Yet by 1450 the threat posed momentarily by Alberto became a crushing reality when another

Franciscan, Giovanni da Prato, appeared in Ferrara and condemned the books of the pagans to the stake, along with those pedagogues who engaged in the teaching of immoral authors such as Terence to schoolboys. Guarino's lengthy reply, citing the uses of the poets by Cyril, Basil, Jerome and Augustine, and conscripting some of the arguments he had employed in defending his approval of Beccadelli, now includes the explicit avowal that the Muses are *ancillae* of theology.[79] His letter to Giovanni da Prato inaugurated a decade of similar defences of poetry, in some cases directed by members of the clergy against their reactionary brethren;[80] in answer to these defences another former pupil of Guarino, the Bishop of Verona Ermolao Barbaro the Elder, dedicated to the future Pope Paul II in 1459 his *Orationes contra poetas*. Fully conversant with the traditions of defence since the *trecento*, Barbaro struck with remorseless scepticism at the claims for poetry's useful and moral character, pointing to the outcast and abject condition of poets since antiquity, the origin of poetry with the pederast Orpheus and the bestial cults of paganism, the absurdity of the presumption that God would speak in a 'theology' which is 'mendax', 'turpis' and 'flagitiosa', and the idea that poetry was superior to rhetoric for the teaching of eloquence.[81] Poetry is again condemned as a 'sirenarum cantu', and Hesiod in particular was singled out to illustrate the uselessness of ancient didactic poetry.[82]

If this all seems to be taking us rather far away from the paintings, it should be remembered that the process of realising Guarino's programme as a work of art took place largely in the wake of his encounter with Giovanni da Prato and during the debates that ensued. In reacting to the rather fraught fortunes of humanism in the 1450s, a period of considerable personal difficulty for Guarino,[83] some of his followers and colleagues assumed a rather less apologetic attitiude. What role might these followers have played in the realisation of the cycle? I believe that there are indications in their poetic responses to the paintings that their involvement might have gone beyond the function of witnessing and applauding. It is these responses to which we will now turn.

THEODORE GAZA, BASINIO DA PARMA AND THE POETIC RE-FASHIONING OF PAINTING

The controversy regarding the *Hermaphroditus* provides an instance of how a modern poetic practice which initially found acceptance within the community of readers and imitators of pagan authors became indefensible when it had to be justified in the broader public realm. The arguments advanced for the defence of this modern poetic practice did not progress beyond what had already been asserted regarding the study and teaching of ancient poetry – that is, we read such poetry in order to learn from its negative moral exemplarity, not because we take pleasure in its depictions of vice; however it was also acknowledged by Guarino that these licentious passages could also demonstrate the artistry of the poet.[84]

Beyond the formula that scandal is made beautiful by art, the development of a poetic theory – a *De poesia* to match Alberti's *De pictura* – which would give due prominence to the most admired or most imitated of ancient and modern poets, might only court controversy and repression. In the wake of the furore over the *Hermaphroditus*, the pressure towards self-censorship would have been more acute. For these admired ancients were Ovid, Martial, Propertius, Tibullus and Catullus, and it is within the tacit humanist approval of the Latin elegy and epigram, manifest more in practice than in theory, that the Muses of Belfiore acquire a polemically symbolic force. Could painting, especially in the unprecedented and influential form it assumed at Belfiore, have allowed a means of symbolising or representing poetry which was less possible in prescriptive theoretical writing? Poetic practice implies a movement away from the model of the *poeta theologus* – the vatic, visionary poet – to a more autonomous conception of the poetic artefact; a corresponding development can be identified in the image of the Muse. The Belfiore *studio* might then be seen as a turning-point for the re-emergence of the worldly Ovidian Muse from Hesiod's awe-inspiring primitive goddesses.

In an oration delivered before Leonello d'Este in 1450 the young orator Lodovico Carbone, another pupil of Guarino, paid tribute to his Greek instructor Theodore Gaza, singling out especially a series of verses in Greek which Leonello had ordered him to write for the *studio*, or, as Carbone calls it, the *sacrarium* of the Muses. Each Muse received a verse on her name and office which was, presumably, incised beneath the paintings:

> I will speak indeed of that Theodore so worthy of honour, to whom I always devote more than half my soul, whose little verses composed about your exquisite Muses you ordered engraved in that most splendid study. Again and yet again I ask, was Callimachus ever able to speak more weightily, or Propertius more sweetly, or Tibullus more beautifully? For they fittingly relate the name and the office of each Muse, and briefly sing their praises with reference to the image. How noble is the mind of this man, to exhibit so much philosophy in such pleasurable things![85]

Carbone emphasises the element of pleasure and delight in Gaza's verses and connects them explicitly with a specific poetic genre – the elegiac tradition of Catullus, Propertius and Tibullus. More than twenty years later Carbone included Latin versions of two of the verses, those for the lost paintings of *Clio* and *Melpomene*, in his dialogue on the *barco* of Ercole d'Este:

> Clio is my name, who celebrates the deeds of men. Gold is my attire and golden is my mind. I am called Melpomene, the daughter of the mighty lord, drawing men with my voice and the gods with my radiance.[86]

The verses are interesting for two reasons; first, because of the distinction both propose between the Muses as metaphysical ideas or essences occupying a divine sphere, and the Muses as embodied, sensible presences knowable by mortals. Second, Gaza emphasises the Muse's power of attraction ('trahens') through an appeal to sense – the golden robe of Clio, the alluring voice and visual splendour of Melpomene. It is precisely within the poetry of Tibullus and Propertius that the Muses cease to be feminised but disembodied agents and become physically present, seen and heard by the poet. In the fourteenth and fifteenth centuries their presence was likely to have been seen largely through the more fully visualised and colourful personifications of late antique poets and mythographers, especially those of Martianus Capella's *Marriage of Philology and Mercury* and Fulgentius' *Mythologies*. In the latter, Calliope caresses the poet and arouses the 'itch' of poetry within him:

> She smoothed my hair with an encouraging touch of her palm branch, and stroking my neck more tenderly than was becoming, she said, 'Well, Fabius, you are now a new recruit to the sacred rites of Anacreon, and so that nothing may be lacking for my young beginner, receive like praise for your composition and, insofar as my Satire has sprayed you with a wanton dew of words and the allure of love holds you prisoner, give up what you are turning into words as you sleep, and whatever you are pleased to be inscribing on papyrus from the Nile, and take my words into your receptive ears.'[87]

In Propertius III.3 the poet receives a vision of Helicon where he describes the abode, the activity and – fleetingly – the tender arms of the Muses as they weave crowns of roses or ivy or touch the lyre. Calliope, recognisable from her face ('ut reor a facie, Calliopea fuit') accosts the poet and berates him for attempting to write epic rather than love poetry – 'to you is entrusted', she says, 'the song of garlanded lovers, furtive encounters, adultery and drunken flight'.[88]

The Muses are frequently associated with the poetic strategy which enables the lover to possess his beloved through the seductive power of his art, as in Propertius I.viii 41–2: 'Apollo and the Muses are not slow to aid lovers; I love, trusting in them, and the precious Cynthia is mine!' Tibullus also introduces the Muses in erotic contexts, notably in the elegy to Priapus (I.iv), and in his second book he impatiently threatens to dismiss the Muses if they have no aid for the lover, since he has not summoned them so that he can sing of wars or the motions of the heavens (II.iv 13). In Propertius again the Muses are closely associated with the person of the beloved – she and they appear to him in dreams to remind him of his debt of service; in the first elegy of the second book, the beloved has become the poet's own Muse: 'Neither Calliope nor Apollo sings these songs to me; the girl herself is the cause of my genius' ('Non haec Calliope, non haec mihi cantat Apollo/ingenium nobis ipsa puella facit').

We are at the beginning, in Augustan love poetry, of an internalisation of the Muse by the poet – they are personifications of his *ingenium* or personalities from his own intimate and private world. These Muses stand in marked contrast to the Muses of didactic and epic poetry – Guarino's concepts and intelligences

– external and demonic forces who act upon the poet. In the poetic responses to the Muses of Belfiore, it is possible to see a transformation taking place: the Muses are 'concepts and intelligences' from a divine sphere, but by virtue of being visible, painted images they have a capacity to fascinate, to haunt the poet's fantasy like the image of a lover, a vivid sensation impressed indelibly upon his memory. This is suggested by the two fragmentary verses of Theodore Gaza, but is made more apparent in the remarkable verse epistle to Leonello d'Este by Basinio da Parma, the prodigious young poet who had arrived from Mantua with his mentor Theodore Gaza in 1445. Now the elegiac mode best serves a need to depict the Muses as alluring apparitions or figments of the poet's own fantasy.

The poet contemplates the celebration of Leonello d'Este who has himself led Apollo and the Muses back to the fountain of Parnassus. Passing the prince's *studio*, he sees the marvellous image of Clio, shining like the evening star above the ocean waves.[89] Later the anxious and distracted poet, falling asleep one night as he attempts to write, is roused by a vision of the Muse:

> Hark, there, she says, are you awake, O faithful minister of Leonello? O keep watchful, for it is not right for poets to indulge in long sleep; with sparing rest get ready to proclaim the divine praises of Leonello. Get up, arise, and sound the name of Leonello to the stars. I will attend willingly, nor will your Muse abandon you, for I am the shining Clio who Leonello ordered to be painted, Clio the most joyful of the Muses. Look at my beauty, sweet friend, my countenance, my cheeks, my sparkling eyes, and remember that you saw my face painted thus. Isn't there a man of our times, one who will rank with the Roman ancestors in benevolence and might, who might be willing to assist your genius?[90]

By means of the painting Basinio introduces a visual and strongly sensual dimension, a kind of ephemeral, private 'elegiac' experience into a poem which constantly alludes to more serious panegyrical intentions. An economic arrangement proposed by the poet is given the form of a desire – the prince's desire for fame and, more implicitly, the poet's desire to be read by the prince. This desire is objectified in the appearance of the Muse who displaces the real object of the poet's desires (Leonello) into a disembodied second register, while she appears as the most strongly and vividly characterised image of the poem. What interests me here is less the 'real', political content of that desire, but the fact that in its poetic expression it transforms a convention of inspiration by the Muses. The convention is transformed in the referral to the power of painting, to female beauty and sensual artifice – the Muse's painted face. The referral to painting implies something here about the nature of poetic language and expression – its inscription in the domain of desire – about which characterisations of poetry by the humanists, or of the relations between poetry and painting, cannot afford to be explicit.

By the mid-*quattrocento* elegiac poetry appears to have interested its authors and readers as a poetry of sensual experience in which appeals to the visual had a prominent place. Perception is appraised within this poetry not as a form of knowledge, but for its vulnerability and undependability, its acute sensitivity to the chaotic workings of desire – the gaze of the poet is invariably the distracted, spasmodic and fallible gaze of the lover. It can be shown that the cycle of the Muses at Belfiore, both in subject and design, originated in the 'elegiac' responses to an earlier work of art in which the ambiguity or arbitrariness of a poetic perception was central. Examining this takes us into a cultural domain which pre-exists and is somewhat disjunct from Guarino's meditation on the secular disciplines in 1447. The question to be considered is what poetry and the Muses may have meant to Leonello, the *de facto* initiator of the Belfiore cycle.

LEONELLO D'ESTE AND GIOVANNI MARRASIO: 'SIC IN AMORE FURENS'

Modern assessments of the character and cultural outlook of Leonello have depended heavily on Decembrio's *De politia litteraria*, in which the prince is described in a series of conversations with Guarino, Tito Vespasiano Strozzi and others on topics of chiefly literary interest. The book is written by a partisan of Guarino and hence may be seen to offer only a rather calculated picture of Leonello's views on art (painters lack *scientia* and their art, unlike poetry, has nothing to do with *ingenium*), vernacular literature (which he is shown to exclude from his ideal library) and the defence of poetry against the friars (poets should be read principally for their moral and historical content). As was discussed in chapter I, such views may represent a careful stage-managing of publicly expressed opinions on Leonello's part, or an appropriation of the prince as a mouthpiece for the opinions of Decembrio.

Decembrio's portrayal of the prince needs to be weighed against the evidence that the historical Leonello was on intimate terms with the painter Pisanello and himself the author of love poetry in the vernacular, of which a couple of fragments survive. Certain examples of Leonello's personal imagery in Pisanello's art, and these poetic remnants, present Amor assuming the custodianship of the faculty of poetic speech. In 1444 Pisanello struck a medal for the marriage of Leonello with Maria, daughter of Alfonso of Aragon, the reverse of which shows a lion playing close attention to a musical score held by a naked winged child. The lion clearly represents Leonello, whose *impresa* of the sail appears above, beside the Este eagle. What we are being shown here is the lion, the noble tyrant of the world of beasts, being made docile and taught to sing by Amor (plate 33).[91]

The theme of love may be an idealisation of the political ambitions which were explicitly bound up with the marriage and declared on the obverse of the medal, where the portrait of Leonello is captioned GE RE AR (*gener regis aragonarum*), but the romantic posture corresponds to Leonello's poetic persona, over which Amor also presides. One of the surviving sonnets deals

33　Pisanello, medal of Leonello d'Este. Washington, D.C., National Gallery of Art. Bronze.

explicitly with the vulnerability of the lover's sight: the poet is blinded by a cruel god of love and is unable to find his way.[92] In the other sonnet the poet attempts to bathe his hands and face in the sacred spring of the Muses on the cliffs of Helicon, where he is mocked and menaced by Amor with his arrows. The cruel god taints the waters of the spring with his poisoned arrows, so that as the poet drinks the burning thirst he had sought to quench only becomes worse:

> The horse strikes the mountain rock, and makes the fountain spring from Helicon, where one bathes his hands and another his brow, according as Honour or Love inclines him more. I, too, often approach the divine and wondrous water of that mountain; threat laughs Love, who lurks there in pilgrim wise, with ready darts; And whilst I advance and stretch out my lips to drink, he with the venom of the point stains the stream and makes it poisonous; So that the water, which of its nature should refresh me, inflames me more, and the more I bathe, the more the burning grows.[93]

Thus, as a poet, he can only sing of love. Leonello's poetic persona, then, has a sensual aspect which his character in *De politia litteraria* – who, while praising the Latin elegiacs is disparaging about Boccaccio and Petrarch – tends to obfuscate. However, the prince's self-presentation as a lover may have influenced his later portrayal as a hot-blooded libertine by historians from the reign of Ercole I onwards.[94] The image of husband and lover may have played a role in the portrayal of the Belfiore Muses, and may lie behind the accent on their venereal character. One of the primary antique *loci* for the Muse's

association with Venus is the *Precepts on Marriage* by Plutarch, and it is possible that the act of undressing evoked by some of the figures was inspired by an association between this Plutarch text and Lucian's description of the painting of the *Marriage of Alexander and Roxana*, as mentioned above. The synecdochic representation of marriage in terms of sexuality, however, if this is what is happening in the images, utterly diffuses the moral point of Plutarch's text, and cannot be seen in terms of a privileging of honest over dishonest loves. Moreover, the cycle was continued and elaborated by Tura under Borso, for whom the theme of marriage distinct from venereal themes in general could have had no conceivable interest.

The association of the Muses, the Helicon fountain and Venus has an interesting history in the early *quattrocento* which may have had a bearing on the poetic interests of Leonello d'Este. The image of Eros unleashing his arrows from the fountain of poetic eloquence occurs in an elegy composed in Siena by the Sicilian poet Giovanni Marrasio, who subsequently spent some years at the court of Ferrara. The poem is dedicated to Leonardo Bruni and celebrates the great civic monument of Siena, the Fonte Gaia, completed by Jacopo della Quercia a few years previously.

The Fonte Gaia, like the legendary fountain of youth, invigorates those who drink from it, but its effect on the poet is different, for Venus has concealed her son within the fountain along with his burning darts:

> Freezing they burn and raging with love are those who first drink a cup of the sweet water. Come, O Leonardo, and draw the sacred liquor; if you would be young, so rage in love. After

I first bathed in the marble-cooled fount my heart was full of bitter anguish; I wished that divine furies would seize my heart, furies which those of yours, O divine poet, urged upon me.[95]

The poet, having introduced the menacing Cupid as a figure for the transformative power of poetic inspiration and speech, introduces an image far more redolent of ambiguous fascination, of a beautiful and deadly power which invades the mind through the senses, with the epithet 'Gorgoneus' to designate the Helicon spring:

For that which the poets first called the Gorgonean fountain is called in our times the Fonte Gaia. If my words bring any pleasure, if there is any violent passion in our verses, all praise is due to Venus, all glory to the fountain. Those verses I sang were uttered by the waters, and through the waters I can number myself among the followers of Tibullus.[96]

Among those who read the poem were Carlo Marsuppini, who wrote enthusiastically to Marrasio with a newly completed translation of the pseudo-Homeric *Batracomiomachia*, which he had been inspired to write after reading the poem:

I asked of the Muses that if, as the poet sings, a crow might suddenly become a swan, they might inspire me a little and anoint my lips, if not with the holy spring of Parnassus, then with the water of that Fonte Gaia about which you wrote recently the most exquisite elegies, and I promised them a hecatomb. That night in a dream I saw myself taken away to the bosom of the Muses, immersed in the Fonte Gaia. Wherefore on waking shortly after, with great alacrity of mind, I got down to writing and translated this little work into our [Latin] language. If there is anything elegant to be found in it, it is to be attributed to Homer, the greatest of all poets, and especially to those waters with which, you say, your poem is drenched.[97]

Marrasio responded with a long poetic elaboration of Marsuppini's vision of the Muses, who now emerge from the fountain to claim Carlo's promise of a hecatomb in the form of a translation of the *Iliad* and *Odyssey*. These beautiful and somewhat menacing Muses, who carry weapons and are adorned with jewels and serpentine hair, now receive an extended *descriptio* and are characterised in strongly visual terms:

It is wondrous; the sisters come armed from the fountain and the splendid cohort enters my bedchamber. They bring with them charming and lascivious words of idleness, praise, and, above all, delight. They are accustomed to garland their companions with snowy privet, and to adorn their own foreheads with a gold crown interwoven with green olive, while in golden dresses they shine by art. A skein of gold snakes through their shining hair, and bright jewels adorn their hands. Now they bring shields, and bright bucklers, and bear in their arms a fearful spear.[98]

Thalia tells the poet how the fountain was named in honour of the wife of Tarquinius Priscus: 'And the fountain where they honour the nine goddesses was called Gaia, with the approval of the sisters.'[99]

In the progressively more vivid identification of the Fonte Gaia with the Muses which emerges from this poetic correspondence, Marrasio must have been prompted by the fact that Jacopo della Quercia's sculptural programme includes nine female figures enthroned in niches. The 'numina sacra novem' honoured at the fountain are in fact the Virgin Mary with the figures of Faith, Hope, Wisdom, Humility, Prudence, Justice, Temperance and Fortitude.[100] Marrasio's transformation of the nine figures into the pagan Muses is perhaps an inevitable *topos* in a poem about a fountain, but it also seems an audaciously secularising move. The association with the Muses proposed by Marrasio seems to have adhered to the fountain in later poetic citations, and two epigrams from the mid-fifteenth century testify to its pervasiveness.[101]

In 1433 Marrasio moved his home from Siena to the court of Niccolò d'Este at Ferrara, and there composed an elegy describing theatrical *larvati* (masques) and the spectacles of carnival. Guarino wrote an answering elegy on behalf of the marquis, to which Marrasio responded in turn.[102] Theatre is invoked by both authors under the aegis of Bacchus, Venus and the Muses and is associated with qualities of *procacitas*, *lascivia* and *licentia*.[103] Here, in lyric form, the poets could give vent to their nostalgic fantasies of ancient theatre as an experience of *voluptas*; this was not something which could be expressed at this time within the moral and religious strictures of the epistle, the oration or the dialogue. There is only the merest token appearance of the Stoic/Christian censure of the theatre.[104]

Marrasio's first poem is also a solicitation of patronage from Niccolò and his son Leonello:

The fair and lovely maidens seek your house, which has honour and a gleaming hearth, as well as all the beauties nourished by your Ferrara (if beauty goes with golden garments) so that they might join their fingers with ours and each might move her feet to the lyre. If you so wish it I will lead the Muses from the Fonte Gaia to the long arm of the shining Po, and I will sing the praises and titles and deeds of yourself and your ancestors, of your illustrious house and of you, O Leonello. Let the gods give you what you will and whatsoever you ask for, and let Amor be gentle to you, harsh though he has been.[105]

The first elegy was recited at a magnificent mythological spectacle which he organised for Leonello and Niccolò and which was witnessed by, among others, Ciriaco d'Ancona. As described by Niccolo Losco, a pupil of Guarino, the masque was characterised by all those qualities which made the poetry of the stage so abhorrent to its clerical opponents; it was comic and profane and featured some of the more notorious pagan divinities.[106] The dancing *larvati* included a 'radiant Apollo', Bacchus bearing a thyrsus (played by Marrasio himself), then Asclepius, Mars, Bellona, and Mercury in his winged sandals; Priapus appeared

suddenly and chased away some birds. Then came Venus and Cupid, the Furies, the Fates, and Hercules with Cerberus. After a dance, Cupid recited Marrasio's elegy on spectacles,

We know little else about Marrasio's activity at the Ferrarese court, beyond the fact that he appears to have stayed until 1442 when he returned to Sicily.[107] It can now, however, be shown that over the following decade the Virtues of his beloved Fonte Gaia began to appear in the work of Angelo da Siena, transformed into the Muses of Belfiore. Jacopo della Quercia's sculptures are in a ruinous condition, but even from the rather schematic notion which can be formed of the original, the correspondence with the Muses is striking. Apart from the comparable attenuated proportions, long, swelling torsos and small heads, specific figures such as *Faith* (plate 35), with her right leg folded behind the left, provided a model for the *contrapposto* of Urania, while Urania's heavenward glance is matched by that of the figure of *Hope* (plate 36). Michele Pannonio's *Thalia* repeats the pose of della Quercia's *Prudence* (plate 37) in reversed form, while *Terpsichore*, inclining to the right and with raised forearms, descends from the figure of *Justice* (plate 38). The original design for Tura's *Calliope* also recalls both Prudence and Justice.

Apart from the family of Leonello's mother Stella dell'Assassino, a kinswoman of the Tolomei, the Sienese presence at the Ferrarese court was strong in these years. In addition to Marrasio and Angelo da Siena, there were the physicians Ugo Benci and the engineer and occasional sculptor Giovanni da Siena. Both of these wealthy individuals were among the principal donors towards the expenses of Leonello's wedding in 1435 to Margherita Gonzaga.[108] All of these would have been in a position to recommend the most famous contemporary monument of their native city as a model for the artistic self-imaging of the Marquis of Ferrara, but the capricious and idiosyncratic characterisation of the fountain by Marrasio must have been the most decisive influence of all.

The first humanist mythological cycle of the *quattrocento* originates in an elegiac response to a famous public work of art, the vehicle for the earlier poetic celebration now becoming the literal subject of the new work. Marrasio's wilful mythologising of a civic monument with prominent Christian imagery could be seen as another example of elegiac 'fascination', the representation of the poetic vocation in terms of an enchanted response to visual or to visionary experience. An aspect of works of art which brings them into a closer relation to the language

of elegy is important from this point onwards: both proceed by appeals to sense, by evoking associations and memories which may finally become anarchic and ungovernable – seeing a painting as a speaking woman in a vision, seeing the Virgin Mary and the Virtues in terms of Venus and the Muses, are both effects of erotic *furor*. Finally, images, especially when unusual in form or content, are *sine litteris*, as Guarino complained, and it is this unlettered ambiguity, combined with their power of sensual attraction that leads him to regard them as specious.

★   ★   ★

37 (*above left*) Jacopo della Quercia, *Prudence*, from the Fonte Gaia. Siena, Palazzo Pubblico.

38 (*above right*) Jacopo della Quercia, *Justice*, from the Fonte Gaia. Siena, Palazzo Pubblico. (Photograph of 1858)

35 (*facing page left*) Jacopo della Quercia, *Faith*, from the Fonte Gaia. Siena, Palazzo Pubblico. (Photograph of 1858)

36 (*facing page right*) Jacopo della Quercia, *Hope*, from the Fonte Gaia. Plaster cast made in the nineteenth century. Siena, Palazzo Pubblico. (Photograph of 1858)

> Now purification of the soul ... consists in scorning the pleasures that arise through the senses, in not feasting the eyes on the silly exhibitions of jugglers or the sight of bodies which gives the spur to sensual pleasure, in not permitting licentious songs to enter through the ears and drench your souls.
>
> St Basil, *To Young Men: On how they might derive profit from pagan literature*[109]

> We do not concern ourselves with whether the beak of a live bird is properly carved or not, but we do with whether the mane of a bronze lion spreads beautifully, whether the individual fibres or vessels are visible on the leaves of a stone tree, or whether the sinews and veins are shown in the stone leg of a statue. These are the things that men take pleasure in ... And the beauties of statues are not unworthy things to behold; rather do they indicate a nobility in the intellect that admires them. It is looking at the beauties of women that is licentious and base.
>
> Manuel Chrysoloras[110]

So far I have identified the Muses with the promotion of a defensive self-image by the humanist Guarino. I have argued furthermore that this self-imaging attempts to mediate and transform an original intention on the part of the prince. In prescribing the representation of the Muses through an unusual iconography of liberal and mechanical arts, with possible allusions to the theme of good government and prosperity, Guarino is representing the pedagogical formation of the ideal Christian prince. I have argued that his conception, which we might term 'civic', had to assimilate a more aesthetic, more spectacular idea of the Muses attuned to the interests of the prince Leonello and the poets Marrasio, Basinio and, perhaps, Theodore Gaza. A dual level of beholding hence appears here, which might be characterised in terms of the 'public' or 'civic' – the ideal self-representation of a humanist prince – in contrast to the 'private' – the more restricted, intimate expression of the individual poet-lover. A precedence for this duality is manifested by the Fonte Gaia, which presents itself as the symbol of the prosperity of a city, but also became known through its private, elegiac 'mythologisation' by Marrasio. What becomes important in the 1450s is a particular ideological configuration which co-opted sexuality and the allegorical female body for the imagery of court spectacle, of poetry and of painting. A particular concern of a prince with self-representation may have enabled humanists to symbolise their challenge to censorship in defiant and transgressive ways. I will examine this humanist resistance in the particular fortunes of poetic *licentia* almost two decades after Guarino's repudiation of the *Hermaphroditus*, at a time when Guarino had not only distanced himself from erotic poetry but was producing some of his most negative statements about painting.

Guarino generally wrote about painting in positive terms when it was rhetorically expedient; the visual arts, for instance, could be shown to have the same exemplary and moralising force as poetry, bringing remote and bygone things before the eyes of posterity. Even in the famous poem on Pisanello, which initially appears to celebrate a morally indifferent visual delight, the artist is praised for making images of saints and not of pagan gods.[111] Guarino's reservations about painting are set forth most systematically in a letter to his son Battista in 1452, where the young scholar is complimented for a prose portrait of the great founding father of Greek studies in Italy, Manuel Chrysoloras:

> So it seems to me that you supersede Zeuxis, Apelles, Polykleitos and, from our time, Gentile, Pisanello and Angelo da Siena in the art of painting, primarily because they paint or painted with colours which decay and vanish with time, or because their portraits are mute and the artist claims more praise than the characteristics of the person. But you have expressed and painted and coloured my Manuel so vividly and so permanently and firmly, that in time he will spring to greater life and immortal fame.[112]

There is one quality of painting about which Guarino is particularly mistrustful and concerning which he is at pains to make a distinction between painting and poetry:

> You warn us well and prudently of the greater power and dignity of the use of writing than painting, for the latter lies silent while the former is always alert and speaking; the former also inspires us to an imitation of the good and towards the imbibing of honesty, but to the latter only remains the power of feeding the eyes. Therefore Cicero referred to painting as a pastime for boys, and Virgil wrote 'painting is fodder for empty minds'.[113]

Guarino's more favourable assessment of the analogy between painting and poetry – that both can encourage virtue and the desire for knowledge – is not invoked on this occasion.[114] Following his experience with Giovanni da Prato two years previously, he was probably now even more concerned to redeem literature from any taint of the voluptuous or worldly. As has been pointed out, Guarino's various objections to painting were probably accommodated by the adoption of particular and sometimes novel forms in the visual arts. The addition of inscriptions to the paintings of the Muses ought to make them less easily misunderstood, while portrait medals were more durable than paintings and the *impresa* permitted a neatly abbreviated combination of the resources of word and image.[115]

If the Muses were thus displayed in the *studio* with Guarino's inscriptions, presumably accompanied (or maybe even replaced in some instances) by those of Theodore Gaza, what must their overall effect on the beholder have been? Would the terse statement of name and function have somehow contained and made anodyne the worldly gorgeousness and eroticism which Tura's Muse must have foregrounded in the others following her inclusion in the group? Or would an ironic tension have been generated between text and image? In dealing with these questions, we will need to consider further how the Muses were coming to be perceived during the last years of Leonello and the early reign of Borso d'Este, when such a perception may have been 'read back' into the images already completed by Angelo and determined their evolution under Tura and Michele Pannonio.

In 1450, while Giovanni da Prato fulminated against the *licentia* of pagan poetry, two precocious young poets were dedicating themselves to a revival of the libertinist mode of Beccadelli. One was Janus Pannonius, resident in Ferrara as a pupil of Guarino from 1447 to 1454; the other was Gian Gioviano Pontano, a friend and colleague of Beccadelli at the court of Naples who was in Ferrara on a mission from Alfonso in March 1451. Janus took Martial and Catullus as his models among the ancients and Beccadelli among the moderns, and his early verse composed at this period is mainly in the form of satirical epigrams directed against courtesans, unfaithful lovers and lustful pedagogues – all subject-matter familiar from the *Hermaphroditus*. The most recurrent note, however, is the expression of contempt for clerical hypocrisy and for those who heeded the empty fire-and-brimstone rhetoric of the preachers. In the poem *Galeotti peregrinationem irridet*, composed in 1450, a poet friend is mocked for joining the hordes of pilgrims heading to Rome amidst the euphoria of the Holy Year. Why, he asks, had his friend abandoned Parnassus with his pilgrim's staff and cap, and become part of that mob of hypocrites and credulous foreigners terrorised by the preachers?[116]

The poet reminds him of the pagan philosophers, above all Epicurus and 'Theodorus who denied the existence of God'. Why should Galeotto now subject himself to the daily preaching which Fra Alberto (da Sarteano) and Fra Roberto (da Lecce) bellow hoarsely from the pulpit, fit only to draw tears from old women? Say goodbye to the Muses then, he concludes, and to Apollo, for 'no one is both pious and a poet' ('nemo religiosus et poeta est').

The poem seems to invert completely the characterisation of pious oratory which Guarino set forth in his letter on Alberto da Sarteano in 1447, and to reject the reconciliation between piety and pagan learning which, it must now have seemed, Guarino had too readily assumed to be possible from the enemies of Beccadelli. Janus' poem might be seen as an extreme and hyperbolic example of the counterattack on the clerics launched by Guarino's followers in the early 1450s, of which Timoteo Maffei's *In sanctam rusticitatem litteras impugnantem libellus* and part of Decembrio's *De politia litteraria* were the more typical examples.[117] Such poems may only have been playful posturing with a limited audience, but they serve to indicate how this younger generation may have started to conceive of their roles as scholars and poets as acquiring definition or symbolisation through a practice of poetic *licentia* rather than through a defence of poetic *probitas*. Janus' challenge to clerical censorship and Guarino's professions of propriety did not end there. He mocked the preachers' worst suspicions when he claimed that he himself had been led to writing lascivious verse by Guarino's teaching of the classics.[118]

In 1448 Pontano had begun work on his book of verses *Pruritus, sive de lascivia*, the final version of which he dedicated to the young Ferrarese poet and Guarino pupil Tito Vespasiano Strozzi in 1451. Among Pontano's debts to the *Hermaphroditus* was a scandalous characterisation of his Muse which he could have found, for instance, in the tenth poem of the first book, where Beccadelli defends the Muse against the slanderous pedagogue Mattia Lupi:

My Muse would not normally seem too lascivious as far as he is concerned. Yes, in that respect she corresponds exactly to his own life. He is an obscene man, and my Muse is shameless. She is lewd with her verses; he is lewd from the moral point of view.[119]

The book is figured throughout as itself being hermaphroditic, possessing male and female genitalia and constantly menaced with 'castration' by Beccadelli's critics. The title is also a synecdoche for the author in his various personae, whose sodomitical exploits render him hermaphroditic. By virtue of her sex the Muse is identified with the partly female body of this androgynous persona. She is either identified with the author and his writing, appearing 'drowned in a sea of wine' (I.iv), or 'lewd with her verses' in the poem on Lupi, or she is the possessor of one of the sets of paired male and female genitalia which appear throughout the text:

Mino, you advise me to take the penis out of my verses. You reckon that in such a guise my poetry would please everyone. Mino, I certainly have no wish to castrate my little book; even Phoebus Apollo has a penis and Calliope has genitals.[120]

The sexually active and voluptuous Muse of Pontano's poetry also represents the poet and his writing, but usually she serves rather to introduce an eroticised element into a relation of power or friendship between men which, by being feminised and objectified, can be placed at a safe symbolic distance. In one poem of the *Pruritus*, to the Muse Thalia, the poet employs the Catullan motif of the *basia mille* (which he requested of his Lesbia) and bids the Muse bear these thousand kisses to an unnamed friend.[121] In the introductory poem to the Muse, based on some of the most notorious motifs in Catullus, the Muse does not, as in Beccadelli, personify the poet's own sexual ambiguity, but rather herself becomes the passive object of the poet's aggressively active lust: 'If it is asked, why you speak in such a filthy manner, say it is because I fuck you, fuck you and fuck you.'[122]

However defiant and provocative the revival of Beccadelli, the chaotic gender ambiguity of the earlier work – or the hermaphroditic motif itself – is not reproduced. The experiment in *licentia* is only sustainable with a reinscription of gender difference and sexual norms. As a dependant and dependant-to-be on court employment, Pontano and Janus may not have wanted to risk attracting the scandal which had adhered to Beccadelli. Further, it may have been unwise to circulate poetry on sodomitical themes into the society of Borso d'Este, whose court was organised around exclusively male hierarchies of power and the promotion of younger male favourites of the marquis. Perhaps the pictorial and poetic cult of the voluptuous Muse could be seen as holding the Hermaphrodite at bay in a world of predominantly homosocial energies.[123]

The poetic activity of Janus and Pontano, the continuing popularity of elegy, the reawakening of interest in Beccadelli and the apparent veiling or silencing of the hermaphroditic persona define possible parameters for the beholding and reception of the paintings of the Muses in the reign of Borso, while Tura was working for the *studio*. It is from the humanists that the images must have solicited the richest and most complex levels of response. In their assessments of these and other paintings, and of the role of the painter Cosmè Tura, a re-negotiation of the relation between poetry and painting may be seen to take place. In the appearance of what we might call an implicit theory of the poetic image, the very reservations which Guarino's defence of poetry had led him to express about painting – that paintings were merely sensual, that paintings are *sine litteris* and hence mute, and that paintings are ephemeral – begin to figure as positive values which become analogous with the project of the poet.

EPHEMERA: TITO VESPASIANO STROZZI ON TURA

> Truth is immortal, fiction and things beyond the nature of truth do not last; that which is feigned quickly reveals itself and becomes evident. The hair dressed with the greatest care is tossed by the slightest breeze; the artful colours placed on the face with masterly hand easily fade as they run down the face with every drop of sweat, and so too are cunning lies conquered by truth. And whoever wants subtly and diligently to examine [truth], will perceive that it is a transparent thing, that is, just like a very black thing encased in the purest crystal.
>
> Petrarch, *De vita solitaria*[124]

The non-lasting quality of painting finds its way into poetry only indirectly; most poems on painting seek to praise, and the destructibility of painting is not easily presentable as a virtue. It is frequently implicit, moreover, that the poet's art will outlast the painter's, or that the fame of the painter depends on the poet.

However, painting proferred its charms through fragile and perishable artifice, and its subject-matter, as a Franciscan theologian reminded Borso, consisted of transitory and insubstantial beauties, the ornaments and colour-changing draperies of women.[125] Painting was thus situated in the realm of dreams and apparitions, ephemeral and mortal objects of desire. This transitoriness is figured in the subject-matter of artful mimesis in Ferrarese poems in praise of painters – less because painters actually depicted Arcadian landscapes or pastoral *loci amoeni*, abounding in flora and fauna at different times of the year or hours of the day, than because painting was generically part of the same tantalisingly impermanent realm of experience.

The motif of pictorial ephemera – its material nature and content – occurs with particular suggestiveness in the poetry of Tito Vespasiano Strozzi, a member of the great Florentine family living in exile at the Ferrarese court, where he and his brother Lorenzo enjoyed considerable favour. Two poems in Strozzi's *Eroticon* refer to paintings by Cosmè Tura. Both praise Tura's skill, but also tacitly invoke the *topos* of pictorial ephemerality in order to celebrate the immortality in posterity of the poet's treatment of the same subject-matter. The superiority of painting to poetry according to the traditional comparison is, however, rendered ironic. In one poem, Strozzi contemplates 'a beautful portrait, so well painted, and true to life, by the hand of Cosimo'.[126]

The personage portrayed has died; after reflecting on his life and exploits, the poet meditates on the mutability of fame – all the works of human hands come to nothing, and the memory of illustrious men falls into obscurity, unless seized and preserved for posterity by a poet. If the Muses therefore will permit him to drink from their sacred fount, Strozzi will have the power to summon back the dead friend's spirit from Hades, and will inscribe an epitaph on his tomb. Such claims are rendered outrageous, however, by the fact that the commemorated individual is Bagarino, the poet's favourite hawk. The greater longevity of the poem to Tura's painting is implied, but the mock-serious commending of a dead hawk to posterity places the poet's artifice similarly within the realm of the trivial and ephemeral, since it would ascribe virtue to a creature which epitomises the courtly pursuit of leisure and the vanity of the chase.[127] Competing with a painter for the portrayal of a hawk has a levelling effect, and the books of the *Eroticon* show Strozzi wantonly conferring immortality on the most morally indifferent and trivial subjects – a hare escaping from its mistress, other pets and menagerie animals, a night of insomnia, a painted coat of arms. Decembrio's 'Dialogue on Art' concludes with Strozzi displaying a miniature portrait of 'a golden-haired maiden', another ephemeral beauty whose death he had lamented in a 'tearful elegy'.[128]

The other poem (IV.xxx) is believed to have been written in the late 1450s, just as Tura was making his initial impact on the *studio*. The Aldine edition of 1513 includes the poem under the title *Ad Cosimum pictorem*, but an earlier manuscript edition is entitled *Ad Anthiam, quod stulta admodum et inepta sit, quae faciem suam in tabella depingi tantopere desideret*.[129] The titles in fact correspond to two distinguishable levels of address in the poem. One is to the poet's unfaithful mistress, whom he berates for having herself painted and failing to realise that the poet's art can more effectively commit her image – and character – to posterity. The other addressee is Tura, whom Strozzi salutes, but who has been placed by Anthia in a competitive relation to the poet.

While Tura will represent Anthia, according to her choice, as one of the seasons, Strozzi will make her into a Thais, a notorious courtesan. Anthia's self-representation in posterity is impeded in this case not because of the ephemerality of painting, but because of her own inconstancy and the anarchic passage of time as she adopts the costume of one season or another. Painting here is bound to the representation of fleeting appearances, but these become even more unstable and erratic when the artist confronts the highly unstable artifice of feminine vanity.

But this inconstancy, this play of ephemera, is precisely what the elegiac poet has been seduced by, and is that which he also strives to represent. Although reintroducing the Guarinian *topos* of painting's muteness – the painter can never represent his subject's mores as the poet can – the particular inscription of character here is clearly made evident to be the outcome of the vengeful jealousy of the poetic persona. When the poem is read in sequence with the other Anthia poems of the *Eroticon* it can be seen as a near-climactic statement of the poet-lover's frustration. The poet's rage ironically signifies the triumph of the indifferent, narcissistic Anthia, and indicates the threat of her artifice of self-representation when it joins forces with painting's unlettered ambiguity.

'FEEDING THE EYES': THE METAPHOR OF PICTORIAL SENSUALITY

On entering the *studio*, beholders found themselves confronted with an interior lavishly outfitted with costly majolica tiles, *intarsia* work and, above eye level, nine imposing female figures seated on thrones. Reading the inscriptions, or having them translated, the viewer is made aware of the Muses' attribute and function, which explains, to a certain extent, why they are portrayed as they are. The Gaza inscriptions, however, if they were present, drew the viewer's attention to a duality – the Muses as both 'concepts' and 'intelligences', existing beyond the sensible world, and the Muses as visible, embodied, arrayed by dressmakers and hairdressers and finally made present by the hands of an artist.

In the figures of *Erato*, *Calliope*, *Thalia* and *Terpsichore* viewers might have recognised qualities which they could have read of in Ovid and the elegists, in Pontano and Beccadelli. Here, it is obvious that the choice to view the Muses in terms of the inscriptions simultaneously presented to the gaze, or in terms of the circulation of the Muses in contemporary poetry, depends on the viewers' particular formation and interests, their relation to the worlds of humanist pedagogy or to the humanist Latin poets of the court. The relation of women to the image will clearly differ from that of male spectators; as Guarino's praise of Isotta Nogarola shows, woman's relation to the Muses is invariably figured as one of mirroring, but the Muse on which the educated woman models herself is entirely different in character to those of the Belfiore *studiolo*.[130] Such a Muse is, above all, a type of chastity, exemplified in the anodyne, interchangeable figures dancing under male direction in the later *studiolo* decorated by Mantegna for Isabella d'Este.

Women of the court, should they have been allowed within the *studio*, may have found in the Belfiore Muses a reflection of their sumptuary privilege as court ladies. The Muses are attired with a luxurious extravagance which, in the very year 1447 in which Guarino composed the programme, may have exceeded what was deemed legally allowable to the ordinary women of Ferrara.[131] Only two categories of women would have been exempt from this provision of the sumptuary law: women of the prince's household – and prostitutes. This double connotation would not have been lost on a viewer whose curiosity has been directed towards poetic *lascivia*.

Whoever intervened between Guarino and the artists of the *studio* was exploiting a particular instability or ambivalence which attended on the representation of mythology and poetic fable (especially the Muses following their condemnation in Boethius), on the representation of women embellished by cosmetics and sensuous materials, and on the art of painting itself. Poetic fable, the adornments of women which could signify both nobility and harlotry, painting as an art of illusion and sensuous ornament, are classically linked in the western Stoic and Christian tradition as arts of lying, of deceptive and dangerously seductive appearances.[132] When considered in relation to Guarino's text, the figure of Calliope with her corporeally expressive twist, her opened dress, her plucked brows and her eyes coolly averted from the observer, seems to exult in the same dangerous equivalences which Guarino had been anxious to displace:

Muse = poetry = *vanitas* and *lascivia*.

An observer might grasp the abundant presence of flowers and fruit as a panegyrical theme, a celebration of prosperity under the house of Este. However, the cherries and roses in the hands of Calliope and Erato might make a more dominant impression and more fully determine the tenor of his response to the other images, for flowers and fruit recall the sensuous imagery of Latin and neo-Latin erotic poetry. In Pontano's 'De amore coniugalia' of 1461 the poet does not invoke one of the canonical Muses, but is approached by the seductive nymph Elegia. She wears a loose white robe of silk fastened with a golden brooch at the shoulder (perhaps as we see in the *Thalia*), a golden girdle, chains of gold and a pearl on her breast, from which, as she sings alluringly to the poet, roses, hyacinths, violets and lilies pour forth in profusion.[133] In the same poet's eclogue *Lepidina* gifts of roses, cherries and other fruits are exchanged between the nymphs and their lovers and worshippers; frequently they are given explicit sexual meanings and associated with the 'ripeness' of nubile girls.[134]

Poetry and painting here employ the same pictorial metaphors for voluptuousness. The eye is 'fed' not only with appeals to taste and smell, but to touch (in the hardness of Tura's figures which menace with monstrous spikes and teeth) and to hearing (the uproarious dancing children, the music of the lost Melpomene).

The sensual qualities of painting are affirmed in a genre of poetry which flourished in Ferrara and which we have already encountered in Guarino's poem on Pisanello. Guarino, however, continued to assert the superiority of word to image, and sought to redeem the sensual, illusionistic immediacy of Pisanello's art by pointing to his facility in making images of holy saints rather than pagan gods; Tito Strozzi, in his own poem on Pisanello, follows Guarino in praising the painter's skill in depicting the natural world, but the landscape differs from that of Guarino's poem in that it now contains the presence of two hunting nymphs, and the *pater aeternus* of Guarino's poem is given the more ambiguous name Jove, whose painted image compels the beholder to a potentially idolatrous adoration:

Who does not marvel at the gestures and venerable persons of men, who no one would deny to be inwardly alive? Or who would not bow down before the painted face of Jove, judging it to be an image of true divinity?[135]

The world of artifice which arrests our sense of sight is now rendered in more fictional and pagan terms, and encompasses the beauties of women.

In a later poet of this tradition, who emerged in the reign of Borso's successor Ercole, painting more explicitly becomes a model for qualities pursued by the elegiac poet. In the figure of Lodovico Bigo, who took the name 'Pittorio', the figures of poet, lover and painter are all metaphorically combined. In one epigram, he reproaches his fellow poet Tebaldeo for attributing a non-painterly sense to the name 'Pictorius'. He is called this name, he writes, because a poet must render like a painter the kind of amorous fires which consume him, which, in his case, all the waters of eternal Helicon could not extinguish.[136] Poets, like painters, in other words, must appeal to the sense of sight, and make use of vivid and sensually compelling images. With this pictorial self-consciousness, Pittorio embellished his verses with copious *descriptiones*, among which are colourful vignettes of the Muses. In one poem, Calliope stands thoughtful by the fountain while Polyhymnia combs the dust from her hair and Erato washes the perspiration from her cheeks. In another the Muses steer the ship of poetry – Calliope mans the sail, Urania and Polyhymnia steer, Euterpe holds the tow-chain, Terpsichore lifts the oars, while Melpomene bestows pearls and cereals from the rowing bench.[137] It is perhaps no wonder that Pittorio 'collaborated' with Tura by providing the inscription and possibly also iconographical advice for the Roverella altarpiece.

'SINE LITTERIS': TURA'S *CALLIOPE* AND PICTORIAL AMBIGUITY

Even when clearly captioned, paintings are *sine litteris* in the sense of being ungovernable as signs; the effect which Guarino referred to as 'muteness' is additionally one of ambiguity, the deficiency in the image of the supposedly more stable kinds of referentiality which, for Guarino, made painting incapable of the accuracy and specificity of the written word. The paintings may have originated in a didactic scheme devised by Guarino and have been seen, on one level, as the beautification of abstract ideas of human knowledge through metaphorical female bodies

and through the skills of celebrated painters. Yet in this secular domain, and in a pictorial subject without precedent, there is less ideological pressure on a beholder to accept poetic invention in painting as allegory, as standing in place of a specific didactic text beyond the image. The gaze of the beholder may require no more of the image than that it conform to a particular ideal of female beauty and erotic appeal, and he may attribute yet other meanings to that beauty.

As we saw with Marrasio's rapturous 'misrecognition' of the Fonte Gaia, it is this polysemy in poetic beholding that enabled the Muse cycle to be conceived, through the adaptation of a particular model, in the first place. Moreover, in the theatricalisation of power and the replacement of political action by allegorical spectacle which characterised the reign of Borso d'Este, the polysemous response found its way into official records and eye-witness accounts of the duke's own ceremonial self-presentation. In the lavish allegorical tableaux described by the chronicler Fra Giovanni da Ferrara, which accompanied his triumphal entry as duke into Modena and Reggio, Borso was constantly identified with personifications of the Virtues. While Giovanni on the one hand underscores Borso's chastity and faith, he describes the Virtues in curiously sensual and pagan terms. At Modena Borso is met by the Virtues, riding in a chariot, 'adorned to the likeness of Venus'; at Reggio some days later Julius Caesar appeared before Borso on a chariot, 'presiding over seven shapely nymphs who were clearly to be recognised as the Virtues'.[138] Borso appears as a male ruler for whose gaze and pleasure the spectacle of female personification is produced. Yet in the ambiguous poetics of state spectacle, Borso could also assume a feminised personification; his entry into Reggio Cathedral was described by Giovanni as 'like a bride being led to her spouse'.[139] Charles Rosenberg has argued that in the Hall of Stuccoes in Palazzo Schifanoia the figure of Justice is absent from the stucco cycle of six female Virtues because her place was assumed by Borso himself when enthroned within the room.[140] Giovanni's chronicle indicates something of an epidemic pervasiveness of ambiguity – of gender, of the representation of virtue – in the circuit of self-representations around Borso d'Este.

It was the ambiguity of visual representation which had prompted some of the most recurring motives of the attack on painting in the *quattrocento* – the fact that it was capable of improper levels of suggestiveness, and that an artist's privileging of novelty and skill over convention and didactic meaning could stimulate an impure level of curiosity in the observer. Around mid-century St Antoninus of Florence denounced the irrelevance of decorative and picturesque details, such as dogs, hares and monkeys, in religious painting, while the Ferrarese Dominican Girolamo Savonarola would later attack painters who imbued the images of female saints with an ambiguous, worldly sensuality.[141] Among the humanist commentators on painting, both Alberti and Filarete were concerned that in rendering figures in movement, artistic virtuosity ran the risk of making figures appear like mimes and acrobats of the public stage, thus censoring pictorial licence with one of the grounds for the attack on poetry – its theatricality.[142] Figures of pronounced

artifice, of the monstrous or grotesque, also fell under suspicion as forms of excess which endangered a moral and didactic meaning.

Filarete's *Trattato* of 1460–64 offers a blatant example of the excision of the quintessential figure of monstrous, licentious ambiguity – the Hermaphrodite – whose most famous classical exemplar (exemplified by the version in the Museo Capitolino, Rome) exploited the duplicitous, incomplete and unreliable nature of human perception.[143] Book XIX mentions a painting of the sculptor Alcamenas, 'a disciple of Phidias, with an image of a Hermaphrodite – that is, a Venus, that he carved in marble and placed outside the walls of Athens, even though there were many other figures made by his hand in the city'.[144] The Hermaphrodite is evoked as a token of artistic mastery only to be subjected to a verbal gender reassignment operation, cancelling its ambiguity. In a *studio* decorated a generation later for an Este princess, Andrea Mantegna painted a Hermaphrodite being banished from an allegorical Garden of Virtue along with a host of other grotesque hybrid beings.[145] Some of these beings, above all the centaur, evoke the licence of painters as it was denounced by Horace in his *Ars poetica*, celebrated by Cennino Cennini in his *Libro dell'arte*, and appropriated by Donatello with the centaurs bearing his signature *cartellino* on one of the San Lorenzo bronze pulpits in Florence.[146] Guarino would have approved of the fact that these figures of pictorial extravagance or excess are in most cases assigned a specific meaning through inscription, in order to be identified, unambiguously, as Vices; the Hermaphrodite is labelled IMMORTALE ODIUM, FRAUS ET MALITIAE (undying hatred, fraud and malice).

Mantegna's painting could be seen as a purgation from the art itself of the vices imputed to it when humanists compared painting with poetry. His contemporary at the court of Mantua and Ferrara, Mario Equicola, had written dismissively of painting with the Horatian adage that painters 'fall into various errors, allowing their licence to become like Africa, which continuously brings forth monstrous progeny'.[147]

Yet this is precisely the notion of artistic licence that Tura's painting affirms, manifesting it in the decorative *copia* of Calliope's throne with its incongruously juxtaposed forms – shells, classical mouldings, golden mutant dolphins, fruit and vines. An observer literate in Greek would not have been oblivious to the fact that the Greek word for dolphin, *delphinos*, also signifies 'womb'; the fact that these *delphinoi* have intimidatingly sharp spikes and opened mouths with exposed fangs may have had enough of a psychological impact even without such knowledge. Their effect, along with the snake-like coils of tubular folds around the lower portions of the figure, give her a Gorgon- or Scylla-like aspect, a beautiful terribleness which in this century caused the art historian Benedict Nicolson, marvelling at the hardness or tactility of the figure, to fantasise about the wounding and drawing of blood from his 'finger' as he attempted to play with the coils of her hair.[148]

The excess of pictorial artifice and invention in the embellishment of the figure points towards a male fantasy of excessive and even monstrous sexuality. This monstrosity could be seen as

the trace of a concealed or displaced Other – the Hermaphrodite, the contemporary poetic figure of *licentia* and artistic mastery, with distinct social connotations of sexually deviant behaviour.[149] Although menacing, the Siren-like Muse offers a covert means of representing an eroticised and transgressive impulse in humanism which had previously represented itself in the sexual anomaly of the Hermaphrodite. The Muse is presented as *object* – that is, of more conventional forms of desire for a gendered gaze, and hence as a reassurance of orthodox masculine desire; she also appears, subliminally, as a *refracted image* of the viewing subject, her grotesque ambiguity standing for the bisexuality of a marginal but powerful humanist self-image.[150] This is not to say that Tura's Muse has characteristics which we might see as explicitly hermaphroditic or androgynous, and her gender seems guaranteed in the sexual signal of the unlaced dress. However an ambiguity, which I regard as an evocation of the fantasy of hermaphroditism, returns in this very inscription of sexuality and in the monstrous ornament which surrounds the figure. The Muse is thus drawn into realms of meaning, erotic and menacing, which cannot be stabilised by the imposed text.

Now it might be asked, would this dichotomy between the more sobre office of the Muse and her sensual presentation, or between the didactic precision of the original inscription and the extravagance of the figure, have been apparent to contemporary beholders? There is evidence to suggest that it was apparent, and that the dichotomy was moreover seen as a creative tension which could serve the ends of humanist self-fashioning. Around 1469, on the laureate medal of the Ferrarese rhetorician and writer of erotic verse Lodovico Carbone, we find a similar apparent resistance between an image and an inscription (plate 40).[151] The Latin inscription on the reverse, MUSIS GRATIISQUE VOLENTIBUS, celebrates the poet's indebtedness to the Muses and the Graces, while the image is that of a Siren, conceived in the form of a female sea-monster who pulls her fish-tails apart in a gesture of ominous sexual invitation – the motif of the opened dress taken to extremes. The juxtaposition seems bewildering, even shocking, a flaunting of the expectations set up by the word 'Musa'. Boethius had identified the Muses with Sirens, but in a vehemently negative sense which could hardly have legitimised the use of a Siren-Muse as personal *impresa*. The blatancy of the substitution seems designed to provoke; Pontano, in his funerary poem on his mentor Beccadelli, placed both Muses and Sirens in mourning around the grave of the poet of the *Hermaphroditus*.[152] In the medal and in the paintings, however, the monstrous or siren-like element could be seen as encoding a warning – the spines and teeth of the dolphins, the roses held by Thalia and Erato, remind us of St Basil's and Eneo Silvio Piccolomini's warnings about the study of profane poetry – pluck the flowers, but be careful not to seize the thorns. None the less, this dangerous element only makes what is seen more fascinating; we are directed towards the prurient solution of Odysseus, who hears the Siren's song while cunningly averting its destructive consequences.

Carbone's self-imaging as Poet Laureate would have seemed

40 Sperandio, medal of Lodovico Carbone, Poet Laureate. London, Victoria and Albert Museum. Bronze.

a boldly defiant and transgressive vindication of his poetic vocation, directed against those very parties who had censured his
mentor Guarino and his poetic precursor, Beccadelli. And not
only did Carbone choose the Siren as personal *impresa;* one of
Janus Pannonius' poems, by way of facetious compliment, refers
to him as a Hermaphrodite, because he excelled in the arts of
Mercury and Venus (i.e., rhetoric and poetry).[153]

   The afterlife of Tura's Muse did not end with Carbone's
medal. A century later, the subtle erotic menace of the Belfiore
Muse was reworked with a ferocious degree of literalness in an
illustration used for textbooks on human generation and gynae-
cology (plate 41). The Muse's slightly menacing invitation to
contemplate her inwardness has been pursued with a surgical
zeal; the open dress is now an opened abdomen, the sea-
monsters of the throne are more explicitly male and even more
phallic in form.

   Carbone thus exploits the suggestiveness of an image and its
resistance to total inscription by the *litterae* to represent the
voluptuous and morally ambiguous qualities of his own art.
Carbone's poetry may be placed under the aegis of the Muses,
but these Siren-Muses are figured as overwhelming reason and
moral judgement with their seductive power. Such equivocation
suggests why humanists may have become particularly interested

41 Woodcut from Jacob Ruff, *Ein schön lustig trost Büche von den
Empfengtnussen und Geburten der Menschen* (Zurich 1569), fol. XVIII. Ann
Arbor, University of Michigan, Taubmann Medical Library.

in the ambiguous, sensual unletteredness of painting at this time. It provided them with a visual symbol of that desire also figured in their own poetry, a symbol which could assume the form of sensual experience without being reducible to the narrow alternatives of virtue or vice. Lacking any modern poetics which could take the place of the fundamentally unsympathetic prescriptions of Horace, painting could be said to truly represent an *Ars poetica* for the literary professionals of the fifteenth century.

HISTORY, POETRY AND SPECTACLE

The Muses of Belfiore testify to a recognition of the capacity of images as a means of negotiating identity which appears to acquire a particular importance during the reigns of Leonello and Borso d'Este. The cycle enables both princes to extend their official and public self-image as providential rulers and patrons of culture. The paintings are a manifesto of the alliance between humanist pedagogy and the enlightened prince; they also participate in Leonello's more private promotion of himself as poet and lover. Again on a more restricted level, they affirm the more tangible, but less idealisable fruits of humanist pedagogy – the formation of humanist courtiers, writers of elegant and witty verse in which licence (and licentiousness) is a token of educational and social privilege, provoking clerical philistinism and pedagogical prudery from the safe vantage-point of the court.

It could be said in addition that by the 1450s the image acquires a crucial currency in the political culture of the Ferrarese court. The political fortunes of the duke and his retinue depended more than ever on the manipulation of appearances; this may have provoked reflection on the power of the image, including those aspects considered specious or duplicitous (if only because there were no more positive terms available). While, for instance, Borso portrayed himself as the enemy of idolatry, and his triumphal entry of Reggio was accompanied by the ceremonial toppling of a figure of *Idolatria* from its column, he also realised the power of the effigy on the pedestal; a massive column was subsequently raised from which his own enthroned likeness in bronze surveyed the main square (and gallows) of Ferrara.[154]

The chief events of Borso's cautious and precariously peaceful reign were moments of spectacle and ceremony – his becoming Duke of Modena and Reggio in 1453, his investiture as Duke of Ferrara by Pope Paul II in 1471 – rather than more dynamic and dramatic instances of military prowess, the matter of classical history or epic. Unlike Leonello, Borso was not noticeably distinguished for his education or for his patronage of humanists of the calibre of Guarino. The lack of occasions or qualities to celebrate posed a challenge for Tito Vespasiano Strozzi who spent many years trying to write an epic on Borso, for which he mainly resorted to long non-narrative digressions and allegorical amplifications.[155] Borso's official humanist historians and panegyricists had little option but to

devote extensive space to the ceremonial self-fashioning of the duke, so that the visual artifice of spectacles assumed a central importance as historical events.[156] Borso's own relation to the Virtues was of a highly theatrical nature, enacted in the allegorical scenography of triumphs and formal receptions as much as actualised in practice. Some contemporaries evidently cared about this distinction, among them Pius II who wrote acerbically of Borso's desire 'to seem rather than to be' magnanimous and magnificent.[157]

Historians resorted constantly to ornate poetic descriptions, focusing on the theatrically visible manifestations of Borso's splendour and magnificence. For Fra Giovanni da Ferrara, an apparent concern regarding the taint of artifice or fictionality led him to begin his work with nothing less than a defence of poetry. His assertion that 'poetae et scriptores' provide knowledge of mankind and the deeds of great men is coupled with a note of admonition directed at Borso – it is by writers that one's image is best transmitted for posterity rather than through the masterpieces of great artists alone:

> It is not enough that the brush of Protogenes or Apelles, or the workshop of Scopas or Lysippus were dedicated to being the ornament of the splendour and perfection of the great men of their time, O most magnanimous Duke Borso, unless the light of letters was added to the images and statues in marble and shining gold of the ancient heroes.[158]

At the very end of his history the friar directs to the duke a meditation on the ephemerality of the goods of fortune: 'Imponendum est, mi Borsi, felicitati frenos' ('A bridle must be placed upon pleasure').[159] For what could be more foolish than to place one's faith in things which Fortune gives and takes away – 'in rebus fluxis ac mobilibus stabilitatem ac aeternitatem quaerere?' Yet at the same time, the political imperative of being Borso's panegyrist means that his text is constantly contaminated by the sensuality and ambiguity of the ceremonial spectacles it records – its voluptuous, Venus-like allegorical personifications, the duke's appearance as a 'bride of Christ'. The most striking feature of the text is the constant affirmation of visual experience; poetry defeats painting only because it has greater longevity as a mode of picturing – its purpose is to tell us how things used to look. Giovanni's characterisation of what can be learned from poetry is almost entirely visual: 'the deeds of man, his habits of body, his crimes, his manner of gesture, his mode of walking, whether quick or slow'.[160] Spectacle is finally affirmed as a kind of *voluptas*, but one which feeds the soul and not the eyes alone:

> And so that they should all exhibit pleasure in the spectacles, he ordered all to be still; and with ears alert, the powers of the spirit attentive, the mind feasted [*animum pascebat*] in contemplating the arrangement and embellishment of so great a variety of marvels.[161]

Consciously or not, Giovanni is answering Guarino's charge that the spectacular image only fed the eyes. For Giovanni da Ferrara the defence of poetry is the only remaining strategy available for dealing with the spectacular fictions of Borso's reign. Borso's pre-occupation with vainglorious spectacle can be gently admonished but its omnipresent manifestations which replace the actuality of Virtue with its semblance are transformed into the realm of poetry and history in order to be affirmed. Even while rehearsing the usual distinctions between the didactically justifiable artifice of poetry and the more sensuous artifice of spectacle, Giovanni's own strategies again suggest the growing sense of a collusion, of an identity of means and ends, between poetry and painting in Ferrara by the late 1450s.

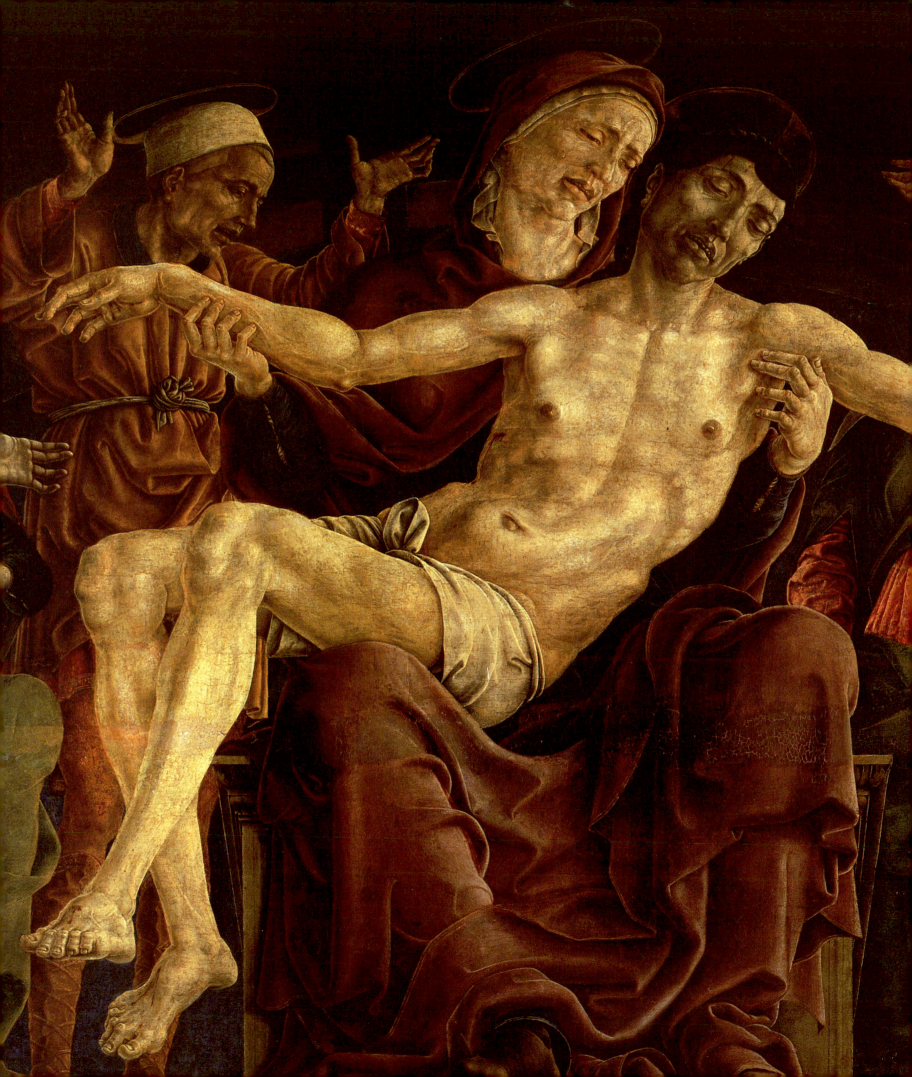

III

'O SACRO CORPO': DEVOTIONAL IMAGES
AND THE ART OF SANCTITY

THE DEVOTIONAL IMAGE, ranging from the small panel for private worship to large, multi-panelled altarpieces, was the standard product of the fifteenth-century painter's workshop, and it is as a painter of religious pictures that Tura is primarily known from his surviving work. Few panel paintings by Tura as we encounter them now are complete in themselves, but are fragments of larger polyptychs. Apart from two altarpieces in the convent church of San Giorgio, almost nothing is known of the original form or location of these works. The polyptych remained a popular form throughout northern Italy until the 1490s, when it was largely being superseded in the larger centres by the single-panelled altarpiece; figures of saints and the Virgin, previously represented on separate panels, were now grouped together in a coherent pictorial space and a unified architectural setting; Ercole de' Roberti's San Lazzaro altarpiece from around 1480 is an early Ferrarese example (plate 99). Tura appears to have designed works of this *sacra conversazione* type, and to have produced at least one modest example (plate 43). A drawing of just such a work (London, British Museum; plate 44) may be a model drawing submitted to a patron, establishing the subject, ornaments and the colours to be used; given the demand for Tura's style, however, manifest in the number of surviving works by Tura imitators, it could have been made for the use of another artist.[1] The heavily damaged but imposing canvas (Ajaccio; plate 43) probably served as an altarpiece for a chapel of the Cicognara family. It bears an inscription recording its dedication by Antonio Cicognara, a notary who had served as *giudice* of the communal magistracy known as the Dodici Savi: ANTONIO CICOGNARA VERGINE PURA/DEPINGER FECE QUESTA TUA FIGURA (Antonio Cicognara had this your image painted, O pure Virgin).[2]

We know of other polyptychs only in the form of gold-ground single panels with the image of saints who very commonly appear in *quattrocento* religious painting and as such offer little clue as to their original purpose and location. A number of attempts have been made to reconstruct the original polyptychs by grouping these fragments in various combinations, often relying on the rather liberal criteria of attribution of later writers such as Girolamo Baruffaldi and Cesare Cittadella, who identified various polyptychs by 'Tura' in the churches of the city.[3] Images of *St Jerome* (London and Milan; plates 62 and 61) and *St Anthony* (Modena; plate 60) claim a special distinction among these fragments by virtue of a more monumental scale and a remarkable, visionary landscape setting. The drawing in the British Museum could in fact be seen as an experiment in combining the traditional 'iconic' portrayal of saints on a gold ground with a view of open-air space.

Apart from sparse information on the San Giorgio altarpieces, little or nothing can be determined about the commissioning of any of these works. Surviving court records show only one devotional image, a small polyptych with an elaborately inlaid frame, being produced under direct ducal commission;[4] Tura's supplication to Ercole d'Este in 1490 refers to 'una anchona da altaro' which he had produced for the duke's secretary, and a painting of *St Anthony of Padua* for Niccolò Maria di Gurone d'Este, Bishop of Adria.[5] More research is needed on the general demand for altarpieces in Ferrara, and on how the presence of a court may have affected production differently from that in other Italian cities, but it is demonstrable that Tura's clientele would have embraced a spectrum of patrons wider than the court, including the clergy (in Tura's case, the cathedral canons and the Roverella) and the professional classes (such as the Cicognara). The city's confraternities, for instance, provided a steady market for devotional images, and the conventual church of San Francesco housed several chapels and oratories which were decorated by confraternities and private patrons.[6] A busy and uncelebrated painter like Bonzohane, whose oeuvre has never been identified, served all of these categories of client, producing Madonnas for the ducal audience chamber, a *gonfalone* with Sts Francis and Sebastian for the confraternity of Santa Maria della Scala, images for cells at the Certosa, the *cappella maggiore* decorations at San Giacomo and a painting of the *Twelve Apostles* for the cathedral. Records of commissions to

43   Tura, *Virgin and Child with Sts Jerome and Apollonia*. Ajaccio, Musée Fesch. Canvas mounted on panel (152 × 101 cm).

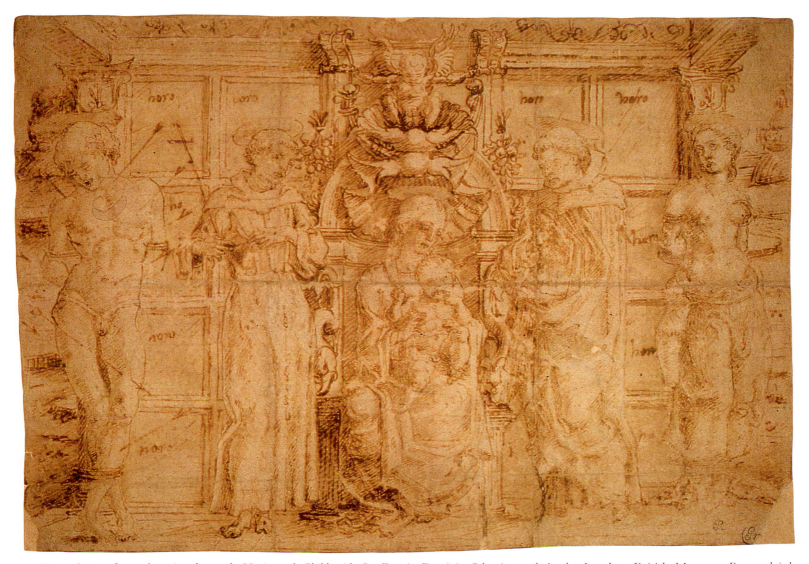

44   Tura, design for a devotional panel: *Virgin and Child with Sts Francis, Dominic, Sebastian and Agatha*. London, British Museum. Pen and ink with wash on paper (14.9 × 21.5 cm).

Bonzohane and to painters like Titolivio and Gherardo da Vicenza indicate a fairly constant demand for religious art in the city in the later fifteenth century, but it is evident that these painters provided a much cheaper product than Tura, more within the spending capacity of craftsmen and confraternities. Tura received 48 ducats in 1469 for painting the organ-shutters of the cathedral. Bonzohane was paid only 40 ducats three years earlier for a considerably more extensive cycle of paintings in San Giacomo (including materials and labour); the patron was a carpenter, Peregrino Punzinella.[7] There is one early record of Tura repainting a *gonfalone* for the Arte dei Sarti (Guild of Tailors) in 1456; thereafter, to judge from the documents, he accepted more financially rewarding commissions from more élite clients.[8]

The original destinations of the small devotional images, including the *Pietà* (plate 57), two of the *Virgin and Child* (plates 9 and 11), *Sts Peter and John the Baptist* (plate 45), the *Crucifixion with St John and the Virgin* (plate 46) and the *Annunciation with*

Sts Francis and Louis of Toulouse (plate 48), are also mysterious; we know, however, that there was a demand for small devotional images at court.[9] Within this group there are notable variations of handling, suggesting that Tura varied his investment of labour according to the client's financial outlay. The four Washington panels are characterised by a cursory if vigorous treatment of the figure, its drapery and its setting; the *Sts Peter and John the Baptist* show by contrast an extreme refinement of handling, with the delicate brushwork and minute detail characteristic of book illumination. There is a subtlety in the *contrapposto* and elaborate drapery of St John which is lacking in the more formulaic gestures and draperies of the Washington figures. A marble statuette of *St Maurelius* has recently been attributed to Tura on the basis of its distinctive physiognomy and drapery style (Ferrara, Museo del Duomo; plate 47). As there is no documentation that that Tura worked as a stonecarver, it is not possible to be conclusive on this point: strong affinities with Tura's painting suggest that the statue may have been designed by him; or it

45　Tura, *Sts Peter and John the Baptist*. Philadelphia Museum of Art, Johnson Collection. On panel (each 22 × 10.8 cm, including frame).

could be a highly competent evaluation of the artist's calligraphic style. The statue appears to have been commissioned by the bailiff Vincenzo de' Lardi in 1458 for an overdoor in the cathedral sacristy, and Tura painted a *Nativity* for de' Lardi in the same location, also in 1458, which disappeared in the eighteenth century.[10]

Despite the daunting lack of evidence for specific commissions, there are other ways of thinking about Tura's devotional images, particularly those of saints. A sense of their meaning and function, and a context for certain artistic choices, is obtainable if one places these images in relation to contemporary beliefs and local practices surrounding sainthood in Ferrara. One can also think of sainthood as involving a particular set of representational problems which have implications even beyond the pro-

duction of images. In the first place, the cult of saints was a visual culture; sanctity was manifest in visible gestures and behaviour, perhaps most powerfully in signs produced by the saintly body, before and after death. Images of the saints, not unlike the saints themselves, acted as channels of communication between the divine and the human sphere. The saints served the faith by inspiring wonder through visible manifestations of miraculous power; they also provided the faithful with types of exemplary piety.[11] What then, for Tura and his contemporaries, were the visual characteristics of sainthood? Second, I want to consider the ways in which Tura's manner of painting may have answered to the devotional requirements of contemporary beholders. So far, Tura's style has been discussed in terms of the extremely secular values of humanist poetics and courtly self-fashioning.

46 Tura, *Crucifixion with St John and the Virgin*. Cambridge, Fitzwilliam Museum. On panel (50.2 × 30.5 cm).

47 Follower of Tura, *St Maurelius*. Ferrara, Museo del Duomo. Marble (80 cm).

Given that the audience for devotional paintings would be constituted differently, or at least more widely, what would be the status for beholders of pictures which clearly so assert the mediating role and virtuosity of their maker? It could reasonably be answered that an expectation would have been fulfilled; human artifice, like precious materials adorning a reliquary, could serve the pious function of honouring the saint.[12] Yet what if the artist was concerned to claim a greater authority for the 'man-made-ness' of his own art, and was conscious, as were Alberti and Leonardo, of the dependency of images which commanded devotion on the skills of the human artist? For Alberti, the ability to stimulate piety through the image testified to the God-like power of the painter; Leonardo would write of the power of

painting by referring to the behaviour of the devout before the image, 'throw[ing] themselves to the ground, worshipping and praying to Him whose image is represented for the recovery of their health and for their eternal salvation, as if the deity were present in person'.[13] Whether or not Tura consciously concerned himself with such radical conceptions of the artist's status, I want to consider the ways in which art that manifestly does not conceal art could also have generated a claim of authority for itself. The issue is treated more fully in chapters IV and V, where I show how two works by Tura explicitly raise questions about this very issue. In Tura's lifetime, the devotional efficacy of his art may finally have been found wanting: there are signs of a reaction in northern Italy against the artfully wrought,

48   Tura, *Annunciation with Sts Francis and Louis of Toulouse*. Washington, D.C., National Gallery of Art. On panel (each 30.7 × 11.5 cm).

ornamented manner epitomised by Tura, Zoppo, Crivelli, Bartolomeo Vivarini and others, which is examined at the end of this chapter.

Evidence which can securely place fragmentary paintings in relation to documented saint cults in Ferrara is at best circumstantial, but taken as a group, the images of the saints share certain features which will sustain comment and interpretation in the light of this milieu. The grounds for the linkage I am proposing lie less in the specific identities of the saints than in Tura's distinctive handling of the human figure. As discussed below, Tura's stylisation of the body could have enhanced the efficacy of his portrayals for an audience who believed that sainthood itself resided in a transfiguration or even embellishment of bodily form.

In the absence of firm historical facts, scholars have been silent about these panels except to comment on the expressive qualities of the figures. What has been most striking to modern commentators may, in fact, be the most historically significant feature of these images. I have already observed that the forms of jagged and flowing linear embellishment characteristic of this artist, manifest usually in drapery in the silhouettes and outlines of figures, in pseudo-inscriptions and passages of decoration, are often transposed to the forms of the body itself. To the erratic rhythm of broken drapery folds, Tura will often counterpose an articulation of the body surface with bones and sinews graphically expressed under taut skin, or sometimes the sparse flesh covering will gather and furrow around the solid skeletal core (plate 49). Once again, the incisive quality of line is the key instrument here. Tura's adaptability to the requirements of various audiences who would have encountered his paintings is also implicit in his calligraphic style; for the very means by which Tura generates a visual experience of opulence, curiosity and virtuoso display are equally effective in the imaging of values which may appear to stand as the opposite of these – a visual experience of impoverishment, restraint and austerity.

VISUALISING SANCTITY: THE SAINTLY BODY

The most recent commentators have seen Tura as primarily engaged, in his depiction of saints, with the expression of emotion.[14] Such an observation is generally connected with assumptions about stylistic influence, which would place Tura as a follower of Donatello or Mantegna.[15] The expression of emotion in fifteenth-century art is often seen in a progressive light, as part of an emerging modern conception of the individual inner self and in terms of a deepening psychological engagement of the beholder. Yet the 'expressive' personalities produced by Tura are misunderstood if they are taken as attempts to represent a newly discovered human condition. The qualities expressed by Tura's saints do not add up to realistic character studies of individuals, but are distinguishing attributes of a class of mysterious and transfigured beings. Tura may in fact be closer to older contemporaries such as Paolo Uccello, Vecchietta or Giovanni di Paolo, who populated their religious paintings with

49 Tura, *St Dominic* (fragment). Florence, Galleria degli Uffizi. On panel (51 × 32 cm).

wiry and emaciated, even cadaverous figures; these seem pointedly distinguished from the elegant or heroic figures of the Florentine tradition. Two Ferrarese painters who worked in a manner different from Tura indicate that an emphasis on certain bodily characteristics is not necessarily dependent on style; an anonymous painter working at the convent of San Andrea around 1450 conceived *St Christopher* and *St Sebastian* as vigorous and agitated figures (plates 52 and 53); *St Sebastian* adopts an animated and abandoned physical comportment rarely if ever encountered in representations of this saint. Michele Pannonio painted the Franciscan saints *Louis of Toulouse* and *Bernardino of Siena* with the bodily attributes of the ascetic (plates 54 and 55), yet any notion of corporeal realism is called into question in the

50 Tura, *St Anthony of Padua*. Paris, Musée du Louvre. On panel (72 × 31 cm, without addition).

51 Tura, *St James the Greater*. Caen, Musée des Beaux-Arts. On panel (74 × 31.3 cm, without addition).

52 Ferrarese, mid-fifteenth century, *St Christopher*. Ferrara, Pinacoteca Nazionale.

53 Ferrarese, mid-fifteenth century, *St Sebastian*. Ferrara, Pinacoteca Nazionale.

use of illusionistic techniques to generate fantastic and paradoxical conceits, which place the figures beyond earthly time, space, gravity and materiality; shell niches viewed from different angles hover behind the saints in a zone of spaceless gold, while the IHS monogram of Bernardino hovers weightlessly before his gaze. Even in this timeless, spaceless zone, the saintly body bears the marks of its earthly trials – emaciation, the executioners' arrows – but at the same time seems curiously energetic, triumphant and impervious to mutilation.

The conception of sanctity as identifiable in physical and visible phenomena is reinforced by the culture of the religious image, as in the promotion through images of the cults of the stigmatic saints Catherine and Francis; such images could claim to be authentic 'portraits' of individuals whose bodies had been

miraculously transformed by divine intervention.[16] Yet the power of the image to propagate sometimes controversial beliefs – even, in some cases, to create saints – was not uncontested; the authenticity of Catherine's stigmata was impugned by the Franciscans, and in the 1470s Pope Sixtus IV prohibited the painting of the saint's mystical wounds.[17]

Underlying the notion of sainthood as a miraculous yet visible and representable phenomenon was the idea of the body as material which could be shaped by invisible and immaterial forces. Such a belief with regard to the body was not confined to the realm of the supernatural, but underlay Aristotelian (and theologically orthodox) accounts of human generation and growth. The human person was defined in terms of his or her soul; the body is the mere material which takes its form from

54 Michele Pannonio, *St Louis of Toulouse*. Ferrara, Pinacoteca Nazionale.

55 Michele Pannonio, *St Bernardino of Siena*. Ferrara, Pinacoteca Nazionale..

the soul, and the expression and animation of the body are outward manifestations of the soul's movements. The Aristotelian position underlay various scholastic formulations of human identity;[18] it also informed the science of physiognomy – the decipherment of interior character from bodily appearance – which by the later fifteenth century had claimed the attention of art theorists such as Alberti, Leonardo and Pomponius Gauricus.[19] Most artists would have had a casual knowledge of what would have anyway have appeared to have a rational and common-sense basis – that there is a dependable continuity between the characteristics of the face and the character of the person, the latter determining the former. For Leonardo, it is the soul's role in fashioning the body that enables the artist to fashion other human figures, which are no more than imagings by the soul of itself at second hand.[20]

Tura's saints would have had to assert a continuity of outer appearance with inner spiritual condition, a classic problem of representation not only for the artist, but also for the saint. As one Ferrarese bishop stated, basing his remark on Ecclesiastes, chapter 2, verse 19: 'A man shall be known from his countenance, and the wise man by the quality of his face.'[21] Yet there are signs that Tura was responding to a physiognomical tradition which was not acknowledged by Alberti, Leonardo or Pomponius Gauricus.

Physiognomic expression in Renaissance art theory is premised on the soul's disposition of the body from within. The influence is held to proceed unidirectionally, from soul to body, while classical physiognomic theory had posited a capacity of the body to affect the soul.[22] Tura could have been aware of the later possibility through acquaintance with the court physician Michele Savonarola, whose treatise on physiognomy addressed this matter.[23] Yet such knowledge may only have reinforced an entirely independent conception of the soul's dependency on the body in contemporary devotional literature. In this alternative account, ideas of the soul as 'first mover', or of the soul as artist, are modified by less systematic, long-standing beliefs underlying the cult of the saints and the visibility of sanctity, beliefs which accorded a special and far from secondary status to the body. The body was still material to be worked on, but what now guaranteed sanctity were the signs of workmanship *from without*, where the body is identified as the recipient of rigorous physical discipline and of marks and signs more supernatural in origin. There is even a sense that sanctity is expressed according to a process in which the immortal soul is conceived not as the stable and continuous basis for identity which gives form to the body, but as itself shaped and transformed by forces acting upon the body. What is designated as the 'soul' in the mystical literature is refashioned, purified and purged through acts of penance, through mortification of the body, and through martyrdom.[24] According to one Ferrarese mystical writer of the mid-*quattrocento*, Caterina Vegri, the goal of Christian discipline is 'the refashioning of the beauty of the soul, returning it to its original state of innocence'.[25] The degree of the soul's purity is measured primarily by the visible neglect or active mortification of the flesh. As Giovanni Tavelli wrote:

Your beauty shall be internal, just as those who inwardly are peaceful, are outwardly deformed and pallid through privations and vigils and prayers and other disciplines and discomforts of religion. You thus conform to the nature of your spouse [i.e. Christ], thus extolled in the words of Isaiah: We will take him for a leper, stricken and humiliated by God, and through his lividness and pallor we are cured.[26]

This ascetic refashioning of the soul is sometimes, as in the case of Francis and Catherine, finally authorised by divine and mystical forces which leave their trace on the surface of the body, altering it in some way – aureoles or effulgences of light, the stigmata or wounds of Christ, signs of mysterious sickness. Even the 'interior beauty' which writers like Tavelli attributed to the saintly soul was literalised in reports of miraculous pictures or golden letters found in the saint's internal organs – allegedly the case with St Bernardino of Siena.[27]

The soul as a philosophical postulate was very different from the soul as it was conceived in the devotional writings and lived religious experience of fifteenth-century men and women. The terminological precision of scholastic theology tended to give place to a series of less precise and often poetic labels (*anima, cuore, mente, intentione, volontà*) all approximating to what might be called the 'inner self' and often giving the soul a more strongly corporeal and visible cast:

[Charity] causes the soul to have its conversation in heaven; it crucifies the soul in the world and the world within it . . . it causes the soul to desire nothing except suffering, it leads the soul into an abyss of divine illumination . . . it is a fiery furnace, which burns but does not consume, and in fact tempers and hardens, giving comeliness, health and beauty . . . O vehemence of delight, O violence of charity, O excellence and supereminence of perfect love, which penetrates the heart, inflames the affection and animates it to its very marrow, so that it truly can say: 'I am wounded in charity and by charity.'[28]

The body, as Carolyn Bynum has demonstrated, had long provided a much more tangible principle according to which human identity could be grasped, even at the level of more technical philosophical discussions;[29] the damned and the blessed of necessity reclaimed their unique individual bodies on the day of the Last Judgement, and the cult of saints' relics would have had to be deemed without foundation if the venerated bodily part did not somehow participate in the essence or selfhood of the saint – impossible if the saints were conceived of only as disembodied souls. In Ferrara, according to the Inquisitor Tommaso dai Liuti, the question of the soul's dependency upon the body was debated at the court of Borso d'Este; Borso himself, like other princes before him, was concerned to know whether the soul, when separated from the body, retained its sensory capacities; if it did, the question implies, why was there then a need for bodily resurrection, and could the damned suffer torment before the Last Judgement?[30]

Sanctity manifest in the alteration of the body, through

extreme asceticism or through supernatural influence, carried a tremendous weight of conviction among the laity; the church endorsed such criteria of sanctity only with caution, and was generally disposed to approve sainthood in less sensational (and more institutionally useful) guises.[31] The Inquisition took steps to forestall popular credulity before such radically physical demonstrations of piety, which could often lead to posthumous cults, popular and unapproved. The body of one popularly acclaimed saint, Armanno Pungilupo, had been exhumed and burned by the Inquisition in Ferrara in 1301. The 'theatrical' display of holiness was described in satiric terms by the Inquisitor General of Lombardy and Ferrara, Tommaso dai Liuti, in his *Liber petitionum animae* of 1466: 'many are the ways of simulating sanctity, and thus the devil finds many stipendiaries in hypocrisy.' He attacked the 'spiritelli' who disdained all non-pious speech, the 'saint-eaters' who voraciously kissed saint's relics or images, 'abstracti' who faked trances, the 'barbati' who grew their beards long and feigned contempt for the world, the 'beati in piaza' who wore chains and practised acts of discipline in public, and the 'afflicted ones' who cultivated mournful expressions.[32] The Inquisitor may have been reacting to the undoubted popular impact of spectacles like the following, which the Ferrarese diarist Zambotti described as occurring on Christmas Day of 1487:

> Giovanni Novello of Siena, who went about barefoot and bareheaded with a long beard, dressed like an apostle in the skin of a wild beast, and bearing an iron cross one *braccia* in length, like St John the Baptist, preached in the Piazza with wondrous grace, warning of many future calamities; and he collected much money for the love of God, using it with the approval of citizens to provide clothing for poor children, showing himself to be a good-living and merciful man.[33]

For another local theologian, the saintly bishop Giovanni Tavelli da Tossignano, the outward show of piety was a pursuit of vain *singularitade* and hence was one of the degrees of *superbia*, the very antithesis of the saintly quality of humility. The signs of this characteristic were defined by the bishop almost entirely in negative terms, as abstention from any purposeful singularity in gesture, action and behaviour.[34] Both comments provide an insight into the modes of performing sanctity and its regulation within the religious milieu of the city: dai Liuti seems to imply a distinct separation between 'authentic' sanctity and the popular iconography of painting and religious drama, with its haloes, instruments of martyrdom and histrionic gestures and expressions. Yet his comments would also seem to give a particular weight to mystical proofs of sanctity, to the divinely induced bodily signs which are beyond human simulation; Tavelli moreover implies that holiness can be recognised in bodily signs which are 'earned' through rigorous discipline. And Tura's painted figures also make their claim to saintliness on just these corporeal grounds – through the signs of mystical bodily alteration in elongated limbs and fingers, through the coexistence of death-like emaciation with feverish animation, a possessing force which

also makes drapery turbulent or causes it to cling with static energy.[35] Once again, Albertian prescriptions for the movement of bodies and drapery, where natural causality and intention have to be in evidence, would have been little use to the artist who sought to do this; drapery, says Alberti, is moved by wind, and its source and direction should be consistent and evident for the viewer. Alberti is also mistrustful of artistic renderings of frenzy and ecstatic gesticulation; if his remarks censuring the depiction of figures who adopt the frenzied 'movements of actors' referred to Donatello's sacristy doors at San Lorenzo (as Filarete clearly thought they did), then he was choosing not to recognise that the agitated movements and tumultuous draperies made sense in terms of a rendering of divine inspiration or possession – the furious animating power of charity we have seen described above by Tavelli.[36] Tura's representations of the Dead Christ indicate that the painter may actually have perceived and responded to a conflict between the physiognomic logic of Alberti and the rhetorical requirements of the devotional image (plates 7, 8, 57, 81 and 85).[37] The Christ in the Roverella altarpiece *Lamentation*, together with that in the *Pietà* and in a tapestry designed by the artist, is dead according to the literal sense of the Passion narrative. Yet Tura's depictions of Christ seem, in their strangely animated poses and expressions, to be paradoxically alive and still suffering, to lament along with his mourners; in the tapestry, the Dead Christ stares back at the beholder. There seems no doubt that Tura's images respond to a theological controversy which asserted that Christ's body between death and resurrection was not merely cast-off matter, but still participated in the essence of his divinity; relics of the blood of Christ, as the Pope finally affirmed in 1463, could thus be venerated.[38] Christ's body in these images is in a liminal state between life and death, a condition which affirms the potency and venerability of his dead flesh and the imminence of the resurrection; the representation of such a state is in all respects contrary to the decorum of the body as set forth in *De pictura*: 'in the dead man there is no member that does not seem completely lifeless; they all hang loose; hands, fingers, neck, all droop inertly down, all combine together to represent death. This is the most difficult thing of all to do, for to represent the limbs of a body entirely at rest is as much the sign of an excellent artist as to render them all alive and in action.'[39] As in the case of the bodies of the saints which emulate that of Christ, the liminal body has undergone a strange metamorphosis through its suffering, leading to an erratic proportionality which, point for point, violates Alberti's strictures in a passage immediately preceding that just quoted:

> In the composition of members care should be taken above all that all the members accord well with one another when in size, function, kind, colour and other similar respects they correspond to grace and beauty. For, if in a picture the head is enormous, the chest puny, the hand very large, the foot swollen and the body distended, this composition will certainly be ugly to look at.[40]

Art historians hasten to explain away Tura's apparently cruel and licentious approach to anatomy and proportion with an appeal

57 Tura, *Pietà*. Venice, Museo Correr. On panel (45 × 31 cm).

to Northern influence. Even if we were to allow that such artistic effects could be explained as a more or less passive absorption of influences, no Man of Sorrows or Dead Christ in Northern art provides a counterpart for the anatomical characteristics of Tura's Christ, with his large head, shrunken torso and elongated hands and feet (plate 57). If such a counterpart could be found, Tura's adoption of it would have to be understood in terms of a rhetorical purpose, which I believe to be a conscious deviation from the principles of the normative human body as codified by Alberti.

In Ferrara by the mid-fifteenth century, the recognition of sainthood tended towards uncanny bodies, living or dead, which underwent mysterious alteration. Saints were recognised not through pious actions and demeanour alone, but through involuntary bodily phenomena which could not in any obvious way be simulated. Ferrara's cherished bishop, the *beato* Giovanni Tavelli, who died in 1446, was alleged to have had a seraphic countenance, radiant with light. Among the older cults were that

of two female *beate* of the house of Este itself, both fortuitously named Beatrice. The sanctity of the younger Beata Beatrice was attested by the signs miraculously produced by her body after death, renewed annually in the washing and bearing in procession of her corpse by the nuns of San Antonio in Polesine.[41] The body of Beata Beatrice II d'Este would on occasion intervene in contemporary political events, as when Duke Ercole believed himself to have heard his holy ancestor groan aloud in her tomb on the occasion of his dishonourable pro-Florentine and anti-Neapolitan ventures in 1478.[42] Tura's active career is bounded on one side by the sensational death of the saintly Ferrarese Caterina Vegri in Bologna in 1463, and by Ercole's long but ultimately successful attempts to draw the stigmatist Lucia Broccadelli to Ferrara in the 1490s. Vegri's corpse had been mysteriously animate for several days after her death, attracting vast crowds to the convent of Corpus Domini; the body exuded fragrant oil, the face became radiant with joy in the presence of the Eucharist.[43]

Conceptions of sainthood by an artist, and perceptions of it by his audience, could have been determined primarily by the charisma of contemporary holy men and women, especially those who had a place in the living memory of those Ferrarese beholders who encountered Tura's images of the more 'classic' saints and martyrs: Francis, Dominic, Sebastian, Christopher, Jerome, Anthony. In addition to Vegri and Tavelli, these would have included such saintly mendicant visitors as Giovanni da Capistrano (in Ferrara 1434 and subsequently), Bernardino of Siena (1423, 1428, 1431, 1438 and 1443), who had been offered the Bishopric of Ferrara, and Bernardino da Feltre (1480s). All of these contemporary saints and *beati* were noted for their asceticism, which is given considerable emphasis in their biographies and in their cult iconography. Both Vegri and Tavelli produced authoritative works on ascetic discipline, emphasising the conquest of the will or the *anima* and drawing on physical metaphors of warfare, combat and struggle to overcome the 'self', which is achieved through bodily means.[44]

Many of Tura's saints show the signs of extreme discipline and self-privation; asceticism is manifested even in the barren and cavernous landscape of wilderness within which the saint is placed. Sanctity is associated with a literal reduction of flesh on the bodily frame, described in a linear mode which seems also to mark the flesh it describes. Tura's saints and martyrs sometimes register the effects of pain and suffering, to an extent unusual even in fifteenth-century Italy; at times the artist seems to equivocate between rendering the effects of torture and of a rapture more supernatural in origin. It had become commonplace in Italy and throughout Europe by the later fifteenth century to show saints accepting martyrdom serenely, as if fortified against pain by an outpouring of divine grace. Carolyn Bynum has argued that one of the functions of the image in the cults of the saints was to provide an image of wholeness and reintegration beyond the mutilations and agony of their martyrdom and beyond the processes of physical corruption. Aquinas and other theologians had written 'that the martyrs were enabled to bear up under pain exactly because the beatific vision flows

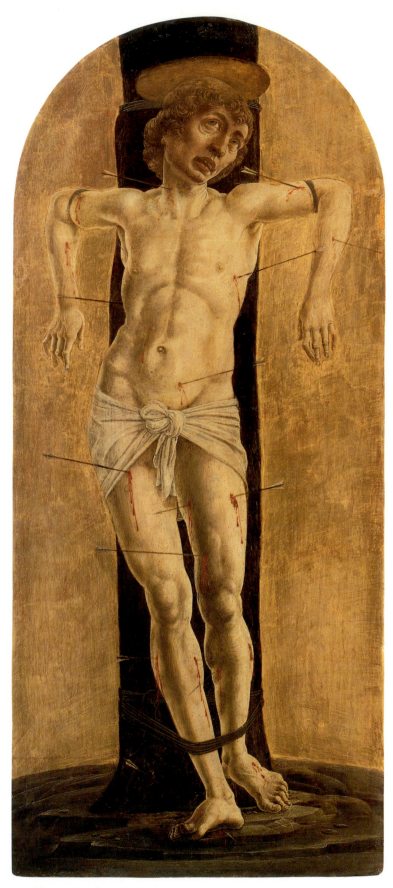

58 Tura, *St Sebastian*. Berlin, Staatliche Museen, Gemäldegalerie. On panel (75.7 × 33.1 cm).

59 Tura. *St Christopher*. Berlin, Staatliche Museen, Gemäldegalerie. On panel (76.8 × 34 cm).

over naturally into the body. Both artistic representation and hagiographical story depicted saintly heroes and heroines as unaffected psychologically (and often even physiologically), by graphic and remarkable tortures.'[45] She adduces images of the martyrs Agatha and Sebastian to illustrate the latter point, drawn from Swiss and German art of the late fifteenth and the early sixteenth centuries. Relatively serene images of St Sebastian could certainly be cited from late fifteenth-century Italy, such as those by Botticelli or Antonello da Messina. But consider the representation of these same saints by Tura, in the drawing for a *sacra conversazione* (plate 44), in which St Sebastian appears to writhe and grimace in pain, and Agatha opens her mouth, rolling her eyes as the pincers clutch her left breast. The *St Sebastian* (Berlin, Gemäldegalerie; plate 58) may suggest the experience of divine rapture, but does so in highly physical and sensational terms, with the saint grimacing as he gazes heavenward. The companion image of *St Christopher* (Berlin, Gemäldegalerie; plate 59) bears an equally ambiguous expression, both grin and grimace. It could signify the pain or effort which could relate to the unnaturally heavy burden of the Christ Child on his back, as related by *The Golden Legend*, or to the impending martyrdom of which that burden is symbolic. Only the images of St Sebastian by Mantegna, working nearby in Mantua, come close to Tura's in the extravagence and ambiguity of their expressions of pain. As in the case of the martyrs, there is also in the *St James* (plate 51), *St Jerome* (plate 62) and *St Anthony of Padua* (plate 60) a sense of agitation or feverish restlessness, in which might be recognised the quality of 'disquiet' identified by Richard Kieckhefer as a distinguishing characteristic of sainthood in this period.[46] The suggestions of pain in Tura's images point to their destination not as therapeutic reassurances of delivery from suffering, but rather to an idea of martyrs as examples of *ascesis* – the body is privileged as the means through which harsh and painful discipline will produce sanctity; frequently, the voluntary suffering of saintly figures like Tavelli, who are not martyrs in the true sense, was referred to as 'martyrdom'.[47]

Tura's representations of the saints participate in both local and more widely diffused conceptions of sainthood, manifestations of which we will now explore in specific paintings. The bodies of his saints bear the marks of both physical and mystical transformation, although it is hard to establish any distinction between these: both together constitute *admiranda*, wondrous signs by which sainthood becomes manifest in the flesh. It will be suggested further that Tura's figures also suggest an analogy between this fashioning of the body, with the aim of beautifying the soul, and the artistic processes of stylisation and embellishment. As ascetic discipline produces a refashioning and beautification of the soul, so the resources of Tura's *maniera* inscribe this process of beautification in the surface of the ravaged body. Yet Tura, as we shall see, grounds his representations of sanctity not in artistic *fantasia* alone, but in the authorised contemporary likeness of a saint.

★ ★ ★

60 Tura, *St Anthony of Padua*. Modena, Galleria Estense. On panel (178 × 80 cm).

It is truly astounding how the incorporeal mind can
be defiled and darkened by the body. Equally
astonishing is the fact that the immaterial spirit can be
purified and refined by clay.[48]

John Climacus

While I lived thus, the companion of scorpions and
wild beasts, ofttimes I imagined that I was surrounded
by dancing girls, and in my frozen body and moribund
flesh the fires of concupiscence were lighted. For this I
wept unceasingly, and subjugated the rebellious flesh
with week-long fasts. Often I joined the days with the
nights, nor stayed from beating my breast until the
Lord restored my peace of Spirit. I dreaded to enter
my cell, as if it were aware of my thoughts, and
angered and stern with myself I sought the desert
wastes alone; and as the Lord is my witness, after all
my weeping I sometimes seemed to be among the
choirs of angels.[49]

St Jerome

More than any other image, Tura's *St Jerome in Penitence* (London,
National Gallery; plate 62) makes explicit the continuity between
ascetic practices and the divinely authorised self-transformation
which is their goal.[50] Jerome is a ferocious ascetic, represented
in an act of violence against the self which, in its physical vigour,
is unparalleled in contemporary painting. The aim of Jerome's
penitence is not mere mastery over the flesh, or carnal desire,
but the rapturous vision of the crucified Christ which replaces
the crucifix normally contemplated by the saint; Christ appears
in place of the heavenly choirs specified in Jerome's own account
of the ordeal. Tura's panel has been cut down drastically from its
original format, and the portion bearing the vision of Christ,
whose cross is composed of a hovering beam of light, is now in
the Pinacoteca di Brera, Milan (plate 61).[51]

Although Jerome is one of the most commonly represented
saints in fourteenth- and fifteenth-century Italian art, depictions
of him receiving a vision of the dead or suffering Christ are
extremely rare; to my knowledge, the sole extant examples are
the panel by Tura, another Ferrarese work by Ercole de' Roberti
(London, National Gallery; plate 63) and Castagno's famous
fresco at SS Annunziata in Florence.[52] Jerome's own account of
his vision is not very specific as to its contents, which explains
the iconographic variation among these works (and occasionally,
the pictorial identification of the Virgin Mary as the subject of
the vision[53]). Castagno presents Jerome contemplating the Trinity,
while the Ferrarese artists show a vision of Christ alone; this suggests that Jerome's vision is here being patterned after that of St
Francis, who is represented with Jerome in both works.

Another disinctive feature of Tura's painting is Jerome's
dynamic posture and his emaciated physique, homologous in
many respects with that of the apparition of Christ; the notion
of a saint's self-fashioning as mimesis, as an 'imitation of Christ',

61   Tura, *Christ Crucified*, fragment of *St Jerome*. Milan, Pinacoteca di
Brera. On panel (21.5 × 17 cm).

seems directly evoked here. Only Leonardo da Vinci's treatment
of the subject (Museo del Vaticano, Pinacoteca; plate 65) comes
close to Tura's, in the vehemence of expression, the dynamic *contrapposto* where the weight-bearing knee is the pivot, and the
pursuit of extreme relief effects.[54] The figure is in both cases
placed against a dark mass close to the picture plane which is
defied by the thrust of the saint's knee, while an Albertian church
appears in the distance to the left. Jill Dunkerton has recently
drawn attention to analogies of technique between the two
artists – in the later *quattrocento* it is these two artists who show
the most highly developed use of monochrome undermodelling
to establish the volume and lighting of figures.[55]

Although usually dated slightly before Leonardo's departure
for the Milanese court in 1482 or 1483, the Vatican picture might
be reconsidered as a response to a typically North Italian treatment of the penitence of St Jerome in which Tura's image occupies a key place.[56] Marco Zoppo (Bologna, Collegio di Spagna),
Ercole de' Roberti (London, National Gallery) and a Paduan follower of Mantegna (Washington, National Gallery of Art) all
conceived Jerome according to the dynamic *contrapposto* of the
single weight-bearing and pivotal knee, a solution seldom
encountered in Tuscany (plates 63 and 64). The posture suggests

62   Tura, *St Jerome in Penitence* (fragment). London, National Gallery. On panel (101 × 57 cm).

63 Ercole de' Roberti, *Dead Christ with Sts Jerome and Francis*. London, National Gallery.

a particular physicality and sense of abandon, identifying Jerome as a radical ascetic beyond the margins of society and the limits of bodily decorum; the same spirit is apparent in another small panel by Roberti, in which Jerome is displayed in a manner 'unusually indecorous, with the crucifix thrown over one arm,

64 Marco Zoppo, *St Jerome*, from the predella of the Collegio di Spagna altarpiece. Bologna, Collegio di Spagna.

and his knee thrown up revealing his *mutande*' (Los Angeles, J. Paul Getty Museum; plate 66).[57]

Yet Leonardo's work also rationalises and critiques this tradition, above all in the register of emotional expression. Like a good Albertian artist, Leonardo pursues a psychological decorum; he approaches Jerome as a study in the expression of religious fervour and of physically demanding effort, psychological states on which the artist dwells in his theoretical writings. He is interested in the visible response to two sensations – the sight of the image, which registers in the saint's intense gaze, and the effort of scourging, manifest in the straining muscles and sinews, in the tension of the neck and of the mouth. The body signifies according to a mechanical logic of causality, of stimulus and reaction. The affective response to an image and the pathetic reaction to pain are both operations of the organic soul, which controls cogitation and sensory experience.

However, in the conception of the saintly body as a kind of ideogram of the divinely enraptured soul, the naturalistic epistemology of Aristotelian psychology is inadequate. By contrast, Tura's figure has an excessive character, a hyperactive

65 Leonardo da Vinci, *St Jerome*. Museo del Vaticano, Pinacoteca.

66   Ercole de' Roberti, *St Jerome*. Los Angeles, Calif., The J. Paul Getty Museum.

quality which suggests animation from a supernatural source, and an emotionalism which is not merely a response to physical pain or the sight of an image, but to a privileged mystical vision which is felt in the body as much as seen. Physical pain and mystical phenomena are given the same terms of reference in Jerome's expression and his euphorically abandoned pose.

The saint's action is no mere performance; it is authenticated in the image by a visionary experience. His expression, like that of Tura's martyrs, is equivocal; it is a response to the physical ordeal and a sign of divine *furor* or possession. Several of Tura's saints express a kind of gratuitous movement, where the soul no longer appears as the 'first mover' of the living being. A supernatural force seems to animate and transfigure the body, expressing veins and sinews and recessing cheeks, throat and eyes, and this same force reverberates in drapery which clings statically to the limbs or convulses independently of bodily movement, as in the figures in the *St James* or the *St Anthony*.

The association of sanctity and the mortification of the flesh had acquired particular prominence in the religious life of the laity of Italian cities through the permeation of lay devotion by the confraternities of *disciplinati* or *battuti* – the flagellant groups, active in Ferrara from the later thirteenth century. The passive, suffering body as an agent of religious meaning was framed as such chiefly through the activities of these groups. Among the ten or so flagellant confraternities active in Ferrara by the mid-fifteenth century, the most distinctive appear to have been the Compagnia dei Battuti Neri, also known as the Compagnia della Morte. The bodies of its members were sacralised by acts of violent self-discipline, to the extent that they were sometimes regarded as living saints, to the great alarm of ecclesiastical authorities; steps had to be taken to prevent the shed blood of the flagellants from being venerated as a precious relic.[58] Actual drawing of blood in the public penitential exercises of this group was thus confined to very select occasions, such as the Good Friday procession, but the devotional activities of the Battuti Neri had a particular gravitation to a more recurrent spectacle of pain and death in everyday urban life, in the rituals accompanying the execution of condemned criminals. The function of the group was to mediate the spectacle of the passive and suffering body for its own members, for the victims themselves, and for the witnessing crowds. Its devotional practices could assimilate the body of the condemned to the body of the martyred saint.[59] In its collective devotions, the Battuti Neri used the pictures from its *Martirologio* (Venice, Fondazione Cini), which includes an exceptionally gruesome series showing the violent deaths of many saints.[60] The image provides a psychological conduit between past and present, sacred and profane – it provides the means by which modern execution gives dramatic reality and pathos to the hagiographical account, while the saint's death gives a sense of structure and purpose to the violence of the scaffold, especially as such executions were scrutinised for signs of conversion or demonstrations of pious resignation.[61] The physical signs of pain or persecution in the images of martyrs could only make the image more rhetorically effective in responding to the present reality. The activities of the flagellants commanded considerable attention in the ceremonial life of the town, and important members of the Battuti Neri were prominent in other confraternities, such as those associated with the basilica of San Francesco.

On the basis of available evidence, none of Tura's works can be connected with the Ferrarese confraternities, but his attention to the agony of the martyrs (in the British Museum drawing and the Berlin panels; plates 44, 58 and 59) may be engaging some of the extreme forms of asceticism, and the ascetic mediation of public execution in Ferrara. The very action performed by the London *St Jerome* calls to mind the strong presence of *disciplinati* groups in the religious life of the laity. The painting includes an unidentified donor portrait; could he have been a member of one of these flagellant confraternities?

The provenance of the painting before its apparent removal in the seventeenth century to the Carthusian monastery of Ferrara is not known, but I will consider here what I believe to be the strongest possibilities.[62] One would be to associate it with a Minorite foundation noted for the lay patronage of art, such as the conventual church of San Francesco.[63] The image features two figures attired like Franciscan friars; I have identified one of them, who accompanies the donor of the image portrayed in the right background, as Francis himself, sharing in St Jerome's ecstatic vision of the crucified Christ. But whatever its original location, the image must reflect the fact that the cult of Jerome had a particularly prestigious focus in Ferrara. Near San Francesco is the oratory of San Girolamo, maintained by the order of the Gesuati who maintained a special devotion to the saint.[64] San Girolamo was a site of special distinction because it was the burial place of Giovanni Tavelli, who had been a particularly distinguished Gesuato Bishop of Ferrara; records of the church's interior appearance refer to the presence of memorials to lay donors in the form of paintings or wax effigies, including one dedicated by Rinaldo d'Este in return for a miraculous cure.[65]

In Ferrara in the fifteenth century the ideal of the ascetic, long part of the heritage of Christianity, was manifest among the laity through the activities of the *disciplinati*; the ideal was also invigorated by the writings, sermons and exemplary life of Tavelli.[66] Tavelli is perhaps most significant historically for having achieved official respectability and recognition for his own order of ascetic extremists; he himself attained a renown beyond Ferrara from his addresses to the Councils of Basle and of Ferrara-Florence. His widely diffused writings include works of hagiography and of spiritual exhortation; they draw upon a range of Greek as well as Latin sources, which reflects his acquaintance with humanist scholars of Greek such as Guarino and Ambrogio Traversari. Tracts such as the *De perfectione religionis* refer not only to Thomas Aquinas, Gregory and Jerome, but to the Byzantine abbot John Climacus, in whose writings Tavelli would have found some of the richest theological considerations of the disciplined body as the manifestation of a spiritual condition, as well as reflections on the malleability of the soul through the physical alteration of the body. Tavelli's *De perfectione religionis*, composed for a community of Benedictine nuns at

67 Tura, *St Anthony of Padua*. Detail of plate 60.

Siena, is a work in the same genre as the text by John Climacus known in Latin from the fourteenth century as *Scala paradisi*, in which the marvellous physiognomy of asceticism is described in terms strongly redolent of Tura's *St Jerome*:

> They ate dust and ashes instead of bread; their bones stuck to their flesh and they were dried up like grass . . . With knees like wood, as a result of all the prostrations, with eyes dimmed and sunken, with hair gone and cheeks wasted and scalded by many hot tears, with faces pale and worn, they were no different from corpses. Their breasts were livid from all the beatings, which had even made them spit blood . . . Compared with this, what are the sufferings of the possessed, of those mourning the dead, of the exiled, or of those condemned for murder? These are suffering involuntary torture and punishment. But this is nothing in comparison with suffering deliberately sought. Believe me, brothers, I am not making all this up.[67]

In his life of Giovanni Colombini, the founder of the Gesuati, Tavelli followed John Climacus in dwelling upon the spectacular qualities of asceticism:

> There were many of their number who, inflamed by charity, thenceforth despised the earthly realm, and shunned the pleasures of the flesh, so that although still living in the flesh they appeared already to have put the flesh aside. While still inside the flesh, they knew nothing of the use of the flesh, and while their 'conversation was in the Heavens', with mind directed towards the summit they held the earth they trampled beneath their feet to be but dung, so that they would receive Christ as a prize. They took consolation in hunger, thirst, cold and nakedness, the many discomforts and the mockery and hatred of the world, sustained in the love of Jesus Christ the Saviour. Indeed it was a wondrous spectacle to see these free-born men, formerly so prudent in the care of the body, now become foolish in order to be wise.[68]

In Tura's painting, Jerome's self-mortification produces a wandering of the spirit, a 'conversatio in caelis' made visible in the vision of Christ. That Tavelli's own penitential physiognomy had a supernatural aspect is attested in a eulogy by Giovanni Peregrino from 1448:

> I will leave out how much he despised his earthly life, the telling of the pains and martyrdoms that his afflicated flesh endured. With an infinity of harshness he wasted his flesh down to the blood. O Holy Body, to how much good you enjoin us . . . His face was that of a cherub, his words were sweet honey, his outward being like a sun, and his teaching was from Heaven.[69]

Tavelli achieves saintliness through the alteration of his body, through physically debilitating practices such as fasting and flogging. As he wrote to Niccolò d'Este: 'Twice a day I punish my body, sometimes drawing blood, unless my own frailty prevents me.'[70] The emaciated body thus acquires a supernatural aura, a cherubic radiance which the poet identifies with beauty and splendour. This inverse conception of beauty, an aesthetics of pri-

vation, is a recurrent feature of hagiographical literature, especially in accounts of famous ascetics.[71] It is this aesthetics to which Tura responded in his linear stylisation of figures such as *St Dominic* (Florence, Uffizi; plate 49), where physical wastage coincides with a visual richness, a rhythmic play of spiralling forms defining the complex relief of the face. Artistic technique re-codifies the wasted body as beautiful, an effect further enhanced by the radiance of light etched into the gold ground around the saint's head.

The imagery of Tavelli's exhortatory writings is specially suggestive for certain paintings by Tura, above all *St Jerome*. Tavelli recommended intense devotion before the crucifix, and his own constant 'prostration' before it was mentioned in the eulogy by Giovanni Pellegrino.[72] Another image favoured by Tavelli, with which he himself also came to be identified after his death, was that of the 'athlete of Christ'; he employed it most vividly in a letter to the Council of Basle in 1433:

> Ho! vigorous soldiers, labour for your Lord; toil without weariness, for you is destined unassailable glory and the crown of Justice . . . Watch that you do not return empty handed; now rush, rush, encourage your friends, comfort the weak-minded, strengthen [*roborate*] those weak knees; . . . O dearest ones, are your faces not already exhilarated, have your souls not already rejoiced with lightness of heart in that infallible truth of the Gospel . . . ? Think of how the greatness of the reward lightens the burden and sweetens the work. Athletes of Christ and strongest of warriors, do not fear the coming struggle, but stand in the forefront of the battle lines, like the forces of the armies of the Lord God, and girdled with the sword of the spirit, which is the word of God! So be fortified [*roborate*] struggling in the battle, dearest shepherds and watchmen, and do not, I beg you, do not flee like a hired mercenary, do not turn your back, nor let your countenance be shamed in the presence of the good shepherd, if you have neglected any of the sheep of the flock which he entrusts to you . . .

Tavelli calls for the castigation of negligent clerics, and a general renewal of the church:

> sending sharp, potent arrows after those who flee, with burning coals which we will heap upon their heads, in order to pluck out and destroy all that is wickedly planted and rooted in their hearts, so that there shall be a new planting and new construction built upon the foundation of the Apostles and the prophets, in the construction of the new Jerusalem which descends to us from the heavens.[73]

The image of the heroic cleric invoked by Tavelli's *exhortatio* corresponds closely to Tura's *St Jerome*: the expression is both triumphant and suggestive of the endurance of a trial; the disposition of the limbs in an elaborate *contrapposto*, and in particular the vigorous gesture of the right arm, suggest a heroic and athletic physicality without precedent in depictions of this saint, who is usually old and frail, more submissive and abject in appearance. The adjective applied to such a heroic individual is

68 Tura, *St Jerome in Penitence*. Detail of plate 62.

69   Antonio Marescotti, medal of Giovanni Tavelli da Tossignano. Turin, Museo Civico. Bronze.

'roboratus', which carries the metaphoric dimension 'fortified with oak' (*robur*), and this may explain the massive hollowed tree-trunk against which the saint has been placed. The hollow tree may be a replacement for the saint's usual grotto; by dwelling within it, Jerome could be very literally described as 'roboratus'. The saintly hero is also characterised as a pastor and as one who rebuilds the church according to the likeness of the heavenly Jerusalem; in the background of the painting, to the left, a pasture with sheep can be seen, and to the right a pair of habited figures bear building materials up a steep mountain path towards the monumental Albertian building.

The tree metaphor suggested by 'roburatus' occurs in a varied form in the medal of Tavelli struck by Antonio Marescotti after the bishop's death, in 1446 (plate 69). In a striking visual conceit, the *beato* is converted into an olive tree, surrounded by the legend EGO SICUT OLIVA FRUCTIFICAVI SUAVITATE ODORIS IN DOMO DEI (I, like the olive tree, flourished with sweet odours in the house of God).[74] Metaphorically, at any rate, Tavelli was a source of precious oil, which was literally the case with other saints such as Beata Beatrice and Caterina Vegri. It may have been these poetic associations – the soul fortified with a body callused and toughened like oak, or transformed into a fruitful olive tree – that Tura was evoking when he conceived another saint, his *St Anthony*, as a tree-like form; the saint's robe solidifies like wood, and assumes tubular folds, suggestive of roots, by his feet (plate 60).

70   Antonio Marescotti, tomb slab of Giovanni Tavelli da Tossignano. Ferrara, Oratorio di San Girolamo.

71 Antonio Marescotti, *Giovanni Tavelli da Tossignano*. Ferrara, Ospedale di Sant'Anna. Terracotta. Detail.

72 Antonio Marescotti, tomb slab of Giovanni Tavelli da Tossignano. Detail of plate 70.

But more might be said regarding Tavelli's influence on Tura's representation of the saints. Tavelli's own particular likeness was commemorated not only in poems and medals, but in a terra-cotta figure also by Marescotti now preserved at the Ospedale di Sant'Anna which Tavelli had founded in Ferrara (plate 71).[75] The face is no mere artistic fabrication, having been cast directly from Tavelli's face after his death. Particularised description has been given a relic-like status, and also an exemplarary one: this now became the prototype for other images of Tavelli, and also a definitive image of how the saintly body should look. In his portrayals of saints, Tura was playing on his audience's familiarity with the portrait of Tavelli; the countenances of Dominic, Jerome and James seem contrived to echo that of the *beato*. The *St Anthony* seems to respond more to another authoritative icon of the Tavelli cult – the relief portrait on the saint's tomb in San Girolamo, which shows the same unusual stylisation of the throat and neck (plate 72); these features are also found in the statue of *St Maurelius* (1458) for the cathedral, a sculptural essay in

73 Follower of Tura, *St Maurelius*. Detail of plate 47.

Tura's manner, its force for fifteenth-century beholders probably deriving from an evocation of Tavelli (plate 73). The culture of the devotional image in Ferrara, in other words, participates in a hierarchy of authoritative likenesses, in which the image taken directly from the body of the saint assumes a precedence over all artistic invention; Tura's artifice is grounded or authorised in the truth of the saintly body.

ST MAURELIUS

The Este did not notably identify themselves with the cult of Tavelli until late in the century, when Ercole I began to actively promote his candidacy for sainthood. This was also the case with regard to another local saint who also affected the contours of religious life and civic identity – St Maurelius, the patron bishop and martyr whose relics were preserved at San Giorgio outside the city.[76] The attempts by Ercole and his heir Alfonso to associate these cults with Este rule appears as a systematic appropriation with a political basis, corresponding to a growing pervasiveness and centrality of the court in all aspects of civic life. These saints had hitherto been the symbolic property of the clergy and the city.

The cult of Maurelius had been revitalised with the 'invention' and 'translation' (discovery and reinterment) of his relics at San Giorgio in 1419. The twelfth-century hagiographic romance of St Maurelius and the supplementary account by Matteo Ronto of the finding of his relics (1439–42), can be seen as a response to perceived deficiencies in the cult of patron saints such as St George.[77] There was a need to promote a martyr saint with a local connection, whose ongoing presence and tutelage is manifested in miraculous relics. His cult was given more active promotion in the later decades of the century. Probably in response to initiatives by the Roverella family, the saint's chapel was newly outfitted in the old cathedral of San Giorgio, where the martyr's relics were also housed, and an altarpiece was provided by Tura – two tondi survive showing the martyrdom of the saint (plates 75 and 76).[78] A vernacular life of Maurelius was printed in 1489, with a woodcut frontispiece probably deriving from the main panel of Tura's altarpiece (plate 74).[79] Here, the drapery of the saint clearly emulates Tura's draughtsmanship, while the pose recalls the Modena St Anthony (plate 60) and the flanking of the saint by kneeling figures shows an affinity of conception with the Roverella altarpiece. Maurelius holds a miniature castle to denote his protectorship of the state; there is no apparent acknowledgement of Ferrara's secular lordship. The kneeling ecclesiastics, probably Olivetan monks, suggests that it is his authority alone that is countenanced by the clergy.

Both accounts emphasise virtues and saintly behaviour which are completely concurrent with the ideals of sanctity already encountered in Tavelli and his writings:

For the following period the precious pearl of Christ, blessed Maurelius, in living flesh beyond the flesh, appeared an angel

74 After Tura, *St Maurelius*, frontispiece to *Legendario e vita e miracoli de Sancto Maulerio* [sic] (Ferrara, Lorenzo Rossi, 1489). Ferrara, Biblioteca Comunale Ariostea, 516.4.6.

and not a man; prudently he despised the world while looking at heaven, he humbled his own nature seeking after the remaker of humility; violently scorning worldly things by snatching at eternal joy, in the power of his clean heart in all the times of his sincere life he stood forth in the bloom of his virginity, zealous in his pursuit of divine contemplation. From the body rising to the spirit, from the spirit rising towards God, chastising the flesh – which subdued in castigation, became the servant of the spirit.[80]

The condition of the body once again becomes the sign that the spirit is elsewhere, already in the Divine Presence.

As with the woodcut, there are suggestions of a political dimension in the story of Maurelius, whose life is a polemical exemplification of the rights of the clergy. Maurelius is distinguished by royal blood, through anointing by the Pope (at the prompting of St George), and consecration by the visible hand

75   Tura, St Maurelius altarpiece. *Trial of St Maurelius*. Ferrara, Pinacoteca Nazionale. On panel (diameter 53.5 cm).

76   Tura, St Maurelius altarpiece. *Execution of St Maurelius*. Ferrara, Pinacoteca Nazionale. On panel (diameter 53.5 cm).

of God himself. His designation as *pater patriae* placed him figuratively as a sovereign power in the state. A significant topos in the *Vita*, especially given the interests promoting his cult, is his rejection of the court and of princely honours and his submission to the Pope; this renunciation is underlined by the association of the court with paganism. The dramatic dichotomy in his life is between the worlds of spiritual perfection and Papal jurisdiction on one side, and the inimical massed forces of court, tyranny and idolatry which bring about his death (his tyrant brother Rivallo bids him renounce that Christ who the Jews had 'justifiably executed' and to worship the pagan idols). As a bishop saint, Maurelius represents the authority and autonomy of the church; the *Vita* even incorporates the supremacy of the church to the empire – Maurelius appears in a dream to Henry II, informing him that he had himself been a prince but had forgone worldly honours in favour of the eternal kingdom.

This is the world evoked by Tura in the surviving tondi of the St Maurelius altarpiece (plates 75 and 76). Tura shows Maurelius consigned to execution by the tyrant, who is seated on a raised stool and surrounded by his minions, his falconers and his pet ape. Through an *all'antica* archway, a contemporary cityscape is partly visible. Courtly decadence is evoked with an economical precision; moreover, the image of a ruler with a staff on a raised stool, although not uncommon in martyrdom scenes, may have echoed for some viewers the bronze statue of Borso d'Este as Justice which overlooked the scaffold in Ferrara. The scene of execution shows a transformation of Rivalo's men; pugnacious and grotesque in the judgement scene, they are now more noble, docile and even reverent as they contemplate the saint's passive acceptance of martyrdom. The pair of tondi gently encode the notion of a tension between court and clergy, and the conquest of souls by the latter through humility rather than force. This tension, which here may signify no more than the drawing of a boundary, will be explored further in the following chapters.

ST JAMES

Where circumstances of patronage are known, Tura's production of altarpieces shows no involvement with Este initiatives; the exception is a commission for the Este Bishop of Adria, which was presumably an altarpiece. Beyond this otherwise unknown work, is there any aspect of Tura's output of religious panel painting which might even speculatively be identified with the rulers of Ferrara? I believe that the regally enthroned *St James* may have formed part of such a work (plate 51). The saint's enthronement, and his unusually direct and urgent address to the beholder, suggest a dominant, central position within a polyptych which also included the Louvre *St Anthony* and the Uffizi *St Dominic* (plates 50 and 49), and possibly another pair of panels with near-similar dimensions, the Berlin *St Sebastian* and *St Christopher* (plates 58 and 59); a combination of martyrs with mendicants also appears in the London drawing (plate 44). The provenance of none of these panels is secure before the nine-

teenth century, but the common origin of the *St James* and *St Anthony* (and hence of its obvious companion panel, *St Dominic*, now cut down from its original form) is indicated by the fact that they have uniform, possibly sixteenth-century, borders of *grotteschi*.[81] It is conceivable that the Este could have commissioned an altarpiece dedicated to St James, since they maintained a devotion to the saint from at least the late fourteenth century when, in 1393, a chapel in San Francesco was dedicated by Alberto d'Este to 'San Giacomo di Galizia'. Subsequently another chapel of St James was dedicated in the cathedral by Niccolò d'Este. Both foundations were referred to as 'Capelle degli Estensi'.[82]

The shrine of St James at Santiago de Compostela was the great pilgrimage destination of western Europe, and there was a dignified tradition of pilgrimage to such sites among the Este princes. Alberto d'Este's promotion of himself through the role of pilgrim, following a trip to Rome, is manifest in his memorial statue on the cathedral; Niccolò III had made a celebrated pilgrimage to Jerusalem and to the shrine of St Anthony at Vienne. Contardo d'Este, a minor saint, had died while undertaking a pilgrimage to Compostela in 1249.[83] In 1487 Ercole I, after an elaborate and tearful request for the consent of the communal officials, himself embarked for Compostela, apparently in fulfilment of a vow. The pilgrimage had to be cancelled, however, as the duke was immediately summoned to Rome by Innocent VIII under pain of excommunication.[84] But what was this vow, and why had Ercole chosen to renew his family's earlier association with this saint? The answer can at best be a hypothesis, but it may lie in the fact that two significant events in Ercole's life had occurred on the Feast of St James, 25 July. In 1467, while fighting as a *condottiere* for the Venetians, Ercole had received a wound in the foot which afflicted him for the rest of his days, and often required him to walk with the aid of a stick. Furthermore, on 25 July 1484 the terms of the peace between Venice and the Italian League which ended the War of Ferrara were publicised, delivering Ercole from the greatest crisis of his reign. Either of these events, conceivably both of them, could have resulted in a vow to make the pilgrimage honouring the saint, or soliciting a cure. Could the polyptych be related to Ercole's sense of a special indebtedness to St James, possibly an ex-voto in substitution for a pilgrimage not undertaken? If the reconstruction of the polytych to include the panels of *St Dominic* and *St Anthony* is accepted, then there may be additional grounds for identifying the work as an Este commission from the mid-1480s. The work would have counterposed a Dominican with a Franciscan saint. This may on one level reflect the fact that both Dominic and Anthony, like James, were at the centre of pilgrimage cults; the remains of both were preserved much closer to hand, in Bologna and Padua. In 1478 tumultuous disputes occurred in Ferrara, between the Franciscans and Dominicans, with regard to the Immaculate Conception of the Virgin. The controversy polarised the people of Ferrara as well as the Mendicant orders:[85] Ercole directly intervened in the controversy and brought it directly beneath his auspices, calling on one occasion for the debate to be staged within the court itself. The altarpiece with the centrally enthroned Este patron saint may signify the duke's interest in the theological differences between the orders, and his own posture of engaged neutrality.

LINE AS FORM AND SYMBOL

The emphasis on skill, virtuosity and ornament in Tura's religious painting might lend support to the view that the early Renaissance was a period of increasing secularisation in attitudes to the image among élite patrons, in which the image as product of a distinguished artist supersedes the primary role of the image as object of piety.[86] If this tendency exists, and Tura's painting reflects it, it does so in a rather ambivalent way; Tura's assertions of skill seem designed to play a rhetorical function, convincing the beholder of the authenticity of the saintly body. Line, for instance, operates as more than an aesthetic principle; its aesthetic possibilities are enabled by its connection with the culturally privileged form of writing. Reduced to the calligraphic flourish or even scribble, 'writing' is re-converted to the more basic function of a distinguishing mark. That which is distinguished is the artistic product, together with the hand which commands the prime cultural instrument of control and demarcation. Yet for a broader audience, Tura's line may have been read less as personal stylisation than as marking bodies, cutting profiles, inscribing the distinguishing marks of physiognomy, age, experience and expression. All of these were conceivable as forms of inscription or marking upon living as well as represented bodies: 'There can be nothing in Man that is not marked on his exterior, through which one may discern what is within the person bearing the Sign.'[87] The figurative habits of homilectic and hagiographic rhetoric would have encouraged Tura's audience to think of the bodies of saints as the products of style, of fashioning, even in terms of metaphors of artistic process. No less a personage than Ercole d'Este wrote in defence of the authenticity of Lucia Broccadelli's stigmata, using the Lactantian trope of the 'artisanship of God' as reported in a tract entitled *Spiritualium personarum feminei sexus facta admiratione digna*. For the strengthening of the Christian faith in the present 'tempests', says the author, God 'wondrously manifests Himself in many spiritual, pious and religious persons, especially of the feminine sex'. Ercole's testimony on Broccadelli and on other nuns in Ferrara 'rapt in ecstasy by the divine spirit' is then cited: 'These things are shown by the Supreme Craftsman in the bodies of His Servants to confirm and strengthen our faith, and to remove the incredulity of pious men and hard of heart.'[88] The point of such artisanship is 'to bear witness to us that this our Catholic Faith is true, and that the Holy Roman Church is the Mother of the Faith'.

Recent scholarship has demonstrated that by the fifteenth century this 'divine artisanship', the manifestation of sanctity through bodily alteration, is more typically a characteristic of female saints and mystics. Although treated as living saints by their contemporaries, few had their cults approved by Rome, and with a couple of exceptions (for instance, Donatello's *Mag-*

dalene) the spectacle of the female ascetic body does not leave its mark in religious art.[89] Relatively few images of female saints by Tura survive;[90] although there is no reason to doubt that more once existed, one might wonder whether this gender imbalance in his painting of the saints might not be addressing the need to assert or appropriate the corporeal manifestation of sanctity for saints who were male and officially approved. This would coincide with a reassertion of asceticism in the hagiography and iconography of recently deceased male saints and *beati*: Lorenzo Giustiniani, Giovanni Tavelli, Bernardino of Siena and Bernardino da Feltre; very few of the generally controversial female mystics of the period achieved canonisation or commemoration by the image; Sixtus IV's prohibition of images of Catherine's stigmatisation, referred to above, suggest that when image cults did develop around holy women, bodily distinction was de-emphasised.

Tura's images of *St Anthony* and *St James* are shocking visualisations of bodies transformed by ascetic practices and mystical ardour, yet they are notably lavish, even luxuriant, in the decription of bodily emaciation. The same resources of linear elaboration, which draw attention to manual facility, are expended on the faces, hands and draperies of these figures of exemplary piety as on the capricious golden dolphins of the throne of Calliope. Such works present themselves for consideration on two levels simultaneously: as products of worldly art, to be evaluated by fellow artists or by patrons, and as visions of divine craftsmanship, manifest in an ascetic or mystical transformation of the body. Given the predominant role of holy women in these physical manifestations of the spiritual, it is perhaps not surprising that one of Tura's images of the Virgin Mary is imprinted with the signs of dual 'artisanship'.[91]

The Bergamo *Virgin and Child* may originally have formed the central panel of a small polyptych (plate 77). Lacking the obvious opulence of Tura's other paintings of this subject, the image may have struck the praying beholder by its solemnity, by an apparently tragic conception of the Virgin Mary. Unlike the serene or even smiling versions in Washington, London or Venice, here she has an emaciated, livid, even haggard appearance. Yet even with this solemn figure, ascetic stylisation may speak equivocally of courtly or poetic standards of feminine beauty. Her otherworldy character is produced by an elegant linear description of her body and its adornments – above all by a spiral motif which appears in the hair, is picked up by the ears, and recurs in the fall of linen on her shoulders. A similar pathos is manifest in the expression and extravagently elongated hands of the Annunciate Virgin in London (plate 78).

The coincidence of artifice with the imaging of the ascetic body is also evident in the active poses adopted by some of Tura's male saints, since the saintly ascetic, in his abandoned posture or startlingly foreshortened limbs become a proving ground – as Alberti would have recognised – for artistic displays of skill. The *contrapposti* and foreshortenings of figures such as the *St Jerome* and *St James* fit well within the general extravagance of Tura's style. It is also noteworthy that the saints themselves flout a contemporary social decorum of the body, just as Tura himself resists

77   Tura, *Virgin and Child*. Bergamo, Accademia Carrara. On panel (45 × 30 cm).

78   Tura, *Virgin Annunciate*. London, National Gallery. On panel (45 × 34 cm).

Alberti's standards for pictorial movement and expression, or the invisibility of artifice. In the Ajaccio panel, Jerome plants his foot in an offhand manner on the Virgin's dais; *St John on Patmos* shows the saint sprawled on the ground while he reads.[92]

That an asceticism of bodily renunciation should coexist and even coalesce with an ornamented and extravagant mode of representation is perhaps less surprising given the oxymoronic tenor of contemporary spirituality, where bodily debasement and disfigurement, material impoverishment, and sensual renunciation were all relished and extolled in terms of their opposites, in terms of beauty and splendour; St Maurelius was the 'precious pearl of Christ', while mystical writers conceived of the body as something to be 'formed and tempered' by pain, remade as 'a beautiful robe'.[93] The Este themselves, like other European ruling families, collected *joyaux* in which images of martyrs, of the Passion of Christ and the Pietà in enamel and precious metal were encrusted with pearls, rubies and other precious stones.[94]

That conceptions of the aesthetic splendour and preciousness of the suffering body were at work in Tura's imagery is suggested most strongly by the British Museum drawing (plate 44), where a copious display of fantastic architectural ornament in the Virgin's throne coexists with an *ostentatio vulneris* in the suffering bodies of the two nude martyrs. Artistic ornament is equated with and sustained by the artistic rendering of bodily pain and mutilation, enabling a rich yet entirely orthodox play of symbolism; both martyrs and Virgin together form the *fabbrica* of the church, the martyrs acting as its pillars, the Virgin its Tabernacle. Distinguished by wounds or by precious embellishment, both saints and Virgin together form part of a greater work of artifice.[95]

Finally, the paradoxical status of Tura's style can be associated with a systematic and progressive compression of ascetic values with a policy of display in later fifteenth-century Ferrara. The Este, like many European ruling families, cultivated an identification with their hierarchial opposite: what was least prestigious in terms of 'worldly' hierarchies carried tremendous authority in terms of spiritual scales of value; the holy pauper as opposed to the prince, the hermitage as opposed to the palace. The Ferrarese court in the fifteenth century may have generally failed to produce an effective, all-embracing apparatus of statehood, but this was because the Este gave greater priority to symbolic and charismatic kinds of authority which they pursued in its various manifestations – feudal, juridical and religious. As Richard Gordon Brown has demonstrated, in the later fifteenth century 'signorial interest in public ceremonies gradually took precedence over all other affairs of state';[96] none the less, the charisma which was often being sought through such materialist display was often a spiritual one. The Este pursued more sacralised forms of authority not only through a lavish and visible endowment of Carthusian and Observant foundations (the Carthusian monastery more literally fused the princely palace with the hermitage), but through acting out a saintly and ascetic charisma for themselves; Borso requested that he be interred at his death in a condition of austere mendicant nudity, and the populace behaved at his funeral, as one chronicler reported, 'as if Eternal God had died once more'; 'God', the chronicler added, 'had certainly gathered his soul among his Blessed Saints'.[97] Ercole's aspiration to a central place in the spiritual welfare of the state seems yet more programmatic.[98] It is manifest in the above-mentioned pilgrimage activities, themselves an occasion for a lavish display of his court. He instituted the annual princely custom of door-to-door 'begging' on the Feast of the Epiphany, in which donations of provisions were solicited for the Ferrarese poor. He involved himself in the confraternal life of the town, and took the role of Christ in an annual Maundy Thursday commemoration of the Last Supper where he washed the feet of twelve Ferrarese paupers. The 'poveri vergognosi' (shamed poor) become instruments of a signorial policy which constantly sought new areas of collective religious experience, like the devout provision of charity – in order to associate them with the persona of the prince.[99] Ercole competed with the relic cults of the Ferrarese diocese by instituting the worship of a miraculous image of the Virgin within the palace itself. All of these gestures had their own theatrical and aesthetic form; gold, jewels and artistic embellishment played their part, underlining the assertion of an identity between princely piety and princely extravagance, the enhancement of princely lustre through what might be called 'spiritual imperialism'.

Tura's style, then, may also speak of this more general conversion of world-renouncing piety to world-affirming splendour. Yet their coalescence in his art may have prepared the way for other less obviously paradoxical artistic solutions which could have made his style obsolete in the eyes of his élite patrons. The patent artificiality of Tura's style gives way to a new idiom in which manual virtuosity and the display (or simulation) of precious materials are considerably less emphasised. In the works of the later Ercole de' Roberti and Lorenzo Costa (plate 91), of Michele Coltellini, Gian Francesco Mainieri and Domenico Panetti, Tura's artificial and curious *maniera* seems deliberately avoided along with any attempt at 'self-stylisation' on the part of the artists.[100] The tremendous success of the new *maniera devota*, the style of Francia and Perugino, among the sophisticated clerical and princely consumers of the Papal State, including the Este, probably lay in its effacement of conspicuous manufacture, at least in the precious and extravagant form in which it had appeared in the artists of an older generation – Carlo Crivelli, Marco Zoppo, Cosmè Tura; this was a recurrent characteristic of painting in the age of Savonarola, the nephew of the Ferrarese court physician with whom Ercole d'Este maintained a reverential correspondence. Along with craft, something else disappears from the devotional image – the rhetoric of extreme pathos, of the ascetic or suffering body rendered through artistic stylisation gives place to a new serenity, restrained composure, and normative physical beauty in the rendering of the Dead Christ and the suffering saints; this is apparent in any comparison of a Dead Christ or Pietà by Crivelli with one by Giovanni Bellini. Pathos, perhaps, became too obvious as a 'craft', a fashioned thing which disappears from the image along with the artist's self-conscious and spiritually expressive stylisation of the body.

THE ROVERELLA, THE JEWS AND THE IMAGE OF ECCLESIASTICAL STATEHOOD

BY 1471, THE YEAR DURING WHICH his patron Duke Borso d'Este died, Cosmè Tura could be said to have reached the height of his wealth, professional success and social prominence. His association with the court had brought him particular fame; when the literary men of the court – Guarino, Tito Vespasiano Strozzi, Lodovico Carbone (and, later, Lelio Gregorio Giraldi) – wanted to refer to the most illustrious artist of the period, they invariably named 'Cosmè'. The painter's social ambitions are revealed by his will of 14 January 1471, with its charitable bequests and grandiose schemes to erect a memorial church.

In the same year, Tura was completing his most important monumental commission for Borso – the chapel in the castle of Belriguardo. The chapel decoration emulated that painted around 1420 by Gentile da Fabriano in the Broletto at Brescia, which Tura was sent to examine in November 1469; it consisted not only of paintings in oil of God the Father with the Evangelists and four Church Fathers, but also of gilt stucco friezes with seraphim and Borso's heraldic date-palm. Probably executed by two assistants mentioned in the documents, the frieze would have demonstrated Tura's skills as a designer of elaborate decorative work, for which he was most appreciated at court.[1] These skills were called for again when Borso died, and a painted wooden catafalque was erected for his funeral in the Carthusian monastery of Ferrara.[2]

Tura had also by 1468 decorated a chapel at San Domenico with a *Nativity* for the Sacrati family, relatively recent arrivals among the ranks of the Ferrarese nobility who had enlarged their fortune by famine profiteering in the 1460s.[3] In 1469 he had produced his only monumental painting of the decade which still survives relatively intact – the organ-shutters for the canons of Ferrara Cathedral. Tura continued to work for Borso's successor Ercole I, until at least 1485, ten years before the artist's death. As we saw, however, there are signs of a shift in the artistic preferences of the new duke and his wife Eleonora d'Aragona, and of a demand for a different kind of painting to

which the artist might not easily have adapted. The pious Eleonora was a collector of devotional paintings; an inventory of 1493, the year of her death, records images of the Maries and the Virgin and Child by Mantegna, a Flemish Madonna, a Christ by Bellini, with images of the Passion and the face of Christ predominating among the remaining thirty-five items.[4] It seems likely that these pictures typified the styles which dominated court painting in the 1480s and 1490s, when images of the Man of Sorrows and the Holy Family were rendered in a soft, atmospheric, northern-influenced manner by Domenico Panetti, Michele Coltellini, Gianfrancesco Mainieri and the later Roberti. Tura remained in demand as a portraitist and as a designer of decorative arts – bedcovers, tapestries and the ducal silverware; one of these tapestries, a *Lamentation over the Dead Christ*, survives in two versions (Cleveland, Museum of Art, plate 81; Lugano, Thyssen-Bornemisza Collection, plate 82).[5] The format and iconography of both versions indicate that they were to be used as altar frontals, possibly commissioned as votive offerings by the ducal couple themselves. The prominent central couple have been identified as portraits of the duke and duchess; such a mode of self-imaging is characteristic of Ercole's reign, when religious ceremony and iconography were constantly appropriated to produce an aura of sacrality around the prince. Eleonora wears a garment with a laced front, which, given the solemn context, can only designate her as pregnant; this detail indicates that the design of the tapestry precedes the birth of Ercole's son and heir Alfonso in 1476, when the ducal household accounts record the completion of 'a tapestry altar frontal' ('uno palio da altaro di razo') depicting the 'Dead Christ with the Maries' ('Jesus morto con le Marie') by the tapestry-maker Rubinetto di Francia. There are, nevertheless, differences between the two tapestries, notably in the design of the sepulchre and the more orientalising costume of the figure to the left of the structure in the Cleveland version; we will return to the significance of these differences at a later point.

Apart from the 'naked women' produced for Ercole's *studio* in

81 After Tura, *Lamentation over the Dead Christ*. Cleveland, Ohio, The Cleveland Museum of Art. Tapestry (97.8 × 192.4 cm).

1477, there are no records of monumental commissions comparable in scale or expense to the chapel Tura had decorated for Borso. The new artistic preferences of Ercole and Eleonora might explain Tura's final disappearance from court records after 1485, around which time he was generating an income from investments in shoemaking, wool and fuel production, and other trades. From the end of Borso's reign, Tura also seems to have cultivated an association with other socially eminent Ferrarese patrons. A ponderous library decoration for the counts of Mirandola, with allegorical personifications of the genres of poetry and numerous portraits of famous poets, may be a literary fabrication by the humanist who described it in the 1520s, but it does indicate the extent to which Tura was associated even then with subjects of a literary or humanist nature.[6] Ongoing links with the Sacrati are suggested by a lease of land in 1485 and by the nomination of Jacopo Sacrati as guardian to Tura's son Damiano in the will of 1491. During the 1470s, commissions for two large altarpieces were provided by or through the Roverella family, who for a short period were scarcely less important in local and national prominence than the Este themselves. The Roverella were a family of what might be called professional ecclesiastics, two generations of whom dominated the church in Emilia and the Romagna in the second half of the fifteenth century, as well as occupying important positions at the Papal court and in the service of the Emperor. The association with the Roverella may be said to begin around 1467 with the organ-shutters for the cathedral (to be discussed in the following chapter) and to con-

clude about ten years later with the altarpiece of St Maurelius, which has been dated to 1479. This altarpiece was painted for the church of San Giorgio – the original cathedral of Ferrara – in the Olivetan monastery outside the city, a foundation which had come to be heavily associated with the Roverella; at its reconsecration in 1479 it was jointly dedicated to St George and St Lawrence – the name-saint of the late Bishop Lorenzo Roverella. It was at San Giorgio that Tura himself would be interred at his death in 1495.[7] In the mid-1470s, however, at a time of particular crisis in the family's fortunes, he produced for their chapel at San Giorgio the work with which this chapter is concerned – the great polyptych known as the Roverella altarpiece (plates 83–90).

'A CALAMITY HAS BEFALLEN THE HOUSE OF ROVERELLA'[8]

The enormous altarpiece, originally over 4 metres in height, was in the private chapel of the Roverella – which appears to have been little more than an altar in the north aisle – until 1709, when, during the occupation of the monastery by invading Prussian forces, it was partly destroyed by Papal artillery. In its original state, the impact of the work on visitors to the church must have been specially striking; the altarpiece would have been fully visible, at close range, immediately to the left of the Reli-

82 After Tura, *Lamentation over the Dead Christ*. Lugano, Thyssen-Bornemisza Collection. Tapestry (97 × 207 cm).

quary Chapel of St Maurelius, the main focus of the laity's devotional interest in the church.[9]

Tura's painting, with its strident colours and profusion of curious detail, could even be said to clamour for attention. The dominating image is the spectacularly enthroned *Virgin and Child with Musician Angels* (London, National Gallery; plate 83). The Virgin is seated in a marble niche raised on an architecturally implausible tier of stone blocks, surrounded by Hebrew inscriptions on horned tablets, angels and golden vines, gigantic shells and the four creatures of Ezekiel's vision in the Jewish Bible. Musician angels flank the throne, dressed alternately in robes of high-toned pink and green, a colour chord repeated in the architectural elements of the throne and the barrel-vault, piers and entablature of the great temple-like structure which contains the heavenly court; the Virgin's robe, and the sky beyond the throne, are painted in a brilliant ultramarine. The asymmetry of colour seems perversely insistent: Tura, in fact, repainted the right-hand pier green having first rendered it, like the left-hand pier, in pink. Before the throne two wingless angels operate a curious organ with pipes arranged 'a chiocciola' – in the spiral form of a snail shell – which may record the design of an organ made for Leonello d'Este and noted by Ciriaco d'Ancona during his visit of 1449. The twittering sound it evokes adds an aural dimension to the stridency of the colour.[10]

The festive effect is in marked contrast to the great lunette of the *Lamentation over the Dead Christ* (now Paris, Louvre; plate 85) which originally surmounted the main panel; the eternally young figure of the Virgin with the sleeping Child was aligned with an aged version of herself supporting her lifeless adult Son,

his arms and legs disposed to evoke his death on the cross. This *Pietà* group is accompanied by six gesticulating mourners, all crowded together around Christ's sarcophagus beneath a green coffered vault. Apart from three predella panels only one of the other main sections of the altarpiece survives – the commemorative portrait of a kneeling Roverella prelate, accompanied by Sts Paul and Maurelius, in one of the two panels which originally flanked the scene of the heavenly court (Rome, Palazzo Colonna; plate 84).

Tura's work for the Roverella coincides with a particularly important phase of the family's history. In his paintings for the cathedral and for San Giorgio, the artist obtained prestigious public exposure within the city's most important ecclesiastical foundations.[11] Moreover, in the family's sudden promotion of themselves through monumental works of art, the employment of the leading painter of the court is significant. In the painting there is an emphatic presence of those qualities which a court audience associated with painterly skill; in the sinuous tracery of drapery borders and folds, and in the elaborate decoration of the architectural setting, we might identify the quality which Guarino called the 'Daedalian hand', the masterly calligraphic line of painters and scribes, or observe a primacy of the 'colours, edges and outlines' which Decembrio associated with painting for princes. If the painting could be said to invoke Tura's courtly persona and the house style of the Este court, this could indicate more than the emulation of princely fashion by another aristocratic patron – it could also, as I hope to demonstrate, signify a competitive dimension, the taking possession of a highly valued cultural property.

Beyond its possible reference to the court, the issue of style raises some interpretative considerations which will inform any understanding of the work. In the decoration of the architectural setting Roberto Longhi perceived an elaborate and fantastic quality which he characterised as 'barocco'.[12] Longhi also used the term 'salamonico', referring to the tablets on either side of the Virgin inscribed with the Hebrew Ten Commandments from the Book of Exodus. Rather than identifying what was written on the tablets, he chose to see their inclusion as a stylistic feature, an anticipation, as it were, of the orientalising fantasies of the *seicento*. Longhi's indifference in this instance to the possible iconographic meaning of motifs he chose to see as decorative or stylistic touches on a recurrent problem in the interpretation of fifteenth-century art, and one which, as we have seen, is constantly raised by Tura's works – the problem of the inseparability of programmatic and decorative elements. No confident distinction can be made between the work's 'iconography' and 'style', or between the meaning of the work and elements which might be said primarily to advertise the artist's skill. This is because, as the previous two chapters have already suggested, artifice itself is not a mere packaging of content, but is actively and self-reflexively set forth as a matter for the beholder's critical concern. Artifice itself has a metaphoric function.[13]

It will be central to the following investigation that the image, as a totality of form and meaning, presents an argument by visual means, that it speaks for the interests of those for whom it was produced, and that this argument can to some extent be paraphrased. If the image mounts an argument, however, to whom could it be said to be speaking? In answering this question, I will show that the work addresses divisions within its possible audience, and that it employs a multi-levelled strategy to engage the interests of different kinds of viewer. One kind of viewer, for example, might have been content to be amazed by the artful display of exotic writing and paraphernalia around the throne of the Virgin. Other viewers, however, recognising or even reading the Hebrew tablets, might have made the connection with issues of considerable political urgency during the 1470s – issues involving the church and the Estense state, and concerning the Jews of Ferrara, their religion, their writing and their property.

Although citizens of Ferrara since 1393, the Roverella family maintained its base in the Imperial territory of Rovigo.[14] Giovanni Roverella was employed there in the Este adminstration, and in 1444 he received the title of Count Palatine and a coat of arms – the oak and Imperial eagle – from the Emperor Frederick III. Twenty-four years later the Emperor was received at the Roverella palace in Rovigo, and he bestowed similar honours on Giovanni's grandson Lucio Antonio, along with the governorship of all Imperial castles and lands in the territory. On the same occasion, Giovanni's son Bartolomeo received an Imperial fief in Germany.[15] Residing mainly in Ferrara, Lucio Antonio was a member of the ducal council from 1472 and served as an Este ambassador to Rome, where he had several useful family connections.

The extraordinary prominence attained by Lucio and Giovanni's sons appears to have depended primarily on their con-

83 (*facing page*) Tura, Roverella altarpiece. Central panel: *Virgin and Child with Musician Angels*. London, National Gallery. On panel (239 × 102 cm).

84 Tura, Roverella altarpiece. Right-hand panel: *Sts Paul and Maurelius with Cardinal Bartolomeo Roverella*. Rome, Palazzo Colonna. On panel (154 × 76 cm).

nections with Pope and Emperor, rather than on the favour and patronage of the Este. Courtly honours, such as Borso's apparent promotion of Bartolomeo's elevation to the purple, might themselves be seen as a recognition of the Roverella's standing with the Papacy.[16] Unlike their Gonzaga and Sforza neighbours, the Este were not successful in having a member of their own family placed strategically at the Curia, despite the imposition of ecclesiastical offices on three of Borso's brothers.[17] Borso had his mind set on his Papal investiture as Duke of Ferrara, and thus he stood to gain a great deal in cultivating Bartolomeo whom he hoped to see elected Pope with the death of the generally ill-disposed Paul II.[18]

Giovanni's son Florio served in a professional and military capacity on behalf of the Pope from the time of Eugenius IV. According to Bucelino, Paul II elevated him to the highest rank within the Knights of Jerusalem, and he served thereafter as Papal ambassador to the Naples court. Pietro his brother was Senator, Praetor and Consul of Rome, while Giovanni's remaining sons Lorenzo and Niccolo, like Bartolomeo, pursued highly successful careers within the ecclesiastical hierarchy.

Bartolomeo Roverella studied with Guarino at Verona and Ferrara,[19] and in the 1430s he appears in the service of two scholarly bishops; first Niccolo Acciapiccia, Bishop of Tropaea, and then Scipione Mainenti, Bishop of Modena, whom he accompanied to Florence. In Florence Bartolomeo came to the attention of Pope Eugenius IV, whose butler and secretary he became in 1442. Eugenius appointed him Bishop of Adria in 1445, and Archbishop of Ravenna shortly afterwards. Under Eugenius' successors Bartolomeo undertook a series of important military and diplomatic commissions on behalf of the Papacy.[20] He was created cardinal by Pius II in 1461 while active on behalf of the Papal interest in Naples during the Angevin wars. In 1471 he came close to being elected Pope, and in 1474, two years before his death, he was in Ferrara with Lorenzo for the wedding of Ercole I and Eleonora d'Aragona, whose father he had crowned King of Naples in 1468.[21]

It was through the special favour of Eugenius IV that Bartolomeo came into possession of the principal ecclesiastical benefices of the Este state. Given the fluctuating relations between the Este and the church, these were politically sensitive appointments. The Este in theory were only Papal Vicars of Ferrara, holding the city and its territory from 1329 as a fief from the Holy See. Borso d'Este's desire for the Papal title of Duke of Ferrara led him to pursue an obsequious but non-committal policy towards the Papacy in the 1450s and 1460s, which taxed the patience of Pius II.[22] Pius at one point threatened Borso with excommunication for failure to pay certain vicarial taxes; in the same letter, the Pope berated Borso for his failure to provide his promised support for the Papal crusade against the Turks, for his harrassment of the Bishop of Ferrara Francesco dal Legname, for his negligence as a prince and addiction to hunting, horse racing and 'the vain judgements of the astrologers' and for his courteous reception of the Pope's enemies Sigismondo Malatesta and the envoys of the King of France.[23]

Pius' successor Paul II was eventually won over into granting

Borso the title of Duke of Ferrara in 1471, following Borso's military support of the beleaguered Papacy in the war against Rimini.[24] However, we find the same Pope admonishing Borso over his non-payment of vicarial tithes in 1470.[25] During the 1470s Sixtus IV's various expressions of disregard for Este sovereignty culminated in his donation of certain Este territories to the Republic of Venice, whose occupation of the Polesine in 1482 unleashed the War of Ferrara (1482–4).[26]

Since becoming *signori* of Ferrara the Este Dynasty had been locked in territorial struggles with the ecclesiastical lordships, the dioceses and abbeys of the Po valley. These included in particular the abbeys of Vangadizza and Pomposa near Rovigo, and the episcopal sees of Ravenna, Adria, Cervia and Comacchio. By the early fifteenth century a substantial part of the Este territorial possession had been formed from the takeover of church property, either by forcing bishops and abbots to grant them fiefs on favourable terms, or by obtaining the right to appoint secular 'protectors' of the various religious foundations.[27] As a recent historian of Ferrarese feudalism notes, by the middle of the century the lands of the abbey of Vangadizza had been almost entirely annexed by the Este and their followers; the abbey was struggling to take legal action against the nobles who reneged on the payment of rent, or to sequester their property.[28]

The See of Ravenna was the most formidable opponent to this territorial expansion.[29] As Archbishop of Ravenna, and subsequently Cardinal of San Clemente, Bartolomeo Roverella enjoyed ancient feudal rights and was also able to accumulate benefices in the Este territories. These included the *commendae* of San Romano in Ferrara, of the abbey of San Pietro degli Umiliati near Rovigo (renamed San Bartolomeo in the 1470s, just as San Giorgio was dedicated to San Lorenzo) and of the abbey of Vangadizza.[30] In this latter capacity Bartolomeo received an annual payment (a feudal obligation?) from the Marquis of Ferrara.[31] If there was a relationship of clientage between Borso and Bartolomeo, the cardinal held the upper hand; on certain territories of the Este state – Lugo, Argenta, Villa San Potiti – the rulers of Ferrara were feudal subjects of the Archbishop of Ravenna.[32] Given Bartolomeo's prominence within the church, the Este's honouring of the cardinal could be seen to have a propitiatory character. This is more so the case because Bartolomeo with his brothers Lorenzo and Niccolo commanded what amounted to a state within the Este state, and Bartolomeo could appeal to a feudal authority more sacred and more ancient than any which could be claimed by the princes of Ferrara.[33]

The office of Bishop of Ferrara was held by Bartolomeo's brother Lorenzo from 1460 until his death in 1474.[34] In the recent past this position had itself been beset by controversy. Lorenzo's predecessor, Francesco dal Legname, had been imprisoned in 1458 by Borso, who claimed he was acting under Papal orders. The Papacy meanwhile passed to Pius II, whom Borso petitioned to have Francesco removed from office. Pius conceded with great reluctance, and later accused Borso of tyrannising the clergy.[35] Lorenzo himself had trouble with Borso; Pius II reprimanded the prince for preventing Lorenzo from disposing of

85　Tura, Roverella altarpiece. Lunette: *Lamentation over the Dead Christ*. Paris, Musée du Louvre. On panel (132 × 267 cm).

a benefice which had become vacant at the death of the humanist Giovanni Aurispa.[36] Apart from diocesan synods in 1465 and 1466 and pastoral visits in 1470 and 1474 the bishop was seldom present in the city. Lorenzo remained, like his brother, principally a member of the Papal court. He was personal physician to Pius II and listed as a *famiglio* of Paul II. Like his brother he was active as a Papal legate, undertaking missions to France, Burgundy, Hungary and the Imperial court. As *datario* Lorenzo was active in the internal administration of the city of Rome, and it appears that Sixtus IV had intended to appoint him senator before his death in 1474.[37] Lorenzo died at the mother house of the Olivetan order, Monte Oliveto near Siena, and was interred at San Giorgio in Ferrara in a grandiose tomb by Antonio Rossellino and Ambrogio da Milano, completed between 1474 and 1479 (plate 103).[38] It is with Lorenzo that Tura's first San Giorgio altarpiece is most frequently connected.

Two further members of the family remain to be introduced. One is Niccolo, brother of Lorenzo and Bartolomeo, who was Prior General of the Olivetan order from 1472 to 1476 and Prior of San Giorgio in Ferrara several times during the 1460s and from 1478 to 1480, the year of his death. As Prior General, Niccolo had the *commenda* of the abbey of San Pietro near Rovigo ceded to him by Bartolomeo in 1472 and by 1476 the foundation was annexed by San Giorgio in Ferrara. In 1488, the abbey divided its goods and lands with the Roverella family.[39] Bucelino claims that Niccolo was twice offered a bishopric by Sixtus IV, but that he refused, modestly preferring the life of the cloister to the *cursus honorum* pursued by his brothers.[40] Niccolo

is of special significance here because he was appointed the executor of both Lorenzo and Bartolomeo, and was resident at San Giorgio during the years of its renovation, the period of the family's most significant involvement with the monastery church.

In their nephew Filiasio the three brothers had a dynastic continuation of their own ecclesiastical power. Filiasio had been married and fathered a son, Philos (later Bishop of Ascoli and Governor of Rome under Julius II). With the death of his wife Filiasio must have realised the considerable advantages to be gained by joining his uncles in Holy Orders. When the Cardinal Bartolomeo died in 1476 he was succeeded immediately as Archbishop of Ravenna by Filiasio, who had obtained a guarantee to this effect from Sixtus IV. Filiasio contributed to the renovation of San Giorgio, in particular the re-erection of its campanile in the 1480s, and it was he who re-dedicated the church to Saints Maurelius, George and (in honour of his uncle) Lawrence in 1479.

By the time of this re-dedication it is possible to think of San Giorgio as a family shrine of the Roverella, and the seat of its interests within the Este state. This had been possible first and foremost because of the considerable autonomy the monastery had enjoyed for several decades.[41]

The ancient church of San Giorgio had been the original cathedral of Ferrara until the twelfth century. The civic cult of St George and of St Maurelius, whose relics had been found in the church in 1419, must have confirmed the monastery's status as a symbolic centre of ecclesiastical autonomy. The tomb of St

86   Tura, Roverella altarpiece. Fragment of left-hand panel: *St George*. San Diego, Museum of Fine Arts. On panel (32 ×
28 cm).

Maurelius bore the inscription 'Hic pater est patriae qui lassas demone mentes sanat et auxilium civibus ipse gerit' ('This is the father of the fatherland who cures the diabolically possessed and proffers aid to this city'). The title *pater patriae* is particularly charged since it was also bestowed on Niccolò III d'Este.[42] This joint reference of the title to secular lord and patron saint establishes an interesting symmetry or bipolarity between the centres of sacred and secular authority.

Relations between the monastery and the Este were untroubled during this period of the Roverella's greatest power.[43] Between the government of Ferrara and the Holy See, however, beyond the continuing charade of diplomatic courtesies, there was ongoing controversy and jurisdictional strife. One such controversy concerned the taxation of the clergy – although here the Este could pretend that this was imposed by the *comune* and not themselves. In 1469 Pietro Landi, a member of the communal magistracy known as the Dodici Savi, had died and his funeral was about to take place at San Romano (a commendatory church of Cardinal Roverella). A message arrived from Rome forbidding religious offices to those who had extracted taxes from priests and friars as Landi had done.[44] Another point of contention in Ercole's reign was the ducal interference in ecclesiastical appointments. On 24 November 1476 a ducal proclamation declared that no-one could claim an ecclesiastical benefice without the approval of the duke.[45] In addition to these matters the Este collided with the Papacy over the tolerance and protection of Jewish usury, of which more will be said in due course. But first we must look more closely at the altarpiece, the work which chiefly expresses the Roverella family's identification with San Giorgio.

RECONSTRUCTION AND DATING

All we know of the work's original appearance comes from the descriptions by the Ferrarese cleric Girolamo Baruffaldi.[46] In the version of the life of Tura dating from 1706, Baruffaldi described a polyptych in eight parts, with the *Virgin and Child with Musician Angels* in the centre. To the right of the Virgin were Sts Peter and George with a 'monaco ginocchione'; on the other Sts Paul and Maurelius with another kneeling monk. In the upper compartments were the figures of Sts Benedict and Bernard, the whole surmounted by a *Lamentation* with St John and the Maries. The predella featured scenes from the lives of Sts Bernard and Benedict. In his collected lives of Ferrarese artists, written after 1709, Baruffaldi associated a damaged inscription on the organ played by the angels in the centre foreground with a couplet in the *Tumultuaria Carmina* of the Ferrarese poet Lodovico Bigo Pittorio, a book of Latin verse published in 1492.[47] The couplet is entitled 'Imago Virginis excitandis filium' and the lines read: 'Surge puer. Roverella fores gens pulsat./Apertum redde aditum. Pulsa lex ait, intus eris.' ('Arise boy, the Roverella family are knocking outside. Let entry be given unto them. The Law says "knock, you shall be admitted." ').

Baruffaldi now claimed that the figure in the left-hand panel, which he had previously described as a kneeling monk, was in fact Lorenzo Roverella, and that the bishop was identifiable from the effigy on the Rossellino tomb. The dead man was shown knocking on a door, in accordance with the action described in the inscription. When Baruffaldi subjected the altarpiece to this second scrutiny it may have been in a severely mutilated condition. After being damaged in a bombardment by Papal forces in 1709 it was taken to pieces, and portions gradually left the sacristy of San Giorgio over the next two centuries.[48] Roberto Longhi's identification of a group of scattered panels with the altarpiece described by Baruffaldi has been accepted by most subsequent scholars (plate 87).[49] Longhi associated three small tondi of the *Circumcision*, the *Adoration of the Magi* and the *Flight into Egypt* with the three main panels, showing how the centralised composition of the *Circumcision* aligns comfortably with the axis of the main panel (plates 88–90). There was also, he noted, a stylistic correspondence between the 'Salomonic' architecture of the Virgin's throne and the horned tablet of the *Circumcision* tondo. Objections to Longhi's reconstruction largely arise from Baruffaldi's statement that the predella contained stories of Sts Benedict and Bernard.[50] Neither of these objections provides sufficient grounds for dismissing Longhi's reconstruction. Baruffaldi is often quite laconic in describing works of art, and liable to omit mention of that which he does not find remarkable. The presence of these three Gospel episodes beneath the central panel does not preclude the possibility that the complete predella according to Longhi's reconstruction could have featured as many as four additional tondi devoted to the two saints. The iconographic logic of placing the Circumcision on axis with the sleeping Christ in the central panel and the Dead Christ of the lunette is also very compelling. The sleeping child, together with the infant Christ whose blood is shed for the first time in the Circumcision, both allude proleptically to Christ's Passion and death; the three episodes define a visible axis of redemption to which the two Roverella prelates direct their gaze. There is other circumstantial evidence in the form of works of art which respond stylistically or iconographically to the Roverella altarpiece, above all in the association of the Virgin and Child with Jewish ritual.[51]

For instance, the Ferrarese painter Lorenzo Costa, who began his career as a follower of Tura, painted for a Bolognese patron the *Presentation in the Temple* (plate 91),[52] in which the frontal iconic image of the Virgin and Child is combined with a narrative of the Circumcision. Costa's painting proposes a number of symbolic equivalences which, as we shall see, also occur in Tura's altarpiece – the identification of the Virgin with the Ark of the Covenant – denoted by the altar with the ciborium.

On the basis of Baruffaldi's identification of Lorenzo, Tura's altarpiece has always been considered a memorial to the deceased Bishop of Ferrara and dated 1474. More recently, Giordana Mariani Canova has suggested that the work could have been commissioned by Lorenzo as a personal memorial during the years preceding his death, perhaps around 1470 when he made a pastoral visit to Ferrara.[53] The Latin inscription on the

87   Tura, Roverella altarpiece. After the reconstruction by Roberto Longhi.

88 Tura, Roverella altarpiece. Predella: *Flight into Egypt*. New York, Metropolitan Museum. On panel (38 × 37 cm).

89   Tura, Roverella altarpiece. Predella: *Circumcision of Christ*. Boston, Mass., Isabella Stewart Gardner Museum. On panel (39 × 38 cm).

90 Tura, Roverella altarpiece. Predella: *Adoration of the Magi*. Cambridge, Mass., Fogg Art Museum. On panel (38.8 × 38.6 cm).

91 Lorenzo Costa, *Presentation in the Temple*. Formerly Berlin, Kaiser–Friedrich Museum (destroyed).

altarpiece, however, could be taken as evidence of a later date. This refers not necessarily to Lorenzo alone, but to the *gens Roverella*. More than one member of the family, this implies, is knocking on the door of heaven. If Baruffaldi was right in his identification of Lorenzo, then the prelate represented in the Colonna panel is likely to be Bartolomeo.[54] This figure, who wears a long, trailing garment of red, closely resembles the portrait of the cardinal on his tomb in his titular church of San Clemente in Rome, carved by Antonio Bregno and Giovanni Dalmata in the late 1470s (plate 92).[55] The iconography of the Virgin enthroned is common to both, as is the presence of Sts Peter and Paul, who represent the power and authority of the Papacy.[56] Both brothers, then, were shown in a moment of suspense, awaiting judgement and the bestowal of grace.

It is also possible that the altarpiece was commissioned in the late 1470s, during the campaign of renovation of San Giorgio undertaken by Niccolo and Filiasio, when the St Maurelius altarpiece was presumably also installed. The family fortunes must have seemed precarious following the deaths in close succession of Lorenzo and Bartolomeo and the need for visual propaganda more urgent. The work may reflect Niccolo's and Filiasio's sense of themselves as the inheritors of a mandate to maintain the prominence that had been won for the family, and to secure its memorialisation for posterity. Niccolo, moreover, is the one member of the family that we know of as a discerning patron of artists. As Carl Strehlke has observed, his term as Prior General at Monte Oliveto coincides with the period when Francesco di Giorgio and Liberale da Verona worked for the order.[57] Finally, as I have already indicated, certain themes invoked in the altarpiece acquire a greater purposefulness and motivation if the work is seen in relation to events which would have influenced church-state relations around the time of Bartolomeo's death.

A PSALM, ITS EXEGETICAL TRADITION AND A FERRARESE POET

As a monumental painting with a commemorative purpose, the Roverella altarpiece is almost unprecedentedly dramatic in character. In the action performed by the cleric who knocks, in the exhortation to the sleeping Christ Child, in the gesture of his mother whose head inclines slightly towards the source of the knocking, there is a clear element of temporality and suspense which has no parallel in other representations of the Madonna with donors. Furthermore, in its invocation of theological authorities (Paul and Bernard), in the use of specific metaphors (the door of heaven), in the centrality of the dramatic gesture (the mourners in the harrowing *Lamentation*, Lorenzo's act of knocking) there are analogies with humanist homilectic oratory, such as that which characterised sermons at the Papal court from the time of Nicholas V onwards. With its 'amplification' of a biblical text, the painting parallels the homilectic citation and expansion of scriptural passages, which constantly invokes dra-

92 Antonio Bregno and Giovanni Dalmata, tomb of Cardinal Bartolomeo Roverella. Rome, San Clemente. Detail.

matic action and direct appeals to the emotions and to the visual imagination.[58] This Roman context is specially appropriate for the Roverella brothers, with their ties to the Papal court and their scholarly interests.

There are, at any rate, clear analogies of content. John O'Malley has shown that this oratory reflected the centrality of the theology of Incarnation, especially the links between the Incarnation of the Saviour, his Passion and the redemption of mankind. 'Each even in the life of Christ', he writes, 'could be interpreted both as an extension or reflection of the Incarnation and as having redemptive value',[59] Certain ekphrastic passages attributed to St Bernard which cast the audience in the role of a beholder, a visual witness to Christ's outpouring of

grace, provided a model for several preachers.[60] Some of the most celebratory rhetoric of the Papal chapel was devoted to the redemptive significance of the Epiphany and the Circumcision, both events which appear in the predella of the altarpiece.

The sleeping Child in the lap of the Virgin forms a thematic and visual axis with the Dead Christ above and the bleeding Christ of the *Circumcision* below (plate 89). The ritual of the circumcision takes place before an altar which bears a horned tablet repeating the form of the Tablets of the Law. It bears an unusual monochrome image, resembling an outline drawing in black chalk, of a kneeling figure with the face of God the Father overhead (plate 93). From its association with the Tablets above, and from other painted narratives of the Circumcision, such as that by Mantegna (Florence, Uffizi), dated 1473, this can be identified as Moses, at the moment of the institution of the Law when the tablets of stone are received from God.

The redemptive interpretation of the Circumcision was in the *quattrocento* specially characteristic of the sermons preached annually on New Year's Day in the Papal chapel. A number of these sermons use imagery that corresponds to what I have called the dramatic or theatrical character of the altarpiece; they allude to the Circumcision of Christ as a prerequisite for salvation. In his oration of 1460 Antonio Campano stated:

> Until now we were in the chains of the old law, and today, for us hitherto emeshed in its bonds, He began to open the door to make accessible the entry unto life. At the moment the boy was circumcised, the weapons for our salvation appeared for the first time in the blood of that infant.[61]

And, in a sermon by Antonio Lollio from 1485, we find:

> Today is opened for mankind the book of the Circumcision, the first volume of the most bitter Passion. Here issues the first blood of our redemption . . . Circumcision is the figure of the Passion of Christ and its beginning, and we observe it in our hearts. Let us enter through the gate which Circumcision has opened for us, which today lies open wider through Baptism, in the most sacred waters of which all are reborn and in which the grace of God is restored to us . . . It appeared harsh that we should cut the flesh, and the father does not wish to punish his holy ones with pain. He found a new remedy, and gave openly of the precious balm . . . Let us venerate this most sacred day of the Circumcision, which we can call the gate that opens the way to Paradise.[62]

The door to Paradise is also invoked in the inscription on the altarpiece, on which Lorenzo was supposedly shown to be knocking in the lost portion of the left-hand panel. The rousing of the child from sleep also has a redemptive significance, as is implicit from the words SURGE PUER in Pittorio's couplet, which evoke a text from II Chronicles 7 and from Psalm 132, a prayer spoken by Solomon at the consecration of the Temple in Jerusalem. If the hypothesis that the painting was completed

93 Tura, Roverella altarpiece. Predella: *Circumcision of Christ*. Detail of plate 89.

close to the time of the re-dedication of San Giorgio in 1479 is correct, then the theme of consecration is highly appropriate. Verses 8–10 of the Psalm run as follows:

> Arise O Lord and go to thy resting place
> Thou and the Ark of thy might.
> Your priests shall be clothed with justice and your holy
>   ones will rejoice.
> For thy servant David's sake, do not turn away the face of
>   your anointed one.[63]

In Christian exegetical tradition this text was understood as prophetic of the Resurrection, and in St Augustine's commentary on this Psalm the sleep or rest of the Lord is seen as prefiguring Christ's death and the Ark as prefiguring the Church.[64] Is there more evidence that the forgotten poet who composed the inscription, and the unknown author of the programme, may have had this Psalm and its commentators in mind? There is strong evidence that this is the case: at some point in his career Pittorio wrote a vernacular commentary on the Psalter which was published in 1547. In his comment on the eighth verse, Pittorio provides a typological exegesis on the Ark in Solomon's Temple. The Lord is exhorted to ascend to 'la celeste patria',

> And not only you but also your church, which you have sanctified with your blood. You have established it as the Ark – no longer of the manna, but of the Eucharist; and within it are the Tablets, that is the Evangelical Law, and the rod of Aaron, the sign of priestly authority.[65]

In the altarpiece the inner space dominated by the Virgin's throne is the domain of 'la celeste patria', of the Heavenly Jerusalem. The Virgin sits enthroned in a niche adorned with shells and the Tablets of the Law, on a tier of steps consisting of classical entablatures. The rich ornament of the throne is actually an assemblage of motifs taken from Psalm 132. On the tablets a lantern-like motif appears four times, evoking a line from the end of the psalm (17): 'I have ordained a lantern for my anointed' ('paravi lucernam Christo meo'). The form of the Hebrew tablets with their horn-like protrusions is taken up by the shells, in the viols played by the angels, and by a sarcophagus-like form above the throne which is framed by the symbols of the Evangelists. On either side of the throne there are yet more horns, *cornucopiae* from which living grapevines and other fruit-like forms burgeon forth. The *cornucopiae* might be glossed once again from Psalm 132: 'I make a horn to sprout forth for David', ('Illuc producam cornu David') a line which Augustine interpreted as an exhortation to 'spiritual loftiness' and faith in Christ.[66] Likewise Pittorio understood horns in terms of the aspiration of the faithful towards heaven and the image of the Divine Countenance:

> For in my Church, says the Lord, the horn of David shall revive and endure, that is the lofty nature of my son and of my Church, so that his faithful shall not cast their gaze upon the earth, but like mighty horns shall raise them towards heavenly

things, and in so doing shall finally deserve to see him face to face in whom for centuries they have believed.[67]

Horns occur throughout the Old Testament as attributes of victory or glory; the sacrificial altar of the Temple was referred to as having horns, and horns have a long association in Christian tradition with the iconography of Moses and the synagogue.[68] As a number of modern studies have shown, however, horns were at best an ambivalent symbol of Judaism by the fifteenth century; they figure in blatantly racist characterisations of the Jews and were connected with notions of the Jews as allies of Satan. In fact, the Virgin's throne in Tura's altarpiece is crowned with two golden lamps in the form of bearded heads wearing the *pileus cornutus*, the 'horned cap' imposed on Jewish males in many parts of Europe throughout the Middle Ages and a constant signifier of 'Jewishness' in Christian Bible illustration (plate 95).[69] In the *Rappresentazione ciclica* performed by the confraternity of St Jerome in Bologna in the late fifteenth century, Synagogue appears as a horned woman mounted upon an ass, just as she would appear, in 1523, in Garofalo's fresco of the Living Cross for the Augustinian church of Sant'Andrea in Ferrara (plate 94).[70]

Claudia Cieri Via has proposed that the architecture in the painting is to be identified as the Temple of Solomon; the reason for this was not, however, as the same author suggests, to celebrate the Este.[71] Borso's emblem of the *steccato* (stockade) may be alluded to in the crozier of St Maurelius, which is ornamented with a sheep bearing a banner and enclosed with a rustic fence. A routinely courteous acknowledgement by the Roverella of the secular lords of Ferrara is possible – Borso's unicorn appears almost imperceptibly in the clouds above the saint – but the pastoral and hence ecclesiastical dimensions of the crozier device would in this context more effectively designate the Roverella than the Este. Evocations of the Este, in short, are either ambiguous or very difficult to detect.[72] One other discreet reference to the Este is the red, white and green ribbon worn by St George (plate 83).

By considering Psalm 132 and other literary sources for the image of the Temple it is possible to specify more fully the significance of the Temple in the altarpiece. For instance, the prayer of Solomon and Psalm 132 refer to the transferral of the Ark of the Covenant into the Temple. The throne can plausibly be seen as a representation of the Tabernacle, long established in Christian exegesis as a type of the Virgin Mary herself. Just as the Ark contained the manna which prefigured the Eucharist, so the body of the Virgin contained Christ; a similar symbolic equivalence is proposed, as we have seen, by Costa's painting (plate 91).[73] The golden angels who appear over the throne stand accordingly for the cherubim who watch over the Ark in the Holy of Holies. In the tapestry of the *Lamentation* designed by Tura around 1476 (plate 81) the sepulchre provided by the Jew Joseph for Christ's burial has pointed or horned architectural elements which resemble those of the Virgin's throne. The common architectural forms may have been suggested by the joint allusion of both the throne and the tomb to the eucharistic tabernacle.

94   Garofalo, *Allegory of the Crucifixion*. Fresco. Ferrara, Pinacoteca Nazionale.

The Second Book of Chronicles describes Solomon's Temple as ornamented throughout with golden cherubim; in the architecture of the altarpiece Tura has included golden angelic forms above the throne and in the Corinthian capitals. The four Evangelist symbols refer also to the visions of the prophet Ezekiel who also describes a vision of the temple decorated with many cherubim (Ezekiel 41: 18–26). Horns, cherubim, the Ark and the tablets serve to invoke the context of Synagogue and Temple, and this evocation in Tura's altarpiece does not appear as blatantly vituperative as it clearly is in Garofalo's fresco painted several decades later. The few art historians who have commented on the Hebraic imagery of the painting have seen it as a rather innocuous statement of the harmony of the Old and New Testaments.[74] Like the curial sermons on the circumcision, however, Pittorio's commentary is not about harmony but, more accurately, the termination of the Jewish ritual. On verse 7 of the Psalm – 'Introimus in tabernaculum eius. Adorabimus in loco ubi steterunt pedes eius' – Pittorio writes:

Let us go with devotion no longer into the Synagogue but into the Holy Church, and make sacrifices not of animals but of ourselves, offering our will as victims to the Lord, and there inside we will worship where once were the feet of the Lord, which are the ceremonies which are used to consecrate a church.[75]

On closer inspection the painting itself reveals a darker side, a more aggressive or militant relation to its Jewish Biblical sources. This aspect becomes apparent in a couple of easily missed details, the understanding of which is dependent to a large extent on viewing within a particular historical situation and with a certain kind of viewing competence.

★ ★ ★

95 Tura, Roverella altarpiece. Central panel. Detail of plate 83.

'ADVERSUS IUDAEOS':
THE METAPHOR OF PAINTING

In the representation of the Tablets of the Mosaic Law,[76] Tura's altarpiece mounts an attack on the Jewish religion which explicitly calls into play the power and legitimacy of human artifice and the painted image as a weapon of the Christian faith.

The verses from Psalm 132 quoted above make particular reference to the 'facies Christi' ('Christus' being Jerome's translation of the Hebrew word for 'anointed'), and in his commentary Pittorio refers to the Divine Countenance in the vision of the Blessed. In the painting the face of Christ becomes an element of extraordinary importance because of its juxtaposition with a particular Hebrew text. Precariously balanced on the lap of the Virgin, the sleeping Child leans off to the left so that his head partly obscures one of the Tablets of the Law (plate 96). What is no longer visible is the Second Commandment in the Hebrew version, which reads 'Thou shalt not make to thyself a graven thing, nor the likeness of anything that is in the heaven above, or in the earth beneath, nor of those things that are in the waters under the earth' (Exodus 20: 4).

In Rabbinical interpretation the Second Commandment was seen as prohibiting every kind of visual representation.[77] Christians had adapted and assimilated this commandment to the first, 'Thou shalt not have strange Gods before me', as if it merely amplified the injunction against idolatry. But the Second Commandment remained troubling for many Christians in the early Middle Ages, and it was the focus of fierce contention from the Carolingian Empire to Byzantium. The attack of the iconoclasts was frequently countered by referring to the Incarnation; the prohibition of images under the Old Law reflected the fact that God then had no image. This was the view of the Franciscan Nicholas of Lyra, a standard authority in the fifteenth century, who conceived his exegesis as an argument with the Jews.[78] Yet we need to move away momentarily from fifteenth-century Italy in order to understand the full force of the theme of image-making in Tura's painting.

In the Eastern church a more elaborate form of the Incarnation argument was employed against the iconoclasts: this was the metaphor of artistic process as a means of explaining the supremacy of the New to the Old Testaments by analogy with the supremacy of image to word. In his commentary on a text from the Epistle to the Hebrews, 'For the Law contains but a shadow, no true image, of the things which were to come' (Hebrews 10: 1), St John Chrysostom likened the Old Testament to an outline drawing which is not only completed but obliterated when layers of colour are applied:

> As in a painting, so long as one only draws the outline then it is a sort of shadow [*skia*]; but when one has added the bright paints and laid in the colours, then it becomes an image [*eikon*]. Something of this kind also was the Law.[79]

Cyril of Alexandria made the comparison more pointed by introducing the term 'skiagraphia' (drawing) in place of 'skia'; he maintained that just as the painted image covers up and completes a drawing, effectively obliterating it, so the New Testament, in fulfilling the Old, renders it obsolete.[80] The topos of *skia/eikon*, as Herbert Kessler has pointed out, was re-formulated by the iconodules to further denote the supremacy of the painted image of Christ over the written word of scripture. The Incarnation itself, in which Christ is substantially and visibly manifest, becomes justification for the existence of holy images: 'Why might one not describe Jesus Christ our Lord with the brilliance of colours as legitimately as with ink?', wrote Methodius in the ninth century, 'He was never presented to us with ink, but was manifested as a true man, truly endowed with form and with colour.'[81] Hence, for Christians, before the abstract form of the letter stands the sensible form of Christ made man.

The fact that Christ had existed in human form justified the existence of icons; it secured the legitimate use of appearance, of image, for Christian contemplation and worship. In the exegetical tradition of the Epistle to the Hebrews, Christ's iconic image also signified revelation, liberation from the abstract form of the letter and the exclusive and occult character of Jewish ritual: 'The blood of Christ makes us free to enter boldly in the sanctuary by the new living way which he has opened for us through the veil of his flesh.'[82] In this light, the juxtaposition of the face of Christ with the written word of the Law invokes a theological and iconographic tradition of long standing: Christ's completion of the Law in his Incarnation and sacrifice, Christ's obliteration of the Law, and, through his own holy image, of the Law's provisions against the making of images. A number of image-cults in Italy and in the Greek East celebrated the triumph of the icon over the Tablets of the Law. The titular church of Cardinal Bartolomeo Roverella was the basilica of San Clemente in Rome; a record from 1462, the year after Bartolomeo's elevation to the purple, shows that on the Feast of the Assumption the famous Lateran icon of the true face of Christ paused at San Clemente in the course of a triumphal procession from the Lateran to Santa Maria Maggiore. Unpainted by human hand, the image was seen to legitimate the cult of icons; it normally resided in the Papal chapel known as the 'Holy of Holies', a designation which explicitly evokes the resting place of the Ark in the Jerusalem Temple.[83]

In the Roverella altarpiece, human artifice triumphs, in the image of the Christ Child and in the re-creation of the Temple. In the predella panel of the *Circumcision* we find an even more dramatic reprise of the *skia/eikon* trope. Before our eyes, the colourless outline drawing of Moses – which now substitutes for the writing of the Law – is counterposed with the painted, coloured form of the living and presumably bleeding Christ Incarnate (plate 93). Once again this relates to the theme of completion and fulfilment. Just as the Law was instituted by God through Moses, so, in the Circumcision of Christ, it had its consummation. Christ's submission to circumcision represents not only his abidance by the Law but also his liberation of those who came after him from its observance.[84] Moses may be intended here as a *figura* of Christ, and his raised arms might prefigure the eucharistic elevation of the Host, yet Moses has no other validity except as the sign of a covenant which has been completed and fulfilled; his precedence and prefigurative capacity are also a sign of his obsolescence. This aggressively polemical use of typology was especially characteristic of the fifteenth-century Papacy, as is clear from the violent depictions of Jewish history and ritual in the Sistine Chapel. Just as a newly invested Pope at this time first revered, and then cast down the Torah proffered to him by the Jews of Rome, so the importance of the Jewish Law for sacred history is to be recognised by Christians, while its prescriptions are to be rejected.[85] That this is the sense intended here is suggested by the Child in his vigorous turning away from the *mohel* and from the image of Moses.[86] The composition has a clarity which, I would argue, would make the narrative action intelligible not only to those with close access to the altarpiece – such as members of the family, of the Olivetan order, and the celebrant of daily Mass – but to those visitors to the church who merely saw the work from the nave.

The revival of a centuries-old polemic in favour of icons in late fifteenth-century Ferrara might seem not only incongruous but bizarre. One key to its reappearance, however, lies in the intellectual culture of San Giorgio. At least one member of the community was literate in Greek and a student of the Greek fathers. This was Girolamo Bendedei, who preceded Niccolo Roverella as prior of the monastery in 1474–6, and, in this capacity, acted as agent for Niccolo in concerns such as the annexation of San Bartolomeo near Rovigo. Among the manuscripts annotated in Greek by Bendedei are a Latin translation of Chrysostom's sermons against the Jews and 'iudaizantes christianos' and another of Chrysostom's commentaries on the Epistles of St Paul. As the surviving copies are in the Latin translations of Ambrogio Traversari, they would have been accessible to the larger monastic community.[87] As we need not assume that Bendedei's knowledge of Greek patristics extended no further than the works of which copies survive, he seems a possible theological adviser for the altarpiece. Beyond San Giorgio, Ferrara's main link to the intellectual world of the exiled Greek scholars in Italy was Guarino, who had died in 1460. On Palm Sunday 1447 the humanist had presented Bishop Francesco dal Legname with a Latin translation of sermons by Cyril of Alexandria.[88]

While this suggests how the programme was conceivable in late fifteenth-century Ferrara, it does not answer the question, Why? An argument against Christian iconoclasts would have been somewhat redundant in the 1470s. The Jews, however, were

96 Tura, Roverella altarpiece. Central panel. Detail of plate 83.

still very much an object of theological and jurisdictional concern for the church and for secular powers, and the remainder of this investigation will focus on that particular dimension to the imagery of the altarpiece.

The episode of the Circumcision unites the two central themes which have figured so far. The representation of the event is inseparable from its exegetical tradition, where the themes of redemption and of the obsolescence of Judaism intersect. In his Epistles St Paul writes of how the physical circumcision according to the Law is superseded by spiritual circumcision, 'circumcision made without hands' in Christ.[89] On the Mosaic Law, Paul provided some of the main scriptural support for countless Christian polemics against the Jews and their religion for nearly two millennia. The Second Epistle to the Corinthians contains the much-quoted verse 'the letter killeth, but the spirit giveth life'. In the same chapter Paul addresses the ministry of the church: 'Ye are manifestly declared to be the epistle of Christ ministered by us, written not with ink but with the Spirit of the living God, not on tables of stone but in the fleshy tables of the heart.'[90]

The passage from Corinthians could be said to underlie the opposition between word and image, writing and the body, and the association of writing with violence which underlies the imagery of the painting. While the body is conceived as a sign figuring the spiritual, the written word is fallen, basely material, not only redundant but finally even illegible. With the deadliness of the written word is expunged the violence of inscription on the body, the incision of the sign of God's covenant in the flesh of the new-born: the behaviour of the Infant in Tura's rendering of the ritual explicitly renders it as a scene of violence. It is noteworthy that the Tablets of the Law are rendered in the painting as produced through carving or incision, rather than as painted on the stone. The Virgin's right hand makes a gesture as if to rouse the sleeping Child, at the same time drawing attention to his genital area and the intactness of his flesh. There may be some metaphorical play here on the notion of arousal suggested by the words SURGE PUER, which some few of Tura's audience adept at the Latin vocabulary of *lascivia* may have appreciated. The carnal associations of the verb 'surgere', and of the idea of 'resurrection', is actually given an almost shockingly literal form by Tura. The Christ Child himself does not display any obvious signs of sexual excitement, but this sexual response has been displaced on to two other infantile figures: the golden angels over the Virgin's throne (plate 97). For a modern viewer this startling appearance of ithyphallic angels may seem to breach the rather taut web of theological correspondences proposed in the image; its significance for a beholder of Tura's time will be considered more fully at the end of this chapter.

In any case, Christianity had had to accommodate the fact of the Jewish ritual of circumcision. In the economy of the body as a theatre of rebellious and unspiritual appetites, through which Christianity in its origins had distinguished itself from the ethos of the pagan and Jewish world, circumcision was bound to evoke an anxious sense of shame and repugnance. The ritual could be

97 Tura, Roverella altarpiece. Central panel. Detail of plate 83.

viewed in a positive or a negative light, sometimes depending on how a Christian commentator viewed its sexual connotations.

St Bernard composed three sermons on the Circumcision of Christ in which he appears to celebrate the cutting of the foreskin as a form of spiritual castration: the knife of the priest castigated that part of the body in which 'Leviathan' resides (Bernard, interestingly, uses the word 'surgere' to characterise the involuntary behaviour of the male organ). He also regarded circumcision as the primitive form or *figura* of baptism; like Augustine he considered circumcision as having the same sacramental function, marking the remission of the sin inherent in generation.[91] Certain fifteenth-century commentators on the Circumcision, such as the orators of the Papal chapel, followed St Bernard in stressing the moral interpretation of the Jewish Law and of this ritual in particular, which they identified with purification and with sacraments such as baptism.[92] This interpretation had been favoured by St Thomas Aquinas, who had become the near-canonical authority for the theology of the Roman Curia by the *quattrocento*.[93] Yet in the centuries intervening between St Bernard and the humanists and Thomists of the Papal court, an important paradigmatic shift had occurred in the perception of the laws and rituals of the Jewish tradition and their persistence among contemporary Jewry. The impetus came in the thirteenth century with the rise of the preaching orders, the Franciscans and the Dominicans. Now, under the impulse of a missionary and Inquisitorial zeal, the Jews, their culture, and especially the corpus of post-biblical rabbinical texts, were subjected to intense and hostile scrutiny.[94] Furthermore, by the fifteenth century the dependence of the wealthy and of rulers on Jewish usury had become an important concern of the church in its struggle with secular authority.

PRINCES AND JEWS: CLERICAL ATTITUDES

> Nobody is allowed to preach against the viciousness of the Jews . . . because princes and magistrates corrupted by financial gain normally practice censorship . . . The infidel dogs themselves dare approach magistrates and so influence them that they obtain letters of licence and protection. I have no part in this. Nowadays the nonsense of the Jews is believed over the truth of the clergy . . . The magistrates have no anxiety about keeping the preachers from making sermons.
>
> Giacomo Ongarelli, *Contra perfidium modernorum Judaeorum* (1490s)[95]

> This is the true Israelite, in whom there is no guile.
>
> Comment on Niccolo Roverella attributed to Sixtus IV[96]

The first important Christian Hebrew scholars since St Jerome were invariably proselytisers or anti-Judaic polemicists. One of the first Italian humanists to study Hebrew, Gianozzo Manetti, was writing at his death in 1457 a treatise 'for the confusion of the Jews'.[97] Along with the intellectual scrutiny of the humanists, which reflects real dialogue and cultural exchange, went the more traditional surveyance of the Jews by the Inquisitors. Conversion was not always the sole concern; the Inquisitors held themselves responsible for seeing that the Jews obeyed the Law of Moses only in the form in which it was recorded in the Jewish Bible. Long attacked for being 'people of the letter', the Jews were now legally prevented from being anything else. The Talmud was seen as a corrupt, abominable mystification, devised by the rabbis to prevent the Jews from ever recognising the christological significance of their own Bible.

In 1435 Eugenius IV renewed the mandate to the Inquisition, authorising it to proceed against the Talmud, against false Jewish converts and against those who denied the sinfulness of usury.[98] The Inquisitor for Lombardy and Emilia was based in Ferrara by the reign of Borso d'Este. Although Ferrara enjoys a much-lauded reputation for tolerance in the history of the Jews of Italy, there are signs that this presence of the Inquisition may have forced the Este on occasion to fulfil the obligation to police the orthodoxy of their Jewish subjects. The nineteenth-century historian Abramo Pesaro noted with surprise that in 1461 the Jews were fined 'for having prevaricated the Law of Moses on certain matters'.[99]

Through the propaganda of the Inquisition and the preaching orders throughout Europe, the ritual of circumcision acquired specially negative connotations as a token of the depravity of Judaism. Preachers and theologians stressed its shameful aspect along with its redundancy. The most influential polemicist in this regard was the Dominican Raymond Martini who in the second half of the fourteenth century produced a vitriolic attack on Judaism and Islam entitled the *Pugio Fidei* ('The Dagger of the Faith'), in which he mined the Talmud for material to scandalise Christians and portrayed the persistence of the Jews in their observance of the Mosaic Law as the work of diabolical influences: 'The devil returned the Jews to the observance of the Mosaic commandments', he wrote, 'which God had intended to nullify through the Roman persecution.'[100]

Circumcision was singled out as patently inspired by demonic forces. Martini attributed it to 'the spirit of fornication which is in their midst' who restored to them 'circumcision, the sabbaths and other rituals which God removed through the agency of the Romans'. Martini was scandalised by the genital aspect of circumcision, especially by the custom of drawing blood orally from the wound of the circumcised child, which the rabbis justified on hygienic grounds: 'For as often as they circumcise an infant or an adult, they suck the penis orally for as long as blood emerges from it, desiring to obey the aforementioned mandate of the rabbis.'[101]

The *Pugio Fidei* had become a standard sourcebook for the Dominicans and for the Inquisition by the fifteenth century. Gianfranco Fioravanti has traced the influence of Martini's work (together with some fifteenth-century Spanish Dominican tracts written in the same fanatical spirit) on a series of Italian anti-Jewish treatises, some of them printed in the 1470s, which emerged not only from the preaching orders but from the jurists and the humanists.[102]

The obscene and even vampiric character which Martini infers from circumcision reflects a broader tendency to fantasise about Jewish rituals in terms of horror, perversion and conspiratorial secrecy. In *quattrocento* Ferrara the slaughtering of animals according to Jewish dietary laws was regarded with distaste by civic officials who reported that the Jews butchered their meat 'cum maledictis et diabolicis ceremoniis'.[103] The allegations of Jewish ritual child-murder which brought about a wave of persecution in Italy during the 1470s may have originated in Christian fear and suspicion of such practices, especially as seen through the lurid characterisations of the preachers. The child Simon, whom the Jews were supposed to have tortured and bled to death at Trent in 1475, instantly became the centre of a cult, and, according to the reported testimony of the Procurator of Trent, the Tridentines could be seen 'to worship their blessed [Simon] as if he were a second Christ or second Messiah'.[104] A representation of the Circumcision of Christ in a church may for some beholders have evoked the cult images of 'Simonino', some of which show the child carrying a knife and tongs, a bowl at his feet collecting the blood flowing from his partially amputated penis, or explicitly evoke the ritual of circumcision (plate

98 Gandolfino di Roreto d'Asti, *Martyrdom of Simon of Trent*. Jerusalem, Israel Museum.

98).[105] If this scenario can be accepted, it may confirm a recent argument that assertions in Renaissance painting of the 'sexuality of Christ' may not only manifest a new incarnational theology which celebrated the body, but might also give visual form to more sinister Christian fantasies of pollution, sacrilege and abuse – of the Host, of the Christ(ian) child – which were displaced on to ethnic and religious 'Others'.[106]

As well as being exposed to manipulation by the preaching orders, Christian consciousness of the Jewish minority in their midst could also have been influenced by resentment arising from the principal form of commercial contact with the Jews. In Ferrara, as elsewhere, this was the practice of usury, in which the Jews received the active support and protection of the Este princes.

As early as 1376 the poet Francesco da Vanozzo had written satirical verses directed against the princes of Ferrara and the city's Jewish community. Vanozzo wrote that the people of Ferrara themselves were 'all of them gloomy and dismal, backward, bitter and badly nosed. They are not recognisable as Gauls, Germans or Latins, but as members of the Jewish sect.'[107] Another sonnet by Vanozzo attacks the hangers-on at princely courts and alludes to the Jews 'who have placed on the crest of Justice's helm a great burden of corruption, all disguised and obscured in the Hebrew tongue'.[108]

By the 1470s, the Este were having to resort to violence to ensure the protection of the Jews. The tax burden imposed by the princes on their subjects, especially the provincial *comune*, made them heavily reliant on Jewish moneylenders, a dependency which produced bitterness, constant complaints to the Este, and finally outbreaks of bloodshed. The murder of a son of the banker Zinatan in Reggio in 1474, and of the banker Solomon Noah Norsa in Ferrara in 1480, brought the imposition of the death penalty for the murderers in each case. However, this could only be imposed in the first instance following the direct intervention of Duke Ercole himself; there was tremendous popular and juridical support for the young assassin, and it was reported that enormous crowds, including professors of the university, had followed his funeral procession.[109] Ferrara had a blood libel case of its own in 1481,

and Ercole could disband the crowds preparing to ransack the Jewish banks only with his drawn sword and the threat of the death penalty.[110] The Jews, in other words, had become a major point of tension and dispute not only between the Papacy and the Este, but between the Este and the *comune* and people of Ferrara.

The financial structure of the Este state was heavily dependent on the availability of Jewish credit. In Ercole's own household accounts for the year 1475 numerous transactions involving at least nine different banking foundations or pawnshops are recorded. The bankers were also an important source of revenue; those who operated in Ferrara each paid a formidable 700 lire every year for a licence from the prince.[111] Nicholas V had formally authorised Leonello d'Este to give licences to Jewish moneylenders in 1448. In the same Papal bull, Jews were also conceded freedom of worship, immunity from attacks by preachers, and the Inquisition's jurisdiction over them was limited to the monitoring of 'heresy' and of attacks on the Christian faith.[112] The polemic of the friars against usury, and their power to manipulate popular sympathy against the Jews, remained a constant source of anxiety for the Este rulers. Following the preaching of Fra Giovanni da Prato in 1452 Borso attempted to secure a copy of the Papal edict permitting the licensing of bankers,[113] and in 1459 another Papal mandate had to be issued in an attempt to control the anti-Jewish preaching of the Franciscans.[114]

By the 1470s, with the reign of Ercole I, relations between the Papacy and the Este concerning the management of the Jews were placed under a renewed strain. Ercole had granted privileges to certain moneylenders of Ferrara, including the right not to wear a distinguishing sign, the yellow badge which had been imposed by Eugenius IV in 1432 at the instigation of Bishop Giovanni Tavelli.[115] More controversially, Ercole had exempted his Jewish subjects from the payment of the *vigesima*, the Papal tax imposed by Pius II in 1460 which bound the Jews to contribute one-twentieth of their property value to the Papal treasury. In 1476 Ercole was formally commanded by Sixtus IV to refrain from obstructing the collection of this tax from the Jews in Este dominions, territory which the Popes constantly claimed and referred to as their own in these communications.[116] The clerical pressure against usury must have increased with the successful foundation of a Monte di Pietà in nearby Bologna in 1473, a Christian loan bank which the Franciscans constantly advocated as a means of bringing an end to Jewish usury.[117]

The formidable anti-Jewish ideologue Fra Bernardino da Feltre, one of the ringleaders in the persecutions at Trent in 1475, emerged in the 1480s as the champion of the Monte di Pietà throughout Italy – in Ravenna in 1487 he received the support of Archbishop Filiasio Roverella.[118] The Venetian government had intervened at Ravenna in 1475 and 1480 to prevent 'injuries, beatings, and other insults' to the Jews. Now with the allied forces of the friar and the Roverella archbishop the Republic was unable to prevent the foundation of a Monte di Pietà and the subsequent devastation of the Jewish community. By accusing the Venetians of being more of a friend to the Jews than to the city, Bernardino was able to merge the interests of ecclesiastical authority and communal solidarity.[119]

Following the slaughter of innocent Jews in Trent, the rulers of Ferrara and Mantua and the governments of Venice and other states were forced to take special measures to prevent the bloody uprising from spreading to their territories, and were themselves attacked by the preachers for their efforts. Ercole banned all sermons against the Jews of Ferrara, intervened to impose restraint on the Franciscans who were harrassing the Jews of Modena, and in 1479, when absent from the city, he directed the Duchess Eleonora to ensure the continuing protection of the Jews from the preachers.[120]

In the light of the resolute (if hardly disinterested) protection by the Este of their Jewish subjects, it can be seen that any form of anti-Jewish gesture or utterance, whether religiously, economically or racially motivated, would have had a charged political significance. Such activity could be seen not only as anti-Jewish, but as anti-Este. For the heavily taxed populations of Ferrara, and especially for the *comune* of Modena and Reggio, the Jews who flourished through usury would have been identified with the Este and possibly seen as the exercise of tyrannical will over subject city-states.[121] The Roverella altarpiece does not seem at first sight to manifest anything like the intense anti-Judaism of the preachers or the ideologues of the Inquisition (nor, for that matter, of an almost contemporary work of art, Uccello's predella of the *Miracle of the Host* (Urbino, Palazzo Ducale)). Moreover, the allusions to icon theology would seem rather subtle and abstruse for observers without the required background in Greek patristics. However, I believe that the altarpiece can be seen as providing cues to its audience, or more properly audiences, in its manipulation of signs which could have acquired a certain resonance in the crisis-ridden relations of Jews and Christians during the first decade of the reign of Ercole d'Este.

The first of these signs is Hebrew writing. The writing of the Jews was one of the most identifiable signs of Jewishness in the Ferrara of the 1470s. Following the relaxation of the laws requiring the Jews to wear yellow badges or earrings, signs to ensure their demarcation from Christians, the Hebrew language, especially in its written and visible form, would have been one of the more evident manifestations of cultural difference. Christians had long been encouraged to see Hebrew writing as a form of gibberish, a token of Jewish obscurantism and confusion and even as a sign of blindness.[122] This attitude had been promulgated in the *quattrocento* by Leonardo Bruni and others.[123] This enigmatic writing, sometimes suggestive to Christians of an insidious secrecy (as in Vanozzo's attack on those who conceal their 'corruption' in the 'Hebrew tongue') would have again been encountered principally through the trade of money-lending. Legislation against the bankers keeping accounts in Hebrew characters was apparently difficult to impose. In 1474 the *comune* of Reggio had to appoint a specially trained official to scutinise the records in Hebrew.[124]

Two other Ferrarese paintings from the 1470s feature Hebrew writing. One of these is considered the earliest surviving work of Lorenzo Costa, the *St Sebastian* (plate 17), which bears the signature 'Master Lorenzo Costa' in Hebrew characters on the shield leaning against the column to which the saint is tied. The other is Ercole de' Roberti's altarpiece for the Lateran Canons of San Lazzaro (plate 99), which, in its conception of the Virgin enthroned, has been considered a response to the Roverella altarpiece. Here, writing has a clearer relation to subject-matter. The figures of Moses and David appear above the throne, identified by their names in raised Hebrew characters on the entablature. Rendered as lifeless figures in grisaille (without colour as in Tura's figure of Moses) these personages appear lost in melancholy contemplation of the Books of the Law or the Psalms, oblivious to the festively enthroned Virgin and Child. David, rather shockingly, is presented as a corpulent, naked, crowned figure who appears to be a close relative of Mantegna's *Allegory of Ignorance* (plate 100), generally dated some years later.[125] Hebrew characters here seem more explicitly to figure not only the redundancy of the word before the image, but also, in its perceived cryptic or mystifying quality, the perpetual bewilderment and even ignorance of the Jews who remain absorbed in its domain. For an attentive lay observer of the altarpiece, therefore, I propose that the Hebrew script produced a set of associations which were largely negative and that the representation of the Circumcision may have provided a further cue to this kind of understanding.

Let us suppose, however, another kind of viewer, a member of the clergy with some theological education who might grasp the references to the Ark of the Covenant and the Temple of Solomon. Such a viewer could have been aware that such imagery pointed to one of the apparent contradictions of the Jewish religion which was frequently deployed in anti-Judaic polemic – that the Jews maintained a prohibition of the image according to their Law, but that one of their greatest leaders had ornamented the Lord's Temple with representations of cherubim. This became an occasion of formal debate at least once in the *quattrocento*, when in 1418 the rabbi Ahron Aboulrabi appeared before Martin V to defend the aniconism of the Jews.[126] Jewish behaviour with regard to Christian images was carefully

99   Ercole de' Roberti, San Lazzaro altarpiece. Formerly Berlin, Kaiser-Friedrich Museum (destroyed 1945).

100 After Mantegna, *Allegory of Ignorance*. London, British Museum, Department of Prints and Drawings.

10, 'On behalf of David your servant do not turn away the face of your anointed':

> And through the merits of your son, he of the seed of David who took the form of a servant, do not totally turn your shoulders away from the Jews withholding from them the news of your incarnate word, but concede that at least one time in the last days those who remain shall be saved.[131]

Pittorio's exegesis suggests that we might now see the face of Christ in the painting as turned towards the Jews in a move to redeem them from the strictures of their Law, at the same time rendering illegible the portion of the Law which deprives them of the image of his face. But what kind of literate Jew would it have been who would come into contact with sacred images in a Christian church? The answer lies, I think, in that part of the community of Ferrarese Jews who converted to Christianity. Their number is impossible to gauge, and their very existence is attested to only by the briefest of references. An unpublished entry in the ducal accounts for 1458 records a gift of alms 'to a Jew who is becoming Christian ('ad uno hebreo che se fece cristiano').[132] It is known that elsewhere the Olivetan order was charged with the supervision of converted Jews.[133]

In 1476, the year in which which Christian anti-Jewish propaganda was banned by Ercole, the Ferrarese chronicler Zambotti records that a converted Jew preached in the cathedral, where all the Jews came to hear him: 'he proved using Hebrew arguments [*per raxone hebraiche*] that our faith was better than the Hebrew, and this was a remarkable thing for the faith.'[134] It is just such a proselytising intention that is manifested in the Roverella polyptych. Like the sermon referred to by Zambotti, it speaks to those about to convert or recently converted, convincing them 'per raxone hebraiche' of the faith of the Christian majority and its ascendancy over theirs.

monitored in Ferrara; in 1449 the bishop's deputy received two separate notarised testimonials exculpating Jews for the deterioration of Christian images frescoed on walls of houses they were renting.[127]

The imagery of the Temple or Synagogue and its colonisation by the triumphant Mother of the Church may also invoke another controversy involving the Jews of Ferrara in the 1460s and 1470s – their right to a place of worship. In 1458 the Inquisition fined the Jews of Ferrara and Modena for attempting to establish a synagogue (it may have been this that occasioned Pius II's mandate of 1459 confirming the Jews freedom of worship).[128] In 1466 a formal request from the Jews for permission to erect a synagogue was treated with typical caution by Borso, who wrote to his *referendarius* Ludovico Casella that he could allow him not to impede the construction of a synagogue, but that he himself did not have the authority to give formal permission. In 1476, the likely year of the commission for the altarpiece, Ercole I gave full permission for the Jews to open a synagogue in the city of Ferrara. By showing the colonisation of the Temple/Synagogue by the Virgin/Ecclesia, the painting may reflect a particular clerical response to the Jews being granted freedom of worship.[129]

In its evocations of the Temple, in the justification of image-making taken from the Bible of the Jews who attempted to repudiate representational art, and in its explicit obliteration of the Second Commandment, the altarpiece occupies a position in a traditional and conventionalised dialogue between Jews and Christians.[130] On a more current and immediate level, however, I believe that the altarpiece addresses the Jews of Ferrara themselves. The dramatic juxtapositioning of the face of Christ with the Second Commandment must have been conceived to be intelligible to at least a few of those who encountered it in the 1470s. Moreover, this detail closely corresponds to a passage in Pittorio's commentary on Psalm 132 where the poet prays for the conversion of the Jews. This occurs in the section on verse

'EBRAISMO' AND CURIOSITY: THE EMERGENCE OF ARTISTIC PERSONA

We have not, however, exhausted the possible significances the Roverella altarpiece could have had for its audiences. For some viewers, motifs such as writing, horned tablets, cherubim, sprouting *cornucopiae* may have had less significance as anti-Jewish polemic and been more appreciated for their evocations of Jewish culture as spectacle. Although harassment, repression and proselytisation hardly diminished, by the later *quattrocento* Judaism had emerged as an object of curiosity; this had many manifestations in the domains of humanist study, the self-representation of the Papacy, and in the world of aristocratic fashion and taste. Among the first we might think of Giovanni Pico della Mirandola, the son of an Este vassal, who began the Christian study of the cabbala, or of Poliziano who undertook the philological study of Hebrew in the 1480s.[135] Regarding the second, there is the aforementioned story of Moses, explicitly incorporated within the genealogy of the Papacy, in the Sistine Chapel cycle of the 1480s.[136] It may be observed regarding the Sistine Chapel frescoes that the selection of episodes from the life of Moses emphasises the violence of the Jewish Law, with the constant depiction of scenes of transgression and punishment. This view of Judaism is promulgated by Paul's reference to the Law as 'a handwriting of ordinances that was directed against us' (Colossians 2: 13–14) and similarly underlies Tura's conception of the Circumcision of Christ. The Roverella altarpiece and the Sistine Chapel frescoes both correspond to a programmatic marking of distinctions between Christianity and the Jewish 'Other' which characterises the image of the Papacy and the triumphant church in the reign of Sixtus IV; the altarpiece would thus also assert Ferrara's inclusion within the States of the Church.

North Italian court society also shows a preoccupation with Jewish culture and antiquity in the late fifteenth century. The consolidation of the signorial states may have led to a concern with the status of marginal or enclave communities, although manifest in the apparently more benign form of antiquarian curiosity. Both Borso and Ercole d'Este were interested in the works of Flavius Josephus, and a certain Fra Alessandro Ariosti of Ferrara dedicated a work entitled *Topography of the Promised Land* to Borso in 1469.[137] Lodovico Gonzaga, ruler of neighbouring Mantua, ordered a Bible in Hebrew from Vespasiano da Bisticci in 1461, but was outraged at the report that it was being transcribed without proper respect for Hebrew punctuation.[138]

The Cleveland version of the *Lamentation* tapestry designed by Tura (plate 81), with its exotic 'Hebrew' architecture and costumes, can be seen as one visual manifestation of a kind of philo-Semitism in Ercole's later years. So too can the record of a commission for another tapestry design from the artist in 1478, which was to show the story of Solomon. Tura's style may have been identified with a kind of exotic antiquarianism which could have been identified as 'Asiatic' or even 'Jewish'.[139] The duke surrounded himself with a Jewish doctor, Jewish musicians, a Jewish swordmaker, Jewish gambling companions and a Jewish dancing-master. The dancing-master, Guglielmo Ebreo, seems to have been a specialist in Hebrew exoticism. At Pesaro in 1475 he organised a lavish spectacle for the marriage of Costanzo Sforza and Camilla of Aragon, at which Jews in oriental costume performed dances, the Queen of Sheba riding on an artificial elephant, and King Rehoboam on a 'Monte degli Ebrei' gave orations in Hebrew to the couple requesting tolerance for their Jewish subjects.[140] Jewish ethnicity became on such occasions a theatrical spectacle in which the Jews participated on terms dictated by Christians. Such apparent 'philo-Hebraism' does not, however, indicate a relaxation of what Christian princes saw as part of their spiritual jurisdiction. On the contrary, the increased visibilty and 'fashionability' of Jewish culture in the late *quattrocento* may testify to a more thoroughgoing concern with its control and surveyance by secular and ecclesiastical authority. The Jews were induced to play the role of living antiquities, to perform and make visibly manifest their ethnic difference, their anachronistic status under Christendom. Such performances included the spectacle of the Jews' inevitable defeat in religious argument. In 1487, for instance, we find Ercole d'Este organi-sing a theological debate before the court between a rabbi, a Dominican and a Franciscan.[141]

I believe that it is on a spectrum which encompasses philology, mysticism and court spectacle that we can locate Costa's *St Sebastian* (plate 17). Here the signature draws directly on the association between Hebrew writing and mysterious meaning; in the disguising or encrypting of his name, the artist makes of his own identity a form of exotic masquerade. The lavish Solomonic allusions of Tura's altarpiece may also be said to show a simultaneous concern with the demonstration of marvellous artifice and a particular construction of the persona of the artist. For part of its audience the programmatic meaning may have been secondary to aesthetic effect, rather as it has been for Longhi and for generations of nineteenth- and twentieth-century art historians who have regarded this painting entirely in terms of the idiosyncrasies of style, the capricious individualism of Cosmè Tura. Elements to which I have ascribed programmatic meaning could also be seen as a particular staging of self-conscious artifice through continual reference to the work of the hand, to virtuoso craftsmanship – writing, goldsmithing, carving, drawing. The repetition of the horn motif is just such a sign which extends through repetition and formal arrangement into a possible realm of 'pure' artifice; the rhythmic repetitions of the horn shape, and the mimicking form of the shell above the throne and the viols played by the angels, suggest the kind of decorative embellishment later called the grotesque, of a similar kind to the decorations on the Corinthian piers and to what we know of the appearance of decorative arts produced for the court. An artistic persona also calls itself into being through what might be called provocation of the viewer through refusals of norms or violations of expected symmetries, as in the violent coloristic *contrapposto* of the classical architecture and the garments of the angels.

Artifice is continually thematised through allusion to the paradoxes of representation – the particular ambiguity, for example, of artifice within artifice. In the decoration of the throne we are invited to see not merely architecture but a literal shell, perilously suspended over the head of the Virgin on a delicate ribbon by two curiously animated angels, and 'real' fruit sprouting forth miraculously from gold cornucopias.

All of this may correspond to a particular kind of virtuoso display expected from a painter of Tura's stature, and in modern criticism this has been at the root of characterisations of the artist as a 'mannerist' or as a wayward provincial eccentric. Yet Tura's 'individualism', if it can ever be so-called, has also in a sense been pre-written for the painter; it makes itself known through a persona which has been borrowed from elsewhere. Tura's self-presentation is structured or predetermined by the symbolic context: once the imagery of the central panel is read allusively, he comes into being only by wearing the mask of King Solomon's divinely ordained artificer in the Jewish Bible. Moreover, the foregrounding of artifice can be seen as demanded by the iconographic context with its metaphors of artistic process and its assertion of the supremacy of the image over writing. In Ferrara the fashionability of an imaginary Hebrew antiquity

101 Lodovico Mazzolino, *Circumcision*. Vienna, Kunsthistorishes Museum.

can be seen as sustaining the emergence of the grotesque in painting. A generation after Tura, Lodovico Mazzolino produced numerous versions of the *Circumcision* and of *Christ among the Doctors* which can be seen almost as biblical genre pieces, oriental fantasies involving bizarre architecture, Hebrew script and a profusion of grotesque ornament (plate 101).[142]

Grotesquerie and theology become particularly undecidable in the case of the two cherubim who flaunt their infantile arousal over the head of the Virgin. I have already proposed a de-emphasis of their outrageous character by seeing them as symbolic of the 'resurrection of the flesh'. This may be appropriate for a religious painting with such a pronounced genital emphasis, firstly in the circumcision and secondly in the manner in which the Virgin's gesture recalls Pittorio's title 'Imago Virginis excitandis filium'.

The possibility of the relation of this motif to a funerary context is suggested by the appearance of similar ithyphallic putti on an exactly contemporary monument, the tomb of Lorenzo Roverella in the same church (plate 103). The putti here, who

clutch bunches of grapes and recline on the exterior arch (plate 102), are the work of Ambrogio da Milano who oversaw the assembly and completion of the tomb which was sent in pieces from the Rossellino workshop.[143]

But is the extension of the 'programme' the only means of interpreting this detail? Could we see it as related instead to a code of figuring artistry, a thematising of artistic licence through the metaphor of sexual licence? Although the erections can be seen by anyone close enough to read the inscriptions on the tomb or on the altarpiece, it is conceivable that they would easily elude the gaze of most viewers; despite careful restoration in the 1950s, the National Gallery catalogue entry on the panel of the *Virgin and Child with Musician Angels* is written as if in complete innocence of the painting's assertion of angelic sexuality.[144] Perhaps to an ordinary, uneducated worshipper the sexuality of putti (whether children or angels) is unproblematic, undisturbing, and hardly likely to strike the attention. Perhaps, on the other hand, the recognition of such a detail would have been self-implicating for a fifteenth-century viewer. To see an angel with the characteristics of a satyr would have been to surrender

102 Ambrogio da Milano, tomb of Bishop Lorenzo Roverella. Ferrara, San Giorgio. Detail of putto on extrados.

103 Antonio Rossellino and Ambrogio da Milano, tomb of Bishop Lorenzo Roverella. Ferrara, San Giorgio.

to the potential impurity of sensual perception, the sinfulness inherent in the intrinsic libidinousness of the gaze.

Such a detail appeals above all to a curiosity which detaches itself from the portraits, the Virgin, the predella scenes and all the activity at centre stage; it presents itself as a surprise or shock for the distracted or roving eye of the viewer. The cherub is 'discovered' with most facility by those who view other aspects of the painting as manifestations of visual curiosity, of the exotic or bizarre, who could appreciate the facetious character of the motif. Lodovico Carbone's collection of *Facezie*, dedicated to Borso d'Este in 1466, includes an anecdote which suggests that such incongruous details – the attribute of 'Santo Priapo' – are presented for the appreciation of a sophisticated, urbane and possibly irreverent wit, the capacity to perceive and to laugh at what others would not dare:

> Master Blasius of Parma, the greatest mathematician and astrologer, was notable for his playfulness. In reading a book, whenever he found anything worthy of note, he marked the spot not with a pointing hand but with Holy Priapus, saying that that member was more noteworthy than the hand, hence better for the recall of important points by the memory.[145]

In the most famous fifteenth-century account of pictorial curiosities, the censorious attack by St Antoninus of Florence, the painting of *curiosa* is particularly associated with a quality of excess which distracts the observer, and with the intrusion of strange, absurd or 'superfluous elements' in painting.[146] The motif of the cherubim, then, might be the one point in the painting where the assertion of artistic mastery points to its own fallen nature; while painting can reproduce the face of Christ, it also contains a dangerous sensual power, a snare for the beholder's attention, which might even be equated with the fallen theology of Judaism. Another way of thinking about this is that once the body is placed in opposition to the sign, or to inscription, an excess is produced which cannot be reduced to the rhetorical purpose. Although the new traditions of Renaissance realism in the rendering of the body gave a new force to visualisations of an incarnational the-ology, there are other irrepressible connotations which an artistic language of excess, like that in which Tura worked, might even be said to exploit. The body as truth is an unstable prescription within the Christian association of the body with inauthentic desire and deceitful appearance; it has ironically perverse implications for which this marginal motif might be the figure. The most famous deployment of the body as a sign of artistic licence and as an assertion of the Christian prerogative of representation occurs in the ceiling of the Sistine Chapel a generation later; once again, this is in the context of a programmatic refutation of Judaism, which is similarly characterised in terms of violence, rituals of bloodshed, the assault on bodily integrity. Yet the polemical assertion of the body on behalf of Christianity proved once again destabilising, with more far-reaching consequences. Michelangelo, who like Tura also grounded his claim to truth on the principle of licensed artifice, would finally encounter crisis, reaction and censorship in response to his own ambiguously sexual imagings of the human form.

On several possible levels, therefore, the Roverella altarpiece participates in the cultural conflicts and exchanges of Jews and Christians in late fifteenth-century Italy. It is a document of the cultural appropriation of Judaism and an ideological projection upon Judaism by religious and secular authority. It accomplishes this through a subtle transformation of the philo-Judaic, even philo-Semitic fashions of the court, and by co-opting the theatricalising of artifice in the work of the court's chief painter for its own rhetorical ends. Although seen by more than one scholar as yet another manifestation of court art in Ferrara, the employment of Tura should now perhaps be seen as a gesture of political competition by cultural means. In the memorialising of the Roverella family, proprietors of a virtual ecclesiastical state within the territories of the Duke of Ferrara, the altarpiece speaks from an independent political domain, one whose independence is being negotiated at the expense of the centralising, secular power of the court. The painting appeals to a viewer's curiosities and also, in the case of some beholders, it would have engaged their prejudices – against the Jews of Ferrara, and ultimately against the Este who protected them.

V

PAINTINGS FOR
THE CATHEDRAL OF FERRARA:
VISUAL POLEMIC AND THE USES OF
ART THEORY

THE FOUR CANVAS PANELS BY Cosmè Tura for the organ-shutters of Ferrara Cathedral (now in the Museo del Duomo) form part of a monumental commission of considerable importance, which required negotiation and co-operation among the leading civic and ecclesiastical authorities of the city. On 27 April 1465 a committee – consisting of Bishop Lorenzo Roverella, two canons of the cathedral, a member of the civic magistrature known as the Dodici Savi, a prominent citizen representing the *comune*, two musicians of the Este court, and a representative of Borso d'Este – drew up a contract with the organ builder Fra Giovanni da Mercatello. Fra Giovanni was to have made for the cathedral, within two years, 'a good and beautiful organ, elegantly embellished, having all the perfections one could want from an organ, as much in beauty as in the harmony of its voices'.[1] The friar, in fact, was to bear the responsibility and expense of everything pertaining to the construction and decoration of the organ except for the paintings on the shutters, which would be commissioned separately by the cathedral clergy.[2] The paintings were subsequently provided by Tura, to whom a payment is recorded on 2 June 1469.[3]

The organ was installed by 1470 'in the chapel behind the choir above Jesus Christ and the Twelve Apostles'.[4] Three years later the organ was provided with a new platform for the organist 'with inscription and mouldings in the antique manner' ('cum littere et cornixe a la anticha') and a new painting of the Twelve Apostles by the painter Bonzohane was added below. These alterations probably indicate that at this point in 1473 the organ was moved from the choir to a location of far greater public visibility where it appears in later records – over the eighth arch of the nave on the left from the main entrance. The organ was finally removed from this position and dismantled in 1712.[5]

Despite some surface losses and repainting, the four canvases are the most intact of Tura's monumental paintings.[6] They are somewhat sombre in tonality, because the canvas has tended to absorb the thin layers of oil paint; the areas of shadow in the strongly modelled figures appear more dense and opaque than was probably once the case. With large areas of purple, golden yellow and ultramarine, and accents of vermilion, the paintings would originally have presented a more opulent appearance. Beyond condition, obtaining a sense of how the paintings would have appeared in their original context presents additional problems: a prominent site in the cathedral, a famous instrument on which the cathedral's flourishing musical culture was centred, a group of sparsely documented inscriptions and images aligned with the organ – all of these would have affected how Tura's paintings were conceived and understood. The imposing twin diptychs of the *Annunciation* and the *St George* nevertheless provide a unique example of how Tura organised narrative compositions on a large scale, and how, through the command of gesture and expression, spacing and overlap, through unexpected internal symmetries and repetitions, the artist generated kinds of meaning which emerge directly from a concern with pictorial *scientia*, with the rhetorical properties unique to images. No other surviving works by Tura so fully manifest the artist's command of the techniques of pictorial illusion, of classical architectural ornament, of the principles of weight shift and the movement of the nude and draped human figure, and of a sculptural *all'antica* figurative style comparable with that of Mantegna.

The paintings have been relatively well served by interpretations. While critically examining some of these, this chapter will seek to re-situate Tura's imagery within the contemporary concerns of his audience and his clients, which are clearly alluded to in the paintings, and not least of which is the status of painting itself. Three claims of previous scholarship will be subjected to particular scrutiny – first, the relation of the images to a presumed 'absolutism' of Este self-imagery in works of art commissioned for non-courtly institutions; second, the relation of the images to contemporary events; third, the issue of secret meaning or enigma, the alleged relation of Tura's work to mystical or occult traditions.

In the first and second cases, with the depiction of St George, the city's patron saint, the image raises the issue of symbolic authority within the urban community. Who, in the case of this pictorial commission, might have best exploited the opportunity to appropriate the central figure of civic cult imagery as their own? In other words, how can we best characterise the involvement of the Bishop of Ferrara, especially drawing on the conclusions of the previous chapter regarding the Roverella family, their employment of Tura and their partisan co-opting of styles and symbols in their own public self-imagery?

In the third case, as with other works by Tura, the abundance of imagery which we might loosely and unsatisfactorily characterise as 'marginalia', and of depictions of human craftsmanship, raise questions of meaning, of the potentially metaphoric effects of ornament. Just as the allusions to calligraphy in Tura's painting bear the effect of both decorative pattern – the 'Daedalian hand' – and of secret writing, so too might the profusion of masks, dolphins, animals and fruit with which Tura embellishes his sacred narratives and Madonnas produce at least the *effect* of significance. The extent to which meaning should be pursued in Renaissance painting has been debated in recent scholarship, most usefully in relation to the conditions of beholding, and less so, perhaps, with regard to what artists 'really intended'.[7] Discussions of the requirements of patrons are frequently grounded on the very narrow specifications of contracts and throwaway comments in letters, rather than in the unique qualities of the image which are thereby rendered invisible or available only to 'aesthetic' appreciation. Frequently the discussion centres on the viability of distinguishing between ornamental and signifying elements, and it is true that contemporary beholders may have occasionally pondered this problem. We might recall Isabella d'Este's query to a humanist about a sample of hieroglyphic picture-writing he had sent her, where she asks whether 'certain flourishes' accompanying the figures were to be taken as decorative or as significant in the manner of conjunctions, prepositions and punctuation.[8] Yet the distinction may not itself have been valid for all *quattrocento* observers; scriptural exegetes and humanist readers of Vitruvius could on occasion assign meaning to elements of architectural form, but the symbolic association would be provisional and contextually bound. Yet the associations will not therefore be random; given a certain regard for context, there will be a predictability to the period's habit of figurative and metaphoric thinking and reading. Mariological imagery, for instance, had a rich visual poetics of its own, not always dependent on literary traditions; painted images both draw upon and influence the tradition of Marian poetry, which itself mediates between 'scholastic' exegetical concerns and the more vernacular world of romance and Christian legend.[9]

These issues are specially relevant in Tura's paintings because they sometimes seem to present the connection of ornament and significance as a challenge or invitation to the beholder; the effect is often to produce effects of mystification or enigma. Previous interpretation has aimed at an unravelling of the pictures' secrets. Yet Tura's painting may itself be about secret meaning, manifesting a certain indifference to or ironic distance from the content of the secret itself. To a certain extent, Tura's imagery fits the description which Michel de Certeau applies to the painting of Hieronymus Bosch:

> The secret of [the painting] is to make you believe that it possesses some sayable secret – or rather to promise one secret (meanings hidden from the understanding) in place of another (the enjoyment given to the eye). It paradoxically engenders its opposite, namely the commentary that turns each form into script and wants to fill that entire colored space with meanings in order to turn it into a page of writing, of discursive analysis.[10]

For de Certeau, Bosch's painting involves a 'conversion' of signs which imply knowledge or symbolic meaning from a 'referential' function to a 'poetic' one; 'the criterion of the beautiful replaces that of the true' and 'a chart of knowledge is converted into a garden of delights'. Yet de Certeau's account, while it rightly questions both the 'dictionary' and 'esoteric' approaches to iconography, fails to take account of two factors. One is the socially controversial and indeed politicised aspect of the 'chart of knowledge' which can be embedded in painterly fantasy, as we saw in the case of the Roverella altarpiece and the Belfiore Muses. The second is the nature of 'poetry', which de Certeau uses in a distinctly modernist and aesthetic sense. Yet poetry in the fifteenth century has the status of a form of knowledge, which, as we have seen, could be controversial; it is a style of metaphoric thought which while it might be informed by aspiration, desire and a straining against cultural norms – hence the controversial aspect – is systematic and often rhetorical in character. Poetic associations are not necessarily random or unconscious, but present a distinct ideological profile with wider implications. The association of the Christian Virtues of the Fonte Gaia with the seductive Muses of erotic elegy may now appear incongruous or surprising, but is understandable in terms of the humanist polemical concern with the defence of poetry. The association corresponds to a rhetorical trope known as 'catachresis' which can be rendered also as 'transumption', 'misuse' or 'irony': 'Through irony . . . entities can be characterized by way of negating on the figurative level what is positively affirmed on the literal level. The figures of the manifestly absurd expression (catachresis), such as "blind mouths," and of explicit paradox (oxymoron), such as "cold passion," can be taken as emblems of this trope.'[11] Ironic tension arises not just formally, in the unlikeness of the figure and its referent, but in the dissonance between two opposed systems of *cultural* values (in the case of the Belfiore

Muses the disjunction arises between modern ethical norms of self-restraint and the fantasy of pagan sensuality). Catachresis is one of the forms of metaphor available to painters as well as to poets, as we saw in the Ferrarese adaptation of the Fonte Gaia figures, and like its poetic equivalent it may point to broader social tensions – the dangerous contamination of sacred by profane imagings of the female body. The subject of irony is discussed more fully in the concluding section, entitled 'Painting and Irony', below.

Adducing a 'poetic' characterisation for elements of pictorial ornament, marginalia or curiosity does not place these features beyond discursivity, but opens a way of thinking about their significance within and beyond the painting. Poetic texts will be once again referred to here not as 'sources' or as ways of making dumb images speak, but because of common rhetorical (i.e. social) concerns, and because the poetic texts can point us more readily towards the preoccupations of contemporary beholders.

As we shall see, Tura's paintings for the cathedral are engaged with concerns and beliefs which might be termed 'hermetic'. They are not, however, de Certeau's 'hermetic hieroglyphics, interrelated by aesthetic rather than semantic relationships';[12] nor are they the underground, secret hermeticism imagined by several commentators on Ferrarese art and Renaissance astrological imagery. The paintings invoke a hermeticism disseminated and already interpreted in canonical texts well known to theologians and humanists – or in fact to anyone who read Augustine. The paintings furthermore do not necessarily allude to secrets known only to initiates, but engage a broader cultural tendency to recognise at least the outward form of secrecy and mystery. The paintings will be seen to bring together several discursive realms which share a concern with the meaningfulness and efficacy of the image: Christian theology, humanist art theory and poetics, and the controversial science of astrology. The works very 'paintedness' is pressed into service for polemical ends, as in the case of the Roverella altarpiece and the Belfiore Muses, but such a co-opting of the image once again produces a residual excess which is ironic, unsettling and even perverse in its effects. The waywardness of images is finally demonstrated for the beholder – a waywardness, it should be said, which is not recognisable only from the perspective of historical distance, appreciated only at the end of the twentieth century. It is proclaimed, in Tura's own time, by the very writer who is considered the great apologist for the value and dignity of art, but who also appears as an ironic detractor of artifice and its claims to authority – Leon Battista Alberti.

COMPOSITIONAL STRATEGY: VISION, VOICE, MARGINALIA

On a great right-to-left descending diagonal St George's horse lunges at the picture surface while the saint turns back to force the yielding dragon into submission with his lance; the shouting princess, rushing towards the left, away from the horse, turns her head to witness the dragon's defeat, restoring a sense of closure and containment to the diagonal plunge of the composition (plates 105 and 106). On the descending left to right diagonal are a mountain with three ranges of battlements, the uppermost including a monumental triple-arched gateway, beyond which can be seen a castellated enclosure, and, in a more prominent position, a campanile-like structure. The outer margins of this city are further marked by a gibbet with a corpse, the site of executions. On the spiralling mountain path, in a badly abraded portion of the painting, can be seen a small building with a bell-tower, together with the King of Libya and his court. Seven figures can be seen on the left-hand panel; one more is partly visible on the right. The king, father of the princess, is robed in purple and surrounded by dark-skinned figures dressed in red, all with hands joined in gestures of prayer. A kneeling, turbaned and bearded figure sleeps or meditates in the vicinity, his head supported on his arm. To his right three similarly attired figures have turned to flee. One makes a gesture of expostulation towards St George – perhaps because of the danger represented by the dragon, or because of the saint's victory over the monster?

The pious attitude of the court reflects St George's role as described in the Legenda aurea – as an evangelist and militant campaigner against paganism. In this account the king and his subjects are converted and baptised following George's slaughter of the dragon. The agitated figure of the princess might then appear somewhat anomalous against the already converted, unafraid, confident behaviour of her father and his retinue. Although frightened princesses have appeared before in representations of the subject, they have never been set in such pointed contrast with figures embodying immovable faith; it is far more common, in fact, for the princess to embody this virtue herself.[13]

The azure sky is saturated with a golden crepuscular light, which enhances the already detached and self-contained aspect of the St George panel by evoking the tradition of the Greek icon or gold-ground panel painting. On a tilted axis with the princess, the gesturing runaway figures and the gibbet appears a crescent moon. I have referred already in chapter 1 to the prominent surface calligraphy of the red bridle of St George's horse, which finds a counterpoint above right in the intertwined oak and gourd and an inverted reflection in the wings and neck of the dragon, with further echoes in the surface arabesques of the sweeping cliff path, the agitated drapery of the princess, her golden girdle and her long gathered and trailing hair. Two pieces of goldsmith's work are presented with a considerable degree of elaboration – the golden horn-like forms of the princess's headdress, and the saddle of St George, the front of which is adorned with a mask partly composed of plant-like forms which evoke the cusps of the shell in the central panel of the Roverella altarpiece.

On the interior of the shutters appears the Annunciation (plates 107 and 108). Now, between the viewer and the

105 and 106 Tura, Ferrara Cathedral organ-shutters. Exterior panels: *St George and the Princess*. On canvas (each 413 × 338 cm).

107 and 108   Tura, Ferrara Cathedral organ-shutters. Interior panels: *Annunciation*.

unboundaried pictorial space, the wild and labyrinthine landscape and the surface-defying energy of the exterior, a more regimented scheme of architectural and perspective order has been imposed. Cities now appear in the far distance, near the horizon behind the Virgin, or on the crest of a towering rock formation. The landscape, divided by a river yet seemingly barren, is inhabited by shepherds and fishermen. Both intensely plastic figures are variations on the same pose, and in the axial conception of the pose and disposition of the members recall Tura's most significant experiment with the *contrapposto* of the kneeling figure – the London *St Jerome* (plate 62). Since the two panels flanked the pipes of the organ, the Virgin and angel may not necessarily be read as occupying adjacent spaces, but parallel barrel-vaulted aisles or chambers of a temple or basilica, perhaps interrupted by a nave. Or, as Didi-Huberman has written of Giotto's *Annunciation* in the Arena Chapel at Padua: 'These places are different since they are well separated in the church, and since common sense could not imagine that two bodies could occupy the same physical space; but they are also in a certain (virtual) way *the same*, indicating that where the angel's message is uttered, there too the divine Word is incarnated.'[14] The issue of perspective space deliberately rendered implausible or 'mysterious' is discussed more fully below.

The stasis and silence of this interior scene contrasts with the violence and turmoil of the exterior, with its shouting and gesturing people, furious animals, and dynamic diagonal compositions. The one sound, however, constitutes the only apparent action in the scene of the *Annunciation* – the angel's lips are parted as he utters his salutation. The Virgin's role as listener is reinforced by her praying, contemplative pose – she does not look at or even appear to see Gabriel – and by the figuring of Christ's Incarnation as taking place through the Holy Spirit's penetration of her ear. The auricular impregnation of the Virgin, a long-standing theological commonplace based on the scriptural figures of angelic speech and Divine *logos*, is at this time an artistic and theological rarity. Painting had long evolved a metaphorics of its own based on the action of the visible property – light.[15] Among all representations of the Incarnation of Christ, only Tura's so blatantly shows the dove assailing the ear of the Virgin, and underscores the carnal dimension of the miracle through a vocabulary of images imported from secular and even 'pagan' contexts. Tura has surrounded the Virgin with the signs of fleshliness, fecundity and pregnability that he had already employed in the Belfiore *studio* of the Muses. From the spandrels bundles of pears, their leaves withered since the previous autumn, are suspended in two striped white cloths; spiny golden dolphins form the volutes of the Corinthian capitals, and, as the Word becomes Flesh in the body of the Virgin, the laces of her red dress come undone with the instantaneous swelling of her womb.

Yet while dolphins, fruit and unlaced clothing have determinable associations in other works by this painter, what sense, if any, might be intended by the black squirrel, tethered to a column by a red cord and perched above the Virgin?[16] Since the squirrel's symbolic associations – rapacity, appetite, lust – are undesirable or inappropriate for this context, does it signify no more than the painter's (squirrel-hair) brush? Or does its presence signal a kind of errancy in any attempt to read meaning in details, to see the vain trappings of pictorial ornament as having anything to do with the sacred mystery which is being enacted but mystified, revealed but re-veiled, in the pictorial narrative? Can this painting, or any painting, really tell us how the Incarnation happened, or does it not rather symbolically clarify the form of a secret without disclosing its content?[17] *Conceptio per aurem* was itself a figure which served precisely *not* to explain how the Incarnation took place through an irrational proposition. Church fathers like Zeno of Verona had connected the narrative of Gabriel's greeting in Luke 1:28 with John 1:14: 'And the Word was made Flesh and dwelt among us' – with Gabriel understood as the mediator of the Divine *logos* which enters the Virgin's womb through her ear.[18] Such a formulation was given a literal treatment in Marian poetry and art of the later Middle Ages: 'Quod lingua jecit semen est/ in carne verbum stringitur' ('What the tongue uttered is a seed, in the flesh the word is gathered').[19] Metaphor, in other words, is given the status of mystery.

The Christian, however, is counselled not to seek too deeply into this central mystery of the faith; to dwell on the *quomodo* of Christ's conception and birth beyond the metaphors provided by the Fathers of the Church was a form of improper curiosity. The symbolic potential of Tura's marginalia seems itself to indicate this taboo, a caution against reading too far, straying into the margins. It is noteworthy that the Virgin is shown reading, contemplating the written word and giving ear to the Divine *logos* rather than looking at the angelic apparition or the various manifestations of human image-making which surround her, least of all the dancing, gesturing naked figures on the walls of the temple. In all respects she embodies exemplary feminine behaviour, recalling a well-born lady praying from her Book of Hours. Although the kind of noblewoman who might keep a squirrel as a pet, and whose Hours might be embellished with pictorial fantasies which engage and ensnare the eye, it is clear where and how she is focusing her attention.

The apocryphal stories of the Virgin contain several instances of the deadly consequences of curiosity regarding her miraculous maternity.[20] The very narrative of the Annunciation itself in Luke's Gospel shows the angel checking Mary's initial curiosity which turns into submissive assent.[21] The sense of a deadly secrecy which cannot be represented or beheld is suggested by the four petrified faces adorning the dados on which stand the columns of the temple. The stony severed heads, with closed eyes and monstrous snaky protruberances, belong in the realm of fleshliness and sexual power to which the other 'marginal' imagery has already directed us, in that it recalls the 'Medusa effect' in the paintings of the Belfiore Muses. They also, however, recall the *aegis*, the apotropaic armour of a virgin goddess.

A number of connections and analogies might now be referred to between the interior and exterior narratives: a similar carved mask appeared already on the front of St George's saddle;

and the golden dolphins of the temple capitals are only slight transformations of the golden horns worn by the princess. A determinate system of values hence begins to structure the associations produced by particular motifs: dolphins recall the exotic bodily adornments of a pagan princess, while Gorgonesque masks have formed a screen or a shield to the virginity of a Christian knight about to rescue and convert her. Similarly, the masks might signify the protection of Mary's virginity and of the mystery which surrounds it.

As we scan the image, as looking becomes reading, symbols beckon for decipherment while yielding not elucidation but further concealment. At the same time, a range of symbolic parallels and oppositions is beginning to appear: order and tumult, stasis and violent motion, noise and silence, the spiritual word and the sensual image, the haloed virgin saint and virgin mother and the horned pagan princess. Seeing is opposed to listening and inward contemplation, which is the demeanour of the Virgin and of the court of the King of Libya. Seeing is associated with curiosity and with fear – those who see the dragon flee in a panic; those who contemplate the visible stone mask rather than the invisible, inaudible word of the angel are 'mystified', paralysed, understand no further. Bearing in mind that the paintings adorned an organ, the concept which affirms the limits of vision and the special efficacy of listening has a peculiar force.

The location in which the event takes place is not readily identifiable; it appears to combine elements of a domestic and a ritual setting. Given the classical architecture, we might designate the *locus* of the event as a temple.[22] The portion of the structure we can see is ornamented with three green and three red columns, disposed with a coloristic asymmetry employed by Tura for the temple structure he designed for the Roverella altarpiece. The visible walls of the temple each bear four gilded panels with scantily draped or nude figures in grisaille. Although their status as sculpture is implied, the figures flout the logical appearance of both relief and free-standing sculpture as they should be seen under the perspective conditions established by the architecture. Each horizontal pair of figures represents an entire interval of depth represented by the diminution of the background from the foreground column, which suggests that their head-on appearance, if we could look at them from 'inside' the painted space, would present all the distortions of an anamorphosis. If in high relief, the degree of disengagement from the ground is ambiguous (plate 111). The bodies seem to project into 'real' space, almost like free-standing sculptures fastened to the wall, yet their feet seem to inhabit the internal, fictive space within the frame. Whether Tura is intentionally creating a visual paradox or not, something about the inclusion of these figures has necessitated a deliberate suspension of the principals of order and measure normally associated with the geometric construction of space.

The figures are classical pagan divinities represented in an *all'antica* pastiche, in a series of vigorous *contrapposto* variations whose identities and attributes are precisely specified in almost every case. Diana, with an expression of intense concentration, holds her crescent moon aloft; beside her a turbaned Apollo, with

his back turned, shields a firebrand with his mantle (plate 110). Facing them a nude Venus (plate 111), an instance of the *figura serpentinata* thirty years before its supposed invention by Leonardo (plate 109), with hair spiralling upwards like a snake, grimaces in the direction of the Virgin and makes a curious gesture with her crossed arms. Jupiter nearby frowns and draws himself upwards on tiptoe as he prepares to release his eagle (plate 111). Below this pair is a sombre bearded figure, identifiable as Saturn, whose left hand draws attention to the curious knotting of his drapery; beside him a figure without attributes, striking the most complex pose of all, steadies himself against the frame with one foot as he balances on the tip of another, his face a mournful grimace (plate 111). On the other side, behind the angel, appears a rather apathetic Mars bearing a baton, and, almost completely covered by the angel's wing, a figure whose tasseled boots and right-hand gesture are alone visible (plate 110). Although his identification might appear to be obvious from the foregoing, especially as his gesture duplicates that of the angel who eclipses him, it forms what might be considered to be a crucial point of debate about this

109 After Leonardo da Vinci. *Leda and the Swan*. Rome, Galleria Borghese.

painting, and hence will be deferred until previous contributions on the interpretation of the image have been reviewed.

The sense of a disjunction between canonical subjects and Tura's treatment of them has necessitated particular reading strategies on the part of art historians committed to the priority of a unitary and paraphrasable iconographic text. The artist's deforming and defamiliarising technique, the plenitude of intriguing detail and distracting marginalia, are taken to point towards a subtext of 'hidden meanings', as if at some deeper level the undesirable anomalies that haunt Tura's work could be reconciled by assuming an underlying murmur of hermetic knowledge, esoteric beliefs, secrets and heresies. The pioneering study in this regard was Enrico Guidoni and Angela Marino's 'Cosmus Pictor' which appeared in *Storia dell'arte* in 1968.[23] The system of beliefs which the authors maintain to have pre-existed and determined the image of the cathedral paintings is reconstructed by them through an interpretative syncretism which recalls the procedures of Florentine Neoplatonists in the late *quattrocento*. Marsilio Ficino himself is a major figure in their account; not just the Ficino of the *Pimander* (which the authors believe to have been known in Ferrara on the basis of a court library inventory of 1495),[24] but the later Ficino of the *Theologia platonica*, together with various works by Pico della Mirandola, seventeenth-century alchemical texts and a play about St George dating from 1653. Hermes, alchemy, astrology, 'Pythagoreanism' and the tarot are all raided to produce a core of meaning which merely figures the desire that Guidoni and Marino's text interpretative strategy enacts. The painting is finally about harmony, the reconciliation of opposites, the unity of the manifold. The *armonia* of spirit, cosmos and humanity revealed in the miracle of the Incarnation is confronted with and seen to assimilate the temporality, conflict and difference of *storia*, human history, which is represented in the legend of St George.

It is not my purpose to respond here to these and other authors' metaphysical speculations about *armonia*, the confirmation of which ultimately relies on faith rather than demonstration. I wish instead to consider a number of conclusions presented in previous scholarship regarding the painting's relation to contemporary history and culture, before proceeding to an interpretation of the organ-shutters in which Tura's artifice itself becomes rhetorically 'charged' as an agent of meaning.

First, Guidoni and Marino regard the St George scene as a panegyrical celebration of Borso d'Este. According to this assertion, repeated by Marco Bertozzi and Enrica Domenicali,[25] the act of killing the dragon corresponds to Borso's princely wisdom in sponsoring schemes of drainage and land reclamation, by means of which the 'dragon' of pestilence is overcome. The painting is also seen to commemorate the 'Borsian Addition' to the city, completed in 1466, which extended the city walls towards the south-west and the ancient monastery of San Giorgio – the walled mountain in the background of the painting would then be an idealised city-portrait of Ferrara.[26]

Second, St George is seen to represent the rallying of Christendom for a crusade against the forces of Muhammad II, who were menacing the eastern frontiers of Europe and who were believed ready to descend upon a disunified and ill-prepared Italy, whose princes intrigued against each other and ignored the Pope's call for a united resistance against the enemy.

Third, the monochrome figures of pagan divinities represent the seven planets and the Eighth Sphere; the juxtaposition of Gabriel with the planet-god behind him represents, according to the doctrine of the horoscope of religions derived from the astrological works of Albumasar, the conjunction of Jupiter with Mercury which signified the Birth of Christ.[27]

Fourth, the apparition in the rock formation behind the angel is identified as a sphinx, explicitly evoking the religion of ancient Egypt.[28]

ST GEORGE AND THE ESTE

If the combat of the saint and dragon celebrates Borso d'Este it does so in a rather subtle and far from explicit way, which might make one wonder about its effectiveness as dynastic propaganda. In fact, there are no recognisable Este symbols visible on the organ-shutters. The fact that the Este on a rare couple of occasions may have implicitly identified themselves with the patron saint of Ferrara does not provide a basis for assuming that the evocation works in reverse.[29] The cult of the saint in the area of the Po valley which became the Este state has its origins in the sixth century.[30] The saint's image as a warrior and dragon-slayer appears in a portal lunette from the cathedral of Ferrara dating from the early twelfth century, around the time of the transfer of the episcopal seat from the more ancient foundation of San Giorgio outside the city. Thereafter the saint was most strongly identified with the cathedral and its resident clergy; the lay community gravitated towards the cult of another warrior-saint, St Romanus, while the old feudal episcopacy which sought its authority in the arch-diocese of Ravenna developed the cult of St Maurelius, the martyred Bishop of Ferrara, from the old basilica outside the city.

St George, however, continued to figure prominently in manifestations of collective identity by the different orders of Ferrarese society. The famous *palio* race was run on his local feast-day, 23 April. On this day from 1287 onwards an offering of wax was made at the cathedral by the city's subject *comuni* and by religious orders and other groups within the city. St George recurs constantly in artistic commissions for the cathedral, notably in the choral books illuminated by Jacopo Filippo d'Argenta, while on the great choir screen of 1454–66, a joint commission of the bishop and magistrature, gilt bronze statues of George and Maurelius flanked a crucifixion group with the Virgin and St John.[31] The Este certainly benefited from and encouraged the state-centralising impulses generated by the cult; in 1457 Borso decreed that even the various *comuni* of the Este state which lay beyond Ferrarese territory would henceforth participate in the offering of wax on the eve of St George's Day.[32]

111 (*previous page*) Tura, Ferrara Cathedral organ-shutters. Interior, right-hand panel: *Annunciation*. Detail of the planetary divinities and the Eighth Sphere (Pantomorphos) (see plate 108).

This court appropriation of St George nevertheless avoided direct identification, and maintained the appearance of a respectful non-interference in an institution of the *comune*, a familiar feature of Este policy.

I would maintain therefore that the image of St George painted on the organ-shutters represents, to the people and the cathedral chapter of Ferrara, a personified image of their community and its spiritual leadership. The bishop is evoked by the oak branch above the saint's shoulder which denotes the Roverella *stemma*, while the court, if it appears here at all, can only be in the guise of the pious grouping who pray silently for their protection by the saint. A series of ideal social relations might be seen to be figured – ecclesiastical solidarity, together with reverence and non-interference by the secular power. Such themes would have had particular resonance in a decade when church and state in Ferrara were locked in a controversy regarding the municipal taxation of the clergy, the appropriation of church property by the princes and nobility, and the contributions levied on the secular powers by the Papacy towards the war against the Turks.

The harmony of church and state is one of the principal themes of the story of St George and the dragon in the *Legenda aurea*. Following the combat the converted King of Libya caused a great church to be built in honour of the Blessed Virgin and St George, and, before taking his leave, George teaches the king four things – 'ut ecclesiarum Dei curam haberet, sacerdotes honoraret, divinum officium diligenter audiret et semper pauperum memor esset' ('to care for the church of God, to honour the priests, to hear the divine office reverently, and to have the poor always in mind').[33] It is interesting to note in this regard that the cathedral of Ferrara was jointly dedicated to the Virgin and St George.

That the decoration of the organ might have involved the self-imaging of the cathedral clergy is further suggested by the fact that on two occasions the organ is documented as being associated with an image of the Twelve Apostles. The first, in the choir, preceded the installation of the instrument, and the second, probably in the nave, was painted by Bonzohane in 1473. The theme of the Twelve Apostles and its preserved association with the organ was evidently a matter of some importance; the image of the first bishops may be seen as an assertion of identity by Lorenzo Roverella, while the Chapter of Canons could have taken the apostles as the archetype for a clerical brotherhood like their own.

CRUSADE AND CONVERSION

That the image of St George refers to contemporary preoccupations with a crusade is a hypothesis which it would be difficult to resist. St George, the archetypal crusader saint, is synonymous with the theme of military force exercised on behalf of the church. His legend refers to his victories in the sign of the cross, his service in 'the war in Palestine', his apparition to the crusaders during the siege of Jerusalem. The cause of a crusade had been promoted with considerable urgency by successive Popes and by Cardinal Bessarion since the fall of Constantinople in 1453. Pius II had died at Ancona in August 1464, tended by his physician Lorenzo Roverella, while about to lead personally the Christian fleet against Muhammad II. On 17 November the previous year Pius had appointed Lorenzo his official treasurer for the enterprise.[34] Paul II pursued a different strategy, throwing the support of the church behind the princes who fought the Turks on the frontiers of Europe. A proposed levy on behalf of Matthias Corvinus of Hungary (which was to include 20,000 ducats from Ferrara and Modena and 50,000 from Florence) was ignored or defied by the Italian states who demanded unfavourable conditions in return.[35] Paul was moreover constantly alarmed that Naples or Venice had long been prepared to make terms of their own with Muhammad II.[36]

The Pope used the proximity of the Turkish threat to further Papal authority among the disunited forces of Christendom, and to secure collective action against the internal enemies of the Holy See. His reign is noted for actions against the *fraticelli* and the Hussite heretics of Bohemia, for warfare with princes of the Papal State including the Malatesta and the Count of Anguillara, and a final disastrous confrontation in 1469 with the combined forces of Florence, Rimini and Naples. A sense of his priorities is evident from the fact that despite significant Turkish successes in Albania, Wallachia and Slavonia from 1464, Paul chose to prosecute a war against the heretic George Podiebrad, King of Bohemia, excommunicated in 1466. Matthias Corvinus was enjoined to depose Podiebrad instead of uniting with him against the Ottoman advance. By December 1470, however, Paul II was reminding Borso d'Este of the obligations of the Italian princes to contribute 'to the Christian army united against those impious Turkish dogs, for it has been promised to us numerous times'.[37]

Brothers Lorenzo and Bartolomeo Roverella were energetic servants of the Papal cause, both with regard to the renewed commitment to a crusade after 1467 and the more self-seeking moves against those who challenged Papal authority.[38] In 1467 Lorenzo assisted Bartolomeo Colleoni in the command of the armies of Florentine exiles against the Medici, and in 1468 Bartolomeo resolved a territorial conflict with King Ferrante of Naples.[39] On 22 June 1467 Lorenzo was appointed Papal Nuncio to Germany, where he had embarked on a mission concerning the crusade.[40] On the same mission the Bishop of Ferrara proclaimed an indulgence for all who took part in the war against Podiebrad either personally or through donations; he also succeeded in preventing an alliance between Bohemia and Hungary.

Lorenzo's various missions on behalf of Paul II caused him to be generally absent from Ferrara, although he was present for the commissioning of the organ in 1465 and he held a diocesan synod there in 1466; he could therefore have been personally involved in contracting Tura at that point. Between 1470 and 1474, however, Lorenzo was resident for at least one significant period in Ferrara, when he would have seen the organ with its complete decorative ensemble and may have been instrumental in having it moved to the nave.[41] Lorenzo's nephew Filiasio Roverella, the future Archbishop of Ravenna, was a canon of the cathedral and may have served to ensure that his uncle's personal interests and agendas were represented in the proceedings of the chapter.[42]

In the light of Lorenzo's particular services to the Papacy, the imagery of the organ-shutters, which he would have been well positioned to influence, signifies the imperative of Christian unity in the face of the Ottoman threat. For an observer before this painting around 1470, the images of warrior saint, princess and dragon would have had powerful symbolic or literal evocations of recent events. The Turkish threat was constantly figured as a 'venomous dragon', among others by Pius II in the bull which summoned the princes of Europe to the Congress of Mantua in 1459.[43] The ornate headgear of the princess probably alludes to the Golden Horn, the area of water north of Constantinople, while a famous spur on the Bosphorous was called the Arm of St George.[44] While St George alludes to the Papal enterprise of the crusade, the pious king may have recalled the fugitive and supplicant Greek Orthodox princes of the East who had fled the Turkish advance and come to beseech aid from the Pope with pledges of conversion.[45] Thomas Paleologus, 'the Despot of the Morea', was one such fugitive prince; his usurping brother had sacrificed his daughter in marriage to Muhammad II to secure a favourable peace. Another female figure of celebrated pathos was Thomas's niece Charlotte Lusignan, the young Queen of Cyprus, who journeyed through Italy from October 1461 to August 1462 to solicit aid for her beleaguered husband.[46]

The enemy with whom the saint is engaged, however, is not only Islam, but all heretics, rebels and schismatics, including Hussites and Greeks, who undermine the unity of Christianity and its submission to Papal authority. While the pious king and his entourage – held up, I would argue, as an exemplar to Borso d'Este and his court – signify the proper deference of Christian princes, the fleeing 'orientals' might be seen to represent enemies and dissidents routed by the appearance of the holy crusader, or the disarray and despair of the unconverted who scatter at the approach of the dragon: the fatalism of the Greeks was reported by eye-witnesses at the siege of Constantinople as contributing to the quick defeat of the city.[47] An anonymous treatise composed in Rome in 1452, which urges Christians to aid the Greeks notwithstanding their treachery, proposes that 'it is better to tolerate the Greeks, just as the Church tolerates prostitutes for the sake of avoiding a greater evil'.[48]

The groupings of figures in the left-hand panel broadly thematise schism, contrasting faith and confidence with fear and perfidy. The princess herself appears right on the hiatus of this opposition, between the converted/faithful and the unconverted/schismatics. Her posture could even be said to incorporate the division of responses between the two groups – at the same time as she rushes away from the scene of the battle, she turns to witness the saint's victory. I would further claim that her embodiment as the principle of conversion (a leading motif

of the legend of St George) is indicated in the figures behind her, and has implications, as will be shown, for Tura's conception of the *Annunciation*. Tura's portrayal of the princess, with her fantastic headgear, her gold and jewels, her swirling layers of drapery and her serpentine coils of hair underscores the fact that she is an *oriental* princess, a type of exotic otherness bearing associations of paganism, luxury and venery. Horns in particular might have invoked a level of excess in female adornment – horned hairstyles received particular censure from the preachers and in the 1450s were forbidden by the sumptuary laws of at least two cities, Florence and Savona.[49]

The oriental princess presented in such terms has a particular typological resonance, above all because of numerous biblical passages of patriarchal spleen in which such a type personifies a Jerusalem, an Israel, or a Babylon, characterised in terms of a wanton luxury whose punishment and conversion is prophesied. Contemporary preachers such as the famous Roberto da Lecce (who was caricatured by Janus Pannonius, as described on p. 53 above) held up the fate of the wanton Constantinople as a warning to Italy: 'O poor Italy, o dissolute Italy, fear God and do penance. You have the example of unfortunate Greece, in her current state. Constantinople, who was it ever gave you into the hands of the Grand Turk? It was your lack of goodness, your luxury, your infidelity.'[50] A Franciscan chronicler who asserted that 'the city perished through its avarice' found the city's luxury emblematised by one rich male citizen, but more spectacularly by 'a woman [who] could be found there worth 150 million ducats in jewels and silver and fabrics and coin'.[51]

For a contemporary beholder Tura's princess could recall the captive Constantinople, punished for her apostasy and luxury. She may also, however, represent the decadence of a Western church in need of reform, a matter of immediate concern to Lorenzo Roverella with his pastoral visits and synods devoted to the castigation of luxury among his diocesan clergy.[52] Above all, the theme of reform and conversion might have spoken with particular pointedness to the court. Borso and the other Este princes frequently had to endure, with a proper pious demeanour, the 'advice' of their more zealously reform-minded subjects. The homiletic exhortation to shun vainglory and luxury was a constant motif of several modes of literary address to the prince by the end of Borso's reign. The marquis was treated to such exhortations by the Grand Inquisitor of Lombardy, by the Franciscan theologian and chronicler Giovanni da Ferrara, by Pius II and Paul II.[53] His nephew and for a time heir-apparent Niccolo di Leonello received invectives against hunting by the court physician Michele Savonarola, while his favourite Teofilo Calcagnini appears as an interlocuter in a sobering dialogue on divine providence by Francesco d'Ariosto Peregrino, in which he is enjoined to contemplate the struggle of angels and demons for his soul.[54] In 1444, at the court of Leonello d'Este, the same author appears as one of the pioneers of neo-Latin drama with the performance of his play *In Isidis religionem elegia* for the wedding festivities of the prince and Maria of Aragon. Ariosto subsequently dedicated the work to Borso d'Este.[55] The theme of the play is the conversion of the

112 Tura, Ferrara Cathedral organ-shutters. *St George and the Princess*. Detail of plate 105.

beautiful libertine Isis, who relinquishes her wealth, her companions and her several lovers when called to repentance by a 'divine orator' who teaches her 'to disdain this world'. Behind the character Isis stands the shadow not only of the ancient Egyptian goddess but of the orgiastic cults of the orient, now superseded by Christian asceticism.[56] While seen as a form of humanist *sacra rappresentazione* the play is also clearly itself a conversion or rehabilitation of Latin elegy and drama to Christian ends; it is written only three years before Guarino (who was also mindful of the pronouncements of 'divini oratores') produced his description of the chaste and sober Muses. The most substantial speaking part in the play is that of Carinus Adolescens, whose name is derived from the character of a youth in Terence's *Andria*. The characterisation of his interlocuter Isis, however, the converted oriental libertine, is highly suggestive with regard to Tura's princess and how she might have been perceived. Isis presents her conversion as a disrobing from her oriental finery:

> And he taught me to cover my vain hair with veils, and, thus conquered, to tear my purple cheeks. A collar of gems and amulets used to ornament my brow; in place of amulets and gems the holy cross was given to me. He even ordered me to put off my garments of figured embroidery, and their use has been changed to the golden robes of the priests.[57]

Further on she presents herself as an example for other *nymphae*:

> I advise you, O young girls, who are tormented by a vain bitterness, I advise you that Christ, a sweeter lover, will torment you. Forsake, O chaste ones, the coils of the twisting serpent and willingly forsake the paths of the winding labyrinth.[58]

Most strikingly for the analogy with Tura's princess, Isis at one point looks back on her 'impetuous life' employing the term 'petulca' – a word normally translated as 'butting with the head' and applied to horned animals such as goats.[59]

Despite enticing parallels I am not proposing that Francesco Ariosto's Isis was a direct model for Tura's princess, and much of the imagery through which both are characterised is generic to the theme of *vanitas* and *conversio*. Yet the play does show some of the associations the theme of princess and serpent may have held for sections of Tura's audience, above all for the court at which it may have been directed – the redemption from the idolatry of luxury and of false beliefs.[60] The spiralling curves in the landscape and even in Tura's drawing, the sense of barely contained chaos in the movement of the figures, point to an earthly experience figured in terms of errancy, disorder, ambiguity and violence, a premonition of the labyrinthine 'selve oscure' later described by Ariosto's more famous nephew in *Orlando furioso*. The meaning of the princess might also be determined by the contrast of this labyrinthine milieu with the rectilinear structure of the interior and by her contrast with the serene and modestly attired Virgin Mary. It is also striking, in the light of Ariosto's text, that the princess's purple and ultramarine costume has indeed been 'converted', in the scene of the *Annun-*

ciation, into the sacramental vestments of Gabriel and the reversed blue and purple dress of the Virgin.

THE ASTROLOGICAL HYPOTHESIS

The *Annunciation* as enacted in Tura's painting occurs in juxtaposition with a representation within a representation. That the statues represent the planets in the eightfold Ptolemaic division of the cosmos, personified as eight pagan divinities, is beyond doubt, as is the fact that an astrological note is being sounded, an analogy between angelic and astral mediation proposed in the harmony of the angel's gesture with that of the carved deity behind him (plate 110).

What is not evident, however, in the absence of more precise biographical information about the artist and his patrons and advisers, is the kind and degree of commitment to astrology which is being proposed here. This is crucial for the contemporary circumstance of the work's creation, when any public statement of the relation between astrology and theology was problematic, and in which Tura's association of the central mystery of the *Annunciation* with a controversial science and with the images of paganism has no parallel.[61]

Guidoni and Marino, and after them Bertozzi, have provided an interpretation of the painting's astrological argument which is incorrect in its reading of particular details and results in some rather sensationalised conclusions. I would agree that any inclusion of astrological elements in this canonical subject may situate the image in controversial territory, and that Tura's handling of the subject may at times be generative of subversive or ironic effects. However, I will also show in what follows that on the level at which the image may have been comprehensible to, say, Lorenzo Roverella and the canons of the cathedral, the painting is far more cautious, indeed cautionary, regarding the advocacy of astrology. Tura's painting may have satisfied the orthodox requirements of his clients; nevertheless, the image is equivocal, and does not bind all spectators to a single level of understanding.

Guidoni and Marino identify the carved figure behind Gabriel, who repeats the angel's gesture of benediction, as Jupiter – the god with the eagle is somehow to be taken as a personification of the sun.[62] Regarding the figure as Jupiter led them to see in the juxtaposition with the angel the pictorial figure of a planetary conjunction as explicated by Albumasar, the much celebrated and frequently maligned ninth-century astronomer of Baghdad, whose works circulated widely in Latin editions from the late thirteenth century. In their interpretation Mercury, in the person of the angel Gabriel, is seen to conjoin with Jupiter – the figure eclipsed by the angel – signifying and determining the great historical revolution of Christ's appearance on earth and the institution of Christianity. As we have seen, however, Tura's figures are securely recognisable by their attributes; the only possible ambiguity lies in deciding which of the two figures immediately behind the Virgin and the angel represents Mercury, and which the Eighth Sphere. On the basis of the gesture of greeting or blessing appropriate for the messenger of the gods, the figure partly obscured by the angel can only logically be Mercury. Assigning Mercury to this position allows a planetary order to be determined, but rather than the order of the planetary spheres, the sequence is clearly calendrical, following the days of the week. Above the angel we find the order of *dies Solis*, *dies Lunae*, *dies Martiis*, *dies Mercuriis*; behind the Virgin, with a slight change of sequence, are *dies Giovem*, *dies Veneris* and *dies Saturnis*.

The identity of Mercury is, however, not immediately evident, since any reference to his most constant and famous attribute – the *talaria* or winged sandals – is omitted. Instead, this god wears open-toed boots with tassels. Once the structural principal of the days of the week is grasped, however, his identity is unmistakable. Whatever analogy is at issue between the divine messengers of Christianity and Olympus is being proposed in rather discreet terms. Perhaps this serves to restrict the sphere of recognisability, to de-limit the audience who will grasp the analogy among those who view the image. Such discretion may have been occasioned because the visual association between the Incarnation of Christ and a planetary god would have called up a number of potentially heretical notions – chiefly that Christ, and Christianity itself, were subject to astral determinism (or to Fate).[63]

Certain philosophers who had attacked astrology, such as Nicole Oresme, reserved some measure of credibility for the stellar forecasts of great earthly events.[64] On the other hand, theologians such as Cardinal Pierre d'Ailly, who wrote on the harmony of theology and astrology, attacked earlier authorities such as Roger Bacon for pronouncing Christianity subject to the planet Mercury; although d'Ailly accepted stellar 'participation' in the forming of the human nature of Christ, he asserted (perhaps defensively) that Judaism and Christianity were of divine origin and hence transcended the influence of natural law and the stars.[65] Henry of Langenstein and Pico della Mirandola, writing a century apart, both implicitly or explicitly attacked the doctrine of conjunctions, both in relation to secular historical events and to the fortunes of religions.[66] Those who engaged in discussions of the horoscope of the religions, such as Giovanni de Fundis in the mid-fifteenth century and Francesco Padovano in the 1470s, generally did so with disclaimers regarding astral influence on Christ's birth, carefully distinguishing their positions from the determinism of Albumasar and Roger Bacon, and distancing themselves from the pronouncements on Christ's horoscope which had led the astrologer Cecco d'Ascoli to the stake in 1327 and to the posthumous burning of the bones of Pietro d'Abano in the middle of the century.[67] The disclaimer attributed to Giovanni de Fundis, in a treatise which defended astrology against Oresme, is characteristic: Christ, he says, appeared on earth not through the virtue of a conjunction such as marked the appearance of the prophets of other religions, but through the operation of Divine Providence. 'But', he adds, 'if you will not rest content with this but wish to judge concerning our faith, you will calculate the great conjunction which preceded the advent of Christ'.[68]

In 1465, the year in which the Ferrara Cathedral organ was commissioned, James of Speyer (astrologer to Federico, Count of Urbino) challenged the great mathematician Regiomontanus to calculate the year of Christ's birth on the basis of the great conjunction which had preceded it, and to explain the manner of his death and the nature of his teachings from the planetary influences.[69] These questions, which touched on the forbidden question of Christ's horoscope, were probably designed to embarrass Regiomontanus, who had sent James a series of mathematical problems to which the astrologer had responded in a perfunctory and derisive manner. Regiomontanus replied evasively to James's challenge, and with implicit disapproval for the question, referring the astrologer to the standard works on conjunctions, including the planetary tables of Giovanni Bianchini of Ferrara.[70]

Regarding the question of astrology and the Christian faith, it can be said that such inquiry was likely to be less controversial depending on the position adopted regarding the *symbolic* as distinct from *deterministic* effects of the phenomenon. While Divine Providence might legitimately be said to inscribe its intentions in the stars, the attempt to calculate the horoscope of Christ as it determined his life and character was superstitious curiosity, indefensible, like all horoscopes, on scientific grounds, and theologically suspect in making Christ subject to Fate.

How, then, might we locate an image such as Tura's between the alternatives of the figurative and the fatalistic? We need to take account of the divergence of positions by the 1460s regarding the relation of astrology and theology, and the consequent problems for the interpretation of Tura's *Annunciation*.[71] Also to be addressed are the social and political tensions which were bound up with astrology, the fact that in attacks on the art from Oresme to Pico it was identified with the deceit of opportunistic courtiers and with the 'noxia curiositas' of princes. Although the court and university of Ferrara sponsored a number of astrologers who would have been well read in Albumasar (Giovanni Bianchini, Pellegrino Prisciani, Pietro d'Avogaro[72]), the doctrine was well enough diffused to be invoked in a poem by Antonio Cornazzano, *De excellentium virorum principibus*, dedicated to Borso d'Este in both a Latin and vernacular edition.[73] The poem, however, is exactly the kind of moralising *speculum* discussed earlier in relation to Ariosto, which implicitly – sometimes in the guise of flattery – counselled Christian princes to have no dealings with vain pastimes or superstitious quackery. Borso, who observed the prognostications of astrologers at his court (although perhaps rather cynically, as it suited him) and had himself portrayed in the famous zodiacal cycle of Palazzo Schifanoia, might have paid particular attention to this passage in which the poet upholds Divine Providence over stellar influence:

a configuration occurs in the heavens, called a triplicity, and thus with hands conjoined the planets bring about new events. And the astrologer takes account of this, of the diverse sects [the planets] bring into being amongst us . . . But let's leave off from saying such suspect things. I believe rather that Christ was the True God, as the scriptures say, and if he was a mortal man like myself, I don't believe that the stars made him thus, but his own Father.[74]

Is it likely that Tura's painting could be promoting, in a discreet and underhand way, the kinds of belief which Cornazzano's poem rejects? If so, it might be asked how he got away with it, and if not, why the planets were included in the first place. Again, I maintain that what Tura painted had to be acceptable to those he painted for. Leaving aside for the moment the question of the visibility of Mercury's gesture, the presence of the planets had to be explicable and defensible to those that beheld the painting, especially in the full view of laity and clergy, of theological specialists and those who merely knew their prayers, in the diocesan seat of an official of the Papal court.

Of the attitudes of Lorenzo Roverella, inferences can be drawn only from scattered remarks in the *Commentaries* of Pius II, from the assertions of later biographers, from Giuseppe Scalabrini's archival transcriptions (1773) and from a handful of books which survive bearing his *stemma*. The impression that emerges is one of Lorenzo's orthodoxy as a theologian, with a reforming attitude in jurisdictional matters and a scrupulous rationalism in doctrinal questions such as the veneration of relics and the administration of extreme unction. Lorenzo had studied theology at Paris, where, with the exception of Cardinal d'Ailly's polemic earlier in the century, the faculty's long-standing hostility to astrology would culminate in an all-round condemnation of Albumasar and other authors in 1494.[75] Among Lorenzo's surviving books are a splendid illuminated incunabulum of the *Decretum Gratiani*, the standard codification of canon law which is unambiguous in its censorious stance on astrological divination, and a copy of Augustine's *De civitate dei* which was a fundamental point of reference for Oresme, Salutati, Pico and all others who mounted polemical attacks on the creed of the astrologers.

Lorenzo, however, was also a medical doctor, and had been personal physician to Pius II. He would hence have been knowledgeable to some degree of theories of celestial influence on the earthly processes of generation and corruption; such 'natural astrology' had been approved by theologians such as Thomas Aquinas and its general currency in medicine is attested by Bernardino of Siena and others, but it was not regarded as entailing a belief in other aspects of the astrologer's creed – horoscopes or 'nativities', divination (interrogations and elections) and the use of magical amulets or images.[76] Regardless of what Lorenzo might have 'actually believed', however, his attitude as manifested in a publicly visible work of art would have to be considered in the light of a Papal pronouncement of 1468. In the same breath, in early 1468 while Tura was working on the paintings for the organ, Paul II explicitly condemned both astrological divination and the study of pagan letters, in response to a crisis which may have threatened to implicate the Roverella themselves.

A conspiracy against his life had been revealed to the Pope, involving a number of humanists associated with the antiquarian academy of Pomponio Leto.[77] Some of these, such as Platina, had been embittered against Paul II by his wholesale dismissal from the Papal Chancery of men of letters appointed to the office of abbreviator by the previous pontiff, Pius II. Others were alleged to have been dabbling in paganism and to have declared republican sentiments, plotting the removal of the Pope and negotiating with his enemies George Podiebrad of Bohemia and Muhammad II. Rounded up and interrogated under torture, the conspirators were accused of sedition against the Church, of Epicureanism, of sympathising with Mahomet and despising Moses and Christ, of neglect of religious observances, and, on the basis of the discovery of 'disgraceful epigrams and verses and sonnets addressed to boys', of sexual depravity. The ringleader was one Filippo Buonaccorsi, who, like the other associates of the academy, had taken a Latin name with libertine connotations, Callimachus Experiens. The fact that the other alleged leader of the conspiracy, Glauco Condulmer, was Cardinal Bartolomeo Roverella's secretary must have placed the family in an embarrassing position. However, there are no known documents regarding the Roverella family's role in the affair and its aftermath, and the surviving dispatches of the Ferrarese ambassador Jacopo Trotti, which might have provided a local view of the situation, do not appear to mention the event; in all likelihood Lorenzo had probably not returned from his first mission to Germany at this time. What is of interest for our purposes, however, is the report of the Milanese ambassador Giovanni Bianchi to Galeazzo Maria Sforza, dated 29 February 1468, which provides a lengthy account of the 'press conference' at which the Pope briefed the ambassadors of the Italian League. The Pope refers to Pomponio Leto and his presumptive intrigue with the Grand Turk:

> and here His Holiness began to condemn greatly these humanist studies, saying that if God granted him life he wished to undertake two things: one, that it would not be permitted to study those vain histories and poems because they are full of heresy and accursed things; the other, that it would not be permitted to learn or to practise astrology because many errors are born from it.[78]

Paul proceeds to lament the fact that little boys of not even ten years of age are exposed at school to the 'vices' and 'thousand ribaldries' of Juvenal, Terence, Plautus and Ovid, thus proving himself a keen student of the *Orationes contra poetas* dedicated to him ten years previously by Ermolao Barbaro the Elder. In the course of discussion with the ambassadors it is emphasised that priests above all should not study astrology or the pagan poets:

> It is also to be remembered that just as it is forbidden for priests to follow civil law because of the difference between the temporal and spiritual condition, so the study of poetry and astrology could be prohibited, because from these one falls into a thousand heresies, etc.[79]

Although there is no record that the promised interdiction was ever issued, the association of pagan knowledge with astrology, the attitude that priests should not study them, and the Roverella connection with the conspirators provides a suggestive context in which to consider a monumental painting produced under the auspices of Lorenzo Roverella at precisely the same time. For this painting carries an astrological theme, which is set forth through the images of the pagan gods, figures of myth and the poetic fables of the ancients, thus recalling the same linkage of poetry, paganism and astrology as reflected in Bianchi's letter.[80]

I believe that the painting manifests a polemical position against judicial astrology in general which may reflect the attitude of Paul II and other critics of the science. At the same time, certain details suggest that, in a less public mode, the work manifests a more discriminating and even philological attitude towards astrology and its pagan associations.

The case for this interpretation rests on the meaning of Mercury's gesture, and the kind of engagement implied with the astrological identification of Mercury with Christianity. The painting does not show the conjunction of Mercury with Jupiter, as Guidoni and Marino asserted; its astrological proposition is rather based on the belief that one of Mercury's zodiacal houses contains a subordinate sign or decan which from the most ancient times (or so the astrologers claimed) was believed to forecast Christ's Virgin Birth. The astrological claim of the painting will be seen to allow only a predictive agency to the stars.

A comparison, and some important distinctions, might be drawn here between the *Annunciation* and two other paintings by Tura, both of which pertain to a more intimate and private devotional context and are more explicit in their reference to a Christianised astrology. In the little *Madonna of the Zodiac* (Rome, Palazzo Colonna; plate 113) the Virgin adores a reclining Christ Child against a mandorla in which, almost invisibly in reproduction, the phantom-like forms of the signs of the zodiac appear. To the left, from top to bottom, are Taurus, Gemini, Cancer and Leo. To the right, only Sagittarius and Capricorn are visible in photographs, so it must be conjectured that the signs which precede them, Libra and Scorpio, occur just to the left of the Virgin's head, while she herself obscures and replaces the sign of Virgo. In the Venice *Virgin and Child* (plate 11), a golden halo with the signs of the zodiac (now badly abraded) appears over the Virgin's right shoulder (plate 114). The series starts with Virgo, the half-length nude figure of a woman visible just over the Virgin's sleeve.

It was, perhaps, inevitable that the Mother of God would be identified with the Virgin of the Zodiac.[81] For Christian readers of Albumasar, who provided the most fully elaborated form of the analogy, the recognition provided wondrous evidence that astrology contained much that was useful for the vindication of the Christian faith. For seeing the Virgin signified in Virgo, or, more specifically, in one of her decans, did not entail any necessary commitment to astral determinism or entail any meddling with horoscopes. The fullest exposition of how Christians might

113 Tura, *Madonna of the Zodiac*. Rome, Palazzo Colonna. On panel (21 × 13 cm).

understand Albumasar was provided in a text known as the *Speculum astronomiae*, circulated anonymously from the late thirteenth century but widely believed then and now to be the work of Albertus Magnus.[82]

Albertus cites the first chapter of the sixth book of Albumasar's *Introductorius*. What are we to make of this book, he asks, if in it is written 'that the birth of Jesus Christ from the Virgin, as well as the utterance of the name announced by the angel, was figured in the heavens from the beginning?'

And in the first decan (of Virgo) there arises a girl whom he calls Celchius Darostal; and she is a beautiful, honourable,

pure Virgin with long hair, and a beautiful face, holding two ears of wheat in her hand; and she sits on a covered bench, and she nurses a male child, giving broth to him in a place which is called Abrie. And a certain people call this child Jesus, which is translated as *Eice* in Arabic.[83]

Albertus adds that the time of Christ's birth in Virgo can be calculated with tables,

not because the most desired of births, [of him] who had created the stars, was subject to the motions of these same stars or to their judgement, but because when he spread out the heavens, just like vellum, to form the book of the universe, he refused to make the work incomplete; he did not wish there to be missing from it letters which were written according to his Providence in the Book of Eternity – even what was farthest removed from nature: that [he would be] born from a Virgin – in order that by this means he might be recognised as a natural and true human being, who was not born in the natural manner not because the figure of heaven was the cause of his birth, but rather because it was a sign; or rather, as is truer than the truths, He Himself was the cause by which the manner of his miraculous birth was signified by means of the heavens.[84]

Similarly, the well-known poem *De vetula*, whose author claimed to be none other than Ovid himself, was taken as important testimony of the pagan perception of the truth of Christianity before the coming of Christ.[85] The ancient Chaldeans, Babylonians and Indians, says the poet, had recognised in the first subordinate decan of Virgo an image of the birth of a 'humano genere rex' who would be born of a virgin. 'Ovid' finds the notion of a virgin birth incomprehensible, but recognises in it the superior agency of God over nature, and prays that he might live to witness and to celebrate the miraculous advent.[86]

De vetula, Albumasar, Albertus Magnus and the fourth of Virgil's *Eclogues* were all quoted or paraphrased around the mid-fourteenth century by Thomas Bradwardine in his treatise *De causa dei*, an encyclopedic refutation of heretics and unbelievers, in a chapter directed against sceptics who denied the Virgin Birth. The chapter is interesting in its conception of astrology as an aspect of the poetic theology of the ancients, who veiled their dim apprehensions of the impending Saviour with poetic figures. Thomas follows Albertus in proclaiming the heavens a book of signs, a parchment inscribed by Divine Providence, in which a conjunction of Mercury and Jupiter announced the advent of Christ and a sign in Virgo marked the Virgin Birth, but with an important qualification:

Not because such a constellation or such a conjunction preceded Christ, and on that account that Christ was to be born from a Virgin or that the law was to be given, but rather the contrary; these were not the causes of the events but their signs, nor indeed is the Lord subject to the stars and their periods, but these are subject to him.[87]

Thomas identifies astrology with the pagan religion of the ancients, who mistook the sun, moon and planets for first causes and worshipped them in the form of idols. Noah, who some identify with the sage Hermes, was the first to understand that the heavenly bodies did not move themselves but through the agency of the one true God, the First Mover.[88] The implication is that the poetic theology of the ancients, and the signs to which they ascribed divine power in the cosmos, are to be understood figuratively as ciphers of the Divine Will. The writings of Hermes Trismegistus in particular hold a special place among the revelations to the ancients – Thomas, as we shall see, makes Hermes central to his discussion of idolatry. In a philological move which recalls Augustine's citations of Varro in *De civitae dei*, Thomas characterises Mercury not as a god or planetary intelligence, but as a figure of divine speech: 'Mercury is to be also understood as speech, and signifies "running between", for what would be a more apt figure for the speech of God, resounding and mediating between God and man?'[89]

This is the key in which we are to see the gestures of Mercury and Gabriel in Tura's painting. Mercury appears as a statue, hence as a sign or *figura*. He is a poetic personification, and a man-made idol, produced for a theology which preceded and dimly apprehended Christian revelation. There is hence a significant shift of emphasis from the zodiac Madonnas, in which the signs of the zodiac appear as the golden lights of the heavens, to a man-made image of a pagan god. The accent now falls not on the zodiac sign which prefigured the Virgin, but on its presiding planet which signified the speech of God and the mediation of the angelic gesture. The focus on speech and mediation underlines the *symbolic* status of the astrological agency, no longer to be confused with any power of compulsion attributed to the stars by their idolators. Humanist philology seems finally more important here than astrological doctrine.

The planet-gods appear in the painting as a model of the cosmos as the ancients conceived it. No agency is imputed to these personified planets other than that of representation – they are the merely fabricated, poetic representations of agencies which themselves merely represent. Almost half a century after Tura completed the organ-shutters, Raphael designed the vault of the Chigi Chapel as a figure of the dome of the cosmos, in which God appears at the centre surrounded by the seven planets and the Eighth Sphere. The planets are again represented by the divinities from which they are named. These gods, however, are not movers of their own spheres, since each sphere is moved by its own angel who with gestures of restraint monitors and controls the influences of the planet in his charge. The Chigi dome depicts a Christianised cosmos in which the action of the heavens is overseen by Divine Providence; Tura's cosmos, by contrast, presents no Christianising features. It represents pagan knowledge of the coming of Christ, together with indications of the degree to which paganism fell short, misrecognising signs for agents, making idols of secondary causes.

If we look again at the planet-gods, we can see how the realm of paganism has been characterised as fallen and worldly, imprisoned by the sensual domain of vision and representation. Tura's gods have a pronounced fleshly or sensual aspect. Given the solemn event being enacted, they appear to flaunt their nudity with an exhibitionistic vehemence. Drapery is present merely to emphasise the act of uncovering or disrobing, or to suggest sexual innuendo – as in the large Priapic knot which covers the genitalia of Saturn. Apollo's exposed back has an androgynous character which partly mystifies his identity (Guidoni and Marino saw him as a Hermaphrodite Mercury) and evokes the ambiguity of sensory experience which, as we saw in chapter II, was central to the characterisation of pagan poetry and its modern imitations. The nakedness of Venus, immediately above the figure of the Virgin, has a particularly glaring aspect; the goddess appears to grimace, her crossed arms suggest a recoiling motion, and the gesture she makes by bending her left wrist recalls that of the outraged and vengeful Vulcan as he appears in the immediately contemporary *September* fresco in Palazzo Schifanoia – it could be called a gesture of 'negative acclamation', or, given the connection of Venus with witchcraft, it could be read as a mimed malediction (plate 111).[90] It is tempting to see Dosso Dossi's similarly posed *Circe* (Washington, National Gallery of Art) as inspired by Tura's figure with her necromantic connotations.

Several gods wear expressions of baleful gloom – Mars, Saturn – or even pain and anguish – Diana, Jupiter, the Eighth Sphere. What is most pronounced about the gods, however, is their sense of paralysed yet vehement movement, manifest in the elaborate and artful *contrapposti* of Venus, Diana and Apollo, and amounting to a kind of frenzied gesticulation in the cases of the Eighth Sphere, Jupiter and Saturn. The specific connotations of movement are examined later in this chapter. Here, I would like to refer to a little-known text by a contemporary poet and cleric which, although published much later, makes a striking verbal parallel with a number of the themes I am identifying in Tura's idiosyncratic visualisation of the Annunciation. Chief among these are the attitudes of distress or even malice on the part of the pagan gods. The book *De sacris diebus* by the Carmelite Baptista Mantuanus, a series of fables in verse on the feasts of the Christian calendar, was printed in 1518 with a dedication to Leo X. Mantuan, as the poet is better known, was resident in Ferrara for part of the 1460s. In the poem *De annuntiatione beatissimae* the coming of Christ is announced not only to the Virgin by the Angel Gabriel, but by Mercury to the Olympian gods:

> When God wished to weave the ends together with the beginning of time, he sent the offspring of the Divine Mind, and let it assume the image of the human form. Therefore the messenger is sent from highest Olympus, the heavenly being who might bear to the mother the tidings of this eventuality. This new impregnation was borne in the wondrous heavens, from which from the beginning of time direful hell had dragged Phoebus, because banishment was predestined for the ancient gods. Mercury, who then by chance was emerging from hell, saw Gabriel's flight from the peak of holy Mount Carmel towards the bountiful region of Nazareth. He fol-

lowed his tracks stealthily in fear, swiftly to the entrance to the bedchamber of the Virgin, and, remaining beyond the threshold, he heard their dialogue. His ears, however, did not absorb every word, but because he was cunning, he seized upon certain secrets contained within them, which touched upon himself as much as all the gods. Then, hurrying to Rome towards the final battleground [*Leuctra*] of the gods, found them all in an immense throng, and informed them of everything. The gods moreover began to be anxious in a great uproar among themselves. Venus wept, Saturn's daughter Juno lamented, and miserable Pallas mourned with her spear thrown down. And soon she spoke: 'O companions, turn with composed mind to whatever will happen. The kingdom which we hold now already for a great age – let everything be spoken of among us – is stolen from us. We who enjoyed the command of this kingdom as long as he allowed, since we will be stripped of this realm let us turn to other arts, to other deceptions. Nor shall we be without gain in bringing dishonour through cunning and deceits, and let us win over Christ's followers to damnation!'[91]

As the sign of Aries rises in the heavens the earth is engulfed by a miraculous springtime, signalling the passing of the age of the damned and the dawn of the age of saints (32–40). The poet then describes the mystery of the Incarnation itself, employing the figure of *conceptio per aurem*:

> Then God began to join the mortal and the eternal in a perpetual bond, making man and god meet one another, through miraculous conception, in one person. Then pious men began to understand the heavens, a great work suspended over our affairs. Then the newly unborn having entered through timid ears, grew inside her who was innocent of carnal intercourse, in the womb of a woman (49–55).

The poem ends with a prayer of praise to 'the great historical changes, which are willed by the stars and which God brings about, the irrevocable order of the centuries'.

The theme of the rout of the pagan gods at Christ's appearance emerges from patristic and scholastic polemics on the downfall of the idols and the cessation of the oracles at Christ's Nativity. By the fifteenth century the theme was disseminated in the account of the Flight into Egypt in the *Legenda aurea* and received a learned reprisal in George of Trebizond's letter to Muhammad II in defence of Christianity.[92] Tura's painting and Mantuan's poem are, as far as I can determine, unique in associating this epochal event with the moment of the Annunciation, and in combining the characterisation of paganism with that of legitimate forms of astral divination. Mantuan may not have provided the source for Tura's painting, but both are clearly drawing on a common repertory of motifs. Whether or not the painting could itself be proved to have inspired Mantuan, the poem stands as an example of how a learned cleric with humanist interests may have made sense of Tura's painting. At the head of this particular 'public', of course, stands Lorenzo Roverella, but the religious and academic life of Ferrara could provide many others, including Manuel Guarino, one of the canons of the cathedral, and Battista Panetti, a learned Carmelite and possible acquaintance of Mantuan. Keeping this class of beholder especially in mind, we will now proceed to examine the background and the broader associations of Tura's treatment of the theme of idolatry.

IDOLATRY AND 'INGENIUM'

Michael Camille has drawn attention to the wide diffusion of the pagan idol as a theme in Christian art of the thirteenth and fourteenth centuries. Among the factors he adduces to explain this sudden upsurge, he points to 'the image explosion' from the same period, the proliferation of new and traditional kinds of representational art in religious and secular domains, in public and private life, together with the increasing commitment of artists to a more secularising aesthetic of naturalism, sentiment, visual splendour and ornament. Furthermore, 'through sheer over production and . . . increasing lay participation and artistic experimentation, the semiotic strategies by which the holy had been mediated to Christians were overridden. In response, antagonists on all levels of society, not just ecclesiastics, used the word "idol" with increasing fervour.'[93]

Idols as a theme in religious art function to compel the beholder's discrimination between true and false kinds of representation, between the true holy image and the dangerous effigies of profane society, of pagans and heretics, of 'others' such as Jews and Saracens. In his concluding chapter on the fifteenth century, 'Idols as Art', Camille considers the consequences of his findings for Italian art of the *quattrocento*. In a move which runs directly counter to much revisionist thinking on historical periodisation, he reinscribes some of the more celebratory commonplaces about the notion of 'Renaissance', enlisting the opposition of freedom, enlightenment and secularisation to clerical tyranny and superstition − the respective mentalities, supposedly, of the Middle Ages and Renaissance. He sees in Italian art of the *quattrocento* a relaxation of the strictures of the previous epoch:

> [Donatello's] *David* is not guilty. Its nudity transcends even its idol status and makes it something that cannot be categorized in either classical or medieval terms. It does not posit the viewer as an enthralled devotee or a rote reader of meaning but promises instead an infinite series of potentially inhabitable subject-positions. It carries freedom with it as befits an image representative of the *virtù* of the city state of Florence itself with a power to embody ideas in the body that had, for more than a millennium, been banished to the margins of discourse.[94]

The notion of a broadening of the image's sphere of address, of its capacity to speak on several levels to different categories of viewer, is a useful way of characterising a possible transformation in the relation of image to the beholder in the fifteenth century. I have presented such a development as taking place,

and as following from a demand for new and subtle strategies of self-imaging, in the chapters on the Roverella altarpiece and the Belfiore Muses. However, Camille's confidence in the *emancipation* of the image in the fifteenth century, especially with regard to the incorporation of 'pagan' elements and effects, seems rather apocalyptic or utopian and might be called into question. The possibility remains that *David* might in fact be a 'guilty' image, one produced for the particular requirements of private viewers, a private appropriation, in fact, of an image of civic *virtù*; such an appropriation would parallel the poetic conversion of the public Virtues of the Fonte Gaia into the voluptuous Muses of Belfiore.

Within the very decade in which Tura painted for Ferrara Cathedral, Sigismondo Malatesta was attacked by a Pope for erecting demonic images, and by a humanist for venerating the remains of an idolator in the church of San Francesco in Rimini.[95] Borso d'Este performed in 1453 a ceremonial enactment of his virtuous princely opposition to *idolatria*.[96] Among the humanists, especially those who sought to defend the stylistic and moral exemplarity of ancient literature, there are not infrequent expressions of repugnance for the 'diabolical' religion of the ancients.[97]

Idolatry had far from disappeared as a theme in painting, nor had the concern with the corrupting nature of the image; idols appear in the drawing-books of Jacopo Bellini, and in Piero's *Flagellation*, and in the chapel decorated for Filippo Strozzi in Santa Maria Novella, Florence, in the 1490s. In this fresco decoration by Filippino Lippi, idolatry is explicitly associated with a kind of artificial excess, a painterly indulgence in the exotic, the phantasmic, in antiquarian *bizzarria*. This excess culminates in the altar of Mars from which St Philip exorcises the demon who had given the curiously animated and lifelike statue its magical potency. Similar fantastic ornament, however, engirdles the entire chapel with passages of pseudo-architectural decoration commonly held to be among the first *alla grottesca* schemes of the Renaissance.[98]

The 'profane temple' imagery of the Strozzi Chapel has its forebear in the great classical structure in which Tura set his *Annunciation*, with its grotesque masks and the elaborate pictorial *varietas* of the stone idols in their animated postures. In Camille's view of the fifteenth century the *all'antica* mode is exploited by artists for its sensuality and as a means of allowing their virtuosity to come to the foreground. Perhaps, however, this display of *scientia* has a more double-edged or ambivalent aspect, simultaneously evoking quite opposed sets of values for the individuals who conceived them and the audiences who beheld them. In presenting an engaging or distracting motif to the gaze of a beholder, to the ends of viewing pleasure or perplexity, could painters be seen to enfold their gestures of virtuosity with signs of the fallen nature of artifice, demonising pictorial invention while displaying it at its fullest?

Tura's portrayal of *St George and the Princess*, and more particularly his seven *all'antica* cosmic deities, make reference to contemporary codifications of artistic skill and virtuosity. The gods explicitly recall Alberti's remarks in *De pictura* on variety in painting, where he discusses the seven possible movements of bodies and the principles of weight-shift for poses associated with extreme exertion. He also recommended a variety of nude and partly draped figures:

> Everything which changes position has seven directions of movement, either up or down or to right or to left, or going away in the distance or coming towards us; and the seventh is going around in a circle. I want all these seven movements to be in a painting. There should be some bodies that face towards us and others going away, to the right and left, of these some parts should be shown towards the spectator and others should be turned away; some should be raised upwards and others directed downwards.[99]

Tura's figures clearly enact these seven movements, to a pronounced and extreme degree. Pivoting on one foot, the personification of the Eighth Sphere performs the circular movement. In his elaborate *contrapposto*, balancing his raised right arm with his left leg, he corresponds with another recommendation of Alberti on the distribution of weight, together with Saturn, who aligns his head, tilted towards the left, with his right foot:

> I have noticed that the movements of the head in any direction are hardly ever such that [a figure] does not always have some other parts of the body positioned beneath to sustain the enormous weight, or at least he extends some limb in the opposite direction, like the other arm of a balance, to correspond to that weight.[100]

A subsequent remark further defines the movement of the Eighth Sphere, Jupiter and Saturn:

> I have also seen that, if we stretch our hand upwards as far as possible, all the other parts of that side follow that movement right down to the foot, so that with the movement of that arm even the heel of the foot is lifted from the ground.[101]

The specificity of the correspondence in Tura's figures inclines me to believe that they are inspired directly by the humanist discussion of painting which Alberti's treatise represents, rather than having a common origin in a 'workshop practice' which Alberti was merely codifying. In his discussion of movement in painting Alberti was drawing from Quintilian's prescriptions for the gestures of the orator, and not from any established compositional method which can be shown to have been already in use among artists.

Alberti, however, in following the oratorical norm established by Quintilian, was concerned to establish a dignified economy and avoidance of excess in the gestures and movements of painted figures. In this regard, the figures of artists such as Piero della Francesca or Andrea Mantegna would seem to embody the sought-after qualities of poise and reserve far more than do Tura's planet-gods:

> But because [some artists] hear that those figures are alive that throw their limbs about a great deal, they cast aside all dignity

in the painting and copy the movements of actors. In consequence their works are not only devoid of beauty and grace, but are expressions of an extravagant artistic temperament. A painting should have pleasing and graceful movments that are appropriate to the subject of the action.[102]

Alberti's censure of artists who give vent to a kind of violent immoderation in displaying their skill by reference to the 'histriones' carries two related negative moral values.[103] Firstly it relates to his remarks on the falsity of flatterers who surround princes, and secondly to his recurring pronouncements against an excessive ostentation in personal deportment. The reference to theatre is inseparable in Alberti from the notion of masking, of the assumption of false appearances, and in this sense it can be aligned with a well-established tradition of associating the arts of representation with idolatry, the most influential *locus* for which was Augustine's *De civitate dei*.

Augustine identified theatrical representation as a form of idolatry; the demons who were worshipped as the gods of the pagans delighted in 'the abominations of the stage, which chastity does not love'. He approves of the fact that the Romans treated actors as among the lowliest of professions, but deplores their inconsistency in not recognising that gods who commanded worship in obscene theatrical spectacles were unworthy of any kind of reverence.[104] Although Alberti's remarks appear to have been inspired by Cicero and Quintilian, they fully lend themselves to an Augustinian reading; or rather, Alberti's art theory provided Tura with a means of visualising the Augustinian polemic, because of the affinity Alberti and Augustine share within a common tradition – that of the Stoic prejudice against theatricality and extravagant display. Alberti, in the case of Tura's painting, provides the visual vocabulary for the concentration of the manifold associations of the idol in the tradition of *De civitate dei*. From an Augustinian point of view, the potential association of the image fashioned by artists with theatrical representation, pagan religion and idolatrous practices associated with astrology (such as the invocation of demons through images fashioned from particular stones and metals[105]) may have served to maintain an aura of suspicion around images outside their approved use in Christian worship.

In a text composed in the decade before Tura painted the organ-shutters, the *De re aedificatoria*, Alberti discusses the ornamentation of temples (an inclusive term which leads to a curious blurring of pagan and Christian contexts), together with the suitability of different kinds of statues of 'the gods' and their proper arrangement. His remarks indicate very clearly how Tura's figures might have been seen to embody a kind of dissonance or incongruity, and hence a negative meaning, within the temple depicted in the *Annunciation*:

> Each statue of a god or hero should, I suggest, have a gesture and garb that convey, as far as the artist can, his life and customs. Here I do not mean that they should strike some stance like a wrestler or an actor, as some think appropriate, but I would like the expression or the overall appearance of the body to convey the grace and majesty of a god, so that

they seem to give a nod or gesture of the hand, to beckon to those who approach, and appear receptive to the prayers of the supplicants.[106]

A little earlier he had written: 'And then, the severe countenance of the great gods, with their beards and eyebrows, might not go so well together with the soft expressions of maidens.'[107]

The first passage relates the strictures against excess in *De pictura* to statues in holy places – this presumably applies in pagan and Christian contexts. The second statement, however, about the incongruity of situating the rugged images of the gods near the image of a tender virgin, makes little sense in an antique or pagan context. In a setting where the pagan and Christian traditions are dichotomised, however, as in Tura's painting, the principle of decorum introduced by Alberti becomes far more meaningful.

It might be objected here that the animation which Tura's figures manifest *does* follow a principle of decorum consistent with Alberti's; the planets, after all, move in the cosmos, and the Eighth Sphere in particular was noted for its erratic and complex changes of orientation. This understanding might indeed have operated for certain viewers, especially those who noticed and saw the point of Mercury's gesture. For the majority of the clergy and laity who saw Tura's painting, however, the naked human figure represented as a man-made image may not have shed its idolatrous connotations. This may have especially been the case given the contrast between the exhibitionistic, dancer-like aspect of the antique figures and the sober deportment of the Virgin and Gabriel, who with their robust quality and solidly modelled drapery folds may even be seen as evoking an entirely modern Christian tradition of image-making – we might think of the polychromed terracotta figures or cloth-and-gesso groups of sculptors such as Niccolo dell'Arca and Guido Mazzoni.

De civitate dei, one of the most important texts on idolatry in the Christian tradition, clearly associated statue-making with a historicised view of the Christian religion and the cults which preceded it, treating the wisdom of the pagans along with their errors. Augustine's characterisations of idolatry (which in his terms would include astrology) underlie an entire tradition of anxiety and polemic regarding true and false image-making, the legitimacy of visible artifice in a theology which appealed to faith in things invisible. Augustine's readers in the fourteenth and fifteenth centuries would have included churchmen and academic theologians, such as Lorenzo Roverella, and teachers and students of the *studia humanitatis* such as Petrarch and Coluccio Salutati.[108] Augustine's account of the idolatrous image occurs in a lengthy section read by many who consulted the church father for his grudging testimony to the prophetic insights of pagan philosophers and sages. This is Book VIII, where Augustine cites liberally from a text called the *Asclepius*, believed to record the pronouncements of the legendary ancient sage Hermes Trismegistus and to have been written or translated by Apuleius. Before I clarify the relevance of the *Asclepius* and its Augustinian interpretation for Tura's painting, I will digress slightly

in order to draw some distinctions between the disparate cultural and discursive spheres for which the name 'Hermes Trismegistus' and the texts it designated had significance. This brings us to the final point in the review of Guidoni and Marino's account of the painting – the identity of the anthropomorphic form looming in the rocks behind the angel, together with further clarification of Tura's characterisation of the pagan gods.

'DOLOR DAEMONUM': THE HERMETIC HYPOTHESIS

By the middle of the fifteenth century the 'hermetic' texts were associated with an occult sub-culture of long standing. The name 'Hermes' appears in discussions of the celestial decans, of alchemy, of forms of magic including the use of images to harness or repel virtues associated with the planets or the zodiac.[109] As such, this astrological or magical hermeticism was the frequent target of witch-hunters and Inquisitors, and was vehemently rejected by those who defended astrology as a natural or mathematical science worthy of Christians.[110] By the 1460s, however, the Hermetic Corpus was providing a foundation for the humanist mysticism of Marsilio Ficino, a Christian rehabilitation of magic and of the philosophy and religion of Plato and his followers, and Ficino's translations circulated from 1462 under the title *Pimander*. The *Asclepius* had been known since its appearance in late antiquity, when it had been cited by Lactantius and by Augustine. The patristic record and the circulation in Latin of the *Asclepius* constitutes perhaps the most influential encounter between Hermes and the fifteenth century, and it is with this tradition, rather than the Platonic mysticism of Ficino, that we will now primarily be engaged.

While Augustine observed that Hermes 'makes many statements about the one true God, the artificer of the universe, which closely resemble the assertions of the Truth', he generally seeks to demonstrate the errors, inconsistencies and demonic bewilderment of the ancient sage. Lactantius, writing a century before Augustine, had been far more celebratory. Like the ancient Sibyls, Hermes for Lactantius voiced beliefs 'not incongruous with ours, that is, with the prophets in matter as well as in words';[111] he foretold the end of the world,[112] he was 'not ignorant of the fact that man was made by God in the likeness of God',[113] and, most remarkably, he was aware of the Incarnation, of the invisible God becoming visibly and sensibly manifest in his own son. Quoting the *Asclepius*, which he calls the *Logos teleios*, Lactantius writes:

> That there is a Son of the Most High God who is endowed with supreme power, not only the teachings of all the prophets in agreement show, but also the prophecy of Trismegistus and the oracles and foretellings of the Sibyls. Hermes, in that book which is entitled *Logos teleios* used these words: 'The Lord and Maker of all things whom we rightly call God, since He made a second god, visible and sensible – but I do not say that the

same one was sensible from the fact that he himself senses . . . but because he is sent to those sensing and seeing – since therefore he made this one, the first and only and one, he appeared good to him and exceedingly full of all good, he was delighted with him, and loved him perfectly as his own son.'[114]

Charles Trinkaus and others have written of a revival of Lactantius in the fourteenth and fifteenth centuries, especially among the humanists who drew on him in their celebrations of the dignity of man and his creation in the likeness of the divine image.[115] The reading of Lactantius would have legitimised an interest in the Hermetic texts. The ancient writer may also have influenced how Augustine's more critical account of ancient prophecy was understood, enabling a less censorious attitude to texts such as the *Asclepius*. Among the handful of surviving books bearing the *stemma* of Lorenzo Roverella, there are copies of both *De civitate dei*, as mentioned above, and an early incunabulum of the *Opera* of Lactantius.[116]

Through Augustine's polemic the pronouncements of Hermes in the *Asclepius* become central to the conception of idolatry in Christian thought. Paganism is characterised through its irrational veneration of man-made images, which, like theatrical performances and the art of astrologers, Augustine regards as parts of a diabolical apparatus for the misleading of mankind. The core of the pseudo-Apuleian account of this magical process is Hermes' association of religion itself with the institution of image-making and the demonic magical practices that followed. Augustine quotes the following passage from the *Asclepius*:

> And, since we have undertaken to discourse concerning the relationship and fellowship between men and the gods, know, O Asculapius, the power and strength of man. As the Lord and Father, or that which is highest, even God, is the maker of the celestial gods, so man is the maker of the gods who are in the temples, content to dwell near to men.

He then quotes a slightly later passage:

> 'This humanity, always mindful of its nature and origin, perseveres in the imitation of divinity; and as the Lord and Father made eternal gods, that they shoud be like Himself, so humanity fashioned its own gods according to the likeness of its own countenance.' When this Asculapius, to whom especially he was speaking, had answered him, and had said 'Dost thou mean the statues, O Trismegistus?' 'Yes, the statues,' replied he, 'however unbelieving thou art, O Asculapius – the statues, animated, and full of sensation and spirit, and who do such great and wonderful things – the statues, prescient of future things, and foretelling them by lot, by prophet, by dreams and many other things, who bring diseases on men and cure them again, giving them joy or sorrow according to their merits.'[117]

The practice was instituted, Hermes says, because their ancestors had no notion of worship and of religion; images of the

115 Florentine, *c*.1470, 'Mercurius Re d'Egitto' or 'Hermes Trismegistus', from the *Florentine Picture Chronicle*. Pen and ink on parchment. London, British Museum, Department of Prints and Drawings, 1970.3, fol. 32*r*.

gods were fashioned to counter mankind's unbelief and error concerning the gods. This is Hermes as depicted in a unique representation of 'Mercurius Re d'Egitto' in the *Florentine Picture Chronicle*, where he is seen astonishing a young disciple as he holds aloft a moving and speaking nude statue (plate 115).[118]

> For the things which have been said concerning men, wonderful though they are, are less wonderful than those which have been said concerning reason. For man to discover the divine nature, and to make it, surpasses the wonder of all wonderful things. Because, therefore, our ancestors erred very far with respect to the knowledge of the gods, through incredulity and through want of attention to their worship and service, they invented the art of making gods.

Yet this marvellous religion of the Egyptians, with its temples and miraculous images, is destined to come to an end. Hermes' celebration of the greatness of Egypt concludes with a prophecy of its destruction:

And yet, as it becomes no prudent man to know all things beforehand, ye ought not to be ignorant of this, that there is a time coming when it shall appear that the Egyptians have all in vain, with pious mind, and with most scrupulous diligence, waited on the divinity, and when all their holy worship shall come to naught, and be found to be in vain.

Augustine seizes on this passage as testimony to the downfall of the demons and their idolatrous cult with the coming of Christ; for, he asserts, the demons themselves in their anguish acclaimed the advent of the Saviour. Hermes was inspired to make this prophecy by demons; the divinely inspired Isaiah made a similar prediction, writes Augustine,

expressly concerning Egypt in this matter, saying, 'And the idols of Egypt shall be moved at his presence, and their heart shall be overcome in them.' But to this Egyptian those spirits indicated the time of their own destruction, who also when the Lord was present in the flesh, said with trembling 'Art thou come hither to destroy us before the time?'[119]

Augustine confronts further scriptural authorities with the prediction which a 'fraudulent spirit' had spoken through Hermes, among them Psalm 96: 'He is terrible above all gods. For all the gods of the nations are demons, but the Lord made the Heavens.' Even though idols are 'nothing', mere inert matter shaped by craftsmen, they must be regarded with suspicion as potential instruments by which demons seduce both pagans and Christians. Unclean spirits, he writes, associated through a wicked magical art with the idols, can make captives of the souls of worshippers. For this reason St Paul wrote: 'We know that an idol is nothing, but those things which the Gentiles sacrifice they sacrifice to demons, not to God, and I would not ye should have fellowship with demons.'[120]

It is apparent that following Augustine the very signs by which idols manifested their power, through speech and animation, become the marks of their defeat. Their speech is mourning at their impending banishment, their animation is trepidation at the approach of the Saviour. Fulgentius had pronounced on the etymological derivation of 'idol' from *idos dolu* – 'image of grief'.[121] While Petrarch's nostalgic appreciation of ancient sculpture has sometimes been cited as evidence of a 'modern' or 'aesthetic' relation to the material remnants of antiquity, the humanist is equally capable of moments of Augustinian zeal where broken classical statues become signs of the defeated idol cults of paganism.[122]

I have already suggested that the melancholy and disturbed character of the gods in Tura's painting might be connected with the imminent triumph of Christianity over paganism, a theme which the poet Baptista Mantuanus, while making reference to the astrological tradition, had connected with the Feast of the Annunciation. It can now be observed that the anguish of the gods is inspired by Augustine's concluding remarks on Hermes:

But it was the grief of the demons which was expressing itself through his mouth, who were sorrowing on account of the punishments which were about to fall upon them at the tombs of the martyrs. For in many such places they are compelled to confess, and are cast out of the bodies of men, of which they had taken possession.[123]

In fact this encounter of the martyrs and the idols comes to occupy a prominent place in the stories of the *Legenda aurea*, among them those of St George. George is led to his martyrdom for denouncing the worship of idols with the words of Psalm 96, also quoted by Augustine above: 'For all the gods of the nations are demons, but the Lord made the Heavens.'[124] In an episode which was frequently illustrated in pictorial cycles of the life of the saint, the martyr destroys an entire temple and all its idols through his prayers. The theme of idolatry in the painting, a practice which the *Legenda* frequently associates with tyrants and magnates, is given added force through its correspondence with the life and martyrdom of the city's patron saint whose image appears on the outward face of the organ panels.

The Egyptian context of Augustine's account of idolatry is also evoked in one of the most bizarre elements in the painting: this is the giant anthropomorphic form which appears in the rocks of the landscape behind the angel, a unique representation, without precedent or successor until the nineteenth century, of the Great Sphinx of Giza. Although neither Tura nor contemporary travellers in Egypt (such as Ciriaco d'Ancona) could have seen the Great Sphinx, which is thought to have been buried in sand at that time, there is no doubt that the specific prototype commemorating one of the ancient rulers of Egypt is intended. Tura could have reconstructed it from Italian examples such as those that adorn the cloister of St John Lateran in Rome, whose proportions and basic silhouette the painting seems to repeat, right down to the detail of the missing nose (plate 116). Furthermore, Pliny's *Natural History* provides a reasonably particularised description of the Sphinx in its account of the pyramids, in which he describes it as a monstrous rock, insisting that it is fashioned from a crag 'growing naturally' from the ground and is not a statue transported to the site. He reports that while some believe it to be the tomb of King Amasis, the credulous local people venerate it as an idol, a 'god of the fields and forests'.[125]

Pliny's account of the Sphinx includes a moral characterisation which may explain in part why it appears in Tura's painting. The Sphinx and the pyramids are presented as exemplifying the vainglory of the ancient Egyptian kings who sought immortality by erecting tombs and colossi, the meaning or commemorative purposes of which have long been forgotten. The theme of vanity, especially of vainglory identified with oriental sovereignty, would complement the moral connotations identified above with regard to the princess rescued by St George, the baptiser of tyrants and victor over idolatry. The

116 Unknown thirteenth-century sculptor, *Sphinx*. Rome, cloister of St John Lateran.

Sphinx would then serve not only to establish an Egyptian context in the painting; it would also stand as a further example of an idol, of representational art equated with folly and worldly delusion. Its inclusion, together with the desolate landscape which surrounds it, may have been inspired by Hermes' prophecy of the downfall of Egypt and its religion, as quoted once again by Augustine:

> Then this most holy land, seat of shrines and temples, will be filled completely with tombs and corpses. O Egypt, Egypt, of your reverent deeds only stories will survive, and they will be incredible to your children! Only words cut in stone will survive to tell your faithful works, and the Scythian or Indian or some such neighbour barbarian will dwell in Egypt. For divinity goes back to heaven, and all the people will die, deserted, as Egypt will be widowed and deserted by god and human.[126]

Yet the Augustinian reading of Hermes is far from adequate as an explanation for the evocations of Egypt in the *Annunciation*. Why, it may be asked, does the looming presence of the Sphinx, hardly a symbol which would have been even recognisable to most of Tura's audience, have such a 'camouflaged' character? What, moreover, is the force of the allusions to contemporary codifications of pictorial decorum, the insinuations regarding artistic licence, the apparent discriminations between an *all'antica* and a modern stylistic idiom, and the intrusive force and irrepressible associations of the vocabulary of pictorial ornament – the 'marginalia' of squirrel, stone masks, the dolphins and fruit? In the rest of this chapter I will propose that these elements all finally amount to a pictorial reflection on representation and truth, on curiosity and legitimate knowledge.

For the evocation of Egypt provides the key according to which the imagery of the painting, and the very means of representation itself, can be seen to be negotiating the broader question of knowledge and its symbolic communication. On the one hand, the problem of what kind of knowledge should be communicated, and to whom, is posed in the narrative and symbolic argument of the picture. On the other, the devices of painting itself, above all perspective, are employed to problematise communication through images. Tura engages a whole tradition of scriptural and Augustinian prejudices against visual representation, which he then defies, as it were, though the very intensity of his acquiesence.

In the tradition outlined above, 'Egypt' appeared as a universalising term for the civilisation and religion of the ancient world as a whole, together with the *superbia* of paganism and its ignominious end; its evocation in Ferrara in the 1460s signals the threat of a new idolatrous power in the East which must be overcome. Elsewhere, 'Egypt' was understood in terms of a wisdom of great antiquity, and had become central to various foundation myths of the origins of human knowledge and the various arts of civilisation. Thomas Bradwardine in the mid-fourteenth century had associated Hermes with the biblical sages Enoch and Noah.[127] Apart from sharing the name Hermes, all three were mathematicians and astrologers; the third Hermes ruled in Egypt after the flood and was skilled in all the liberal and mechanical arts. He was the first to write about astrology and composed a work on the astrolabe.[128] Regiomontanus, who knew Alberti and who endeavoured to persuade contemporary astrologers to engage in mathematical rather than occult speculations, placed the origin of geometry (and hence also the science of mathematical pespective) in Egypt.[129] In Egypt also was invented the calendrical divisions of time, sometimes attributed to Hermes himself;[130] Lactantius, as well as making Hermes a prophet of divine creation through the *logos*, referred to him on Cicero's authority as the inventor of Egyptian writing and law.[131]

These various characterisations of Hermes – philosopher, prophet, astrologer, deviser of the divisions of time – find their way into Tura's painting and account for one of the perplexing features noted earlier: the presence of Mercury without his regular attributes. For this figure who gestures behind Gabriel, surrounded by the planets in the order of the days of the week, can now be identified as none other than the euhemeristic alias of Hermes the ancient divinity, the historical sage who was identified in later times with the god Mercury. Although Augustine recognised that Hermes Trismegistus and the god Mercury were distinct individuals, Lactantius believed that the god Mercurius or Thoth worshipped by the Egyptians (one of five different Mercuries identified by Cicero) was the deified form of Hermes the sage.[132] The personification of the Eighth Sphere (plate 111) as a god is a motif which may have originated directly from the *Asclepius* itself. The personification is unusual; Raphael, in the vault of the Chigi Chapel, and the more contemporary Master of the Tarocchi, represented the Eighth Sphere as simply that, a sphere with stars. In *Asclepius* 19 Hermes names the presiding god of the thirty-six decans, the sphere of the horoscopes, as 'Pantomorphos or Omniform, who makes various forms within various classes'. Forms are the individual and corporeal variants of universal categories, or classes, which are divine and incorporeal. The generation of variant forms within classes is, strikingly, analogous in Hermes with the rotation of a circle through individual moments and degrees. The gyroscopic movement of Tura's figure, whose *contrapposto* enacts to an extreme degree the potential *varietà* of the body, could have been inspired directly by the following:

> The forms change as often as the hour has moments in the turning circle where the god resides whom we have called Omniform. The class persists, begetting copies of itself as often, as many, and as diverse as the rotation of the world has moments. As it rotates the world changes, but the class neither changes nor rotates. Thus, the forms of each kind persist, though within the same form there are differences.[133]

The Sphinx itself relates to the mythical origins of the human arts according to the humanist theoretician of painting introduced above with regard to Tura's portrayal of the movements of the planets. For the Sphinx as Tura represents it is a conflation of two separate accounts of the origin of image-making as formulated by Alberti in his writings on painting and sculpture. In *De pictura* II.26 Alberti refers to the Egyptian claim to have practised painting 'six thousand years . . . before it was introduced to Greece'. In the Latin edition of the book the very section of the *Asclepius* discussed above is cited as the authority for the invention of painting and sculpture along with religion:

> The ancient writer Trismegistus believes that sculpture and painting originated together with religion. He addresses Asclepius with these words: 'Man mindful of his nature and origin represented the gods in his own likeness.'[134]

The Sphinx stands as a memorial to the ancient Egyptian religion and to the social and cultural origins of art. One of the artist's particular claims to dignity for Alberti had been his ability to fashion the image of the gods (*De pictura* II.25). There are strong Hermetic echoes in Alberti's claims that man fashions the divine nature in his own image, that painting has a divine power to move men, evoke the dead, or stimulate piety, so that painters feel themselves to be almost like God – 'tam deo se paene simillimos esse intelligant.' Many passages in the *Corpus hermeticum* are recalled in this phrase; we need cite only *Asclepius* 6, 'a human being is a great wonder, a living thing to be worshipped and honored: for he changes his nature into a god's, as if he were a god' and *Asclepius* 23, 'Always mindful of its nature and origin, humanity persists in imitating divinity, representing its gods in semblance of its own features, just as the father and master made his gods eternal to resemble him.'[135]

Yet accompanying the 'cultural' account of painting's beginnings in Alberti is a description of its pre-cultural or natural origins. Nature appears in the second book of *De pictura* as an image-maker, who 'often fashions in marble hippocentaurs and

the bearded faces of kings' ('ut saepe in marmoribus hippocentauros regumque barbatas facies effigiet'). Alberti's source for Nature painting itself in marble was Pliny's *Natural History* XXXVI.5; the passage occurs in the very same book as the description of the Sphinx. A more elaborate formulation by Alberti of the natural origins of image-making is the opening of *De statua*. Here, man's observation of 'half-formed likenesses' ('inchoatarum similitudinem') in tree-trunks, clods of earth and other inanimate objects leads to the formation of *effigies et simulacra* by the sculptural processes of adding and taking away. Tura's Sphinx, probably under the influence of Pliny's characterisation of the ancient idol as 'cut from the living rock', is just such a half-formed image. While its camouflaged aspect would have made it unrecognisable as a sphinx to most viewers, some contemporary beholders may have been struck by the curious reflection of Gabriel's profile in the silhouette of the rocks behind him. Such beholders may have been prompted to a different order of reflection – about Nature's curious powers of mimesis, perhaps, or about the bizarre conceits of painters. In the case of not a few spectators the perception may have been bound up with sentiments of perplexity or ambivalence regarding the errancy of mortal vision, or the visible world as a theatre of phantasmic seductions for the gaze in which painting itself is implicated.

Alberti's analysis of the parts of painting provided an effective means of giving visual form to an Augustinian position on astrology, poetry and the arts of spectacle. Tura's painting, then, is polemical, but not in a narrow propagandistic sense; it is also conceived for a viewer who will move from a casual interest in the painting's many novelties to a reflection on the ambitions and shortcomings of the art of image-making. The 'argument' of the painting is not conclusive; it is rather a rhetorical elaboration of a sacred theme – the Word become Flesh. Various topoi are given visual and synthetic form – the creating power of divinity, human emulation of divine creativity, and the human creation of divinity itself. Is image-making mere representation, or is it, by analogy with the Incarnation, a God-like act of creation in itself? The painting presents for the viewer's discrimination the 'pagan' or hermetic position, recently also deployed by Alberti as part of a rhetorical celebration of the nobility of art.

I have argued that the imagery of the organ-shutters should not be seen as princely propaganda or as flattery of the House of Este by the bishop and cathedral chapter of Ferrara, but as a statement of autonomy by the ecclesiastical body. The court was certainly involved in negotiations for the commission, but may have done no more than authorise the advisory involvement of its musical staff and the employment of its household artist. The choice of imagery reflects the joint dedication of the cathedral to the Virgin and St George, and, in its specific nuances, the theological interests of Lorenzo Roverella. The theological argument is far from 'disinterested' but emerges from Lorenzo's concerns as a Papal courtier, with the authority to command the respect and obedience of a secular head of state within the Pope's dominions. With the co-opting of the visual style of the court the prince and his subjects are enjoined to pious obedience, to a foreswearing of vanity and luxury, and to a proper discrimination between true faith and idolatry. The idolatry theme reflects on a broad public level the Papal strictures of 1468 against both astrology and the 'studi di humanità', as well as a more general Augustinian attitude to poets, astrologers and arts of spectacle. On a private and restricted level, the painting reflects a more discriminating position, a certain acceptance of the historical import of astrology and pagan prophecy by means of which unbelievers from Hermes to Albumasar were granted a partial view of the triumph of Christianity. The painting appears to embody a structure of demarcation between general and restricted spheres of knowledge, between that which it is appropriate for the faithful to know and that which should be only the preserve of experts licensed by sacred authority. A curial theologian such as Lorenzo Roverella and his circle can contemplate the astrological testimony of the advent of Christ, supposedly without being drawn into the *noxia curiositas* which leads princes and the astrologers who serve them astray.

Guidoni and Marino had already claimed the painting for the magical hermeticism of the astrologers and alchemists, and for the Neoplatonic hermeticism of Ficino. I am proposing instead that the tradition of Hermes at issue is patristic and scholastic, and this was also characteristic of humanism before Ficino's dissemination of the Hermetic Corpus – through Hermes, the concerns with image-making, astrology and idolatry intersect. The theme of idolatry makes of the painting something more than an instrument of propaganda on behalf of the Papacy and the House of Roverella; it allows the image to be aligned with a position, both ironic and celebratory, regarding the nature of representation in general. In the painting Tura seems to render unstable the distinction between 'true' images sanctioned by the faith and various categories of 'fallen' image – the idol, the *curiosa* of the painterly grotesque. Beyond the idolatry theme, the painting makes uncertain its own claims to legitimacy as representation.

PAINTING AND IRONY

What would it mean for a painting to be ironic? I do not mean to suggest by this that Tura the historical individual was himself sceptical, facetious or intentionally irreverent in his painting. Irony is a rhetorical trope usually associated with literary representation, but it has recently been applied to the analysis of painting for *literati* in another aristocratic milieu, in which the hereditary basis of social privilege was also actively interrogated and challenged. For Chinese *literati* of the eleventh century, to ironise representation entailed an appeal to honesty and integrity in social and aesthetic values, primarily through a repudiation of painting's claims to truth. In the words of Martin Powers, 'a profound skepticism toward the enterprise of accurate representation – in other words, a conscious rejection of similitude – is a necessary requirement for pictorial irony'.[136] There are sugges-

tive parallels at the historical juncture at which Tura is painting, when the formation of states centring on courts, and the ethical re-definition of nobility, created an active concern with personal merit as social entitlement; as we have seen, both pictorial and literary representation became sites of social conflict and aspiration under these conditions. Yet Tura's implicit rejection of the paradigm of 'painting as window', as imitation of the visible, is produced from a tension between social ambitions and ethical values; the ethical self of humanism is ironised along with the other negated claims of 'truthful' representation. Tura's irony does not make him 'sincere'; it does not necessarily censure what it also points to, namely that there can be no visible and social form of the self except as artefact. The 'figure' one produces for others in an urban society cannot establish a basis of authenticity, whether one is exhibiting the flamboyant manners of the courtier or the taciturn restraint of the Florentine merchant: 'Art should be added to art lest anything seem to be done artfully when one is walking about in the city, riding a horse, or speaking. For in these things one must watch on all sides in order not be displease anyone greatly.' So wrote Alberti, better known in a rather different guise as a theorist of the transparency, naturalness and social probity of pictorial artifice.[137]

Like much contemporary discussion of painting, Tura's works frequently drew on the relation of word and image, either to assert their equivalence (chapter I), their analogous poetic ends (chapter II) or the superiority of the image to the word (chapter IV). The authority of Tura's self-representation depended on the analogy of painting with writing, yet also on the suppression of what in actuality enabled writing to possess authority. The 'literacy' of writing is displaced by the concern with form, pattern, flourishing. Similarly, Tura's painting emulates authoritative forms of the image; the irony lies in the distance that then becomes apparent between Tura's act of fabrication, asserted in his style, and the 'truth' being appealed to. To put it more simply, a mode of painting which celebrates human artifice and virtuosity will at this historical point raise questions, even involuntarily, about its claim to truth. Tura's painting constantly alludes to divinely authorised image-making – divine craftsmanship in the bodies of saints, the painted icon of the face of Christ, the Ark of the Covenant – but it lacks this authority for itself. The only authority such painting can appeal to is the highly contestable 'nobility of the artist', repeatedly advertised in the manual ingenuity of line. The sole authority remaining which could be claimed by Tura is the authority of craft, yet the more intensely he lays claim to this the more his art falls into the histrionic 'fashion of actors and mimes' ('pantomimorum consuetudine') denounced by Alberti and Decembrio. It was only in the generation of Raphael and Michelangelo that human *ingegno* could be given the designation *divino* and the extravagances of a licentious style could be authorised as the products of divine inspiration.[138] Tura's contemporary Mantegna saw one of his own works, the *Madonna of Victory*, achieve cult status in the 1490s; Tura, however, may have found his own works always inferior in authority to certain miraculous cult images in the city of Ferrara. One such cult, that of the *Madonna della Corte*, had its centre within the

Ducal Palace itself, part of the process of sacralising princely authority. The image was a recent artistic product, but its man-made nature tended to be bypassed in contemporary accounts and celebrations, including one by Francesco Ariosto Peregrino.[139] Tura's only answer to such miraculous, divinely authorised images is the assertion of human art and non-divinity.

It was observed in relation to the organ-shutters that the very act of seeing has perilous associations with curiosity, fear, confusion and unredemption; hearing is the privileged sense, identified with faith, confidence and the reception of the *logos*. Four blind stone masks align with the surface of the painting, exposing its equivalence with the redundancy of carnal seeing, with the false appearance of a painted face. I have suggested more than once that the painting evokes the aesthetic precepts of Alberti, and it is from Alberti also that this ironic position with regard to the nature of artifice can be most fully demonstrated. Thus we conclude with the paraphrase of an Albertian fable.

Alberti's vision of artistic enterprise in the service of the state, of the prince, and of religion, which tacitly insinuates his own necessary position as humanist adviser to the powerful, is set forth in works such as *De re aedificatoria* and *De pictura*. Such a vision is ironically undermined, however, throughout Alberti's career by a series of essays in imitation of Lucian, most dramatically in the fable *Momus*. The work was completed around 1450, not long before Alberti concluded his treatise on architecture. *Momus* is subtitled *De principe*; while facetiously purporting to offer material for the instruction of princes who read it, the book treats largely of the catastrophic relation between princes and particular beneficiaries of their patronage. These are the practitioners of the 'arts of dissembling' (poets, courtiers, rhetoricians, actors, artists), all embodied in the figure of Momus.

Early in the work the advice vainly proferred by Momus to his princely employer, the god Jupiter, concerns the dangers of the gifts of simulation enjoyed by the newly created race of mankind. Through the agency of the mask and of the arts of representation the order of creation becomes confused as mankind learns to simulate divinity – a rather ominous reappraisal of the potential divinity of artists in the second book of *De pictura*. Ignored by Jupiter and exiled from the court of heaven, Momus demonstrates the dangerous powers of representation among mankind, constantly changing his shape (and parodying the humanist enterprise of Alberti's time) by exploring the theory and practice of such arts of simulation as cosmetics (a reductive characterisation of painting), poetry and 'vagabonding' ('ars erronum'). After many vicissitudes Momus is subjected to a horrific Prometheus-like punishment, indicating that he has overstepped the bounds of legitimate curiosity and become guilty of impiety. At the opening of the fourth and final book, mankind seeks to appease the wrath of the gods by a great rite of purification, and by constructing temples and a great theatre embellished with statues of the gods.

In a startling parody of the Hermetic account of the invention of religion, already cited by Alberti in *De pictura*, mankind charms the gods down from heaven with music and sacrifices. The gods disguise themselves as their own statues in the theatre, and are diverted by a burlesque exchange between a philosopher and an actor concerning the proper piety due to *images* of the gods, which are after all only matter shaped by human hands. The god Stupor is finally mutilated as the philosopher, unaware of the god concealed in the statue, attempts to beautify him with a chisel.

The hermetic topos of the gods inhabiting statues finally gives place to the Christian tradition of the downfall of the idols. Since the gods have consented to be idols, thereby becoming slaves of human artifice (they have also been seduced by the architecture of the theatre and its spectacles, a distinctly Augustinian accent), they neglect their supposed custody of the elemental forces of nature. The gods of the wind, no longer held at bay, also wish to attend the performance and rush into the theatre, unleashing havoc and destruction in which the statue-gods topple from their pedestals and are severely wounded. Fearing to lose the awe of mortals, they flee back to Olympus, leaving behind the goddess Ambiguity ('dearum mendacissima'), who has stolen Apollo's bag of oracles and who henceforth will be the medium of divine communication to mankind.

Ambago can be seen as the presiding goddess of the book, which constantly confuses its readability as allegory, exulting in ironic shifts between an apparent authorial voice and numerous personae who espouse various received ideas and positions. This refusal of the purported pedagogical design troubled the controversial scholar Francesco Filelfo, who wrote to Alberti in 1450 to express bewilderment at the work's uncertain allegorical content.[140] No conclusion can be privileged, no moral can exhaust the dense play of fable, of topoi, of orthodox and perverse points of view that run through the text. Regarding the theatre episode, the gods can be read in an Augustinian sense as the demonic agencies flattered by mankind with worldly and seductive arts, or as an expression of the estrangement of the divine and the human spheres, or in moral sense as the failure of the megalomaniac designs of men whose overestimation of their capacity to fashion societies, institutions and monuments has self-destructive consequences. Insofar as any major thematic principle can be advanced, Alberti appears in *Momus* both to demonise and glorify all human enterprise as arts of fiction and simulation; all representation fabricates its own object, and the figuring of any truth lying beyond this veil of artifice is subject to constant frustration and obstruction. Alberti's assumption of the mode of Augustinian scepticism regarding pagan religion, theatre, art, poetry, cosmetics, seems to undermine the very myths that this Stoical-patristic scepticism had been designed to preserve.

An analogous claim can be made for Tura's painting, which is similarly dense with a tangle of allegorical motifs and anomalous elements. There need be no direct connection between the painting and *Momus* or any other text by Alberti; however, the world in which Tura's paintings and Alberti's writings were produced were far from discontinuous. In the first place there was the common climate of humanist poetry and rhetoric, galvanised by the encounter with Greek scholarship and a new mode of conceiving the subject-matter and adornments of painting. It had been Guarino's translations of Lucian that had led to Alberti's advocacy of the *Judgement of Apelles* as a model for the ideal *historia*. The Lucianic theme of a hall decorated with images, which Tura's *Annunciation* might be seen to recall, was adopted by Alberti for his *Intercenalis* entitled 'Picture'.[141] With regard to other aspects of the painting, Lucian wrote a mock eulogy of judicial astrology and drew up the rules of decorum for the 'histrionic art' of the dance which suspiciously resemble Alberti's precepts for painters.[142]

The *Annunciation* has the same reflexive, self-negating character as the *Momus*. The theme of astrology is introduced and given a 'demonic' characterisation, but on close inspection is partly recuperated. The skill of the painter in his *all'antica* depiction of the figure in movement turns out to be associated with an infringement of artistic norms and with a demonised paganism. Stone masks and other 'marginalia' both compel decipherment and caution against interpretation. Finally, the treatment of perspective in the painting is double-edged: as much as it corresponds to a notion of clear apprehension, of 'seeing through' along a receding vista, it also functions as a means of veiling, thus encoding the incompleteness and partial nature of human perception. Mercury is rendered significant by virtue of his near-total obliteration, and is hence easily missed by the observer. The assumed objectivity of perspective is also assaulted and reveals itself as a trick, a means of visual manipulation – what appears to be the optical convergence of receding parallels is, if read according to the literal premise of perspective, actually the diminution of the architecture. Even the eye alone can tell that the proportion of capital to shaft in the foreground columns is greater than that of those in the background, a device more characteristic of seventeenth-century perspectivists such as Bernini. Too great a diminution of the capital in the background columns would have revealed the anomaly in the depiction of the planets, their lack of any diminution corresponding to the depth of the space. The receding view into depth finally ends up in winding paths, in visual ambiguities and enigmas such as the monstrous semi-human form lurking in the rocks.

Artistic persona, it might be said, is figured once again through excess, through the venality of artifice which appears under the signs of paganism, sensuality, superstition, ambiguity, in the literal carved personae represented by the stone masks. Tura's 'baroque' Hebrew ornament in the Roverella altarpiece, executed for the ancient cathedral of San Giorgio, might even be seen as a pendant to that of the cathedral paintings; in that case too the artist's stylistic self-representation is constructed from the architecture of a fallen theology.

We encounter an instantiation of painting as metaphor in many of the works by Tura that have been discussed – the Belfiore Muses, the Roverella altarpiece, the organ-shutters for the cathedral, the British Museum drawing. Although co-opting a series of common oppositions – painting and writing, visible and invisible, ancient and modern art – this metaphoric status of painting, while it constantly thematises the painting's authorship in terms of a manifest fictionality, does not always work in consistent ways. The grounds for exposing fictionality are constantly shifting, the boundary between truth and representation is never fixed. The flexibility of the boundary is an extremely subtle ideological weapon on behalf of those for whom Tura paints.

Writing manifests a claim to authority and dignity, a guarantee of painting's worth; however, in appropriating for the painted the status of the written, it menaces all writing with mere pictorialism, the generation of surface effects. Against the Jews, artistry is the term valorised against writing, allowing – as Alberti would claim – the imaging of the Divine Countenance itself. Painting has a different status here than it does in the Belfiore Muses, where artifice is defiantly pagan and sensual, and the *Annunciation*, where the centrality of the angel's inaudible message renders the entire pictorial apparatus hollow and incomplete. In all of these works, ruptures and perplexities lie on the edges of vision, bringing the beholder to an impasse in the equation of knowing and seeing. The demonically sexual angels of the Roverella altar preserve this aspect, which is represented more fully in the cathedral panels. Here the viewer's experience is rendered secondary and as a multiplication of distractions. With each change of focus, with the absorption of every new detail, the question of truth and falsity in what the beholder sees is made problematic, as does the kind of readabilty being proposed by the image. Heresies become capable of re-generation. The figure of Jupiter releases a bird from his hands. To the figure's right, the impregnating dove hovers at the ear of the Virgin. What, finally, prevents the beholder from attributing to a pagan agency – planet, god or demon – the authorship of the central creative act in the painting? Curiosity ceases, or damns itself.

NOTES

INTRODUCTION

1 This sentence is rendered in Latin. The full letter runs: 'Veramente, Ill.mo S. Principe et Excellentissimo Signor mio, dele fatiche mie non mi suffragano. Io non scio come potermi vivere et substentare in questo modo, impero chè non mi trovo possessione ó facultate che mi sostentino con la faminglia mia. Altro cha quello che con le diurne opere e magisterio mio de la pictura per mercede alla giornata mi ho guadagnato, ritrovandome maximamente Infermo de tale infermitade che non senza grandissima spesa et longeza di tempo mi potrò convalere, como forsi di havere inteso Vostra Excellentia. Questo dico perchè havendo da Sey anni in qua facto una ancona da altaro a spexe mie di oro, collori, e pictura al Spectabile Francesco Nasello Secretario de la Ex.tia V. la qual è in San Nichollo in Ferrara che me ne vegneriano Ducati sexanta; et havendo similmente picto allo Illustre et Reverendo Monsignor de Adri un Sancto Antonio da Padua con certe altre cosse per le qualle mi resta debitore ducati xxv. Non posso essere satisfato Cossa certo non debita né honesta, et tanto più quanto sono potenti et hano molto bene il modo à satisfarmi, e io sum povero et inpotente et che non ho bisogno perdere le fatiche mie. Per tanto humilmente ricorro alla Excellentia Vostra et supplico, siccome quella per le opere ch'io ho facto per lei gratiosamente si è dignata satisfarmi, voglia dignarsi con quello honesto et conveniente modo gli pare far dir alli predicti mi vogliano con effecto satisfar senza tenermi più in parole overo longeza di tempo. *Hoc enim exigit causa mercedis.* E quando non lo vogliano far per honestate, Vostra prefacta Excellentia voglia pigliarli tal ordine che per debito mi satisfacino. Alla cui gratia humilmente mi ricomando:

> Ferrariae. VIIII Ianuarii MCCCC LXXXX.
> Excellentiae Vestre servitor fidelissimus
> Cosmus Pictor.'

Text in A. Franceschini, *Artisti a Ferrara in età umanistica e rinascimentale: Testimonianze archivistiche* (Ferrara, 1995), Part II, vol. 1: *dal 1472 al 1492*, no. 736. All citations of Tura documents below are to this edition.

2 Some of these reactions find their way into print, as in the case of one of the most commonly used university textbooks on Renaissance art: Frederick Hartt wrote that Tura's Roverella *Virgin and Child* 'is startling in its plastic intensity and coloristic irresponsibility. Why should Renaissance architectural elements alternate between pea-green and poison-pink, or angels be so gaudily dressed?': *History of Italian Renaissance Art* (New York, 1969), 382. The (posthumous) edition of Hartt's book published in 1994 omits this comment. Kristen Lippincott ('Tura, Cosimo', in J. Turner, ed., *The Dictionary of Art*, London, 1996, vol. 31, 432) finds the Modena *St Anthony* to be 'so mannered and tense as to verge on the repellant'.

3 On the conservation of Tura's paintings in the National Gallery, London, see J. Dunkerton, A. Roy and A. Smith, 'The Unmasking of Tura's *Allegorical Figure*: A Painting and its Concealed Image', *National Gallery Technical Bulletin*, 11, 1987, 5–35; J. Dunkerton, 'Cosimo Tura as Painter and Draughtsman: The Cleaning and Examination of his *Saint Jerome*', *National Gallery Technical Bulletin*, 15, 1994, 42–54; and J. Dunkerton, 'La *Vergine Annunciata* di Cosmè Tura', *OPD Restauro*, 5, 1993, 16–22. On the cleaning of the Correr *Pietà* see A. Dorigato, ed., *Carpaccio, Bellini, Tura, Antonello e altri restauri quattrocenteschi della Pinacoteca del Museo Correr* (Milan, 1993). For the Turas in Ferrara see J. Bentini, ed., *San Giorgio e la principessa di Cosmè Tura: Dipinti restaurati per l'officina ferrarese* (Bologna, 1985); on the Poldi-Pezzoli *Terpsichore* see A. Mottola-Molfino and M. Natali, ed., *Le Muse e il Principe: Arte di corte nel rinascimento padano*, exhibition catalogue (Milan, Museo Poldi-Pezzoli, 1991), vol. II, 266–75.

4 The documents of these transactions, involving the trades of silk, woollen cloth and nail-making, refer to sums totalling 750 lire; I am relying on the calculation 1 Venetian ducat = 3.15 *lire marchesine* after 1485, based on C. M. Cipolla, *Studi di storia della moneta, i movimenti dei cambii in Italia dal secolo XIII al XV* (Pavia, 1948), 48–9. For notarial records of Tura's investments in the period 1478–92, see Franceschini, *Artisti a Ferrara*, Part II, vol. 1, nos 206, 382, 513, 514, 525, 526, 543, 550, 572, 576, 600, 610, 616, 658, 662, 663, 696, 714, 716, 718, 773, 775, 785, 809, 810, 853, 854. The investments are of sums between 100 and 200 lire, and which in one year could raise an interest of 10–15%. The ability to command this kind of capital is also indicated by the purchase and sale of houses (nos 313, 330, 331, 412). A property aquired in the Boccacanale district in 1479 for 200 lire was resold by the artist for 300 lire in 1482.

5 G. Baruffaldi's *Vita di Cosimo Tura* exists in two versions: one in the first volume of his *Vite de' pittori e scultori Ferraresi* written after 1722 and published in 1844, and another of 1706 published separately in 1836. Baruffaldi refers to the obliteration of paintings by Tura in the Sacrati family chapel in San Domenico (see R. Stemp, 'Cosimo Tura and the Sacrati Chapels in Ferrara', *Musei Ferraresi*, 17, 1990–91, 61–70), to the dismembering of altarpieces in San Luca in Borgo and San Giorgio, and, in the later text, to the 1709 damage by artillery fire to the Roverella altarpiece in San Giorgio. Other eighteenth-century writers on the churches of Ferrara, for example C. Barotti, *Pitture e sculture della città di Ferrara* (Ferrara, 1770) and C. Brisighella, *Descrizione delle pitture e sculture della città di Ferrara* (c.1710; Ferrara, 1991), tend in most cases to follow Baruffaldi where Tura is concerned.

6 For example L. N. Cittadella, *Ricordi e documenti intorno alla vita di Cosimo Tura, detto Cosmè* (Ferrara, 1866).

7 R. Longhi, *Officina Ferrarese* (Rome, 1934), 34: 'Anch'egli da un interpretazione medievale, irrealistica, del rinascimento, e si educa sognando all'ombra dell'altare criso-cupro-elefantino di Donatello'; and on the next page: 'Una ascendenza medievale lo convince preventativamente che non sia pittura se prima non si concreti in un materiale raro ed eletto (il misticismo medievale delle pietre e delle gemme); si immagini che cosa ne consegue al contatto dei principi organici venuti di Toscana.'

8 B. Berenson, *The North Italian Painters of the Renaissance* (New York, 1952), 58.

9 See for example the characteristic comment by C. Padovani, *Rivista di Ferrara*, 4, 1933, 21: 'Cosmè e prodotto di cento incroci di scuole pittoriche, il frutto selezionatissimo di cento razze, alle quali il soffio del Rinascimento fiorentino ha comunicato un'anima nuova. Ma, come tutti i primitivi, Cosmè possedeva quella forza latente che trasforma tutto quello che tocca. Dalle forme astratte di Piero, dalla romanità del Mantegna, del naturale di Donatello, dalla preziosità dei fiamminghi, Cosmè, il caposcuola della pittura ferrarese del Quattrocento, è salito all'espressione dell'energia e della vita.'

10 For an attempt at a non-pejorative use of such terms see F. Zeri, 'Renaissance and Pseudo-Renaissance', *History of Italian Art*, trans. C. Dorey (Cambridge, 1994), vol. II, 327–72, where Tura is identified as an adherent of the 'superficial' as distinct from the 'essential' Renaissance; E. Battisti, *L'Antirinascimento* (Milan, 1962, 1989), makes an important attempt to define an alternative 'non-classical' tradition. Longhi's famous *Officina Ferrarese* of 1934 was definitive in focusing serious art historical attention on Renaissance painting in Ferrara. Almost all art historical scholarship on Ferrara since its publication has been concerned with vindicating or reverently correcting Longhi's conclusions.

11 For a critique of the notion of the 'classical' in Renaissance historiography see E. Cropper, 'The Place of Beauty in the High Renaissance and its Displacement in the History of Art', in A. Vos, ed., *Place and Displacement in the Renaissance* (Binghamton, NY, 1994), 159–205.

12 On 'symbolic domination' see E. Castelnuovo and C. Ginzburg, 'Centre and Periphery', in *History of Italian Art*, trans. E. Bianchini and C. Dorey (Cambridge, 1994), vol. I, 29–113.

13 Specific studies on 'court art' tend to avoid this pitfall – one might cite the recent proliferation of scholarship on Mantegna – but not always; the 'escapist' interpretation informs even a useful survey like A. Cole, *Art of the Italian Renaissance Courts: Virtue and Magnificence* (London, 1995), and an otherwise indispensable monograph such as that by J. Manca, *The Art of Ercole de' Roberti* (Cambridge, 1992).

14 For an important and deeply provocative incursion against the alleged 'rationalism' and 'simplicity' of Florentine religious art, see G. Didi-Hubermann, *Fra Angelico: Dissemblance and Figuration* (Chicago, 1995).

15 M. Baxandall, *Painting and Experience in Fifteenth Century Italy* (Oxford, 1972).

16 E. Ruhmer, *Cosimo Tura* (London, 1958), 18; Zeri, 'Renaissance and Pseudo-Renaissance', 364.

17 On *aria, maniera* and related terms see Baxandall, *Painting and Experience* 26–7 and 109ff.; T. Greene, *The Light in Troy: Imitation and Discovery in Renaissance Poetry* (New Haven, 1983, 95–7); D. Summers, *The Judgement of Sense: Renaissance Naturalism and the Rise of Aesthetics* (Cambridge, 1986), 117–25; J. Woods-Marsden, *The Gonzaga of Mantua and Pisanello's Arthurian Frescoes* (Princeton, 1988), 154–61; M. Kemp, 'Equal Excellences: Lomazzo and the Explanation of Individual Style in the Visual Arts', *Renaissance Studies*, I/1, 1988, esp. 2–12.

18 As is argued by M. Warnke, *The Court Artist: On the Ancestry of the Modern Artist* (Cambridge, 1993). Artists in Milan competed to serve the Sforza princes despite their negligence in settling accounts. See E. S. Welch, *Art and Authority in Renaissance Milan* (New Haven and London, 1995), 246–55.

19 The demand for virtuosity and novelty may not have been true of all patrons or even all courtly patrons. As far as painting is concerned the Sforzas of Milan, before they hired Leonardo, seem to have preferred that their artists follow the canonical forms associated with the family's dynastic predecessors, the Visconti. See A. S. Norris, 'The Sforza of Milan', *Schifanoia*, 10, 1990, 19–22. Yet the letter on the artists of Florence, written to the Duke of Milan in 1490, employs a careful language of discrimination and classification which indicates an interest in the distinguishable characters of artists, and hence an interest in acquiring a distinguishable aspect for the visual style of the regime. For a discussion see Baxandall, *Painting and Experience*, 26–7.

20 The term supposedly recalls Jacob Burckhardt's invention of the 'heroic' 'Renaissance Man', although many contemporary attributions of this view to Burckhardt overlook the decidedly non-heroic and entrepreneurial character of the 'individualism' he describes. Raymond Williams argues for a distinction in cultural studies between the terms 'individuality' and 'individualism': the latter is qualitative, and 'corresponds to the main movement of liberal political and economic thought'; the former, however, has a 'quantitative' origin in eighteenth-century mathematics and physics, 'stressing both a unique person and his (indivisible) membership of a group'. R. Williams, *Keywords: A Vocabulary of Culture and Society* (London, 1976, 1983), 164–5.

21 Most frequently in feminist studies. See, for instance, the introductions to M. Quilligan, N. Vickers and M. Ferguson, *Rewriting the Renaissance: The Discourses of Sexual Difference in Early Modern Europe* (Chicago, 1986), xvi, and M. Migiel and J. Schiesari, *Refiguring Women: Perspectives on Gender and the Italian Renaissance* (Ithaca, 1991), 1–7.

22 Most powerfully stated in the dialectical formulation of Stephen Greenblatt, whose theory of self-fashioning usefully re-situates some of the insights of Burckhardt: 'If we say there is a new stress on the the executive power of the will [by the sixteenth century], we must say that there is the most sustained and relentless assault upon the will; if we say that there is a new social mobility, we must say that there is a new assertion of power by both family and state to determine all movement within the society; if we say that there is a heightened awareness of the existence of alternative modes of social, theological, and psychological organization, we must say that there is a new dedication to the imposition of control upon those modes and ultimately to the destruction of alternatives.' S. Greenblatt, *Renaissance Self-Fashioning: From More to Shakespeare* (Chicago, 1980), 1–2. On self-fashioning see also Mario Biagioli, *Galileo, Courtier: The Practice of Science in the Culture of Absolutism* (Chicago, 1993). The concern with the individual's active shaping of identity according to type occasionally emerged in art history before its so-called 'literary' turn; for an example, see C. Seymour Jr., *Michelangelo's David: A Search for Identity* (Pittsburgh, 1967).

23 N. Zemon-Davies, 'Boundaries and the Sense of Self in Sixteenth Century France', in T. Heller *et al.*, ed, *Reconstructing Individualism: Autonomy, Individuality and the Self in Western Thought* (Stanford, 1986), 53–63. On the growth of self-consciousness in individual expression see also G. Duby and P. Braunstein, 'The Emergence of the Individual', in Duby and P. Ariès, ed, *A History of Private Life II: Reflections of the Medieval World*, trans. A. Goldhammer (Cambridge, MA, and London, 1988), esp. 535f.

24 R. Weissmann, 'Reconstructing Renaissance Sociology: The Chicago School and the Study of Renaissance Society', in R. C. Trexler, ed., *Persons in Groups: Social Behaviour as Identity Formation in Medieval and Renaissance Europe* (Binghamton, NY, 1985), 40.

25 R. C. Trexler, *Persons in Groups*, 5.

26 Longhi, *Officina Ferrarese*, 34.

27 L. Simeoni, 'Il documento ferrarese de 1112 della fondazione dell'Arte dei Callegari', *Accademia delle scienze dell'Istituto di Bologna*, ser. iii, 7 (1932–3), 56–71. On the guilds of Ferrara see P. Sitta, 'Le Università delle Arti a Ferrara dal secolo XII al secolo XVIII', *Atti e memorie della deputazione Ferrarese di storia patria*, VIII, 1896; W. Gundersheimer, *Ferrara:*

The Style of a Renaissance Despotism (Princeton, 1973), 36–7, and P. T. Lombardi, 'Le corporazioni di arti e mestieri a Ferrara dal 1173 al 1796,' *La Pianura*, 4, 1976, 3–20 (on the *calegari*, 11).

28 '[7 April 1473] . . . fu dato principio ad essere lavorato intorno al Palazzo de la Ragione del Comune, et il Palazo de le Banche di Calegari in Piaza, il quale Palazo de la Ragione et torre de hore fu acconzo, cioè dipinti come sono; poi similiter il Palazo de le Banche de Calegari a paladini fu depinto in dicto tempo, cioè de Magio, et Zugno fu fornito ogni cosa'. *Diario Ferrarese . . . di autori incerti*, ed. G. Pardi in *Rerum italicarum scriptores* (Bologna, 1928), 24, Part 7, no. 1, 88.

29 G. Pardi, *Leonello d'Este* (Bologna, 1904), 80–81; A. Frizzi, *Memorie per la storia di Ferrara* (Ferrara, 1847), vol. II, 38; G. Ferraresi, *Il Beato Giovanni Tavelli da Tossignano e la riforma di Ferrara nel quattrocento* (Brescia, 1969), vol. IV, 190–91.

30 I am thinking here of accounts largely informed by historical anthropology on ritual and religion and by feminist theory: R. Trexler, 'Florentine Religious Experience: The Sacred Image', *Studies in the Renaissance*, XIX, 1972, 7–41; L. Marshall, 'Manipulating the Sacred: Image and Plague in Renaissance Italy', *Renaissance Quarterly*, 47, 1994, 485–532; P. Simons, 'Women in Frames: The Gaze, the Eye, the Profile in Renaissance Portraiture', *History Workshop*, 25, 1988, 4–30; R. San Juan, 'Mythology, Women and Renaissance Private Life: The Myth of Eurydice in Italian Furniture Painting', *Art History*, 15, 127–45; C. Baskins, 'Echoing Narcissus in Alberti's *Della pittura*', *Oxford Art Journal*, 16, 1993, 25–34.

31 For accounts of the Ferrarese *comune* with an emphasis on the Este rulers of the *quattrocento* see Gundersheimer, *Ferrara*; T. Dean, *Land and Power in Late Medieval Ferrara* (Cambridge, 1988); R. G. Brown, *The Politics of Magnificence in Ferrara, 1450–1505: A Study in the Socio-Political Implications of Renaissance Spectacle* (D.Phil., University of Edinburgh, 1982).

32 On the contingent nature of Este power in the fifteenth century, see T. Dean, 'Commune and Despot: The Commune of Ferrara under Este Rule, 1300–1450', in *City and Countryside in Late Medieval and Renaissance Italy: Essays Presented to Philip Jones* (London, 1990), 183–97, with arguments for divergences of policy between the communal government and the *signoria*.

33 For instances of popular unrest see J. E. Law, 'Popular Unrest in Ferrara in 1385', in J. Salmons, ed., *The Renaissance in Ferrara and its European Horizons* (Cardiff and Ravenna, 1984), and Brown, *Politics of Magnificence*, 41–60.

34 As has been argued on several occasions by Trevor Dean, a relentless critic of structuralist accounts of court society grounded on assumptions of absolutist rule; see his 'The Courts', in *The Origin of the State in Italy, 1300–1600*, supplement to the *Journal of Modern History*, 67, 1995, 136–52, and 'Notes on the Ferrarese Court in the Later Middle Ages', *Renaissance Studies*, III/4, 1989, 357–69. Nevertheless I have found certain features of the work of Norbert Elias useful for this investigation, among them his analysis of the neccessity of structural conflicts in the state: *The Court Society*, trans. E. Jephcott (New York, 1983), Appendix 1, 276–83, and his discussion of chivalric etiquette and ritual in the process of turning feudal warriors into courtiers; see 'Towards a Theory of Civilizing Processes', in *Power and Civility* (New York, 1982), 229ff.

35 This is the argument of Brown, *Politics of Magnificence*, and the development is amply documented in T. Tuohy, *Herculean Ferrara: Ercole d'Este, 1471–1505, and the Invention of a Ducal Capital* (Cambridge, 1996).

36 On magnificence as a princely virtue see A. D. Fraser Jenkins, 'Cosimo de'Medici's Patronage of Architecture and the Theory of Magnificence', *Journal of the Warburg and Courtauld Institutes*, 33, 1970, 162–70, and L. Green, 'Galvano Fiamma, Azzone Visconti and the Revival of the Classical Theory of Magnificence', *Journal of the Warburg and Courtauld Institutes*, 53, 1990, 98–113.

37 These aspects of princely spectacle are discussed further in chapter II.

38 On the 'ancestral' tradition of palace decoration showing the Este as hunters see Gundersheimer, *Art and Life at the Court of Ercole I d'Este: The 'De triumphis religionis' of Giovanni Sabadino degli Arienti* (Geneva, 1972). On the authority of such earlier representations and their power to compell imitation among descendants at a neighbouring court, see E. S. Welch, 'Galeazzo Maria Sforza and the Castello di Pavia, 1469', *Art Bulletin*, 71, 1989, 352–75.

39 Among discussions of Tudor and Jacobean spectacle I have found the following to be useful for considering earlier situations: S. Orgel, 'The Spectacles of State', in Trexler, *Persons in Groups*, 101–23, and J. Goldberg, *James I and the Politics of Literature* (Stanford, 1989), 56–85. For spectacle in Ferrara', see C. Rosenberg, 'The Use of Celebrations in Public and Semi-Public Affairs in Fifteenth-Century Ferrara', in M. de Panizza Lorch, *Il teatro italiano del rinascimento* (Milan, 1980), 521–36, and R. G. Brown, 'The Reception of Anna Sforza in Ferrara, February 1491', *Renaissance Studies*, II/2, 1988, 231–39.

40 'Neque parum illi quidem multarum rerum notitia copiosi litterati ad historiae compositionem pulchre constituendam iuvabunt, quae omnis laus praesertim in inventione consistit.' L. B. Alberti, *On Painting and On Sculpture*, ed. and trans. C. Grayson (London, 1972), 94.

CHAPTER I

1 On careerism see L. Martines, *The Social World of the Florentine Humanists, 1390–1460* (London, 1963); on conservatism and normalisation in politics and pedagogy see Martines, *Power and Imagination: City States in Renaissance Italy* (New York, 1979), 191–217, A. Grafton and L. Jardine, *From Humanism to the Humanities: Education and the Liberal Arts in Fifteenth and Sixteenth Century Europe* (Cambridge, 1986), S.H. Jed, *Chaste Thinking: The Rape of Lucretia and the Birth of Humanism* (Bloomington, IN, 1989) and S. Kolsky, *Mario Equicola: The Real Courtier* (Geneva, 1991). For a recent example of a more positive 'post-revisionist' assessment, see Grafton, *Defenders of the Text: Traditions of Scholarship in an Age of Science, 1450–1800* (Cambridge, MA, and London, 1991).

2 For humanism in Ferrara see the account by R. Sabbadini, *La scuola e gli studi di Guarino Guarini Veronese* (Catania, 1896); G. Bertoni, *Guarino da Verona fra letterati e cortigiani a Ferrara* (Geneva, 1921); P. Castelli, ed., *Il Rinascimento del sapere: Libri e maestri dello studio ferrarese* (Venice, 1991); studies of individual figures are cited below.

3 Even a knowledgeable account like that of T. Tuohy, *Herculean Ferrara: Ercole d'Este, 1471–1505, and the Invention of a Ducal Capital* (Cambridge, 1996), 208, repeats the commonplace that Tura was 'replaced' as *pittore del corte* by Ercole de' Roberti in 1486. There appears to be no evidence that either artist was designated by this title or held the kind of office it implies. For fourteenth- and fifteenth-century examples of artists receiving official retainership, titles and honours, see M. Warnke, *The Court Artist: On the Ancestry of the Modern Artist* (Cambridge, 1993), although with similar unwarranted inferences about the regularity of Tura's salary and his tenure of an official court appointment, 137, 147.

4 This scenario, a necessary corrective to the view of Warnke, *The Court Artist*, is described by E. S. Welch in *Art and Authority in Renaissance Milan* (New Haven and London, 1995), 241–68.

5 A. Franceschini, *Artisti a Ferrara in età umanistica e rinascimentale* (Ferrara, 1995–6), Part II, vol. 1: *dal 1472 al 1492*, no. 487n, q.

6 They include the *studioli* of Borso and Ercole d'Este, considered in chapter II, Borso's chapel at Belriguardo, and portraits of Ercole and his children, to be used as diplomatic or betrothal gifts.

7 Gherardo da Vicenza and Trullo appear to have served chiefly as all-purpose decorators for the princely residences, executing borders or repeating patterns of friezes and festoons (*feste all'antica*); Trullo (Giovanni di Antonio Bianchini, also nicknamed 'il Bianchino'), seems to have specialised in whitewashing. For references to documentation on Trullo and

Gherardo as 'depintori della corte' see also T. Tuohy, *Studies in Domestic Expenditure at the Court of Ferrara, 1451–1505* (Ph.D. dissertation, University of London, 1982), 64, 115. For documentation of their activity see Franceschini, *Artisti a Ferrara*, Part II, vol. 1, and for a rather generous estimation of Gherardo's role at court see Manca, 'A Ferrarese Painter of the Quattrocento', *Gazette des beaux-arts*, CXVI, November 1990, 157–72.

8 The gaps in court records referring to Tura in the period 1465–7 may be interpreted not as absences from Ferrara (as was speculated by A. Venturi, 'L'arte a Ferrara nel periodo di Borso d'Este', *Revista storica italiana*, II, 1885, 713–14, who suggested that Tura worked for the Pico of Mirandola at that time), but as periods in which Tura may have been principally dependent on other Ferrarese patrons. This might also be indicated from slender or non-existent records of Tura's court employment in 1468, when he concluded work for the Sacrati family at San Domenico and worked for the cathedral, 1475, 1478, 1479 (no records), 1482 (no records) and from late 1485 (no subsequent records). Other known patrons of Tura include the tailors' guild, the Roverella family, the ducal secretary Francesco Nasello and Antonio Cicognara.

9 Franceschini, *Artisti a Ferrara*, Part II, vol. 1, no. 351 (1480).

10 M. Baxandall, 'A Dialogue on Art from the Court of Leonello d'Este: Angelo Decembrio's *De politia litteraria* Pars LXVII', *Journal of the Warburg and Courtauld Institutes*, 26, 1963, 304–26; Baxandall, 'Guarino, Pisanello and Manuel Chrysoloras', *Journal of the Warburg and Courtauld Institutes*, 28, 1965, 183–205; Baxandall, *Giotto and the Orators*, Oxford, 1971.

11 Warnke, *The Court Artist*, 3–74, provides the most persuasive arguments that the early modern transformation of the status of the artist, and the perception of art as liberal or noble, was owing in large measure to the prestige and possibilities offered by court service rather than guild-regulated practice in the city republics. For other discussions of artists at court, see R. Starn and L. Partridge, *Arts of Power: Three Halls of State in Renaissance Italy* (Berkeley, 1992), and E. Lincoln, 'Mantegna's Culture of Line', *Art History*, 16/1, 1993, 33–57.

12 The oration is preserved in the Vatican Library, Codice Ottoboniano 1153 fols. 155–6. The translation of Carbone's oration which follows is based on the Latin text in G. Zippel, 'Artisti alla corte Estense nel'400', *L'arte*, 5, 1905, 405–7.

13 Baxandall, 'Dialogue on Art', 304.

14 R. Molajoli, *L'opera completa di Cosmè Tura e i grandi pittori ferraresi del suo tempo* (Milan, 1974), 10–12, and J. Bentini, ed., *San Giorgio e la principessa di Cosmè Tura* (Bologna, 1985), 21–41, both include an 'Itinerario critico'

which can be seen to illustrate the successive expressionist, surrealist and even 'existentialist' characterisations of Tura in twentieth-century scholarship.

15 'Nam a veteribus tacitus poema est appelata pictura, et noster Horatius pictoribus atque poetis aequam semper potestatem fuisse scripsit, propterea quod uterque donare immortalitate homines possunt. Mea quidem sententia, nemo unquam magnifico animo et excelso fuit, qui non pictura delectaretur. Possem vobis proferre ac nominare multos reges qui ipsi pingere ac coelare didicerunt, atque imprimis Caesarem Augustum et Neronem Claudium, qui mirifice atque incredibiliter pictura sunt delectati: unde meliores imagines ex omnibus quae quidem in manus meas pervenerint eas indico, quae Octaviani aut Neronis tempore laboratae sunt; quales enim principes, talia subditorum ingenia . . . Plenum enim studiolum meum mille picturis, signis, tabellis, imaginibus. Nunquam illam Leonelli aspicio, quam Antonius Pisanus effinxit, quin mihi lacrymae ad oculos veniunt: ita illius humanissimos gestus imitatur. Tuam vero, inclyte dux, quam Lodovicus Castellanus expressit tanquam reginam in medio caeterarum teneo, quae me ad virtutem, ad sapientiam, ad eloquentiam, ad omne genus elegantiae veneranda gravitate et augusta maiestate hortari videtur.' Zippel, 'Artisti', 405–7.

16 On Galeotto see Venturi, 'L'arte a Ferrara nel periodo di Borso d'Este', II, 625; C. Rosenberg, *Art in Ferrara during the Reign of Borso d'Este (1450–1471): A Study in Court Patronage* (Ph.D. dissertation, University of Michigan, 1974), 119f.

17 See R. C. Tristano, *Ferrara in the Fifteenth Century: Borso d'Este and the Development of a New Nobility* (Ph.D. dissertation, New York University, 1983); Tristano, 'Vassals, Fiefs and Social Mobility in Ferrara in the Middle Ages and Renaissance', *Medievalia et humanistica*, 15, 1987, 43–64.

18 On the distinction between 'zentilhomini moderni' and 'zentilhomini antiqui' see R. G. Brown, *The Politics of Magnificence in Ferrara, 1450–1505: A Study in the Socio-Political Implications of Renaissance Spectacle* (D.Phil. dissertation, University of Edinburgh, 1982), 126.

19 See the case cited by Brown, *Politics of Magnificence*, 436–7, concerning a merchant's successful appeal against sumptuary provisions and his status of *ignobilis* on the basis of personal fortune as well as paternal relatives.

20 D. Fava, *La Biblioteca Estense nel suo sviluppo storico* (Modena, 1925), 54 (wrongly attributing the text to Leonardo Bruni). It seems more likely that the English scholar and Guarino pupil John Tiptoft, who made an English translation later printed by Caxton, would have encountered Buonaccorso's text in Ferrara, where he spent much of the late

1450s, than on a visit to Florence in 1461, as was suggested by H. Baron. Baron, *The Crisis of the Early Italian Renaissance* (Princeton, 1955), 420–23, 557n, and C. Donati, *L'idea di nobiltà in Italia, secoli XIV–XVIII* (Bari, 1988) 10–11, overstate the Florentine and Republican orientation of the dialogue, and neither takes account of the fact that the *Disputatio* was dedicated to a prince, Carlo Malatesta. In her study of Jean Miélot's French translation (1449) and its influence at the court of Burgundy, Charity Cannon Willard aptly proposes that the appeal of the text to Malatesta would arise from the fact that he was, like Borso d'Este, illegitimate, and therefore likely to be more drawn to the claims of personal *virtù*. The appeal of the text at the court of Philip the Good would have arisen from the aspirations of a rising *noblesse du robe* of bourgeois origin, and Miélot also developed elsewhere the idea of ennoblement through the practice of the Liberal Arts. Willard, 'The Concept of True Nobility at the Burgundian Court', *Studies in the Renaissance*, 14, 1967, 33–48.

21 Ugo Caleffini, *Chroniche del Duca Ercole*, fol. 244*v*, cited in Brown, *Politics of Magnificence*, 271.

22 Carlo di San Giorgio is the most outstanding example. The professional scribe Tommaso da Vicenza 'collaborated' with Guarino and Guglielmo Capello on their edition of Pliny's *Natural History*, according to the colophon on a manuscript now in Munich (Cod. lat. Monac. 11301). See R. Sabbadini, *Guarino Guarini Veronese*, 117. G. Bertoni, 'Notizie sugli amanuensi degli Estensi nel quattrocento', *Archivum Romanicum*, II, 1918, 55n, documents the learned Carmelite Battista Panetti working as both scribe and translator of a manuscript of Josephus acquired by the court library in 1472. Bertoni also refers to the career of the scribe Jacopo Landi, who refers in a letter to a volume of orations transcribed by him 'in quibus scripte erant alique orationes manu mea propria' (41).

23 Tristano, *Borso d'Este*, 245–9. On the culture of the *volgare* in Ferrara see also Venturi, 'L'arte nel periodo di Borso d'Este', 690–93; E. Gardner, *Dukes and Poets in Ferrara* (London, 1904), 83–8; for a recent comprehensive account of the production of vernacular editions of the classics see A. Tissoni-Benvenuti, 'Guarino, i suoi libri, e le letture della corte estense', in A. Mottola-Molfino and M. Natali, ed., *Le Muse e il Principe: Arte di corte nel rinascimento padano*, exhibition catalogue (Milan, Museo Poldi-Pezzoli, 1991), vol. II, 63–82.

24 The allegation rests on an over-literal understanding of a complaint to Borso by the scribe-humanist Carlo di San Giorgio regarding the glaring lack of letters in one who was otherwise so highly accomplished. See A. Cappelli, 'La congiura contro il Duca

Borso d'Este scritta da Carlo da San Giorgio', *Atti e memorie delle RR. deputazioni di storia patria per le provincie Modenesi e Parmensi*, II, 1864, 377–8. Carlo's statement should be offset against the fact that Borso continued to be the dedicatee and active patron of numerous humanistic works in Latin. His commissioning books is no proof that he read them; however, his constant promotion of the vernacular and demand for translations is an indication of interest in their contents, and of a desire to make them available to a broader circle of courtiers other than those with classical training.

25 On Carbone see W. Gundersheimer, *Ferrara: The Style of a Renaissance Despotism* (Princeton, 1973), 165–8; Bertoni, *Guarino da Verona*, 112ff. and *passim*; L. Paoletti, 'Carbone, Ludovico', *Dizionario biografico degli italiani*, vol. 19, 1976, 699–703.

26 *Dialogus de amoenitate, utilitate, magnificentia Herculei Barchi*, in A. Lazzari, 'Il *Barco* di Ludovico Carbone', *Atti e memorie della deputazione Ferrarese di storia patria*, XXIV/1, 1919, 34.

27 E. Peverada, 'La tonsura clericale di Cosimo Tura', *Analecta Pomposiana*, 10, 1985, 159–68; document also in Franceschini, *Artisti a Ferrara*, Part I, app. 39. Court musicians and singers were being rewarded with benefices by the reign of Ercole d'Este; see L. Lockwood, *Music in Renaissance Ferrara, 1400–1505* (Cambridge, MA, 1984).

28 Franceschini, *Artisti a Ferrara*, Part I, no. 1235; the church is to be erected on the site of the disused gate of San Pietro. A later, more modest, will of 18 April 1491 names as universal heir a son of Tura named Damiano; ibid., Part II, vol. I, no. 805. The bequest of alms to the Venetian poor may refer to a possible dispute between Tura and the Sindaco of the Ferrarese charitable organisation known as the Poveri di Cristo to which, the will pointedly states, no donations are to be made. Tura had acquired a house from the Sindaco in 1463 but relinquished his claim on it after a few weeks. See the documents in Franceschini, ibid., Part I, nos 1011, 1014.

29 On Mantegna's funerary chapel in San Andrea, Mantua, see R. Lightbown, *Mantegna* (Oxford, 1986), 248–9, 452–4. On Vecchietta's equally elaborate multi-media project in Santa Maria della Scala in Siena see H. Van Os, 'Vecchietta and the Persona of the Renaissance Artist', in I. Lavin and J. Plummer, ed., *Studies in Late Medieval and Renaissance Painting in Honor of Millard Meiss* (New York, 1977), 445–53. Van Os sees Vecchietta's much-vaunted versatility and 'pyrotechnic display' of illusion and artifice in terms of a 'conscious stylization of his persona as artist'.

30 The information on artist's salaries comes from Tuohy, *Herculean Ferrara*, 302. On Carbone's annual academic teaching of 100

lire see G. Tiraboschi, *Storia della letteratura italiana* (Venice, 1795), VI, 849.

31 For the document of 14 July 1464 see A. Venturi, 'Cosma Tura genannt Cosmè, 1432 bis 1495', *Jahrbuch der Königlich preussischen Kunstsammlungen*, 8, 1887, 9.

32 'e da l'altro lato commanda Sua Signoria che per la Camera sia concessa dicta casa al decto Maistro Angello per ragione de feudo pagando ogni anno in la festa de Pascoa de la rexuratione uno belissimo fiore depinto, on voglia roxa, on ziglio, on altro fiore che vorà epso Maistro Anzollo'. Franceschini, *Artisti a Ferrara*, Part I, no. 763n.

33 On Pisanello and Leonello see most recently J. Woods-Marsden, *The Gonzaga of Mantua and Pisanello's Arthurian Frescoes* (Princeton, 1988), 33–6.

34 L. N. Cittadella, *Ricordi e documenti intorno alla vita di Cosimo Tura* (Ferrara, 1866), 10, and Franceschini, *Artisti a Ferrara*, Part II, vol. I, nos 351, 522, 550, 609.

35 Ibid., no. 609.

36 G. Campori, *Artisti degli Estensi: I pittori* (Modena, 1875), 32.

37 The only exception is Baldassare d'Este, referred to as 'commendabili et praestanti viro' and 'nobilem virum' – but his name was an obvious advantage, along with his service in the Este administration. See Franceschini, *Artisti a Ferrara*, Part II, vol. I, nos 93, 665. There are no really comparable references to Ercole de' Roberti, who in the late 1480s appears intermittently in notarial acts with the more modest single designation 'praestans'.

38 For documentation on Baldassare see A. Venturi, 'L'arte nel periodo di Borso d'Este', 719–22; for a discussion of current attributions see A. Bacchi, *Dipinti ferraresi dalla collezione Vittorio Cini* (Vicenza, 1990), 44–52.

39 Documentation of various gifts to Petrecino 'che fu famio de lo Ill.mo N.S.', including the payment of certain debts 'in elimoxena' is included in Modena, Archivio di Stato, Libri camerali diversi, 41 (1463), fols 102, 104. For Petrecino as artist see Venturi, ibid., 731, 743; see also London, 1984, *From Borso to Cesare d'Este*, exhibition catalogue (London, Matthiesen Fine Art Ltd, 1984), 130 (with erroneous dates); Mottola-Molfino and Natali, ed., *Le Muse e il Principe*, vol. I, 80–82.

40 The most sensible discussion of the letter is that by C. Rosenberg, 'Francesco Cossa's Letter Reconsidered', *Musei Ferraresi*, 5/6, 1975–6, 11–16, which qualifies Baxandall's generalisation in *Painting and Experience in Fifteenth-Century Italy* (Oxford, 1972), 1–2, that the Duke of Ferrara paid his fresco painters by the square foot.

41 On the controversy regarding Mantegna's work in the Eremitani, see M. Warnke, 'Praxisfelder der Kunsttheorie: Über die Geburtswehen des Individualstils', *Idea:*

Jahrbuch der Hamburger Kunsthalle, I, 1982, 54–71.

42 For a general discussion of these terms see H. Glasser, *Artists, Contracts of the Early Renaissance* (Ph.D. dissertation, Columbia University, New York, 1965), 84–5. Tura's petition to the duke in 1490 refers to 'magisterio mio de la pictura'; see Franceschini, *Artisti a Ferrara*, Part II, vol. I, no. 736. For 'ornate et artificiose' see Bartolomeo Pendaglia's will of 1462 with its endowment for the decoration of the *capella grande* of San Francesco; ibid., Part I, no. 987.

43 For examples of a princely patron's dissatisfaction with individualising tendencies, see E. S. Welch, 'The Process of Sforza Patronage', *Renaissance Studies*, III/4, 1989, 383.

44 On the competition see N. Grammaccini, 'Wie Jacopo Bellini Pisanello Besiegte: Der Ferrareser Wettbewerb von 1441', *Idea: Jahrbuch der Hamburger Kunsthalle*, I, 1982, 27–53.

45 The evidence for this is in Alberti's *De equo animante* dedicated to Leonello d'Este, in G. Mancini, ed., *Opera inedita* (Florence, 1890), 238–9.

46 For an account of the manuscript, now in the Biblioteca Classense, Ravenna, see Mottola-Molfino and Natali, ed., *Le Muse e il Principe*, vol. I, 167–9.

47 Alberti, in C. Grayson, ed. and trans., *On Painting and On Sculpture* (London, 1972), 64. References to the *pictoris ingenium* occur throughout Alberti's text; early in Book II painting is described as 'worthy of free minds and noble intellects' ('liberalibus ingeniis et nobilissimis animis').

48 'suaves enim et gratos atque ad re de qua agitur condecentes': Alberti, *De pictura*, in Grayson, 84.

49 Alberti, *De pictura*, in Grayson, 83.

50 Alberti, *De pictura*, in Grayson, 84.

51 Alberti, *De pictura*, in Grayson, 66, 67.

52 Rosenberg, 'Francesco del Cossa's Letter Reconsidered'.

53 J. Dunkerton, A. Roy and A. Smith, 'The Unmasking of Tura's *Allegorical Figure*: A Painting and its Concealed Image', *National Gallery Technical Bulletin*, 11, 1987, 5–35; Dunkerton, 'Cosimo Tura as Painter and Draughtsman: The Cleaning and Examination of his *Saint Jerome*', *National Gallery Technical Bulletin*, 15, 1994, 42–54.

54 'Cuius nempe inclytae artis et eximii artificium ingenii egregium equidem imitatorem Angelum Parasium, quem Senensem recens picturae in Latio specimen vidimus.' For Ciriaco's text, actually a celebration of 'Rugerius Brugiensis pictorum decus', see Mottola-Molfino and Natali, ed., *Le Muse e il Principe*, vol. II, 326.

55 Pliny, *Historia naturalis*, XXXV. 65: 'primus symmetrian picturae dedit, primus argutias voltus, elegantiam capilli, venustatem oris, confessione artificum in liniis extremis palmam adeptus. haec est picturae summa

subtilitas. Corpora enim pingere et media rerum est quidem magni operis, sed in quo multi gloriam tulerint; extrema corporum facere et desinentis picturae modum includere rarum in successu artis invenitur.' The Latin text is from the Loeb edition translated by H. Rackham (Cambridge, MA, 1952), 310, 312. Quintilian's reference to Parhassius anticipates Alberti to a greater extent in making him an investigator of light and shade and of 'subtilius lineas'. *Institutio oratoria*, XII.x.4.

56 See H. Van de Waal, 'The Linea Summae Tenuitatis of Apelles: Pliny's Phrase and its Interpreters', *Zeitschrift für Aesthetik und allgemeine Kunstwissenschaft*, XII/1, 1967, 5–32.

57 Another parallel with Parrhasius is suggestive here: the orator Themistius (*Orations*, II.29c) refers to the painter making a portrait of himself in the persona of Hermes, and further mystifying his identity by signing the work with a pseudonym.

58 On Kufic and actual oriental script in paintings see H. Tanaka, 'Oriental Scripts in the Painting of Giotto's Period', *Gazette des beaux-arts*, CXIII, 1989, 214–21, and M. Barasch, 'Some Oriental Pseudo-Inscriptions in Renaissance Art', *Visible Language*, 23, 1989, 171–87.

59 'Principio quod dictum est de libro "prudenter politeque conscripto" non modo de versus genere, sed etiam de librarii opera intelligi: adeo litterarum facies formosa venustaque, et recta et vetusta scribendi formula, quam orthographiam appellant, legentis oculos alliciebant. Tam haec inerat sententia olim ad verbum posita, quantum memoria repetere valet, et nunc astute subducta: "Quid facturum arbitramur Panormitam nostrum, si gravem et auditore quovis dignam nactus fuerit materiam tam ardenti eius ingenio parem, quando in re tam abiecta et petulcis moribus respondere tam polite ludat?"' Guarino of Verona, Letter to Giovanni Lamola, in R. Sabbadini, ed., *Epistolario di Guarino Veronese* (Venice, 1915–19), vol. II, 201.

60 Filarete grounds this observation in the comparison of portraits by different artists of the same individual, which recalls the competition of Pisanello and Bellini at the Este court: 'Che se uno tutte le fabbricasse, come colui che scrive o uno che dipigne fa che le sue lettere si conoscono, e così colui che dipigne la sua maniera delle figure si cognosce, e così d'ogni facultà si cognosce lo stile di ciascheduno; ma questa è altra pratica, nonostante che ognuno pure divaria o tanto o quanto, benché si conosca essere fatta per una mano . . . E così ho veduti scrittori nelle loro lettere essere qualche diferenza. Donde questa sottilità e proprietà e similitudine si venga lasceremo alli sopradetti speculativi dichiarare.' *Trattato di architettura*, ed. A. Finoli and L. Grassi (Milan, 1972), I, 28.

61 The final version was dedicated to Pius II (now Vat. lat. 1794) while the copy recorded as being sent to Borso and illuminated by Taddeo Crivelli in 1466 has not survived. I have consulted the Basle edition of 1540. Passages cited here are from the translations in Baxandall, 'Dialogue on Art', and in J. Pearson Perry, 'A Fifteenth Century Dialogue on Literary Taste: Angelo Decembrio's Account of Playwright Ugolino Pisano at the Court of Leonello d'Este', *Renaissance Quarterly*, XXXIX/4, 1986, 613–43. In addition to the bibliography on Decembrio cited by these authors see P. S. Piacentini, 'Angelo Decembrio e la sua scrittura', *Scrittura e civiltà*, IV, 1980, 247–77; A. Biondi, 'Angelo Decembrio e la cultura del principe', in G. Papagno and A. Quondam, ed., *La corte e lo spazio: Ferrara Estense* (Rome, 1982), vol. II, 637–57; Mottola-Molfino and Natali, ed., *Le Muse e il Principe*, I, 162–5.

62 This is also the opinion of A. Tissoni-Benvenuti, in Mottola-Molfino and Natali, ed., ibid., II, 76–8. In an appeal to Borso from the mid-1460s Decembrio reminds the Duke of an 'opus . . . Artis Oratoriae in quo laudes . . . celeberrimae urbis tuae, . . . et in primis Ill. fratris olim tui Leonelli perpetuae memoriae commendavi'. See A. Della Guardia, *La "Politia Litteraria" di Angelo Decembrio e l'umanesimo a Ferrara nella prima metà del secolo XV* (Modena, 1910), 21.

63 Baxandall, 'Dialogue on Art', 317; on Ferrarese tapestry during the reign of Leonello see G. Campori, *L'arazzeria estense* (Modena, 1876), 10–18, and N. Forti Grazzini, 'Leonello d'Este nell'autunno del Medioevo: Gli arazzi delle *Storie di Ercole*', in Mottola-Molfino and Natali, ed., *Le Muse e il Principe*, vol. II, 53–62. On relations between Ferrara and Burgundy during his reign see E. Kantorowicz, 'The Este Portrait by Rogier van der Weyden', *Journal of the Warburg and Courtauld Institutes*, 3, 1939–40, 165–80, and Lockwood, *Music in Renaissance Ferrara*, 57. The discussion of the ideal library is in Decembrio, *De politia litteraria*, Part I.I.iii.

64 Baxandall, 'Dialogue on Art', 314.

65 Baxandall, 'Dialogue on Art', 316, 317. E. Lincoln, 'Mantegna's Culture of Line', approaches the prints of Mantegna as the artist's means of laying claim to mastery, and to professional domination, through advertising the normative and near-mechanical perfection of his hand. Mantegna's laying claim to *ingenium* is hence through a form of manual virtuosity which conspicuously avoids the capricious linear deformations and variations of Tura.

66 Baxandall, 'Dialogue on Art', 324, 325.

67 Baxandall, 'Dialogue on Art', 325: 'eruditionis et cognoscendi cupiditatis incitamentum pictura scripturaque quam idcirco graeci latinique pariter uno saepe vocabulo scripturam appellavere . . . cum de poetarum et

pictorum ingeniis eandem fere rationem demonstraret.'

68 J. Monfasani, *George of Trebizond* (Leiden, 1976), 30. Guarino himself attacked Uberto Decembrio, the father of Angelo, for claiming co-authorship of Manuel Chrysoloras' translation of Plato's *Republic* 'for Manuel dictated it, and he wrote down what was said, like a professional scribe' (*librarius*). See J. Hankins, 'A Manuscript of Plato's Republic in the Translation of Chrysoloras and Uberto Decembrio with Annotations of Guarino Veronese', in Hankins, Monfasani and F. Purnell Jr., ed., *Supplementum Festivum: Studies in Honor of Paul Oskar Kristeller* (Binghamton, NY, 1987), 149–84.

69 Piacentini, 'Angelo Decembrio e la sua scrittura', 252. On Guarino's *animus* against the Decembrii see Hankins, ibid., 153.

70 M. Carruthers, *The Book of Memory: A Study of Memory in Medieval Culture* (Cambridge, 1990), 196.

71 The classic account of the evolution of *litterae antiquae* is B. Ullman, *The Origin and Development of Humanist Script* (Rome, 1960). For more revisionist and deconstructive accounts of handwriting, subjectivity and the ideology of humanism see Jed, *Chaste Thinking*, and, on post-*quattrocento* developments, J. Goldberg, *Writing Matter from the Hands of the English Renaissance* (Stanford, CA, 1990).

72 'non vaga quidem ac luxurianti litera, qualis est scriptorum seu verius pictorum nostri temporis, longe oculeos mulcens, prope autem afficiens ac fatigans, quasi ad aliud quam ad legendum sit inventa, et non, ut grammaticorum princeps ait, litera 'quasi legitera' dicta sit – sed alia quadam castigata et clara seque ultro oculis ingerente, in qua nichil orthographam, nichil omnino grammatice artis omissum dicas'. Petrarch, *Epistolae ad familiares*, XXIII.19.8, discussed by Ullman, *Humanist Script*, 12–13 and by Jed, *Chaste Thinking*, 66–7. On Petrarch and the scribes see also S. Rizzo, *Il lessico filologico degli umanisti* (Rome, 1973), 195f.

73 P. O. Kristeller, 'The Modern System of the Arts', in *Renaissance Thought II: Papers on Humanism and the Arts* (New York, 1965), 172.

74 Quoted from Baxandall, *Giotto and the Orators*, 125. Between 1442 and 1445 the scribe Biagio Bosoni of Cremona is recorded as making a copy of this text, *De ingenuis moribus*, for Leonello d'Este. See Bertoni, 'Notizie sugli amanuensi', 32.

75 The most daring exploitation of this ambiguity is by the abbot Trithemius of Spondheim, in his treatise of the 1490s which defends the work of the scribe against the inroads of printing. Trithemius draws on the notion that 'writers' are remembered by posterity through their works, and extends this to include scribes: 'Qui autem scribere negligunt, mox ut fuerint, in oblivionem omnium, tanquam non fuissent, cito deveniunt; vestra autem memoria

ex libris quos scribitis cum gloria transibit ad posteros.' Johannes Trithemius, *De laude scriptorum*, Ca XVI, ed. K. Arnold (Lawrence, KS, 1974), 96.

76 On Carlo see Capelli, 'La congiura', and Bertoni, 'Notizie sugli amanuensi', 37–41 (with remarks also on Landi).

77 GUARINUS VERONENSIS JACOBO LANDO LIBRARIO POLITISSIMO

> Ut sileam priscos animi probitate nitentes
> Et quis dedaleas fata dedere manus,
> Quanta Macro et Cosmo nostri pictoribus
> aevi
> Tanta tibi ex calamo gloria, Lande, venit.

Text in L. Capra and C. Colombo, 'Giunte all'epistolario di Guarino Veronese', *Italia medievale e umanistica*, 10, 1967, 214. Having followed the identification of 'Cosmo' as Cosmè Tura, 'La tonsura clericale di Cosimo Tura', 164, Enrico Peverada has since expressed reservations, pointing out that the notarial archives from 1458 to 1475 feature a number of references to a miniaturist known as 'Choxeme' or 'Cosmo Baronio'. However, it is not at all evident that Baronio might have enjoyed a fame so comparable with Tura's as to cause contemporary readers to recall the miniaturist rather than the leading court painter. The documents of 1458 refer to Baronio as a *minor*, and the only reference to him working is from 1471. Unlike Baronio, both Tura and Giraldi were celebrated by other contemporary poets (Tribraco in Giraldi's case; Strozzi, Giovanni Santi and – possibly – Bigo Pittorio in Tura's). See Bigo Pittorio, *Tumultuaria Carmina* (Modena, 1492), I and IV for two poems 'Ad Cosmum').

78 J. Richter, ed., *Leonardo da Vinci: Literary Works* (Oxford, 1957), I, 57.

79 Bertoni, 'Notizie sugli amanuensi', mentions in both capacities Carlo di San Giorgio, Don Francesco di Codigoro (active 1437–45), Simone di Pavia (1446), a Franceschino 'scrittore e miniatore' (1451), Filippo di San Giorgio (1451) and Andrea della Vieze, the head of a team of scribes and miniaturists during the reign of Ercole d'Este, on whom see also H. J. Hermann, 'Zur Geschichte der Miniaturmalerei zum Hofe der Este in Ferrara', *Jahrbuch der kunsthistorischen Sammlungen des allerhöchsten Kaiserhauses*, XXI, 1900, 266–8, and Lockwood, *Music in Renaissance Ferrara*, 214–16. The Olivetan monastery of San Giorgio seems to have been an important centre for scribe-miniaturists who worked on occasion for the court, among them Alessandro da Sesto, prior in 1460. See P. Lugano, *Memorie dei piu antichi miniatori e calligrafi olivetani* (Florence, 1903), 43. The court librarian Pellegrino Prisciani illustrated his own works; for illustrations see Papagno and Quondam, *La corte e lo spazio*, III, plates 114–21. Other scribes of the Po valley working in an ever-expanding technical

competence were Felice Feliciano and Damianus de Moyllis of Parma, on whom see C. Bühler, *The Fifteenth Century Book* (Philadelphia, 1960), 49, and S. Edmunds, 'From Schoeffer to Vérard: Concerning the Scribes who became Printers', in S. Hindman, ed., *Printing the Written Word: The Social History of Books circa 1450–1520* (Ithaca, NY, 1991), 21–40.

80 Under the Este the jurisdiction of the guilds had been curtailed from the mid-fourteenth century, and it is not known which professional organisations, if any, regulated the practice of painters, scribes and miniaturists. In other centres such as Florence there appears to have been a clear division of labour. See A. M. Brown and A. C. de la Mare, 'Bartolomeo Scala's Dealings with Booksellers, Scribes and Illuminators, 1459–63', *Journal of the Warburg and Courtauld Institutes*, 39, 1976, 237–46.

81 Carlo 'gothicised' his humanist hand for his transcription and translation of Michele Savonarola's *Confessionale*; see the frontispiece reproduced in Bertoni, 'Notizie sugli amanuensi', 39.

82 On Felice see C. Mitchell, 'Felice Feliciano Antiquarius', *Proceedings of the British Academy*, XLVII, 1961, 197–223.

83 Modena, Archivio di Stato, Libri camerali diversi, 15, fol.139: 'Domenico Gatto da Bagnacavallo di x a marzo L cinque D quarto LM che sono La valure di L4 di boni moniti li quali se gli sono facti pagare in argento per havere exemplato arte scripture per facti di lo Illu.mo Nro. S. como appare al capo suso nostro registro a Lorenzo a la camera.'

84 Tura himself may have painted the dedication miniature for the presentation of Antonio Cornazzano's *Del modo di regere e di regnare* to the Duchess Eleanora d'Aragona between 1476 and 1484. The various attributions to Tura are reviewed and accepted by J. Manca, 'A Note on Cosmè Tura as Portraitist', *Antichità viva*, 303, 1991, 17–20.

85 On the miniature see *From Borso to Cesare d'Este*, 116–17, and Mottola-Molfino and Natali, ed., *Le Muse e il Principe*, I, 186–89.

86 Perry, 'A Fifteenth Century Dialogue', 631.

87 R. Sabbadini, *Classicisti e umanisti negli codici Ambrosiani* (Florence, 1933), 96. For further citations from Decembrio on this distinction, see Rizzo, *Il lessico filologico*, 200–202.

88 Perry, 'A Fifteenth Century Dialogue', 632–3.

89 Tura's own epistolary hand (see plate 1) is in an elegantly flourished style typical of court communications, and features an assertive graphic and linguistic stylisation of his signature: 'Cosmus Pictor.'

90 As could the career of the polymath Damianus de Moyllis of Parma, the calligrapher-miniaturist who set himself up as a printer and as a ceramicist. See Bühler, *Fifteenth Century Book*, 49, and S. Edmunds, in

Hindman, ed., *Printing the Written Word*, 21–40.

91 An Italian example is preserved in the Lilly Library at Indiana University, made by the scribe Guinoforto di Vicomerchato in Milan around 1450. See J. J. G. Alexander, ed., *The Painted Page: Italian Renaissance Book Illumination*, exhibition catalogue (New York, Pierpont Morgan Library, and London, Royal Academy, 1994), 213.

92 S. H. Steinberg, 'Medieval Writing Masters', *The Library*, 4th ser., 22, 1941–2, 203.

93 M. Baxandall, *The Limewood Sculptors of Renaissance Germany* (New Haven and London, 1980), 145–52.

94 The relation of the writing manuals to humanist pedagogy to the internalisation of 'courtliness' and various capacities of royal service is discussed by Goldberg, *Writing Matter*, 146–55 and 257–72. A. S. Osley, *Scribes and Sources* (Boston, 1980), 19, points out that many writing-masters and humanists regarded 'flourishing', the extreme demonstration of calligraphic skill, as 'a confidence trick played on a gullible public'; he cites Erasmus praising fine writing as akin to painting, but at the same time denouncing common scribes with their 'curves, joins, tails and similar frivolous strokes in which they revel out of a kind of pride' (29).

95 For a survey of attributions to Tura before 1974 see Molajoli, *Cosmè Tura*, 84–91. On problems in the connoisseurship of Ferrarese art, especially with regard to the communal manner of the court artist, see K. Lippincott, 'Gli affreschi del Salone dei Mesi e la problema dell'attribuzione', in R. Varese, ed., *Atlante di Schifanoia* (Modena, 1989), 111–41. The problem of Tura as miniaturist is treated in Mottola-Molfino and Natali, ed., *Le Muse e il Principe*, I, 330–33.

96 Manca, 'A Note on Cosmè Tura as Portraitist', 17–20, discusses the grounds for attribution of all three portraits.

97 B. Berenson, *Italian Pictures of the Renaissance* (Oxford, 1932), 580; Roberto Longhi's decision to follow the evidence of the inscription and regard the painting as a simulation of Tura undertaken by Costa 'per capriccio di committente' was proclaimed by R. Varese, *Lorenzo Costa* (Milan, 1967), 69, to be 'antistorico, arzigogolato e specioso'. Varese assigned the work to an anonymous follower of Tura.

98 For a discussion of these paintings see *From Borso to Cesare d'Este*, 70–71; also V. Sgarbi, *Antonio del Crevalcore e la pittura ferrarese del quattrocento a Bologna* (Milan, 1985).

CHAPTER II

1 For an account of the evolution of the *studio* or *studiolo* from monastic to court space see W. Liebenwein, *Studiolo: Storia e tipologia di*

uno spazio culturale, trans. C. Cieri Via (Modena, 1988).

2   The value of literary studies for those involved in public life is one of the themes of Cicero's *Pro Archaia poeta*; see also Pliny the Younger, *Epistolae*, II.17, V.6, IX.7. Regarding ancient civic prototypes for the *studio*, Anna Eörsi cited the temple dedicated to the Muses, as goddesses of public order and harmony, by Pythagoras at Crotona. Eörsi, 'Lo studiolo di Leonello d'Este e il programma di Guarino da Verona', *Acta Historiae Artium Accademiae Scientiarum Hungaricae*, 21, 1975, 30. J. Pearson Perry discusses the impracticality of using the court *studiolo*, such as that of Federico da Montefeltro, for other than display in 'Practical and Ceremonial Uses of Plant Materials as "Literary Refinements" in the Libraries of Leonello d'Este and his Courtly Circle', *La bibliofilia*, XCI, 1989, II, 121–73.

3   Others include the portrait medal, the equestrian monument to his father Niccolò III d'Este, the revival of Plautinian drama. For accounts of the cultural life of Leonello's court which are not over-dependent on a literal reading of Decembrio's *De politia litteraria* see G. Pardi, *Leonello d'Este* (Bologna, 1904) and E. Gardner, *Dukes and Poets in Ferrara* (London, 1904), 26–66. The ideology of culture and rulership is attested to by many sources from the period such as Guarino's oration for Leonello's second wedding in 1444 (cited by Pardi, 57) which refers to the marquis as the ideal of the philosopher prince.

4   Michael Baxandall connected eight panel paintings with Guarino's letter: five seated female figures (London, National Gallery; Milan, Museo Poldi-Pezzoli; Ferrara, Pinacoteca; Budapest, Szépmüvészeti Museum) among whom he recognised a *Thalia* and a *Terpsichore*, and three standing figures (Budapest and Berlin, Staatliche Museum) which he identified as Melpomene, Euterpe and Polyhymnia. However, the substantial lack of correspondence between the letter and some of the figures led him to the conclusion that the paintings were not from Belfiore. See M. Baxandall, 'Guarino, Pisanello and Manuel Chrysoloras', *Journal of the Warburg and Courtauld Institutes*, 28, 1965, 183–205. Eörsi identified the remaining figures as Urania and two versions of Erato, and believed that the painings survive from more than one cycle of the Muses. She accepted, however, the surviving paintings as evidence, albeit at second hand, for the reconstruction of the Belfiore decoration (see preceding note). Miklos Boskovits, in 'Ferrarese Painting around 1450: Some Recent Arguments', *Burlington Magazine*, 120, 1978, 370–85, accepted the seated figures as all coming from Belfiore and regarded the standing figures as belonging to a different

group. Recent technical examination of the panels has strengthened this hypothesis. It has been established that the seated Muses in London, Milan and the Strozzi Collection, which had originally been executed in tempera, were repainted in oil by Cosmè Tura or a follower – which corresponds to documentation of his work for the *studio* between 1458 and 1463. Moreover, all five poplar panels appear to have been cut from the same tree. The technical findings are summarised in A. Mottola-Molfino and M. Natali, ed., *Le Muse e il Principe: Arte di corte nel rinascimento padano*, exhibition catalogue (Milan, Museo Poldi-Pezzoli, 1991), vol. I, 380–425 and vol. II, 223–279.

5   The passage by Ciriaco is preserved by Giovanni Colucci, *Delle antichità picene* (Fermo, 1792), cxliii-cxlv; repr. in Mottola-Molfino and Natali, ed., *Le Muse e il Principe*, II, 326. The Guarino letter given here is from R. Sabbadini, ed., *Epistolario di Guarino Veronese* (Venice, 1915–19), vol. II, 589–90:

> Princeps illustrissime et domine singularis.
>
> Cum praeclaram vereque magnificam in pingendis musis cogitationem tuam nuper ex litteris tuae dominationis intellexerim, laudanda erat merito ista principe digna inventio, non vanis aut lascivis referta figmentis; sed extendendus fuisset calamus et longius quam expectas volumen dilatandum; deque musarum numero ratio evolvenda, de qua multi varios fecere sermones. Sunt qui tres, sunt qui quatuor, sunt qui quinque, sunt qui novem esse contendant. Omissis reliquis sequamur hos extremos qui novem fuisse dicunt. De ipsis igitur summatim intelligendum est musas notiones quasdam et intelligentias esse, quae humanis studiis et industria varias actiones et opera excogitaverunt, sic dictas quia omnia inquirant vel quia ab omnibus inquirantur: cum ingenita sit hominibus sciendi cupiditas. $\mu\tilde{\omega}\sigma\theta\alpha\iota$ enim graece indagare dicitur; $Mov\sigma\alpha\iota$ igitur indagatrices dicantur.
>
> Clio itaque historiarum rerumque ad famam et vetustatem pertinentium inventrix; quocirca altera manu tubam, altera librum teneat; vestis variis coloribus figurisque multimodis intexta, qualiter sericos videmus pannos consuetudine prisca. Thalia unam in agricoltura partem repperit, quae de agro plantando est, ut et nomen indicat, a germinando veniens; idcirco arbusculas varias manibus gestet; vestis esto floribus foliisque distincta. Erato coniugalia curat vincula et amoris officia recti; haec adulescentulum et adulescentulam utrinque media teneant, utriusque manus, imposito anulo, copulans. Euterpe tibiarum repertrix chorago musica gestanti instrumenta gestum docentis ostendat: vultus hilaris adsit in primis, ut origo

vocabuli probat. Melpomene cantum vocumque melodiam excogitavit; eapropter liber ei sit in manibus musicis annotatus signis. Terpsichore saltandi normas edidit motusque pedum in deorum sacrificiis frequenter usitatos; ea igitur circa se saltantes pueros ac puella habeat, gestum imperantis ostendens. Polymnia culturam invenit agrorum; haec succincta ligones et seminis vasa disponat, manu spicas avarumque racemos baiulans. Urania astrolabium tenens caelum supra caput stellatum contempletur, cuius rationes excogitavit idest astrologiam. Calliope doctrinarum indagatrix et poeticae antistes vocemque reliquis praebens artibus coronam ferat lauream, tribus compacta vultibus, cum hominum, semideorum ac deorum naturam edisserat.

Scio plerosque fore qui alia musarum signent officia, quibus Terentianum respondebo illus: 'quot capita, tot sententiae'. Bene vale, princeps magnanime decusque musarum, et Manuelis filii negotium et labores commendatos ut habeas supplex oro.

6   See A. Venturi, 'Cosma Tura genannt Cosmè, 1432 bis 1495', *Jahrbuch der Königlich preussischen Kunstsammlungen*, 8, 1887, 6–7.

7   A. Franceschini, *Artisti a Ferrara in età umanistica e rinascimentale: Testimonianze archivistiche* (Ferrara, 1995–6), Part I, no. 954a, b.

8   Quoted in E. Gombrich, 'Raphael's *Stanza della Segnatura*', in *Symbolic Images* (London, 1972), 97. On Argyropoulos, see N. Wilson, *From Byzantium to Italy: Greek Studies in the Italian Renaissance* (Baltimore, 1992), 86–90.

9   'Honestas quaque picturas, caesuras ve quae vel deorum, vel heroum emoriam repraesentent. Ideoque saepenumero cernere est quibusdam iucundissimum imaginem esse Hieronymi describentis in heremo, per quam in bibliothecis solitudinem & silentium, & studendi scribendique sedulitatem oportunam advertimus.' A. Decembrio, *De politia litteraria* (Augsburg, 1540), fol. 3*v*.

10   Quoted from J. H. Gaisser, *Catullus and his Renaissance Readers* (Oxford, 1993), 22. Original text in Milan, Biblioteca Ambrosiana, F 141 sup., fol. 68*v*, cited in R. Sabbadini, *Le scoperte dei codici Latini e Greci ne'secoli XIV e XV* (Florence, 1914), ii, 201: 'Publice non legantur Iuvenalis, Persius, Martialis Cocus, Propertius, Tibullus, Catullus, Priapeia Virgilii, Naso de arte amandi et de remedio amoris, sed relinquantur studio camerario videre eos volentium, ut plurima sciantur, non ut quisquam adolescens tyro eorum lectione contaminetur.'

11   For the letter, see n.5 above.

12   '. . . Musarum divis imaginibus suiscumque sacris insignibus et praeclaris ac eximis plurigenis perbelle quidem atque mirifice exornantem.' Colucci, *Antichità picene*, 15, cxliii,

repr. in Mottola-Molfino and Natali, ed., *Le Muse e il Principe*, II, 326.

13 Clio hoc ad basim ex Guarino nostro epigramma conscriptum habet: 'Historiis, famamque et facta vetusta reservo.'

14 '. . . manu levem pulsando citharam, heroidea facie in olympum ad parentem versa honesta gravique quadam alacritate ut chordae melodemati concordem paena cantu perbelle quidem modulari et roseis labiis vocem formare visa . . .'

15 The allusion is to the *fleur-de-lis* of the French royal coat of arms. The right to quarter these with the Este white eagle was granted to Niccolo d'Este in 1431 by King Charles VII to mark a formal alliance between the two courts. See A. Frizzi, *Memorie per la storia di Ferrara* (Ferrara, 1847–8), I, 69.

16 For instance, by D. Benati in Mottola-Molfino and Natali, ed., *Le Muse e il Principe*, I, 404–8.

17 The fundamental study in this regard is P. Rajna, 'Ricordi di codici francesi posseduti dagli Estensi nel sec. XV', *Romania*, II, 1873, 49–58. See also J. Woods-Marsden, *The Gonzaga of Mantua and Pisanello's Arthurian Frescoes* (Princeton, 1988), 136f. For an example of a humanist use of the rose metaphor see G. G. Pontano, *Eclogae*, I.12, in *Poesie latine*, ed. L. Monti Babia (Turin, 1977), 2: 'Has inter frondes virgultaque nota latebas/ cum tibi prima rosam, primus mihi fraga tulisti.'

18 Giovanni Boccaccio, *De genealogia deorum*, III.23 (Venice, 1494; repr. New York, 1976), 28r [on the roses of Venus]: 'illi rosas in tutelam datas aiunt; eoque rubeant atque pungant: quod quidem libidinis proprium esse videtur. nam turpitudine sceleris erubescimus: & conscientiae peccati vexamur aculeo: et sicut per tempusculum rosa delectat: parcoque temporis lapsu marcet: sic & libido parvae brevisque delectationis: & longe poenitentiae causa est . . .'

19 Benati, in Mottola-Molfino and Natali, ed., *Le Muse e il Principe*, I, 383–9.

20 See the evidence from reflectograms discussed by P. Brambilla Barcilon, in Mottola-Molfino and Natali, ed., *Le Muse e il Principe*, II, 266–75.

21 See G. Baruffaldi, 'Cosimo Tura', in *Vite de'pittori e scultori ferraresi* (Ferrara, 1844–6), vol. I, 80–81; C. Cittadella, *Catalogo istorico de'pittori e scultori ferraresi* (Ferrara, 1782–3), vol. I, 54, and Mottola-Molfino and Natali, ed., *Le Muse e il Principe*, I, 396. The figure bore an inscription identifying it as Charity until its recent restoration.

22 For these *ekphrases* see M. Baxandall, *Giotto and the Orators* (Oxford, 1971), 86, 91.

23 Examples include the *Realm of Venus* painted by Titian for Alfonso d'Este, the nephew of Leonello and Borso, in 1519; the putti rendered in an exhibitionistic *sotto in sù* in Mantegna's Camera degli Sposi ceiling;

the appearance of naked and sometimes urinating children on painted salvers, such as that by Bartolomeo da Fruosino in the Metropolitan, New York. See K. Christiansen, 'Lorenzo Lotto and the Tradition of Epithalamic Paintings', *Apollo*, 124, September 1986, 166–73.

24 The analysis is based on determining relations between the organic structure of the poplar panels, thus establishing that they were cut from the same trunk; the results available so far regarding the Berlin panel are to my mind not conclusive. See Mottola-Molfino and Natali, ed., *Le Muse e il Principe*, II, 246–8.

25 Giovanni di Ferrara records a song performed by Caritas in an allegorical pageant for Borso's triumphal entry of Reggio as duke in 1453:

> o unico dilecto
> di miseri mortali! o rosa degna
> Eccote la insegna
> de l'unicorno che como l'acqua el monda
> Cussi tu de li affari nostri rompi l'onda.

Johannes Ferrariensis, 'Excerpta ex annalium libris illustris familiae marchionum Estensium', *Rerum Italicarum Scriptores*, 20, Part ii (Bologna, 1936), 44.

26 Eörsi, 'Lo studiolo', 16, 36–8.

27 J. Dunkerton, A. Roy and A. Smith, 'The Unmasking of Tura's *Allegorical Figure*: A Painting and its Concealed Image', *National Gallery Technical Bulletin*, II, 1987, 5–35. See also Dunkerton, in Mottola-Molfino and Natali, ed., *Le Muse e il Principe*, II, 251–63.

28 See T. Tuohy, Review of *Le Muse e il Principe*, *Apollo*, 134, December 1991, 425–7 and *Herculean Ferrara: Ercole d'Este, 1471–1505, and the Invention of a Ducal Capital* (Cambridge, 1996), 209.

29 Modena, Archivio di Stato, Camera Ducale Estense, Memoriale 33 (1481–1512), c.154 sx.:

> 1481, 31 agosto
> Illustrissimo nostro Signore in libro per conto de Intrà et Spesa, et a Spesa al capitolo delo offitio del spectabile Marco de Galeoto magnifico maistro camarlengo etc., de' dare adi soprascripto L. novantanove, soldi octo marchesani, li quali se fanno boni per la Signoria Sua a Cosme depinctore per resto de la depinctura de tre figure nude de femine depincte ad olio et de la cunzadura de quatro tavole depincte cum quatro figure de femina ad olio, poste nel studio del prefato nostro Signore; como a credito a lui a libro RR de lo offitio del dicto Marco, c.63 . . .

The document is included with others related to the same commission in Franceschini, *Artisti a Ferrara*, Part II, vol. I, no. 362d, v, and in Mottola-Molfino and Natali, ed., *Le Muse e il Principe*, II, 308.

30 If the series included the nude figures, it probably depicted either the Seven Liberal Arts – Pollaiuolo's tomb of Sixtus IV from the following decade represents these as partially draped figures – or the Seven Virtues; a drawing by Tura in Berlin (Kupferstichkabinett) shows a demonic, bird-like *Charity* with her breasts and torso exposed. Giorgio da Sebbenico's standing *Charity* on the Loggia dei Mercanti in Ancona from the 1450s wears a cloak which falls from her shoulders, exposing her completely. Two drawings from the school of Pollaiuolo in the Uffizi show Prudence and Justice as naked to the waist. See R. Van Marle, *Iconographie de l'art profane au Moyen-Age et à la Renaissance* (The Hague, 1932), figs 51 and 52. On iconographic grounds, I find it unlikely that the surviving panels were incorporated into a cycle of Months in the 1481 series, as suggested by Tuohy, *Herculean Ferrara*, 209. It is by no means clear, for instance, what months could possibly be designated by the *Erato*, *Urania* and *Terpsichore* panels.

31 'coll'arbore dactilo et la alicorno della divisa del duca Borso'. C. Corvisieri, 'Il trionfo romano di Eleonora d'Aragona', *Archivio della Società Romana di storia patria*, I, 1878, 650. Unicorns appear in Este imagery at least from the *trecento* onwards and the device was adopted by Este clients such as the Romei family. A unicorn appears on coinage issued by Borso's successor Ercole; however, this is the rampant type found in the earliest versions of the motif. The unicorn with the palm tree, sometimes dipping his horn in a spring, seems to have been original to Borso in the fifteenth century; the first instances of its revival appear to be with his nephew Alfonso in the early sixteenth century. See V. Ferrari, *L'araldica estense nello sviluppo storico del dominio ferrarese* (Ferrara, 1989), 69f.

32 Although the technical examination shows that a layer of smoky grime had built up on the panel before repainting, Jill Dunkerton points out that this need not indicate an interval of more than a couple of years before the re-painting took place. See Dunkerton *et al.*, 'The Unmasking of Tura's *Allegorical Figure*', 31.

33 The connection has been proposed by, among others, G. Mariani Canova, in Mottola-Molfino and Natali, ed., *Le Muse e il Principe*, II, 110.

34 See J. Anderson in ibid., II, 180.

35 There are possible analogies here with the 'natural' throne in Gentile da Fabriano's *Virgin and Child* (Perugia, Pinacoteca).

36 Lewis and Short, *A Latin Dictionary* (1879, 1962) give as a primary definition: 'stuff, matter, materials of which anything is composed, so, the wood of a tree, vine, etc.' *Materia* can also designate timber for building as opposed to wood for fuel (*lignum*). *Materiarius* can be defined as

carpentry or the timber trade, while the rare verb *materio* means 'to build of wood', as in Vitruvius, 5.12,7: 'eaque aedificia minime sunt materianda propter incendia.'

37 The notion could be found, for instance, in the definition of *fabula* in the *Etymologiae* of Isidore of Seville (1.40): 'Fabulas poetae a fando nominaverunt, quia non sunt res factae, sed tantum loquendo fictae. Quae ideo sunt inductae, ut fictorum mutorum animalium inter se coloquio imago quaedam vitae hominum nosceretur.' On the distinction between poetic making and imitation in Salutati see A. Fisher, 'Three Meditations on the Destruction of Virgil's Statue: The Early Humanist Theory of Poetry', *Renaissance Quarterly*, XL/4, 1987, 607–36.

38 For an interpretation of the London figure as Venus, see M. A. Jacobsen and V. J. Rogers-Price, 'The Dolphin in Renaissance Art', *Studies in Iconography*, 9, 1983, 31.

39 See S. K. Heninger Jr., *Touches of Sweet Harmony: Pythagorean Cosmology and Renaissance Poetics* (San Marino, CA, 1974), esp. 179ff.

40 See Plato, *Timaeus*, 47 a–d; *The Republic*, 616c–617b; The association is examined by K. Meyer-Baer, *Music of the Spheres and the Dance of Death: Studies in Musical Iconology* (Princeton, 1970).

41 See Servius on the *Aeneid*, v.864; Servius, *Georgics*, 1.8; First Vatican Mythographer, I.42; Apollonius Rhodios, *Argonautica*, IV.896, refers to Terpsichore as the mother of the Sirens. See also Boccaccio, *Genealogia*, VII.XX, 56r–57.

42 E. R. Curtius, in an important chapter on the Muses in his *European Literature in the Latin Middle Ages* (Princeton, 1953, 1990), 232–41, discusses the anxiety and strategies of camouflage which attended upon the invocation of the Muses by Christian authors.

43 'Whenever [the poets] recount for you the deeds or words of good men, you ought to cherish and emulate these and try to be as far as possible like them: but when they treat of wicked men, you ought to avoid such imitation, stopping your ears no less than Odysseus did, according to what those same poets say, when he avoided the songs of the Sirens.' St Basil, 'Address to young men on how they might derive profit from pagan literature', in St Basil, *The Letters*, trans. R. J. Deferrari and M. R. P. Maguire (Cambridge, MA, 1934), 389. The letter provided a crucial point of reference for Guarino for his defence of the study of poetry in 1450. See Sabbadini, ed., *Epistolario*, II, 523.

44 On the response to Boethius in Renaissance poetic theory see L. Panizza, 'Italian Humanists and Boethius: Was Philosophy For or Against Poetry?', in J. Henry and S. Hutton, ed., *New Perspectives on Renaissance Thought: Essays in the History of Science, Rhetoric and Philosophy* (London, 1990), 48–67.

45 The best survey of the tradition from antiquity through the Middle Ages is Curtius, *European Literature*, 228–47.

46 'Poesis est quae negligentes abiiciunt & ignari est fervor quodam exquisite inveniendi atque dicendi seu scribendi quod inveneris. Qui ex sinu dei procedens paucis mentibus ut arbitror in creatione conceditur. Ex quo quoniam mirabilis sit: rarissimi semper fuere poetae. Huius in fervoris sunt sublimes effectus utputa mentem in desiderius dicendi compellere: peregrinas & inauditas inventiones excogitare: meditatas ordine certo componere: Ornare compositus inusitato quodam verborum atque sententiarum contextu: velamento fabuloso atque decenti veritatem contegere.' Boccaccio, *Genealogia*, XIV.vii, 104. The translation is that of C. G. Osgood, *Boccaccio on Poetry* (Indianapolis and New York, 1956), 39. A discussion of the four kinds of poetic fiction is in XIV.ix, of which the fourth kind, branded as 'deliratium vetularum' is deemed void of truth.

47 On Coluccio's defence of poetry and his conception of its role in education see H. Baron, *The Crisis of the Early Italian Renaissance* (Princeton, 1955), 295–300; E. Garin, *Il pensiero pedagogico dello umanesimo* (Florence, 1958), 53–71; C. Trinkaus, *In Our Image and Likeness: Humanity and Divinity in Italian Humanist Thought* (London, 1970), 555–71, 697–704; R. G. Witt, 'Coluccio Salutati and the Conception of the *Poeta Theologus* in the Renaissance', *Renaissance Quarterly*, XXX/4, 1977, 538–64; Panizza, 'Boethius', 61–3; W. G. Craven, 'Coluccio Salutati's Defence of Poetry', *Renaissance Studies*, X/1, 1996, 1–30.

48 'Forte rectius erat, cum poetica totum trivium, quadrivium philosophiam omnem, humana divinaque et omnes prorsus scientias presupponat, post hec omnia de ipsa tractare. Sed quia iuxta Quintiliani sententiam . . . videtur poetarum enarratio ad grammaticum pertinere, et prout ars et scientia est pars una logice, hoc est sermocinalis scientie . . . non inconveniens est de ipsa cum liberalibus artibus disputare . . .' Salutati, letter to Giovanni Dominici, quoted in Garin, *Pensiero pedagogico*, 64.

49 'fatendum sit artem poeticam inter sermocinales scientias sine dubitatione sublimem quasi celum quoddam cunctas musici concentus armonias, quas celo sive celi speris assignaverunt Platonici.' Salutati, *De laboribus Herculis*, 1.ix, ed. Berthold Ullman (Turin, 1951), 40.

50 Ibid., 43–5.

51 Euterpe signifies pleasure in learning, Melpomene 'meditation', Polyhymnia means 'multa memorantem', Erato the faculty of 'similia inveniens', and Terpsichore represents judgement. Salutati, ibid., 44.

52 Ibid., 46: 'Male igitur fecit Fulgentius qui, ut cetera dimittam, sicut supra retuli, post tot et tantos autores . . . de Musis novum aliquid cogitavit et edidit.'

53 Ibid., 46–7: 'in hoc, ni fallor, omnibus profuturi, quod, si aliquid intactum ab aliis exponemus, poterunt studiosi in melioris explanationis claritudinem pertransire.'

54 'Sed dato, quod hec poetarum figmenta induant apud Varronem multiplex opus nature aut nonnulla hominum facta in deos relata, numquid est per ignaros lectores pueris tradenda? Nullus denique, si sic ait, quod ipse concedo, est huius doctrine capax, qui philosophie naturalis peritia caret . . . Et sic iuniores non transibunt ab ubere matris ad studium poesie, neque poetas docebunt docere nescinetes ignari.' Dominici, *Lucula Noctis*, ed. E. Hunt (South Bend, IN, 1940), Cap. 44, 386. Dominici proceeds in Cap. 45 to attack the 'scenicam et obscenam artem poeticam' (391).

55 Osgood, *Boccaccio*, 94, translating from *Genealogia*, Book XIV chapter xx: 'Altera autem ea est quae ab inhonestis comicis tracta scoenas atque theatra & quadrivia tenet et scaelestibus fictionibus ob mercedem se inerti vulgo placidam exhibet nullo commendabili ornatu conspicua.' On humanist philology as an activity of 'chastening' (*castigatione*) see S. H. Jed, *Chaste Thinking: The Rape of Lucretia and the Birth of Humanism* (Bloomington, IN, 1989), esp. 45–6, 76–8.

56 Panizza, 'Boethius', 55.

57 See the discussion of Salutati in Fisher, 'Three Meditations'.

58 'Aliter est cum de vitiis et voluptatibus praecepta conscribuntur quae omnia fugitanda sunt, ut qui de amandi arte de incantibus et magiis, de saporibus et condimentis conficiuntur libri.' Sabbadini, ed., *Epistolario*, II, 530.

59 On Guarino and Catullus see Sabbadini, 'Se Guarino abbia fatto una recensione di Catullo', *Studi Vergiliani*, 1885, 27–30; W. Ludwig, 'The Origin and Development of the Catullan style in Neo-Latin Poetry', in P. Godman and O. Murray, ed, *Latin Poetry and the Classical Tradition: Essays in Medieval and Renaissance Literature* (Oxford, 1990), and Gaisser, *Catullus and his Renaissance Readers*.

60 For E. Grassi, *Renaissance Humanism: Studies in Philosophy and Poetics* (Binghamton, NY, 1988), 47–63, the most important feature of Guarino's reflection on poetry is the status given to the poetic word as cognitive and creative, a 'language of being' rather than as mere formal vehicle or embellishment of subject-matter. His view provides an imaginative and stimulating counterweight to the 'de-mystifying' view of Guarino's pedagogy provided by A. Grafton and L. Jardine, despite the strength and value of their arguments, 'Humanism and the School of Guarino: A Problem of Evaluation', *Past and Present*, 96, 1982, 51–80.

61 See Janus' 'Panegyric on Guarino Veronese'

published by I. Thomson, *Humanist Pietas* (Bloomington, IN, 1988), l.516–70.

62 N. Wilson, in Mottola-Molfino and Natali, ed., *Le Muse e il Principe*, 83. C. Grayson, 'Studi su Leon Battista Alberti', *Rinascimento*, IV, 1953, 45–62, considers Alberti to be among the first of the *quattrocento* humanists to draw upon Hesiod, in a vernacular text entitled *Villa* from the 1430s, and in his *Theogenius*, dedicated to Leonello d'Este.

63 J. Anderson, in Mottola-Molfino and Natali, ed., *Le Muse e il Principe*, II, 165–87.

64 Gundersheimer, *Ferrara*, 136. Pardi, *Leonello d'Este*, 167, notes that Nicholas V granted Leonello an exemption from the payment of the *decima* on certain marshlands which had been or would be brought under cultivation, and on 6 February 1442 Leonello summoned an engineer from Grenoble regarding hydraulic projects in the Po valley.

65 J. Bridgeman, '*Belle considerazioni*: Dress in the Works of Piero della Francesca', *Apollo*, 136, October 1992, 218. Bridgeman's dating of the style of drawstring dress to the late 1460s neglects the evidence of the Belfiore *Thalia* which must date from around 1450. The Annunciate Virgin on Tura's Ferrara cathedral organ-shutters also has an opening in her dress at the area of the womb, reinforcing the theme of pregnancy or impregnation.

66 It could be argued that the appearance of agricultural imagery in neo-Latin poetry itself served as a vehicle for the exploration of erotic themes; a clear case would seem to be the *Eclogues* of Pontano. The association of rustic and agrarian themes with sexual frankness is clearly manifest in the *Carmina Priapaea*, a collection of poems dedicated to the phallic god of orchards and gardens which enjoyed a wide circulation in this period – Ermolao Barbaro the Elder names the 'Auctor Priapearum' in his *Orationes contra poetas* (see the edition by G. Ronconi, Florence, 1972, 22). On the Latin *Priapea* and their authorship see W. H. Parker, *Priapea: Songs for a Phallic God* (London, 1988), 10–30. Charles Dempsey has treated the *quattrocento* interest in the erotic themes of the rustic writers and the implications for mythological painting in his *The Portrayal of Love: Botticelli's 'Primavera' and Humanist Culture at the Time of Lorenzo the Magnificent* (Princeton, 1992), 20–49.

67 'Has ob res non mediocres Musis gratias debes quibus a pueritia usque imbutus et institus te tuos et urbane negotia negere disponere et administrare, restiuere ac sustenere didicisti. Quo effectum est ut Musas ipsas non modo chordarum et citharae sed rerum etiam publicarum moderatrices esse demonstres.' From Sabbadini, ed., *Epistolario*, I, 263; the translation is that of Grafton and Jardine, 'Humanism and the School of Guarino'. The passage had a key place in Garin's account of the revolutionary aspects of humanist pedagogy and hence it is a starting-point for Grafton's and Jardine's more deflating account of the disparity between the humanists' 'extravagant claims for a natural and self-evident relation between an education in the revived humanities and "preparation for life" as a mature citizen of integrity' and the actual scope of this education. See Garin, *Pensiero pedagogico*, 326–8; Grafton and Jardin, ibid., 53. The passage is cited with regard to Belfiore by Eörsi, who is heavily influenced by Garin's view of Guarino, in 'Lo studiolo', 30.

68 Est domus in media longe spectabilis
urbe concilium Phoebi Pieridumque
vocant . . .

'Ad Herodotum Alicarnasiensem historiographum et Hesiodum Ascraeum poetam celeberrimum ut Guarini Veronensis viri doctissimi et eloquentissimi domum repetunt et ab eo Platonis volumen nomine suo poscunt.' The volume in question is probably Guarino's life of Plato. See Sabbadini, ed., *Epistolario*, II, 423.

69 See Thomson, *Humanist Pietas*, 120, 142.

70 '. . . olim tot emolumentis amicitiis laudibus honestatus fuisset, filius damno odiis difformaretur et ignominia; quamve liberalissimam quondam nutricem incoluerat pater, eam infestam sibi novercam filium experiretur, et quem mihi delicias et senectutis nutritorem educarim et intra musarum sacra sicut meam quandem effigiem effinxerim, ipsum animi mei tormentum reservatum audirem.' Sabbadini, ed., *Epistolario*, II, 497.

71 Guarino continually attempted to mould the opinions of his former pupil – not, apparently, regarding affairs of state, but in order to influence the prince to adopt a favourable line on controversies within the world of letters in which Guarino had become involved. In 1449 he wrote to Leonello 'de lingue latine differentiis' criticising the positions held by Leonardo Bruni and others on the existence of distinct vernacular and literary languages in antiquity. Sabbadini, ed., ibid., II 813, 503–11.

72 Among those addressed were the recently appointed Bishop of Ferrara, Francesco dal Legname, the newly elected Pope Nicholas V, Leonello's secretary Uguccione Abate, King Alfonso of Aragon and Poggio Bracciolini.

73 Sabbadini, ed., ibid., II, 492.

74 Sabbadini, ed., ibid., II, 485: 'Audisse velles, vir insignis, quot quantosque fructus ex doctina orientes fluvius ille dicendi collegit; quam idoneum ad virtutes instrumentum, ad famam ad decus ad gloriam ante oculos posuit, quantam iocunditatem, quantam otii et secordiae fugam; quos honores dignitates praefecturas, quem ordinem quam conditionem quae tempora in disciplinarum gradibus distribuerit, ut aliae ancillae, non-

nullae comites, duces alterae sint, postremo ut cunctarum domina et regina veniat sacrarum litterarum cognitio, ad quam ceterarum vigiliae labores intentio referatur, vel prophetico illo asserente testimonio: "bonitatem et disciplinam et scientiam doce me". Quas ad res accepisses non dico virum lacteo eloquentiae fonte manantem, sed fluvium, immo vero "flumina iam lactis, iam flumina nectaris ibant". Non defuerunt antiquorum veterum priscorum novorum, gentilium hebraeorum christianorum, principum regum, prophetarum sibyllarum exempla et probationes, ut effusis omni cum copia poetis oratoribus historicis doctoribus, nova inaudita inexpectata testimonia, veluti Padus inundans eruperit . . .'

75 Sabbadini, ed., ibid., III, 160: 'Nam ut Augustinum, Hieronymum reliquosque doctissimos ecclesiae principes omittam, ne longior dicendo sim, eruditissimum et illustrissimum Veronensem episcopum Zenonem animadvertite. Num ipsius scripta non dicam Virgilium ceterosque gravissimos poetas, sed etiam lascivos comicos et procaces satyros stili suavitate et orationis decore redolent et mirum in modum effingunt?'

76 See Beccadelli, *Antonii Panormitae Hermaphroditus*, ed. C. F. Forberg (Leipzig, 1908). For the scant bibliography on Beccadelli see the entry in *Dizionario biografico degli italiani*, vol. 7 (Rome, 1965). See also the English translation and introduction by M. de Cossart, *Antonio Beccadelli and the Hermaphrodite* (Liverpool, 1984).

77 Sabbadini, ed., *Epistolario*, II, 201. I have partly quoted this letter in chapter I.

78 Catullus, *Carmina* 16:

Nam castum esse decet pium poetam
Ipsum, versiculos nihil necessest . . .

79 Sabbadini, ed., *Epistolario*, II, 521: 'Hunc nobis ostendit et aperta promittit dextera domina illa praeclara disciplinarumque regina theologia, cui reliquae, velut ancillae, musae artes doctrinaeque subserviunt obsequuntur et ministrant.'

80 For example the treatise by the Augustinian Timoteo Maffei of Verona, *In sanctam rusticitatem litteris*, the Benedictine Girolamo Agliotti's *De monachis erudiendis*, and Antonio Beccaria's *Orationes defensoriae* delivered before Ermolao Barbaro, Bishop of Verona, around 1455. For discussion (with bibliography) see D. Robey, 'Humanist Views on the Study of Poetry in the Early Renaissance', *History of Education*, 13, 1984, 20–21.

81 See Barbaro, ed. Ronconi, and discussion by Robey, ibid., 22.

82 Ibid., 88: 'Nec tum quidem ullo in honore poeticam fuisse ex eo ipsius libro potissimum constat . . . id est opera et dies, cum in eo libro illum ad aratrum et telluris cultum provocet, quasi inopem agricolam ac desidem virum nullique liberali prorsus assuetum

industriae. Quod maximo argumento est nec ea, aetate in aliqua hominum opinione aut auctoritate poeticam fuisse.'

83 His salary was drastically reduced by the new prince Borso d'Este, who also prevented him from leaving Ferrara to take up employment elsewhere, and the initial promise of a new patron for the last great work of his career, his translation of Strabo's *Geography*, was dashed when Pope Nicholas V died in 1455, leaving Guarino without support for over a year. See Thomson, *Humanist Pietas*, 134–6.

84 Sabbadini, ed., *Epistolario*, II, 212, on his defence of Beccadelli, employing the formula of Manuel Chrysoloras (later taken up by his son Battista, see previous note): 'At enim Persius, Horatius, Iuvenalis obscena efferunt: fateor, illi ad instruendum mortalium vitam et as maius vitiorum fastidium ante oculos obiciunt . . . Id et in pictoribus usuvenire cernimus, quorum cum in adumbrando scorpione mure serpente partibusque reconditis et latere volentibus aptitudinem miramur, non tamen non ea fastidimus abhorremusque spectando.'

85 *Patrologia Graeca*, 161.973–4: 'Dicam equidem quanto dignus Theodorus honore, quem plusquam dimidium animae meae semper deligam, cujus versiculos, quos de Musis tuis elegantissime edidit, in sacrario illo pulcherimmo incidi jubeas, etiam atque etiam rogo et obsecro. Quid enim gravius Callimachus? quid suavis Propertius? quid pulchrius Tibullus dicere unquam potuisset? Nam et nomen et officiam Musarum concinne exprimunt, et earum laudam ad picturam alludentes brevius concinnunt. Nobile hominis ingenium, tantum philosophum in hujusmodi deliciis praestare!'

86 Lazzari, 'Il *Barco*', 17:

Clio mihi nomen celebranti gesta virorum
    Aurea mi vestis, aureus est animus.

Melpomene dicor supremi filia Regis
    Voce trahens homines luminibusque deos.

87 Fulgentius, quoted from L. G. Whitbread, ed. and trans., *Fulgentius the Mythographer* (Columbus, OH, 1971), 44. For the Muses in Martianus Capella see *The Marriage of Philology and Mercury*, ed. and trans. W. H. Stahl and R. Johnson with E. L. Burge (New York, 1977), I. xxvii.

88 Propertius, III. 3:

quippe coronatos alienum ad limen amantis
    nocturnaque canes ebria signa fugae,
    ut per te clausas sciat excantare puellas,
    qui volet austeros arte ferire viros.

89 I have used the text of Basinio da Parma's poem in F. Ferri, *La giovinezza di un poeta: Basinii Parmensi Carmina* (Rimini, 1914), 37:

. . . Namque ego praetereo tabularum signa tuarum
    Aonidum decus: ut plena stet imagine miris

Picta tabella modis; viva est qua candida Clio
Clio Pieridum laetissima, qualis ab imi
Lucifer Oceani sacra iubar extulit unda . . .

90 Ibid., 37:

Heus ait, an vigilas, Leonelli fide minister?
O vigila, neque enim somno indulgere
    poetas
Tam longo fas est; divinae parce quieti
Et Leonellus accingere dicere laudes.
Surge age, et ipse tui Leonelli nomen ad
    astra
Tolle. Libens adero, nec te tua Musa
    relinquam;
Neque ego quam pingi iussit sum candida
    Clio,
Clio Pieridum laetissima: cerne venustas,
Dulcis amice, genas, vultus, oculosque
    nitentes:
Hanc faciem in tabulis ipsam vidisse
    memento.
An quisquam nostra vir tempestate Latinos
Vi tanta praestabit avos tantoque favore
Ingenio aspirare tuo volet?

91 For a discussion of the medal and for bibliography see M. G. Trenti Antonelli, in Mottola Molfino and Natali, ed., *Le Muse e il Principe*, II, 33.

92 Lo Amore me ha facto cieco, e non ha tanto
    De Charità, che me conduca in via,
    Me lassa per dispecto en mea balia
    E dice: hor va tu, che presciumi tanto . . .

The sonnet is included with that quoted below in G. Baruffaldi, *Rime scelti de poeti ferraresi, antichi e moderni* (Ferrara, 1713), 20–21. Baruffaldi appears to have seen 'un intero libro MS [of Leonello's poetry], da dov'è tratto il presente saggio'.

93 Translation from Gardner, *Dukes and Poets*, 53.
    Batte el cavallo su la balza alpina,
        Et scaturir su d'Helicona fonte,
        Dove chi le man bagna, e chi la fronte
        Secondo che piu honore, O Amore lo
            enchina.
    An ch'eo m'accosto spexo alla divina
        Acqua prodigioxa de quel monte:
        Amor mi ride, che'l sta li con prompte
        Le sol sagipte en forma pellegrina;
    E mentre el lubro a ben se avanza, et
        stende,
    Ello con el venen della pontura
    Macola l'onda et venenoxa rende.
    Si che quell'acqua, che de soa natura
    Renfrescan me dovrebbe, piu m'accende,
    E più che bagno, più cresce l'arsura.

94 The first such characterisation is in the *Cronica in rima di Casa d'Este* by Ugo Caleffini, who matter-of-factly describes Leonello's impregnation of a daughter of his teacher in the arts of war, Bracio da Montone. Sixteenth-century chroniclers report that he had four or five illegitimate children, of whom all that is known is that Francesco was kept out of the way at the court of Burgundy for most of his life. Giovanni Battista Giraldi wrote: 'Fuit Leo-

nellus natura ad libidinem proclivior, cui cum plus aequo operam daret intempestivam sibi mortem accesivit.' On these sources, see Pardi, *Leonello*, 63.

95 . . . Algentes ardent, et sunt in amore furentes
    Quam primum biberint pocula dulcis
        aquae.
    Huc, Leonarde, veni sacros haustare liquores,
    Sic iuvenis fies; sic in amore furens.
    Postquam marmoribus gelidoque in fonte
        resedi,
    Plena fuere mihi corda dolore gravi.
    Vellem divini raperent mea corda furores
    Ad quos me hortaris dive poeta tuos . . .

For the complete text of 'Marasii Siculi ad Leonellum Aretinum: De laudibus Fontis Gai' see *Carmina illustrium poetarum italorum* (Florence, 1720), vol. VI, 251–2.

96 . . . Nam quem Gorgoneo primum
        appellavere poetae,
    Nunc fontem Gajum tempora nostra
        vocant.
    Cruda voluptatis siquid mea verba tulerunt,
    Carminibus nostris si qua libido fuit;
    Laus omnis Veneri datur: omnis gloria fonti:
    Quos cecini versus haec mihi dictat acqua.
    Quid mihi collibuit me inter numerare
        Tibullos . . .

97 Translated from the text in Sabbadini, *Biografia documentata di Giovanni Aurispa* (Noto, 1890), 176–7: 'Itaque mutato consilio musas invocavi ut mihi aliquantulum inspirarent meaque labra si non Parnasi sacris undis, saltem lymphis illius Gai Fontis de quo nuper quam plures suavissimos elegos edidisti, aspergerent ac, si repente ex corvo (ut inquit ille poeta) cygnus prodirem, eis hecatomben pollicitus sum. Proxima deinde nocte in somnis mihi visum est musarum gremio sublatum in Gaio Fonte demersum. Quamobrem paulo post experrectus alacri animo ad scribendum accessi et hoc opusculum in nostram linguam transtuli, in quo si quid elegans visum fuerit, cum Homero omnium poetarum praestantissimo, tum maxime illis undis, quibus tua carmina uda esse dicis, attribruito; sin autem aliquid ineptum offenderis, id a me editum esse credas . . .'

98 . . . Armatae veniunt, mirum est, e fonte
        sorores,
    Intrant et thalamum splendida turba meum.
    Secum blanditias, lascivaque verba ferebant,
    Otiaque et plausus, deliciaque prius.
    Consuevere comus niveis ornare ligustris,
    Cingebat frontem fulva corona suam.
    Consuevere caput viridi connectare oliva,
    Stabat et auratis vestibus arte nitor.
    Aurea per flavos serpebat spira capillos.
    Ornabat nitidas candida gemma manus.
    Nunc clipeos hastasque ferunt, parmamque
        sudemque,
    Pilaque sunt manibus tela verenda suis . . .

99 Hunc Gajum vocitant certe a probitate
    sororum

Fontem, quem celebrant numina sacra
novem

100 On the fountain and its iconography see A. C. Hanson, *Jacopo della Quercia's Fonte Gaia* (Oxford, 1965), 22–34, C. Seymour Jr., *Jacopo della Quercia, Sculptor* (New Haven and London, 1973), 44–52, and J. Beck, *Jacopo della Quercia* (New York, 1992), I, 81–8, none of whom discusses the Marrasio-Marsuppini correspondence.

101 These both occur among the *Epigrammata* of the exiled Sienese cleric Francesco Patrizi (who elsewhere in verses dedicated to Lodovico Gonzaga and Pius II introduced the Muses as apologists for amorous poetry):

From 'De immanitate pestilentiae':

Est urbis medio Campus quo pulchrior
usquam
Non datur in terris cerni mortalibus alter
Hac qua parte sacer Musis argenteus exit
Fons.

From 'Ad librum suum de Institutione Reipublicae quem Senam mittit':

. . . Quaere iter ad fontem Phoebo
Musisque sacratum
Quo non Castali gratior unda fuit.
Est in conspectu geminos enixa Quirinos
Ilia, marmorei nobile fontis opus.

Full texts in L. F. Smith, 'A Notice on the Epigrammata of Francesco Patrizi, Bishop of Gaeta', *Studies in the Renaissance*, 15, 1968, 100n, 118.

102 The poems by Marrasio and Guarino are published by Sabbadini, ed., *Epistolario*, II, 149–54.

103 For instance, in Guarino's poem (13–16):

. . . Hinc personatae primum sonuere
Camenae;
Nutriit ast larvas insidiosa Venus.
Palpat amans loquitur tractatque licentius
artem,
Dum larva, ut clipeo, retia aperta iacit.

104 In the poem by Marrasio, 20–21:

Censores habeant undique mille senes
Et dicunt quaecumque velint impune
loquentes,
sive iocos velint, sive pudenda velint.

105 Formosae pulchraeque petant tua tecta
puellae,
Est quibus aurata et candida vesta honos;
Et cunctae Veneres, tua quas Ferraria nutrit
Et si qua auratis vestibus una decor,
Ut digitis digitos possint coniungere nostris,
Ad citharam ut possit quaeque movere
pedes.
Haec si praecipias, ex Gaio fonte Camenas
Traducam ad clari brachia longa Padi.
Maiorum laudes titulos et gesta tuorum
Illustremque domum et te Leonelle, canam.
Dii tibi dent quaecumque velis, quaecumque
rogabis;

Asper qui fuerat, sit tibi mitis Amor
(41–52).

106 For Losco's letter see Sabbadini, *Giovanni Aurispa*, 182–3.

107 For biographical information on the poet see Sabbadini, *L'Angineletum di Giovanni Marrasio* (Verona, 1892).

108 Pardi, *Leonello*, 50.

109 St Basil, *The Letters*, trans. Deferrari and Maguire, IV, 417, 419.

110 Original text and translation in Baxandall, *Giotto and the Orators*, 82.

111 Pisanello is set alongside the artists of antiquity, but distinguished from them by the truth of his representations. Sabbadini, ed., *Epistolario*, I, 557:

Deorum
Mendaces illi effigies componere norant;
Tu Patrem aeternum, totum qui condidit
orbem
Ex nihilo, sanctosque viros componis eos,
qui
Religione viam ad superos docuere beatam.

112 Ibid., II, 589–90: 'Quo fit ut ad meum sensum Zeuxim, Apellem, Polycletum et, ut de nostris dicam, Gentilem, Pisanum, Angelum pingendi artificio superaris et eo magis quod primum quidem illi caducis et vanescentibus in dies coloribus pingebant aut pingunt, deinde quia mutas reddebant effigies et in quibus longe magis artificis quam effictae personae laus emineret, tu vero Manuelem meum sic firmiter sic perpetuo duraturum sic viventem exprimis coloras et pingis, ut maior in dies illi vita accedat et nominis immortalitas.' The letter is briefly referred to and described as 'not very interesting' by Baxandall, *Giotto and the Orators*, 88.

113 'Bene igitur mones atque prudenter, plurimum a scriptura potestate usu dignitate distare picturam, cum haec tacens iaceat, illa semper loquens vigeat, illa praeterea ad imitandos bonos et probitatem imbibendam animet, haec ad pascendum duntaxat oculos vix maneat. Unde a poeta dictum est "atque animum pictura pascit inani" et Tullius "oblectamenta puerorum" appellavit.'

114 It is attributed to him by Decembrio; see Baxandall, 'Dialogue on Art', 325: 'cum tamen ad unum intendant: eruditionis et cognoscendi cupiditatis incitamentum pictura scripturaque . . .'

115 The suggestion regarding the portrait medal was made by Baxandall, ibid., 90. On the development of the *impresa* or emblem in the circle of Guarino see K. Lippincott, 'The Genesis and Significance of the Fifteenth Century Italian *Impresa*', in S. Angelo, ed., *Chivalry in the Renaissance* (Woodbridge, Suffolk, 1991), 67f.

116 Hoc plebs credula gentium exterarum
Hoc larvas solitum timere vulgas
Hoc turbae faciant hypocritarum . . .

Full text in Janus Pannonius, *Carmina Selec-*

tiora, ed. T. Kardos (Budapest, 1973), 28.

117 The section of *De politia litteraria* devoted to the defence of poetry – in which Leonello and Guarino confront the monk Augustine – is in Book v.lxiii.

118 Perleges nostrum cum forte, Guarine,
libellum,
Dixisti (ut perhibent) haec ego non doceo!
Non haec tu, venerande, doces, Guarine,
fatemur
Sed quibus haec fiunt, illa, Guarine, doces.

M. D. Birnbaum, *Janus Pannonius, Poet and Politician* (Zagreb, 1981), 31.

119 Illa sibi solita est nimium lasciva videri;
Confiteor, vitae congruit ergo suae.
Est vir obscenus, nostrae est lascivia Musae,
Illa levis versu, moribus ille levis.

Beccadelli, *Hermaphroditus*, I.x, ed. Forberg, 16, 18; English translation by de Cossart, *Beccadelli*, 29.

120 *Hermaphroditus*, I.xxv, 36; de Cossert, ibid., 35:

AD MINUM, QUOD LIBELLUM CASTRARE NOLIT
Mine, mones nostro demam de carmine
penem,
Carmina sic cunctis posse placere putas.
Mine, meum certe nolim castrare libellum,
Phoebus habet penem, Calliopeque femur.

121 Sescentas, age basiationes

da nostro mea, compatri, Thalia,
quem nos plus oculis amamus unum.

The poem 'Ad Thaliam' was re-incorporated by 1457 into the more 'respectable' collection *Parthenopeus, sive de Amores*, Ixxvi. For discussion of the *Pruritus* see Ludwig, 'Catullan Style', 189–91.

122 'Ad Musam, de lascivia libelli', in *Carmina*, II, 405:

Si queritur, quod tu tam spurca voce
loquaris
dic quod te futuo, quod futuo ac futuo.

123 For a theorisation of homosocial desire as regulated through objectification in woman see E. K. Sedgwick, *Between Men: English Literature and Male Homosocial Desire* (New York, 1986), chapter 1. Sedgwick elaborates a schema from an essay by Gayle Rubin, 'The Traffic in Women: Notes on the "Political Economy" of Sex', in R. Reiter, *Toward an Anthropology of Women* (New York, 1975), which proposes an anthropological model of the transfer of women as property between men, a commerce or 'traffic' which symbolises and secures bonds formed on the basis of common male interests.

124 Petrarch, *De vita solitaria*, from the version by Tito Vespasiano Strozzi dedicated to Borso d'Este, quoted in Della Guardia, *Tito Vespasiano Strozzi: Poesie latine tratte dall'Aldina e confrontate coi Codici* (Modena, 1916), xxx: 'La veritade è immortale, la finzione e le cose che sono fuori di sua natura non durano; le simulate subito si manifestano e fannosi

174

palese. Li capelli pettinati con gran studio, da piccol vento son turbati; li artificiosi colori con maestrevol mano sopra la faccia imposti, per ogni poco sudore, per quella discorrendo facilmente si dileguano e lo astuto mentire eziandio è vinto dal vero; e chi vorrà sottilmente e con diligenza bene esaminare quello, il comprenderà esser corpo trasparente cioè tale quale seria alcuna cosa molto negra riachiusa in un purissimo cristallo.'

125 Giovanni da Ferrara, 'Excerpta', 4.

126 Ille hic, Cosmiaca pulcherrima cuius imago
Ac verae similis, tam bene picta manu est.

Strozzi, *Eroticon*, IV.1; Della Guardia, *Tito Vespasiano Strozzi*, 255.

127 For the criticism of the aristocratic and princely pursuit of hunting by the court physician Michele Savonarola, see A. Samaritani, 'Michele Savonarola, riformatore cattolico nella Corte Estense a metà del sec. XV', *Atti e memorie della deputazione provinciale Ferrarese di storia patria*, ser. 3, 22, 1976, 63.

128 Baxandall, 'Dialogue on Art', 325.

129 Ecce novis Helene consumitur anxia curis
Vultque tua pingi, Cosme perite; manu,
Scilicet in longos ut nobilis exeat annos
Et clarum egregia nomen ab arte ferat.
Sed dum consultat quae tantis commoda rebus
Tempora, quos habitus induat, annus abit.
Ver modo laudatur, modo dicitur aptior aestas;
Nunc placet Autumnus, nuncque probatur hiems.
Nunc cupit externis pingi velata capillos
Cultibus, et nuda nunc libet esse coma.
Dumque diem, et varios alternat inepta paratus,
Quod cupit, in longas protrahit usque moras.
Quid tibi vis? quid stulta paras? an forte vereris
Ne levitas populo nota sit ista satis?
Tales totque tibi cum sint in corpore mendae,
Formae pictorem quaeris habere tuae?
Quod si cura novae te tangit imaginis et si
Spectari a sera posteritate cupis,
Edita, quae populus de te modo carmina legit
Illa tuos mores, effigiemque tenent:
Illa tibi poterunt pallorem afferre legenti,
Si tener impuro fugit ab ore pudor:
Forsan et arte mea, longum transmissa per aevum,
Altera venturo tempore Thais eris.

Eroticon, 124–5. For a translation see C. Gilbert, *Italian Art 1400–1500* (Englewood Cliffs, NJ, 1980), 187–8.

130 On Guarino's identification of the humanist Isotta Nogarola with the Muses and its 'chastising' implications, see his letter to Nogarola, Sabbadini, ed., *Epistolario*, II, 308. Grafton and Jardine discuss the containment of female intellectuals in the circles of Guarino and Poliziano through the inscription of such allegorical types of chastity in their *From Humanism to the Humanities*, 29–58, and Lightbown, *Mantegna*, 194f., cites a number of poetic associations of Isabella d'Este with the 'chaste Muses'.

131 On the sumptuary law of 1447 and its sphere of inclusion see Pardi, *Leonello*, 80–81, and on the special conditions imposed on prostitutes by sumptuary laws at Ferrara and elsewhere see D. O. Hughes, 'Distinguishing Signs: Ear-Rings, Jews and Franciscan Rhetoric in the Italian Renaissance City', *Past and Present*, 112, 1986, 26, n.74.

132 On the tradition of Christian misogyny see I. MacLean, *The Renaissance Notion of Women* (Cambridge, 1980). One of the most important equations of painting and female beauty for the Renaissance is *The Hall* by Lucian (an author from whose works Guarino made translations), in which the ideal decoration of a room is likened to the modest attire of the honest woman and contrasted with the cosmetic excess and masquerade of the courtesan. On the portrayal of the beautiful woman 'as a synecdoche for the beauty of painting itself' see E. Cropper, 'The Beauty of Women: Problems in the Rhetoric of Renaissance Portraiture', in M. Ferguson, M. Quilligan and N. Vickers, ed., *Rewriting the Renaissance: The Discourses of Sexual Differences in Early Modern Europe* (Chicago, 1986). On the association of femininity with the seductive deceptions of artifice and the dangerous power of visual fascination see D. L. Clark, 'Optics for Preachers: The *De oculo morali* by Peter of Limoges', *Michigan Academician*, 9/3, 1977, 340–43; J. Lichtenstein, 'Making up Representation: The Risks of Femininity', *Representations*, 20, 1987, 77–87; M. Camille, *The Gothic Idol: Ideology and Image-Making in Medieval Art* (Cambridge, 1989) 298–338.

133 Pontano, 'De amore coniugalia', in B. Soldati, ed., *Carmina* (Florence, 1902), II, 115–16.

134 Intactu florem maturaque poma legenti
servat in occultis virgo iam nubilis hortis...

Pontano, *Poesie latine*, 8. On the offering of cherries, 10.

135 Quis non miretur gestusque et sancta virorum
Corpora, quae penitus vivere nemo neget?
Quisve Iovis faciem pictam non pronus adoret,
Effigiem veri numinis esse ratus?

Full text in Baxandall, *Giotto and the Orators*, 160.

136 S. Pasquazi, *Poeti estensi del rinascimento* (Florence, 1966), 147.

137 Pasquazi, ibid., 144.

138 'cum septem praestanti corpore nymphas praesidebat, per quas Virtutem cumulas clare intelligebatur.'

139 'veluti si sponsa viro suo traduceretur, quae summa cum honestate fieri solet.' Giovanni da Ferrara, 'Excerpta', 41.

140 Rosenberg, 'The Iconography of the Sala degli Stucchi in the Palazzo Schifanoia in Ferrara', *Art Bulletin*, 61, 1979, 377–84.

141 The relevant excerpts are included in translation in Gilbert, *Italian Art*, 148, 157–8. For St Antonino of Florence and painting see also Gilbert, 'The Archbishop on the Painters of Florence, 1450', *Art Bulletin*, 41, 1959, 75–89; on Savonarola's attitudes see M. B. Hall, 'Savonarola's Preaching and the Patronage of Art', in T. Verdon and J. Henderson, ed., *Christianity and the Renaissance: Image and Religious Imagination in the Quattrocento* (Syracuse, 1990), 493–523.

142 L. B. Alberti, *On Painting and On Sculpture*, ed. and trans. C. Grayson (London, 1972), 84; Filarete, *Trattato dell'architettura*, ed. J. Spencer (London and New Haven, 1965), vol. 2, fol. 179*v*. The theatricality of poetry was implied in Boethius' denunciation of the Muses as *scenicas meretriculas*; Augustine's censure of poets occurs in the context of his attack on theatre in *De civitate dei*, II.14.

143 On the image and symbolism of the hermaphrodite in the Renaissance see C. Freccero, 'The Other and the Same: The Image of the Hermaphrodite in Rabelais', *Rewriting the Renaissance*, 145–58; J. M. Saslow, *Ganymede in the Renaissance* (New Haven and London, 1986), 77–96; A. R. Jones and P. Stallybrass, 'Fetishizing Gender: Constructing the Hermaphrodite in Renaissance Europe', in J. Epstein and K. Straub, ed., *Body Guards: The Cultural Politics of Gender Ambiguity* (New York and London, 1991), 80–111.

144 Filarete, *Trattato*, ed. Spencer, vol. 2, p. 206. Facsimile, 155*r*: 'Quello che fece quel di Roma, Alcamene, discepolo di Phidia, con una immagine d'ermofrondita, cioè Venere, lui avea scolpita di marmo, collocata di fuori delle mura d'Atene, non stante che molte altre figure n'avea fatte nella citta di suo mano.'

145 Paris, Louvre. For an account of this picture see Lightbown, *Mantegna*, 186–208, 440–43; see also Jane Martineau, ed., *Andrea Mantegna*, exhibition catalogue (London, Royal Academy, and New York, Metropolitan Museum of Art, 1992), 418–30.

146 '[il] poeta, con la scienza prima che ha, il fa degno e libero di potere comporre e legare insieme si e no come gli piace, secondo sua volontà. Per lo simile al depintore dato è libertà potere comporre una figura ritta, a sedere, mezzo uomo mezzo cavallo, si come gli piace, secondo sua fantasia.' Cennino Cennini, *Il libro dell'arte*, ed. F. Brunello (Vicenza, 1971), 4. I owe the observation regarding Donatello to Mary Pardo.

147 'Ha quest'arte con la poetica affinita grande, donde nacque quel d'Horatio, A Pittori, & a'Poeti e data egual potesta. La quel sententia per non essere al modo, che Horatio la disse, intesa da gl'ignoranti, precipita gran

moltitudine di pittori in varij errori, facendosi lor lecito diventar Africa, che di continovo partorisce novi mostri.' Mario Equicola, *Istitutioni . . . al comporre in ogni sorte di rima della lingua volgare* (Milan 1541), quoted from A. Colantuono, '*Dies Alcyoniae*: The Invention of Bellini's *Feast of the Gods*', *Art Bulletin*, LXXIII/2, 1991, 241.

148 B. Nicolson, *The Painters of Ferrara* (London, 1950), 10.

149 In the fifteenth century the term 'Hermaphrodite' was understood in at least two ways. One was as a category of biologically defined sex, associated with the mutability of the female body and its potential to develop male sexual characteristics. T. Laqueur in *Making Sex: Body and Gender from the Greeks to Freud* (Cambridge, MA, 1990) and P. Brown in *The Body and Society* (New York, 1988) have discussed the 'single sex' model in Galenic medicine, where the female body was regarded as an unstable variation of the male. The Renaissance had its own articulate notion of the phallic woman, expressed in the notion of the reversibility of the uterus and the penis. Stallybrass and Jones, in 'Fetishizing Gender', discuss some reported cases of hermaphroditism in the fifteenth century, one of the them reported by Pontano (based in Naples, but very much an 'insider' with regard to the Guarino circle of Ferrara); all of these are women who have 'turned into' men. Applied to a man, however, the term 'hermaphrodite' was less medical than moral and social, indicating that he had become a sodomite. One ancient authority for such a usage was Strabo's *Geography* (a text translated by Guarino); a more recent one was Dante, *Purgatorio*, XXVI.82. Such a categorisation is understood in Beccadelli's *Hermaphroditus*, in a passage (xxxiii) where his personified book is threatened with castration:

Tuscus es, et populo jucunda est mentula Tusco;
Tusculus et meus est, Marmuriane, liber.
Attamen e nostro praecidam codice penem,
Praecidat simulac, Marmuriane, jubes.
Nec prius abscindam, nisi tu prius ipse virilem
Promittas demptam suggere nolle notam.

150 For a characterisation of the beloved as a fearful Medusa by Tito Strozzi see the poem in S. Prete, *Studies in Latin Poets of the Quattrocento* (Lawrence, KS, 1978), 78. Leonard Barkan has discussed the desire of humanism – in its nostalgic celebrations of the classical past, its idealisation of the pedagogical relationship, its cultivation of élite and exclusive male society – as an anxiously homoerotic one, affirmed yet disavowed in the humanist's co-opting of another sexually transgressive mythological figure as self-image – the rape of Ganymede. See Barkan, *Transuming*

Passion: Ganymede and the Erotics of Humanism (Stanford, CA, 1991).

151 On the medal see G. F. Hill, *A Corpus of Italian Medals of the Renaissance before Cellini* (London, 1930), vol. I, 92, no. 360.

152 Pontano, 'Tumulus Anthonii Panhormitae poetae nobilissimi', *Poesie latine*, 226, 228.

153 Thomson, *Humanist Pietas*, 34, citing Janus Pannonius, *Epigrammatae*, I.xc.

154 On the monument see G. Agnelli, 'I monumenti di Niccolò III e Borso d'Este in Ferrara', *Atti e memorie della deputazione Ferrarese di storia patria*, 23, 1919, 1–32.

155 See W. Ludwig, *Die Borsias des Tito Strozzi* (Munich, 1977) and K. Lippincott, 'The Neo-Latin Epics of the North Italian Courts', *Renaissance Studies*, III/4, 1990, 422–5.

156 Antonio Cornazzano's vernacular poem entitled 'De excellentum virorum principibus ab origine mundi' is a panegyric of Borso which is dominated by accounts of festivals, ceremonies and nuptial processions. For an account see Mottola-Molfino and Natali, ed., *Le Muse e il Principe*, I, 179, and F. Gabotto, *Notizie ed estratti del poemetto inedito De excellentum virorum principibus di Antonio Cornazzano* (Pinerolo, 1889).

157 See A. S. Piccolomini (Pius II), *The Commentaries*, II, trans. Florence Alden Gragg, *Smith College Studies in History*, XXV/4, 1940, 181. The relations of Pius II and Borso d'Este are discussed further in chapter IV.

158 Giovanni da Ferrara, 'Excerpta', 3: 'Parum admodum profecto splendoris atque gloriae Protogenis aut Apellis penicillus, vel Scopae Lisippique officina viris suo aevo illustribus contulisset fuissetque ornamento, Borsi magnanime Dux, nisi illis priscorum heroum signis statuisque, in eorum immortalis gloriae monumentum marmore auro caelatis, literarum lumen accessisset.'

159 Ibid., 44.

160 'hominum res gestae, corporum habitudines, flagitia, mores gestus, incessus, sive citus, sive tardus, sic aptissime descriptus est.' Ibid., 4.

161 'Et ut spectacula voluptatem praestarent, iussit omnes stare; arrectisque auribus, intentis animi viribus, cuncta serio prospiciens, in tanta rerum varietate et mira inter se artis disposicione atque ornatu *animum pascebat*.' Ibid., 42.

CHAPTER III

1 M. Ferretti in A. Mottola-Molfino and M. Natali, ed., *Le Muse e il Principe*, exhibition catalogue (Milan, Museo Poldi-Pezzoli, 1991), vol. I, 337–42, considers an association of the planned altarpiece with the confraternity of San Sebastiano in San Francesco, but concluding that 'l'inconsueta nudita di Sant'Agata' indicates a small altarpiece for private use.

2 Antonio Cicognara was one of the twelve

members of the governing council of Ferrara in 1462. See F. Passini-Frassoni, *Dizionario storico-araldico dal'antico ducato di Ferrara* (Rome, 1904). The possibility that the canvas was flanked by additional portions cannot be precluded; Tura's style of drawing in the faces shows a very strong affinity with the work of Michele Pannonio and Taddeo Crivelli, suggesting a dating in the 1450s, rather early for a single-panel altarpiece. See A. Bacchi, *Dipinti ferraresi dalla collezione Vittorio Cini* (Vicenza, 1990), 5. The painting was in the sacristy of Santa Maria della Consolazione, Ferrara, according to G. A. Scalabrini, *Memorie istoriche delle chiese di Ferrara e di suoi borghi* (Ferrara, 1773), 236, and other accounts; it cannot, however (as Ruhmer assumes in *Cosimo Tura*, London, 1958, 171), have been made for this church, which was constructed by Ercole d'Este for the Servite order in 1501. See Bernardino Zambotti, *Diario Ferrarese*, ed. G. Pardi in *Rerum italicarum scriptores*, 24, Part 7, no. 2. (Bologna, 1928), 304. A possible original site was the monastic church of San Clemente, where the notary Jacopo Cicognara was interred in 1487, although other members of the family were buried at San Francesco. See Zambotti, ibid, 190.

3 The hazards of reliance on Baruffaldi and Cittadella are pointed out by G. Bargellesi, 'Tura o Aleotti ad Argenta?', *Atti e memorie della deputazione provinciale Ferrarese di storia patria*, ser. III, 11, 1972. Cittadella's account of an altarpiece by Tura in the church of San Giacomo at Argenta (near Ferrara) served Mario Salmi as the basis for the reconstruction of a hypothetical altarpiece from the panels now in Caen, the Louvre, Uffizi and Bergamo, whereas Bargellesi shows that Cittadella was in fact referring to a surviving altarpiece by the local painter Aleotti. See C. Cittadella, *Catalogo istorico de'pittori e scultori ferraresi* (Ferrara, 1782–3), vol. I, 55, and M. Salmi, *Cosmè Tura* (Milan, 1957), 40.

4 'una anchona de intaio cum foiami minuti minuti e lavori a l'antiqua'. See A. Franceschini, *Artisti a Ferrara in età umanistica e rinascimentale* (Ferrara, 1995–6), Part II, vol. I, no. 117b, f. Fragments of a portable altarpiece by Tura survive (an *Annunciate Virgin* in the Colonna Collection, Rome; a *St Maurelius* in the Museo Poldi-Pezzoli, Milan; a *St George* in the Cini Collection, Venice) featuring a uniform architectural setting decorated in the Este colours – red, white and green. This cannot have been the small altarpiece Tura made in 1475, which featured eight saints and a *Virgin and Child*, with Este devices, but no *Annunciation*; it may, however, represent an example of a similar work made for the court. See A. Bacchi in *Le Muse e il Principe*, vol. I, 334–7, and the forthcoming exhibition catalogue *La miniatura a Ferrara, dal tempo di Cosmè Tura all'eredità di Ercole de' Roberti* (Modena, 1998).

5 Franceschini, *Artisti a Ferrara*, Part II, vol. 1, no. 736; see also Introduction to the present volume. Tura does not specify the subject of the first panel, but states that it was made for the church of San Niccolò in Ferrara six years previously. G. Baruffaldi, *Vite de' pittori e scultori ferraresi* (Ferrara, 1844–6), vol. 1, 64, and Cittadella, *Catalogo istorico*, I, 51, both record seeing a St Anthony by Tura in the same church. Ruhmer, *Cosimo Tura*, 180, asserts that there is 'no doubt' that this is the panel now in Modena, and that moreover it is the unnamed painting referred to by Tura along with another San Antonio. This allows him to date the painting to 1484. Although this scenario is possible, I am inclined to be more tentative about alligning surviving paintings with available documentation.

6 See P. Gino and M. Zanotti, *La Basilica di San Francesco di Ferrara* (Genoa, 1958); A. Franceschini, 'Associazioni laiche ferraresi di gravitazione francescana nei secoli XIII–XV', *Analecta Pomposiana*, VII, 1982, 185–248; P. T. Lombardi, *I Francescani a Ferrara* (Bologna, 1974–5), vol. 1, 74–8.

7 For documents on Bonzohane, Titolivio and Gherardo da Vicenza, see Franceschini, *Artisti a Ferrara*. For documentation on the *cappella maggiore* of San Giacomo 'di città' see Franceschini, ibid., Part I, no. 1049.

8 Franceschini, ibid., no. 808.

9 See the many images of Christ, the Passion, the Virgin Mary and saints (chiefly Catherine, Jerome, George, Sebastian, Christopher, Francis) in the *guardaroba* inventories of 1493 and 1494; G. Campori, *Raccolta dei cataloghi ed inventarii inediti* (Modena, 1870), 1–3, 15–22.

10 For a discussion of both de Lardi commissions and the attribution of the *St Maurelius* to Tura see R. Stemp, *Sculpture in Ferrara in the Fifteenth Century: Problems and Studies* (Ph.D. dissertation, Cambridge University, 1992), 29–31. The *Nativity* is recorded in C. Barotti, *Pitture e scoltore . . . nelle chiese . . . di Ferrara* (Ferrara, 1770), 44. On the attribution of a terracotta sculpture to Tura, see Ruhmer, *Cosimo Tura*, 36–7.

11 The conception of saintly qualities specific to this period in terms of *admiranda* and *imitanda* follows the account of R. Kieckhefer, *Unquiet Souls: Fourteenth Century Saints and their Religious Milieu* (Chicago, 1984), 8–15.

12 As is most lucidly discussed by R. Trexler, *Public Life in Renaissance Florence* (Ithaca, NY, 1980), above all in his account of 'framing' – both literal, as applied to an image, and figurative, encompassing ritual practices around the sacred: 'The Renaissance frame contained more than rich materials and craftsmanship. . . . It was often studded with discrete objects like jewels – not only valuble commerically but possessing a characterological value . . . The spatially mediating frame thus also mediated material and moral values between devotees and enclosed images' (92).

Applied in a wider sense, Trexler's formulation might be suggestive for considering the place of material value and 'worldly' artifice in a courtly religious milieu.

13 J. P. Richter, *Literary Works of Leonardo da Vinci* (London, 1970), vol. 1, 36.

14 See Ruhmer, *Cosimo Tura*, 6, for an assertion that 'Tura's saints are the complete expression of inner problems', albeit those characteristic of 'ascetics and fanatics'.

15 Ruhmer, ibid., 12, 45, and more recently J. Bentini, ed., *San Giorgio e la principessa di Cosmè Tura* (Bologna, 1985), 45.

16 For the visible signs of sanctity, see A. Vauchez, *La sainteté en occident aux derniers siècles du moyen age* (Rome, 1988), 499ff.; M. C. Pouchelle, 'Représentations du corps dans la *Légende dorée*', *Ethnologie française*, 6, 1976, 293–308; D. Weinstein and R. M. Bell, *Saints and Society* (Chicago, 1982), 156.

17 Vauchez, ibid., 487.

18 See K. Park, 'The Organic Soul', in C. B. Schmitt, ed., *The Cambridge History of Renaissance Philosophy* (Cambridge, 1987), 464–84.

19 On the theory of physiognomic expression in art literature see L. Defradas in R. Klein, ed., *Pomponius Gauricus: De Sculptura (1504)* (Geneva, 1969), 115–26.

20 'Because . . . judgement is one of the powers of our soul, through which it composes the form of the body in which it lives according to its will, when it has to reproduce with the hands a human body, it willingly reproduces the body of which it was the original inventor, and from this it arises that he who loves will eagerly fall in love with things similar to himself.' M. Kemp, ed., *Leonardo On Painting*, New Haven and London, 1989, 120.

21 'Dal viso si cognosce l'uomo et dallo aspecto della faccia si cognosce el savio.' G. Ferraresi, *Il Beato Giovanni Tavelli da Tossignano e la riforma di Ferrara nel quattrocento* (Brescia, 1969), vol. II, 322.

22 For a discussion of Leonardo's art theory in relation to the physiognomical tradition of the pseudo-Aristotle and other texts, see M. W. Kwakkelstein, 'Leonardo's Grotesque Heads and the Breaking of the Physiognomic Mould', *Journal of the Warburg and Courtauld Institutes*, 54, 1991, 127–36.

23 See A. Denieul-Cormier, 'La très ancienne physiognomonie et Michel Savonarole', in *Biologie médicale* 55, 1956, lxviii–lxix.

24 There is a degree to which this may reflect the absorbtion of a paradigm manifest in late antiquity and maintained in the Greek east, for which see P. Brown, *The Body and Society: Men, Women and Sexual Renunciation in Early Christianity* (New York, 1988), 235, who discusses the ascetic refashioning of the soul through the body among the desert fathers. The writings of these sages were acquiring a new importance in Italy in the wake of Guarino and Ambrogio Traversari. But the 'corporeal' paradigm is already implicit in

Western hagiographies such as Jacopo da Voragine's *Legenda aurea*; see Pouchelle, 'Représentations du corps dans la *Légende dorée*', which shows the centrality of bodily trials for the attestation of sanctity in the most widely known hagiographical collections. The sacristy of the cathedral of Ferrara acquired an illuminated *Legenda aurea* during the episcopacy of Giovanni Tavelli. See Ferraresi, *Il Beato Giovanni Tavelli*, I, 504.

25 'Et dal pericoloso stato mondano l'ha diseperata, ponendola nel nobilissimo claustro della santa religione, acciò che in esso purgata dl ogni macula di peccato, & vestendosi lo addornamento delle sante & nobili virtude, riformando la bellezza de l'anima & riducendola al primo stato dell'innocentia, acciò che essi degnamente possa entrare dopppo questa peregrinatione nel glorioso thalamo del suo castissimo & virgine sposo Christo Giesù . . .' C. Vegri, *Le armi necessarie alla battaglia spirituale* (Bologna, 1614), 7.

26 'La bellezza vostra sia dentro, dinanzi a colui che dentro habita e riposa, nel corpo di fuore disformate et palide per li digiuni, et vigili et orationi et altre discipline et fatiche della religione, così conformate al vostro sposo, lo quale tollendo le parole di Isaia: Noi lo reputamo come uno lebroso percossso da Dio et humiliato, per lo cui lividore et palidore noi siamo sanati.' Tavelli, 'De perfectione religionis', in Ferraresi, ed., *Il Beato Giovanni Tavelli*, II, 272.

27 For examples see K. Park, 'The Criminal and the Saintly Body', *Renaissance Quarterly*, XLVII/1, 1994, 21–9. On Bernardino see R. Kieckhefer, 'Holiness and the Culture of Devotion: Remarks on some Late Medieval Male Saints', in R. Blumenfeld-Kosinski and T. Szell, ed., *Images of Sainthood in Medieval Europe* (Ithaca, NY, 1991), 300–301.

28 'Questa fa l'anima avere la sua conversazione in cielo . . . Questo crocifige l'anima al mondo et il mondo a lei. . . . Questa fa che l'anima non desidera se non croce. Questa induce l'anima in uno abisso di illuminatione divina . . . Questa è fornace di fuoco, che arde et non consuma, anzi consolida, rende formositade, valitudine et ogni bellezza . . . O vehementia di diliectione; o violentia di caritate; o excellentia et supereminentia di perfecto amore, il quale così penetra il cuore, infiamma l'affecto et essa anima in tal modo per infino nelle sue midolle trafiggie, ch'essa veracemente possa dire: "Io sono ferita di caritate e dalla caritade".' Tavelli, 'De perfectione religionis', in Ferraresi, *Il Beato Giovanni Tavelli*, II, 332.

29 C. W. Bynum, 'Material Continuity, Personal Survival, and the Resurrection of the Body: A Scholastic Discussion in its Medieval and Modern Contexts', *Fragmentation and Redemption* (New York, 1991), 239–97, further developed in *The Resurrection of the Body* (New York, 1995), especially chapter 6 on

the resistance to and initial condemnation of Aquinas' propositions on formal identity which denied material continuity of the person; the position had, however, found wide acceptance by the fifteenth century.

30 T. Kaeppeli, 'Tommaso dai Liuti di Ferrara e il suo *Declaratorio*', *Archivum fratrum praedicatorum*, 20, 1950, 205. On the highly charged nature of this question, a reprise of the beatific vision controversy of the early fourteenth century, see Bynum, *Resurrection of the Body*, 279–318.

31 Vauchez, *La sainteté en occident*, 472–89, discusses the church's preferred criteria for recognition of saints during a period he characterises as 'the mystic invasion' of the fourteenth and fifteenth centuries, when the canonisation process for 'mystical' candidates for sainthood was frequently unsuccessful, especially in the case of women.

32 'Alii spiritelli appelantur, fingentes non velle amare nec audire nisi celestia verba tristarique videntur si quandoque audiunt aliquos loquentes verba mundana aut aliquod iocosum. Alii dicentur magna sancti, qui vadunt osculando sanctos per ecclesias ut videantur divoti. Alii abstracti nominantur, qui in missa in communione videntur a sensibus alienati, sicut illa bona domina de cremona que cotidie communicabit et post communionem per hora stabat elevata in contemplatione; tandem ex fornicatione concepit plures filios. Hoc temporis meis fuit . . . Alii barbati nominantur, qui barbam prolixam nutriunt ut mundum videantur vilipendere. Alii zarathani dicantur, qui cum mendaciis et fictionibus praedicant bullas et quedam sigilla secum deferunt . . . Alii vocantur beati in piaza, qui per plateis et per civitates se verberant cum cathenis. Alii afflicti nominantur, qui sophistice afflictam faciem ostendunt. Isti sub specie boni multa mala faciunt.' Quoted from Kaeppeli, 'Tommaso dai Liuti', 199.

33 'Zoanne Novello senexe, il quale andava descalzo a zenza bretta, vestita de pelle salvatica a l'apostolica, con la barba lunga, che portava una croxe de fero in mano lunga uno brazo come faceva San Zoanne Baptista, predicò in Piaza con grande gratia, menazando multi mali futuri, e colse molti denari per l'amore de Dio e messeli aprovo de citadini e vestì molti poveri puti: e mostra essere homo de bona vita e misericordioxo.' Zambotti, *Diario Ferrarese*, 191.

34 Tavelli, 'De perfectione religionis', in Ferraresi, *Il Beato Giovanni Tavelli*, II, 322–3.

35 This is not to say that Tura restricted this stylisation to his portrayal of saints (although in general this is the case – compare the more robust figures of the Roverella altarpiece, where saintly asceticism is less emphasised, and the Ferrara *Annunciation*), but that his *maniera* acquires a special force with subjects of a certain character. Tura's narrative works

on a small scale, such as the Roverella and St Maurelius *tondini*, are likely to feature an intricate juxtaposition of very slender figures, but this might be said to arise from modes of multi-figured composition originating in manuscript painting. Diminution here arises from the demand for clarity and articulation within a complex arrangement.

36 Alberti, *De pictura*, 84; for further discussion of this passage, see chapter v.

37 L. Steinberg makes a similar point with regard to the incipient liveliness and eroticism of Michelangelo's dead Christs, in 'Michelangelo's Florentine *Pietà*: The Missing Leg Twenty Years After', *Art Bulletin*, 71, September 1989, 494.

38 On the debate of 1463 prompted by the preachings of the Minorite Giacomo della Marca see A. S. Piccolomini (Pius II), *The Commentaries*, trans. F. A. Gragg, *Smith College Studies in History*, XXX, 1947, 704.

39 'in eo vero qui mortuus sit, nullum adsit membrum quod non demortuum appareat, omnia pendent, manus, digit, cervix, omnia languida decidunt, denique omnia ad exprimendam corporis mortem congruunt. Quod quidem omnium difficillimum est, nam omni ex parti otiosa in corpore membra effingere tam summi artificis est quam viva omnia et aliquid agentia reddere.' Alberti, *On Painting*, 74, 75.

40 'In membrorum compositione danda in primis opera est ut quaeque inter se membra pulchre conveniant. Ea quidem tunc convenire pulchre dicuntur, cum et magnitudine et officio et specie et coloribus et caeteris siquae sunt huiusmodi rebus ad venustatem et pulchritudinem correspondeant. Quod si in simulacro aliquo caput amplissimum, pectus pusillum, manus perampla, pes tumens, corpus turgidum adsit, haec sane compositio erit aspectu deformis.' Alberti, *On Painting*, 72–4, 73–5.

41 *Bibliotheca Sanctorum* (Rome, 1961), vol. II, 995; see also P. Camporesi, *The Incorruptible Flesh: Bodily Mutation in Religion and Folklore*, trans. T. Croft-Murray (Cambridge, 1988), 7, 10, 13.

42 E. Gardner, *Dukes and Poets in Ferrara* (London, 1904), 155.

43 On Vegri see G. Baruffaldi, *Vita della Beata Caterina da Bologna* (Ferrara, 1708); for her death and its aftermath, 68–83. On Vegri's activity as a painter see J. M. Wood, 'Breaking the Silence: The Poor Clares and the Visual Arts in Fifteenth Century Italy', *Renaissance Quarterly*, XLVIII/2, 1995, 272–6. On Brocadelli see D. Ponsi, *Vita della Beata Lucia Vergine di Narni* (Rome, 1709), and Gardner, *Dukes and Poets*, 364ff., G. Zarri, 'Pietà e profezia alle corti padane: le pie consigliere dei principi', in *Il Rinascimento nelle corti padane* (Bari, 1977), 208–21.

44 'che il servo di Giesu Christo sappia, e voglia vincere se medesimo negando la propria

volontade'. Vegri, *Le Armi necessarie*, 20.

45 Bynum, *Fragmentaton and Redemption*, 231.

46 Kieckhefer, *Unquiet Souls*, 180–201.

47 On the case of Tavelli, see the poem by Giovanni Peregrino quoted below (p. 86); on 'metaphoric' martyrdom in the lives of fourteenth-century saints, see Kieckhefer, *Unquiet Souls*, 67.

48 John Climacus, *The Ladder of Divine Ascent*, trans. C. Luibheid and N. Russell (New York, 1982), 169.

49 Jerome, *Epistolae*, 22, to Eustochium, excerpted in Jacobus de Voraginus, *The Golden Legend*, trans. W. G. Ryan (Princeton, 1993), vol. II, 213.

50 The earliest reference to the painting, by then in a private collection, is C. Cittadella, *Catalogo istorico*, III, 308. Giuseppe Petrucci records in a note to Baruffaldi's *Vita di Cosimo Tura* (Bologna, 1836), 37, that the painting, then in the Costabili collection, had come from the Carthusian monastery of Ferrara. The frequent assumption that the painting had thus been made for the monastery was laid to rest by J. Anderson, 'The Rediscovery of Ferrarese Renaissance Painting in the Risorgimento', *Burlington Magazine*, CXXXV, 1993, 543–4, who points out that many Ferrarese paintings were stored secretly in the monastery in the seventeenth century to prevent their removal to Rome. For an account of the picture's provenance, with a report on its restoration in 1993 and new conclusions regarding its original format, see J. Dunkerton, 'Cosimo Tura as Painter and Draughtsman: The Cleaning and Examination of his *Saint Jerome*', *National Gallery Technical Bulletin*, 15, 1994, 42–54. For exegeses of the painting which are largely focused on its animal imagery, see H. Friedmann, *A Bestiary for St Jerome* (Washington, DC, 1980), 173–88, and S. Macioce, 'Il *San Girolamo* di Cosmè Tura e le disputi ereticali del secondo quattrocento', *Musei Ferraresi*, 15, 1985–7, 28–38.

51 On the Brera fragment, see the entry by A. Bacchi in *Pinacoteca di Brera: Scuola emiliana* (Milan, 1991), #52. The fragment passed from the Carthusian monastery to the Barbicinti Collection in Ferrara; an inventory of the collection records that the panel originally formed part of the *St Jerome*, which had been acquired from the monastery before 1783. See C. Padovani, *La critica d'arte e la pittura ferrarese* (Rovigo, 1954), 157.

52 I base this observation on the numerous examples illustrated in four recent studies of the iconography of St Jerome: E. Rice, *St Jerome in the Renaissance* (Baltimore, 1985); B. Ridderbos, *Saint and Symbol: The Image of St Jerome in Early Italian Art* (Groningen, 1984); H. Friedmann, *A Bestiary for St Jerome*; D. Russo, *Saint Jerome en italie: Étude d'iconographie et de spiritualité* (Rome, 1987); also the series of volumes by G. Kaftal, *Iconography of the Saints in Central Italy* (Florence, 1965),

Iconography of the Saints in North East Italy (Florence, 1978) and *Iconography of the Saints in North West Italy* (Florence, 1985).

53 As in the case of *The Coronation of the Virgin* by Antonio Pollaiuolo at San Gemignano, and *The Madonna of St Jerome* by Parmigianino, London, National Gallery.

54 The two paintings are occasionally compared; see W. Meinhoff, 'Leonardos *Hieronymous*', *Repertorium für Kunstwissenschaft*, 52, 1931, 109–14; H. Ost, *Leonardo Studien* (Berlin, 1975), 11.

55 Dunkerton, 'Cosimo Tura as Painter and Draughtsman', 47.

56 The connection of the *St Jerome* with his Milanese period and with earlier and subsequent North Italian traditions has been discussed by W. Suida, *Leonardo und sein Kreis* (Munich, 1929), 80–82. Leonardo's *Jerome* is closest to that painted by Marco Zoppo in the predella of the Spanish College altarpiece in Bologna. Could Leonardo have known of Tura's work? It is worth noting here that not long after Leonardo's arrival in Milan, his employer Lodovico Maria Sforza sent to Ferrara for Tura's designs for a silver table service. The silver vessels were ornamented with various figures including 'uomini selvatici' or 'wild men', which, when they serve as caryatids, are often disposed in the raised-knee position of Tura's *St Jerome*. On the silver service and Sforza's request see Franceschini, *Artisti a Ferrara*, Part II, vol. 1, nos 65h, 70h, 487n.

57 T. Tuohy, in London, 1984, *From Borso to Cesare d'Este*, exhibition catalogue (London, Matthiesen Fine Art Ltd, 1984), 67.

58 Franceschini, 'Confraternite di disciplinati a Ferrara avanti il Concilio Tridentino', *Atti e memorie della deputazione provinciale ferrarese di storia patria*, ser. iii, 19, 1975, 18–19, for a list of *disciplinati* groups operative by 1450; for the prohibition in *battuti* statutes of public bloodletting, 23.

59 For a demonstration of this point which draws on the work of Michel Foucault, see R. G. Brown, *The Politics of Magnificence in Ferrara, 1450–1505* (D.Phil., University of Edinburgh, 1982), 132–249. See also S. J. Edgerton Jr., *Pictures and Punishment: Art and Criminal Prosecution during the Florentine Renaissance* (Ithaca, NY, 1985); Park, 'The Criminal and the Saintly Body', and V. Paglia, *La morte confortata: Riti della paura e mentalità religiosa a Roma nell'età moderna* (Rome, 1982).

60 For the *Martirologio* of the Battuti Neri see *Miniature italiane della Fondazione Giorgio Cini dal medioevo al rinascimento*, exhibition catalogue (Venice, Fondazione Cini, 1968), 44–52; C. L. Ragghianti, 'Il Maestro dei Battuti Neri di Ferrara', in *Stefano da Ferrara* (Florence, 1972), 67–91.

61 For local examples, see Brown, *Politics of Magnificence*, 224–5.

62 T. Tuohy, *Herculean Ferrara: Ercole d'Este, 1471–1505, and the Invention of a Ducal Capital* (Cambridge, 1996), 376, erroneously attributes to the eighteenth-century writer Carlo Brisighella, *Descrizione delle pitture e sculture della città di Ferrara*, ed. M. A. Novelli (Ferrara, 1991), the testimony that Tura's *St Jerome* was in the basilica of San Francesco; the work is never mentioned by Brisighella. (The manuscript of the *Descrizione* dates from before 1710.)

63 On this church and the works of art it contained up until the eighteenth century, extant or otherwise, see P. T. Lombardi, *I Francescani a Ferrara* (Bologna, 1974–5), vol. 1, and Gino and Zanotti, *La Basilica di San Francesco di Ferrara*.

64 The connection between the painting and the Gesuati cult of Jerome was made by Macioce, 'Il *San Girolamo* di Cosmè Tura', but as a starting-point for a discussion of the painting in terms of theologically heterodox views which the order were accused of holding in the 1430s; they had long been exonerated of these charges by the time Tura painted this image. Dunkerton, 'Cosimo Tura as Painter and Draughtsman', 53, n. 25 disparages the connection with the Gesuati on the basis of the colour of the saint's robe. Nonetheless, it should be noted that mendicant habits, which were made of undyed wool, could sustain a wide variation of colour at this time. Even if Tura's work was made under the direct influence of the order, this does not mean, given the diffusion of Tavelli's works, that it could not reflect their presence and promotion of the cult of Jerome in the city.

65 See E. Peverada, 'Attestati di santità nel quattrocento per il vescovo di Ferrara Giovanni Tavelli', *Analecta Pomposiana*, 14, 1989, 75, on the will of the notary Bonfiolo Bagarotti with reference to the church of San Girolamo, which provides for a painting of the Crucifixion with the Virgin, St John, St Jerome and the *beato* Tavelli. The same will also provides for seven wax and cloth kneeling *orans* figures after the model of a figure of Agostino Villa in the same church. Villa had the effigy installed in San Girolamo but was himself interred in the nearby convent of San Francesco (78). On the statue of Rinaldo d'Este see Ferraresi, *Il Beato Giovanni Tavelli*, IV, 397.

66 Tavelli's *vitae*, miracles, correspondence, theological and pastoral writings are all included in Ferraresi, *Il Beato Giovanni Tavelli*, II and IV.

67 Quoted from John Climacus, *Ladder of Divine Ascent*, 123–5.

68 'Sicque plurimi eis adjuncti sunt, qui, flamma charitatis accensi, adeo terrena quaeque spernebant, et carnis oblectamenta vitabant, ut adhuc carne viventes quodammodo jam carne viderentur exuti. In carne quidem positi, carnis usus nesciebant, et quod illorum conversatio foret in caelis, qui quodam mentis culmine constituti mundum sub pedibus calcante omnia arbitrabantur ut stercora, ut Christum lucrifacerent. Famem, sitim, frigus, nuditatem, et incommoda plurima super et opprobria ac mundi ludibria Christi Jesu Salvatoris amore ducebant solatia. Mirandum spectaculum equidem erat videre viros ingenuos, et olim prudentia carnis industrios, stultos nunc factos, ut sapientes fiant.' 'Life of Giovanni Colombini', in Ferraresi, *Il Beato Giovanni Tavelli* II, 45–6.

69 Quanto in dispecto havesse la sua vita
Lasso, perche mancharia del dire
Le pene, e le martire,
Che sosteneva la sua carne afflicta,
Con ruste all'infinita
El corpo macerava
Fin al sangue gittava,
O Sacro Corpo, che al ben far ce invita . . .

Era la fazza sua d'un cherubino
Melle suave erano sue parole,
L'aspecto suo d'un Sole,
E la Doctrina sua del Ciel divino;
Ha popul Ferrarino
Pregulo humilemente,
Et lui, come possente
Pregara Jesu, che po, e vole.

Full text in Ferraresi, *Il Beato Giovanni Tavelli*, IV, 332–5. For further reports of Tavelli's appearance, see the contemporary accounts in the same volume: 84, 120, 129.

70 'Due volte al giorno punisco il mio corpo, spesso a sangue, se la mia debolezza fisica non me lo impedisce.' Ferraresi, *Il Beato Giovanni Tavelli*, II, 428.

71 The fourteenth-century mystic Henry of Suso described patience in suffering as a sweet odour, a valiant knight in a tournament, a cup of wholesome drink, a glittering ruby. See C. W. Bynum, *Holy Feast and Holy Fast* (Berkeley, 1987), 102.

72 'Con tutta la sua mente et ogni senso/Innanzi al Crucifixo estenso.' Ferraresi, *Il Beato Giovanni Tavelli*, IV, 333.

73 'Eya, strenui milites, agonizate pro Domino vestro; indefesse laborate, vobis enim manet immarcessibilis gloria et corona iusticiae . . . Videte, ne redieritis vacui; nunc discurrite, nunc festinate, suscitate amicos vestros, confortate pusillanimes, genua debilia roborate . . . Nonne iam, dilectissimi, exhillarantur faties vestrae, anime vestre iam exiliunt in laetitia cordis ad illud evangelium infallibilis Veritatis . . . Pensata mercedis magnitudine onus levigatur et mitescit laboris. Athletae Christi, et pugnatores robustissimi, imminente iam bello nolite terreri sed in capite acierum consistite fortes; et velut Domini Dei exercituum castra, ac cinti gladio spiritus, quod est verbum Dei! Roborate agonizantes in proelio, pastores carissimi et vigiles, nolite, quaeso, nolite instar mercenarii fugere, nolite dare terga, ne coram bono pastore, qui animam suam posuit pro ovibus

suis, confundatur faties vestrae, si quas sui gregis vobis commisit oves neglexeritis discriminibus exposita . . . Mittentes enim post eos fugientes, sagittas potentis acutas cum carbonibus desolatoriis, quos congeremus super capita illorum, ad evellendum, destruendum et dissipandum omne quod male plantatum et radicatum ac structum est in cordibus eorum, ut fiat nova plantatio et nova structura super hedificata super fundamentum apostolorum et prophetarum in constructione novae Ierusalem, quae nobis descendit de coelo.' Complete text in Ferraresi, *Il Beato Giovanni Tavelli*, II, 446–8, with modifications in G. Dufner, 'Il Beato Giovanni Tavelli vescovo gesuato', in *Il Beato Giovanni Tavelli di Ferrara nel VI centenario della nascita (1386–1446)* (Ferrara, 1987), 177f.

On Tavellii as *athleta* see the anonymous biography of 1502–5 in Ferraresi, ibid., IV, 120.

74 G. Gruyer, *L'art ferrarais à l'époque des princes d'Este* (Paris, 1897), vol. I, 603, associates the inscription with two scriptural texts; Psalm 52, 10: 'Ego autem, sicut oliva fructifera in domo, speravi in misericordia Dei in aeternum', and Hosea 14, 7: 'Ibunt rami eius, et erit . . . oliva gloria eius, et odor eius ut Libani.'

75 For early references to the statue see Peverada, 'Attestati di santità', 92f.; for a poetic eulogy by Lodovico Carbone referring to 'Hanc vero effigiem' see Ferraresi, *Il Beato Giovanni Tavelli*, IV, 336–7.

76 Alfonso d'Este is depicted on the plaques adorning the reliquary in which the relics of Maurelius were finally housed in 1512.

77 Material on the cult of Maurelius is drawn from the essay by M. Tagliabue, 'L'anonima *Vita* latina di san Maurelio martire vescovo di Ferrara e il *De inventione* di Matteo Ronto', *Analecta Pomposiana*, 6: *Studi Monastici*, 1981, 221–63, which contains the text of both hagiographic works.

78 For a recent discussion of the tondi with comprehensive bibliography see the entry by J. Bentini in Bentini, ed., *San Giorgio e la principessa*, 169–76.

79 Laurentius de Rubeis, *Legendario e vita et miracoli de sancto Maurelio episcopo et patrono de Ferrara* (Ferrara, 1489). The connection between the frontispiece and the lost altarpiece was proposed by L. N. Cittadella, *Notizie amministrative, storiche ed artistiche relative a Ferrara* (Ferrara, 1868), I, 698. G. Scalabrini, *Memorie istoriche*, 29, states that the work was a Roverella commission. In his *Vite* of Tura, Baruffaldi states that the polyptych, consisting of images of various saints with 'tondini' showing 'la consegrazione, ed il maritrio di quel santo vescovo in piccole figure diligentemente espresse', was dismembered at the installation of Guercino's altarpiece. See *Vite de' pittori e scultori ferraresi*, I, 698, and *Vita di Cosimo Tura*, 17. Surviving

documents relating to endowments of the chapel of St Maurelius, preserved in the Archivio Diocesano at Ferrara, refer to the installation of tombs by lay donors but not to the Roverella or to Tura's altarpiece.

80 'Sub sequenti tempore pretiosa Christi margarita, beatus Maurelius in carne preter carnem vivendo, angelus videbatur esse et non homo: prudenter terram despexit celum suspiciendo, naturam humiliavit reformatorem humiliatis expectando, dimisit temporalia violenter gaudia sempiterna diripiendo, mundo corde cunctis temporibus vite sue sincere virginitatis flosculo polens divine etiam contemplationis studio insistebat, de corpore surgens ad spiritum, de spiritu surrectans ad deum, carnem castigans, que castigata quietabatur, quietata spiritui famulabatur.' *Vita Sancti Maurelii*, Part 4, in Tagliabue, 'L'anonima *Vita*', 248.

81 It cannot be ruled out, however, that either or both of these two additional pairs flanked the *Virgin and Child* now in Bergamo, which again would find precedent in the London drawing. It is hard to imagine how a single polyptych could have accommodated both the Bergamo and Caen panels, although Salmi, *Cosmè Tura*, 40–41, did propose an ungainly two-tier arrangement. There have been various attempts to regroup these six gold-ground panels into three altarpieces recorded in the eighteenth-century sources, sometimes incorporating two further gold-ground panels, of larger dimensions, depicting *St Louis of Toulouse* (New York, Metropolitan) and *St Nicholas of Bari* (Nantes, Musée des Beaux-Arts); Baruffaldi briefly describes an altarpiece in the church of San Luca al Borgo with the Virgin on a gold ground and *tavolette* of saints, but his confident dating of the work to 1434 might cast doubt on its authorship by Tura; this is also the opinion of S. Ortolani, *Cosimo Tura, Francesco del Cossa, Ercole de' Roberti* (Milan, 1941), 63. Baruffaldi additionally mentions an altarpiece in the sacristy of San Romano with 'alcuni santi a fondi d'oro'. *Vita di Cosimo Tura*, 11, 16–17. Another candidate for reconstruction is the altarpiece allegedly by Tura in San Giacomo ad Argenta, with which several scholars have tried to associate the *St James*; Bargellesi, 'Tura o Aleotti ad Argenta?', mounts a strong argument that the original attribution to Tura by L. N. Cittadella was erroneous, so that the question of 'Tura's Argenta altarpiece' which haunts the twentieth-century literature can be safely laid to rest. The later 'descriptions', in short, are not especially useful for understanding the original setting of these panels.

82 The existence of the Este chapel of St James in the cathedral is known from the pastoral visits of bishops of Ferrara such as Francesco dal Legname; see E. Peverada, *La visita pastorale del vescovo Francesco dal Legname a Ferrara*

(1447–1450) (Ferrara, 1982), 183. On the corresponding chapel in San Francesco, see A. Frizzi, *Memorie per la storia di Ferrara* (Ferrara, 1847–8), vol. III, 349, who refers to 'una sontuosissima capella che Alberto [d'Este] l'anno 1393 fece fare col disegno di Bartolino nella chiesa di San Francesco, e che doto di ricche rendite intitolendola a S. Giacomo'. It should be noted, however, that there were other local foundations dedicated to St James. On the question of San Giacomo ad Argenta as a destination for Tura's painting, see the previous note. Within the city of Ferrara is the former parish church of San Giacomo Apostolo, founded in 1358, where, according to Scalabrini, a group called the Knights of St James held its induction ceremonies. See Scalabrini, *Memorie istoriche*, 251.

83 L. Chiappini, 'Realtà e leggenda di S. Contardo', in *Atti e memorie della deputazione provinciale Ferrarese di storia patria*, n.s. IV, 1946–9, 86f.

84 Zambotti, *Diario Ferrarese*, 182–6.

85 Zambotti, *Diario Ferrarese*, 47.

86 H. Belting, *Likeness and Presence: A History of the Image before the Era of Art*, trans. E. Jephcott (Chicago, 1994), 424.

87 Paracelsus, quoted in Baxandall, *The Limewood Sculptors of Renaissance Germany* (New Haven and London, 1980), 161.

88 Translation in Gardner, *Dukes and Poets*, 367, 375–6; original text excerpted in Ponsi, *Vita della Beata Lucia*, 205–7: 'Non ignoramus ea, quae a summo rerum Opifice in servorum suorum corporibus ostenduntur, ad fidei nostrae consortationem, & robur & impiorum & indurati cordis virorum incredulitatem submovendam, non satis eleganter & digne narrari posse: tamen pro devotione nostra & ut universis pateat, quae sentimus, vidimus & ut habemus.' For a recent comment on the text, see Zarri, 'Pietà e profezia', 217–18.

89 More research needs to be done on this question; it is nevertheless apparent that when female mystics such as Francesca Romana, Fina of San Gemignano, Clare of Montefalco, Angela of Foligno, appear in art, they do not manifest notably ascetic physcial characteristics. For illustrations see Vauchez, *La sainteté en occident*, 470f., and Weinstein and Bell, *Saints and Society*.

90 Eighteenth-century writers attributed to Tura an elaborate altarpiece in the convent church of San Guglielmo, on the altar of Suor Argeride Botti: 'si vede in piccole figure la storia di San Eustachio, di San Giorgio, di San Cristoforo, e il mortorio di S. Chiara colle monache intorno al cattaletto piangenti; di piu lo Sposalizio di S. Caterina col Bambino Gesu; l'ultima cena di Cristo co'suoi Apostoli, e in mezze figure santa Lucia, Apollonia, Agata, Guglielmo et altri santi.' Brisighella, *Descrizione*, ed. Novelli, 257, following references in Barotti, *Pitture e scolture*, 108, and Scalabrini, *Memorie istoriche*, 173.

91 Among the growing body of scholarship on the rise of ascetic communities of women in Ferrara in the *quattrocento* see A. Samaritani, 'Ailisia de Baldo e le correnti reformatrici femminili de Ferrara nella prima meta del sec. XV'. *Atti e memorie della deputazione provinciale ferrarese di storia patria*, ser. 3, 13, 1973, 91–157 and M. M. McLaughlin, 'Creating and Recreating Communities of Women: The Case of Corpus Domini, Ferrara, 1406–1452' *Signs*, 14/2, 1989, 261–88.

92 Madrid, Thyssen-Bornemisza collection; for a discussion see London, 1984, *From Borso to Cesare d'Este*, 59–60.

93 Bynum, *Resurrection of the Body*, 337, on Mechtild of Magdeburg. See also Pouchelle, 'Représentations du corps', 293.

94 See the inventory of the *guardaroba* from 1494 published in Campori, *Raccolta dei cataloghi*, 15–22, with numerous 'Anchonette, Crocete, et figure de Santi de Arzento de Oro et de piu altre sorte'.

95 In his Griffoni altarpiece, painted in Bologna in the 1470s, Francesco del Cossa made a similar metaphoric association between saints, architectural elements and 'the church' in its wider figurative sense. See A. Gentili, 'Mito cristiano e storia ferrarese nel polittico Griffoni', in Papagno and Quondam, ed., *Lo spazio e la corte*, II, 563–77.

96 Brown, *Politics of Magnificence*, 455.

97 *Diario Ferrarese di autore incerto*, 71.

98 The relation of religion and statecraft is discussed by a number of historians, including Gundersheimer, *Ferrara*, 186–8 and *passim*; and A. Prosperi, 'Le istituzioni ecclesiastiche e le idee religiose', in *Il Rinascimento nelle corti padane*; Brown, *Politics of Magnificence*, 9–15. On Ercole's extraordinary campaigns of church-building, one of his motives for enlarging the city in the 1490s, see T. Tuohy, *Herculean Ferrara*, 164–85.

99 On Ercole's involvement with the confraternity of San Martino, see Gundersheimer, *Ferrara*, 189.

100 On these artists see S. Zamboni, *Pittori di Ercole I d'Este: Giovan Francesco Mainieri, Lazzaro Grimaldi, Domenico Panetti, Michele Coltellini* (Milan, 1975); London, 1984, *From Borso to Cesare d'Este*; and Manca, *Ercole de' Roberti*.

CHAPTER IV

1 T. Tuohy, *Herculean Ferrara: Ercole d'Este, 1471–1505, and the Invention of a Ducal Capital* (Cambridge, 1996), 204, proposes that the appearance of the chapel can be inferred from a likely derivation, that decorated by Bernardino Loschi in 1508 in the Castello dei Pio at Carpi. On the Belriguardo chapel, the programme for which was apparently devised by Borso himself, see A. Venturi, 'Cosma Tura genannt Cosmè, 1432 bis 1495', *Jahrbuch der Königlich preussischen Kunstsammlungen*, 8,

1887, 13–22. The documentation is also available in A. Franceschini, *Artisti a Ferrara in età umanistica e rinascimentale: Testimonianze archivistiche* (Ferrara, 1995), Part I, no. 1149a (the commission), no. 1152f (the purchase of colours from Venice), nos 11550, 1188g, 1224e,f,ff, 1231a,b,d, and Appendix 49 (the trip to Brescia); Part II vol. I, no. 1c (the evaluation by Baldassare d'Este and Antonio da Venezia).

2 For the payment to Tura for 'più legnami depincti a la Certoxa per lo osequio de la Excellentia del prefato Signore', see Franceschini, *Artisti a Ferrara*, Part I, Appendix 50g.

3 See R. Stemp, 'Cosimo Tura and the Sacrati Chapels in Ferrara', *Musei Ferraresi*, 17, 1990–91, 61–70, which corrects the longstanding misconception that the Sacrati Chapel contained an entire New Testament (or Old Testament) cycle. On the Sacrati's commerical activity in the 1460s see G. Tagliati, 'Relazione tra al famiglia Romei e la corte estense nel secolo XV', *Il rinascimento nelle corti padane: Società e cultura* (Bari, 1977), 69.

4 For the 1493 inventory see G. Campori, *Raccolta dei cataloghi ed inventarii inediti* (Modena, 1870), 1–3.

5 On the tapestries see the entries by N. Forti Grazzini in A. Mottola-Molfino and M. Natali, ed., *Le Muse e il Principe*, exhibition catalogue (Milan, Museo Poldi-Pezzoli, 1991), vol. I, 246–51.

6 Giraldi, in his dialogue entitled *Historiae poetarum tam graecorum tam latinorum* (1545), employed the cycle as an ekphrastic frame for a dialogue on ancient poetry. Giraldi claimed that the cycle, recently destroyed, had been executed by a certain 'Cosmam . . . qui patrum nostrorum memoria nonulla eius artes opera praeclara reliquit' (from text in *Opera omnia*, 1580, 22). Although in a dedication to the Duchess Renée of France Giraldi seems to refer to his description as a rhetorical invention ('Nec demum quisquam velim hac mihi parte vitio vertat, quod hac nostrae nusquam sint tabulae: occulta enim significatione Picae familiae bibliothecam significavi, ex qua ad sermones hos conficiendos plurima frequenti lectione collegi') his *ekphrasis* was taken from the eighteenth century as the record of a work by Tura. The possibility of literary fabrication was pointed out by L. Capra, 'Tura inventato', *Biblioteca Communale Ariostea: Recenti ingressi*, 5, 1961, 13–16, but the existence of the Mirandola cycle was constantly affirmed in subsequent scholarship before Capra's observation was given greater publicity in Mottola-Molfino and Natali, ed., *Le Muse e il Principe*, II, 178.

7 The record of Tura's death runs: 'Nota che del mese di aprile 1495 morite el Nobile et Excellente homo M.o Cosimo dal Tura Pictor Excelentissimo et fu sepolto a S. Lorenzo oltre Po in una Archa presso

all'uscio del Campanile di detta Chiesa.' From a chronicle quoted in G. Campori, *Artisti degli Estensi: I pittori* (Modena, 1875), 38. For an account of Tura's connections with the Roverella and the monastery see G. Righini, 'Cosimo Tura a San Giorgio', *Atti e memorie della deputazione Ferrarese per la storia patriam*, IV, 1953, 93–110.

8 'Naufragium passa est tunc Roverella domus': from Bernardino Zambotti's elegy on the three deceased Roverella brothers, included in his *Silva chronicarum*, Ferrara, Biblioteca Comunale Ariostea, MS Cl. I, 16, fol. 73v. The published edition of Zambotti's *Diario Ferrarese dal anno 1476 sino al 1504*, ed. G. Pardi in *Rerum italicarum scriptores*, 24, Part 7, no. 2 (Bologna, 1928), includes only a partial transcription of the elegy (77–8).

9 On the location of the Roverella chapel, see the modern editor's comments in C. Brisighella, *Descrizione delle pitture e sculture della città di Ferrara*, ed. M. A. Novelli (Ferrara, 1991), 562.

10 J. Dunkerton, A. Roy and A. Smith, 'The Unmasking of Tura's *Allegorical Figure*: A Painting and its Concealed Image', *National Gallery Technical Bulletin*, 11, 1987, 35. On Leonello's organ, see E. Peverada, 'Un organo per Leonello d'Este', *L'Oregano*, XXVIII, 1994, 1–30.

11 In the time of Vasari Tura seems to have been remembered largely as the painter of the organ-shutters. See Vasari, 'Galasso Ferrarese', *Vite* (1550).

12 R. Longhi, *Officina Ferrarese* (Rome, 1934), 38–9.

13 In *The Truth in Painting* (Chicago, 1987), 37–83, J. Derrida introduces the *parergon* (ornament, frame, 'context') to challenge the oppositionality of the extrinsic and the intrinsic, ornament and substance, the proper and the improper, the inside and the outside in the discourse of aesthetics. Yet the demand for attention to the semiotic function of style is made in different ways by E. Panofsky, *Renaissance and Renascences in Western Art* (New York and London, 1972), and M. Baxandall, *Painting and Experience in Fifteenth-Century Italy* (Oxford, 1972) but generally assuming a congruence of ornament with a prevailing pictorial decorum. A stimulating recent answer to this call is presented by G. Didi-Huberman, *Fra Angelico: Dissemblance and Figuration* (Chicago, 1995). It is a central premise here, however, that the meaning of style is most appropriately addressed through attention to the work's beholders. R. Starn, with L. Partridge, makes a case for multivalency *vis à vis* the attitudes and social position of different audiences in his discussion of Mantegna's Camera Picta in *Arts of Power: Three Halls of State in Renaissance Italy* (Berkeley, CA, 1992), 83–133.

14 The following information on the Roverella family is drawn from a range of sources. The

most comprehensive are listed here, while sources from which more fragmentary information has been obtained are cited in individual notes. Gabriele Bucelino, *Rutiliae longe vetustissimae et illustrissimae inter Romanae urbis principis familiae* (Veldkirch, 1677) – a rarely consulted genealogical history of the Roverella family from its mythical origins to the seventeenth century; Litta, *Famiglie celebri in Italiane*, x (Milan, 1850) [unpaginated]; Vespasiano da Bisticci, *Renaissance Princes, Popes and Prelates*, trans. W. George and E. Waters (New York, 1963); F. Pasini Frassoni, *Dizionario storico-araldico del antico ducato di Ferrara* (Rome, 1904), 492; L. Barotti, *Serie di vescovi ed arcivescovi di Ferrara* (Ferrara, 1781), 93–6. See also the entries on the Roverella in G. Moroni, *Dizionario di erudizione storico-ecclesiastico* (Venice, 1840–61), vol. x, 130, and vol. LIX, 197–8.

15 A. Frizzi, *Memorie per la storia di Ferrara* (Ferrara, 1847–8), vol. II, 57.

16 Alluded to in a letter of Pius II to Borso d'Este, 5 June 1462, Biblioteca Apostolica Vaticana, Cod. Urb. Lat. 404, 148v. 'Optabas Bartholomeum (Roverella) archepiscopum Ravennatem in collegio cardinalium assummi: idque litteris & nunciis & ore tuo saepe a nobis efflagitasti.'

17 These were Meliaduse (famous for suggesting to Alberti that he write his treatise on architecture), commendator of Pomposa and Bishop of Comacchio, but discharged from his vows before his death in 1452; Gurone Maria, who acquired the *commenda* of the abbey of Nonantola on condition that he receive Holy Orders (the record is in Modena, Archivio di Stato, Serie Casa e Stato, Cass. 25, carta 28). Gurone also had a son who became Bishop of Adria and for whom Tura was working in the 1490s; Rinaldo d'Este, who took Meliaduse's place as commendator of Pomposa from 1451 to 1469, is stated in a letter by Jacopo Trotti to be reluctant to receive the Holy Orders into which he was clearly being coerced by Borso (Modena, Archivio di Stato, Ambasciatori: Jacopo Trotti, 15 June 1468). For an interesting collation of biographical data on Rinaldo and his activity as a patron of musicians see L. Lockwood, *Music in Renaissance Ferrara, 1400–1505* (Cambridge, MA, 1984), 112–14.

18 The sentiment is indicated in a letter to Lorenzo Strozzi from Jacopo Trotti in Rome. Modena, Archivio di Stato, ibid., 13 July 1467: 'Prego dio facia il nostro cardinale di Ravenna papa avanti moriamo . . .' On the strength of Bartolomeo's candidacy for the Papacy at the death of Paul II in 1471 see L. von Pastor, *The History of the Popes from the Close of the Middle Ages*, 5th edition (London, 1923), vol. IV, 6.

19 On Guarino and the Roverella see R. Sabbadini, ed., *Epistolario di Guarino Veronese* (Venice, 1915–19), vol. II, 657, 663–5. A copy

of Guarino's edition of Strabo's *Geography* with the *stemmae* of Bartolomeo Roverella and Pius II is preserved in the Biblioteca Apostolica Vaticana, MS Lat. 2050.

20 These included governorship of Perugia in 1448, nunciature to England in 1451–2, governorship of Ascoli in 1452, commanding the Papal forces against the rebels of Viterbo in 1459, Papal legate during the Angevin war in Naples in 1460–64, and legate to Umbria in 1470. Particulars in P. Litta, *Famiglie celebri italiene* (Milan, 1819/1856–85), vol. x [unpaginated] and in Bucelino, *Rutiliae longe vetustissimae*.

21 On the wedding and the presence of Lorenzo and Bartolomeo see *Diario Ferrarese . . . di autori incerti*, ed. Pardi, 89.

22 See Pius' famous grudgingly admiring but more often exasperated account of Borso, his vanity and false promises in [Piccolomini], *Commentaries*, trans. F. A. Gragg, *Smith College Studies in History*, XXII/1–2, 1936–7, 66, 106; XXV/1–4, 1939–40, 179–83 and 226–8: 'Wherever Borso went among his own subjects he was acclaimed by the populace; outside his own realm his reputation was infamous, though he was accustomed to say that Ferrara was the school where Italians learned whatever they knew and that he was the teacher who presided over it. In his own opinion he had great wisdom, in that of others very little. He ruled his state not so much by shrewdness as by luck. The prosperity of Ferrara was the result of the quarrels of her neighbours, not of the industry of her prince.'

23 I have consulted the edition in the Biblioteca Apostolica Vaticana, Cod. Urb. Lat. 404: 'Ad Ducem Mutine eum increpans & mandans sub excommunicationis poena & assignet procuratoribus apostolicis facultatem exigenda decimarum, vicesimarum, et tricesimarum in omnis locis suae dictionis & territoriis', and the text of the letter in Piccolomini, *Epistolae in pontificatu editae* (Milan, Antonius Zarothus, 1481), no. lxxxxiiii.

24 Ercole led the Venetian army on the Papal side against the combined forces of Rimini, Florence and Milan. See Gardner, *Dukes and Poets in Ferrara* (London, 1904), 108.

25 Notice in Archivio Segreto Vaticano, *Schedario Garampi*, 116, 180: 'Paulus II breve quo ducem Borsium Mutinae monet ut solvat censum ab eo de mense Iunii debitum ratione civitatis Ferrariae comitatius territori ab districtus eiusdem, nec non terrarum Bagnacavalli et Mass. Lombardorum.'

26 On the War of Ferrara see the account in G. Cozzi and M. Knapton, *Storia della Repubblica di Venezia* (Turin, 1984).

27 For a comprehensive account of this process in the fourteenth and early fifteenth centuries see T. Dean, *Land and Power in Late Medieval Ferrara* (Cambridge, 1988), 30ff. On the conversion of abbeys to *commendae* and

the expansion of Este control, with an emphasis on the later *quattrocento*, see the important article by A. Prosperi, 'Le istituzioni ecclesiastiche e le idee religiose', in *Il rinascimento nelle corti padane*, 125–63. On 130–33 Prosperi discusses Papal and Este competition regarding the *commendae* of Nonantola, which passed into the hands of Papal favourites after the occupancy of Gurone d'Este, and Pomposa, which had been more thoroughly absorbed by the Este at the end of the century. Borso and Ercole's brother Rinaldo was prior at Pomposa from 1452 until 1484, and from 1486 until 1492 it was a *commenda* of Cardinal Ippolito d'Este. On jurisdictional conflict between church and state, especially concerning the right of the state to prosecute clerics in civil courts, see R. G. Brown, *The Politics of Magnificence in Ferrara, 1450–1505* (D.Phil., University of Edinburgh, 1982), 31–2.

28 Dean, ibid., 34–5. Dean refers to one particularly striking instance of the predicament of bishops who were not Este nominees: by the beginning of the fifteenth century the Este takeover of the lands of Adria was so thorough that the bishop of the time lacked a residence in the town of Adria itself, and he obtained one only when he made further concessions to the marquis Niccolò d'Este (40–43).

29 In 1411, despite the continual complaints of the clergy about Niccolò and his clients in the preceding years, the schismatic Pope John XXIII allowed the marquis to have his own candidate, Tomaso Perendoli, appointed Archbishop of Ravenna. Once elected, however, Perendoli did not act entirely according to Este interests. He used the considerable leverage his position commanded to enforce the collection of tithe arrears and brought Niccolò to a compromise on certain territorial claims. See Dean, ibid., 43.

30 'The *commendam* was an old way of transferring income from a convent to someone who had the title of abbot or prior but who did not in effect occupy the office . . . [The commendator] was often a cardinal, for cardinals were not bound by the normal restrictions on pluralism.' D. Hay, *The Church in Italy in the Fifteenth Century* (Cambridge, 1977), 74–5.

31 The pension increases from 193 *lire marchesine* in 1460 (Modena, Archivio di Stato, Libri camerali diversi, 32, fol. 250) to 231 *lire marchesine* 13 soldi in 1469 (ibid., 71, fol. 99). Apart from this payment to Bartolomeo I have not yet discovered further substantial evidence of grants of cash or land to members of the Roverella family. The *Catasti delle investiture* (Modena, ibid., Catasto 'FG' 1471, fol. 260) record a donation of land near the territory of Santo Stefano, Rovigo, again to the cardinal. In 1479 Eleonora d'Aragona endowed Girolamo Roverella with some possessions

near the village of Copparo (Ferrara, Archivio di Stato, *Notarile*, Notaio Bartolomeo Goggi, matricola 195 pacco 2 1479).

32 These territories were enfeuded to Leonello d'Este by Bartolomeo Roverella on 14 February 1447, 'sub annuo censu recognitioni . . . receptis'. The investiture was renewed by Bartolomeo's successor Archbishop Filiasio Roverella on behalf of Ercole I and his heirs in 1487 and 1501. The documents are transcribed in a late sixteenth-century manuscript history of the archdiocese of Ravenna by Rafael Aquilino; Biblioteca Apostolica Vaticana, Cod. Urb. Lat. 1568, fols 18–24. See also G. Montanari, 'Istituzioni religiose e vita religiosa a Ravenna in età Veneziana', in D. Bolognesi, ed., *Ravenna in età Veneziana* (Ravenna, 1983), 76.

33 A dimension which might be explored further here is the fact that Maria Gigliola Roverella, sister of Bartolomeo, Lorenzo and Niccolo, was the mother of Teofilo Calcagnini, the favourite of Borso d'Este and the most conspicuous and dramatic instance of Borso's 'creation of a new nobility'. See R. Tristano, *Ferrara in the Fifteenth Century: Borso d'Este and the Developmpent of a new Nobility* (Ph.D. dissertation, New York University, 1983), 232. Virtually nothing of the private side of this relationship is known, but his kinship with the Roverella could indicate that there was a political dimension, and that Teofilo was not quite the 'man without qualities' he is sometimes represented as being.

34 More complete biographical particulars about Lorenzo are given in chapter v.

35 The controversy is examined by P. Partner, 'Francesco dal Legname: A Curial Bishop in Disgrace', in P. Denley and C. Elam, ed., *Florence and Italy: Renaissance Studies in Honour of Nicolai Rubinstein* (London, 1988), 395–404. See also E. Peverada, *La visita pastorale del vescovo Francesco dal Legname a Ferrara (1447–1450)* (Ferrara, 1982); also the entry 'Dal Legname' in *Dizionario biografico degli italiani*, vol. 31 (Rome, 1985).

36 Pius II, *Epistolae Pontificales* (Biblioteca Apostolica Vaticana, Cod. Urb. Lat. 404), 117r: 'Ommitimus quam fecisti resistentiam priusque dilecto filio Laurentio Roverellae nunc electo ferrariensi possessionem traderes eorum beneficiorum quem sibi per obitum Ioannis Aurispe vacantia contulimus.'

37 An inscription from the Capitoline dated 1477 commemorating Sixtus IV as *urbis restaurator* features Lorenzo's *stemma* along with those of the Porcari family, Papal civil servants who undertook important public works in the city. See P. Guerrini, 'La *Restauratio Urbis*', in *Un pontificato ed una città: Sisto IV* (Rome, 1986), 465.

38 For a discussion of the tomb in the context of Rossellino's other works in Olivetan churches (San Miniato in Florence, Santa' Anna in Naples) and of the social ties of the Roverella in Naples see E. C. Apfelstadt, *The Later Sculpture of Antonio Rossellino* (Ph.D. dissertation, Princeton University, 1987), 188–240.

39 A. Samaritani, 'Gli Olivetani nella società ferrarese del'400: Tra Estensi e movimenti di riforma', *Analecta Pomposiana*, 6: *Studi Monastici*, 1981, 125. This article, the result of intensive research in the archives of San Giorgio, is the source of most of the following information about the monastery.

40 Bucelino, *Rutiliae longe vetustissimae*, 73.

41 The Olivetans had been introduced at San Giorgio by Niccolò III d'Este in 1415. For the remainder of his reign, and during the reigns of his sons Leonello and Borso, the monastery received no significant patronage from the Este, but also minimal interference. San Giorgio received certain tax privileges in 1441, and bulls from Eugenius IV and Nicholas V confirmed its rights and possessions. It also emerged favourably from a series of legal actions involving the diocese and local landowners. On taxation see Samaritani, 'Gli olivetani,' 106, on legal processes and bulls, 101ff.

42 On the title see Gundersheimer, *Ferrara: The Style of a Renaissance Despotism* (Princeton, 1973), 67–70 and L. Capra, 'Gli epitafi per Nicolò III d'Este', *Italia medioevale e umanistica*, 16, 1973, 197–226.

43 Samaritani, 'Gli olivetani', 122.

44 See *Diario Ferrarese dall anno 1409 sino al 1502 di autori incerti*, ed. G. Pardi in *Rerum italicarum scriptores*, 24 Part 7, no. 1 (Bologna, 1928), 57–8; G. A. Scalabrini, *Notizie istoriche del nobilissimo capitolo della s. chiesa di Ferrara*, Ferrara, Biblioteca Comunale Ariostea, MS Cl. 1, 125, 132r; A. Frizzi, *Memorie*, II, 58–9. On the taxation of the clergy in Ferrara see Prosperi, 'Le istituzioni ecclesiastiche', 130.

45 Zambotti, *Diario Ferrarese*, 26; For an argument which relates Ercole's attempt to control benefices to his patronage of musicians see Lockwood, *Music in Renaissance Ferrara*, 185.

46 See Baruffaldi, *Vita di Cosimo Tura* [1706] (Bologna, 1836), 17–18, and the version in his *Vite de' pittori e scultori ferraresi* [after 1709] (Ferrara, 1844), I, 78–80. For the earlier references to paintings by Tura in San Giorgio see Righini, 'Tura a San Giorgio', 107–8.

47 Lodovico Bigo Pittorio, *Tumultuaria Carmina* (Modena, 1492), III [unpaginated]. For the little that is known about Bigo Pittorio and a selection of his verse, see S. Pasquazi, *Poeti estensi del rinascimento* (Florence, 1966), xxxii–xlii. See also the section 'Feeding the Eyes' in chapter II above.

48 The circumstances of the destruction of the altarpiece in 1709 are described by S. Padovani, *La critica d'arte e la pittura Ferrarese* (Rovigo, 1954), 425. The central panel was acquired from Lady Eastlake for the National Gallery in London in 1867; the right-hand panel went from the Nagliati collection at Pontelagoscuro outside Ferrara to the Colonna collection in 1836, where it still remains. The panels with Sts Bernard and Benedict were lost at some point during this migration. The *Lamentation* entered the Louvre in 1863. The head of St George, now in San Diego, is all that remains of the left-hand wing; it was acquired from the Lanna collection in Prague in 1929 and is thought to have been among a group of fragments from the Costabili collection in Ferrara, sold in Milan in 1885. For a summary of the provenance of the various panels see M. Davies, *National Gallery Catalogues: The Early Italian Schools* (London, 1951), 513–16, and E. Ruhmer, *Cosimo Tura* (London, 1958), 176–7.

49 R. Longhi, *Officina Ferrarese* (Rome, 1934), 37–8; followed by M. Salmi, *Cosmè Tura* (Milan, 1957), 36, and by Ruhmer, *Cosimo Tura*, 39–41, but disputing Longhi's reconstruction of the predella.

50 Ruhmer, *Cosimo Tura*, 40; S. Ortolani, *Cosimo Tura, Francesco del Cossa, Ercole de' Roberti* (Milan, 1941), 70–72. There is still a possibility that the *tondini* have been cut down from larger panels, but it should be noted that an Infancy cycle in round frames is not unique in *quattrocento* Ferrara; the Oratory of the Conception had a cycle of thirteen tondi by Boccaccino of the life of Christ and the Virgin, including a Circumcision, the remnants of which are now housed in the Pinacoteca. See M. Calvesi, 'Nuovi affreschi ferrarese dell'Oratorio della Concezione – II', *Bollettino d'arte*, ser. IV/2, 1958, 309–28.

51 One of these is the *Virgin and Child Enthroned with Angels* by the Milanese painter Butinone (Milan, Gallarati Scotti Collection) from the 1480s; the fantastic landscape and the narrative reliefs on the throne recall the great altarpieces of Cossa and Ercole de'Roberti which imitated Tura's San Giorgio painting, while above the Virgin, on the main axis of the picture, is a golden tondo bearing a representation of the *Circumcision*. Another Milanese altarpiece, by Bartolomeo Zenale, makes an even closer fusion between the *sacra conversazione* with a clerical donor, who in this case actually performs the Circumcision. For illustrations and discussion see Milan, 1981, *Zenale e Leonardo*, exhibition catalogue (Milan, Museo Poldi-Pezzoli, 1981).

52 On this painting, destroyed in 1945, see D. Haitovsky, 'A New Look at a Lost Painting: The Hebrew Inscription in Lorenzo Costa's *Presentation in the Temple*', *Artibus et Historiae*, 29, 1994, 111–20.

53 G. M. Canova, *Ferrara 1474: Miniatura, tipografia, commitenza: Il 'Decretum Gratiani' Roverella* (Florence, 1988), 13, 31, n. 8.

54 He is not wearing the white habit of an Olivetan and hence is almost certainly not Niccolo, as was proposed by Salmi, *Cosmè Tura*, 34, and by Ruhmer, *Cosimo Tura*, 40.

55 The identification was proposed by Canova, *Ferrara 1474*, 31, n. 8, who does not cite the evidence of the tomb portrait.

56 On the tomb see S. Maddalo, 'Il monumento funebre tra persistenze medioevali e recupero dell'antico', in *Un pontificato ed una città*, 441–5.

57 C. Strehlke, 'Art and Culture in Renaissance Siena', in *Painting in Renaissance Siena 1420–1500* (New York, 1988), 55.

58 On the rhetorical premise, expressed by Poggio Bracciolini and others, that audiences are best persuaded by things seen and the employment of *ekphrasis*, see J. J. Mc-Menamon, *Funeral Oratory and the Cultural Ideals of Italian Humanism* (Chapel Hill, NC, 1989), 14, 134–5, and J. O'Malley, *Praise and Blame in Renaissance Rome* (Durham, NC, 1979). O'Malley (49) discusses the demonstrative oratory of praise and blame, the attitude that the most fitting subject for praise in sacred oratory is God and his works, and that the orator should present for veneration holy mysteries beyond human comprehension, such as the theme of redemption.

59 O'Malley, ibid., 142.

60 O'Malley, ibid., 66–7.

61 'adhuc eramus in vinculi tenebamur lege veteri & iisdem quibus antea nexibus ligabamur hodierna dies aperire nobis ianuam cepit: & aditum advitam patefacere: cum primum circumcisus est puer tum primum arma redemptionis nostrae in sanguine illo infantili apparuerunt...' Biblioteca Apostolica Vaticana, Cod. Urb. Lat. 324, 109*v*. L. Steinberg, *The Sexuality of Christ in Renaissance Art and Modern Oblivion* (New York, 1983), 62–3, stresses that the incarnational sign of circumcision was adduced constantly in these sermons against the traditional heretical enemies of the church who denied the humanity of Christ – Manichaeus, Apelles, Valentinus, Apollinarus, who are all 'exorcised for rhetorical effect'. The altarpiece will be seen in this account to mount a parallel argument against other traditional enemies of the church.

62 'Aperitur hodie humano generi circumcisionis liber. Referatur primus codes acerbissi ne passionis emanat et fluit primus sanguis in nostram redemptionam... Est ergo circumcisio passionis Christi atque principium. hanc nos in corde servemus. Intremus per ianuam quam illa nobis aperuit que hodie per baptisma latius xxx In quo renati omnes et hoc sacratissimo abluti liquore dei gratie restituimur... Durum visum est ut carnem scindamus. Noluit pater piisimos suos dolere aliquo affici. Invenit antidotum novum et aperto latere unguentum pretiosissmum edidit... Hunc itaque Pat. Ampl. sacratissimum circumcisionis diem veneremur quem possumus sicut anni principium ita in ianuam per quam ad paradisus ingressus patuit appel-

lare.' *Antonii Lolii Seminianesis oratio Circumcisionis*, n.d., 80*r*, 84*v*.

63   Surge domine in requiem tuam
     Tu et arca sanctificationis tuae
     Sacerdotes tui induantur iustitiam, et
       sancti tui exsultent.
     Propter David servum tuum, non avertas
       faciem Christi tui.

Latin text from *Biblia sacra juxta Vulgatam Clementinam*; English version from *The New Oxford Annotated Bible*.

64 'He saith unto the Lord sleeping, "Arise!" Ye know already who slept, and who rose again ..."Thou, and the Ark of Thy sanctification" that is, Arise, that the Ark of thy sanctification, which thou has sanctified, may rise also ... The Body of Christ, that was born of Mary, hath been understood by some to be the ark of sanctification; so that the words mean, Arise with thy body, that they who believe not may handle ... He was crucified by the Jews; harrassed by them, He slept. He rose to judge those among whose savage hands He slept, and He saith elsewhere, "Raise thou me up again, and I will reward them."' Augustine, *Expositions on the Book of Psalms* ('Ennarationes in Psalmos'), trans. A. Cleveland Coxe (Edinburgh, 1888; Grand Rapids, MI, 1989), 618.

65 'et non solamente tu, ma etiam la chiesa tua, laquale tu hai col sangue tuo sanctificata, e l'hai constituita arca non piu de la mana, ma de l'Eucharista vero corpo tuo, et ivi sono le tavole, cioè la evangelica legge, e la verga di Aaron, cioè la sacerdotale potesta.' Bigo Pittorio, *I Salmi di David per Lodovico Pittorio da Ferrara moralmente in forma di Omelario col latino all'incontro dechiarati, e di sententia in sententia volgarizzati* (Venice, 1547), 340.

66 Augustine, ibid., 622: 'Spiritual altitude is a horn. But what is spiritual loftiness, save to trust in Christ?'

67 'perche ne la chiesa mia perduro e suscitero il corno di David, cioè la sublimita del figliol mio et de la chiesa mia, facendo che i fideli suoi non teneranno gli occhi a terra, ma come corni alti gli alzaranno a le cose celeste, i quelle esercitandosi infino che vengano a meritar di veder a faccia a faccia quello, che al secolo per fede creduto haveranno...' Bigo Pittorio, *I Salmi*, 341.

68 For the horns of the altar see Psalm 117: 'ordinate pompem cum frondibus densis usque at cornua altaris.'

69 J. Trachtenberg, *The Devil and the Jews: The Medieval Conception of the Jew and its Relation to Modern Antisemitism*, 2nd edition (Philadelphia, 1983). For many examples of the *pileus cornutus* in art see B. Blumenkranz, *Le juif médieval au miroir de l'art chrétien* (Paris, 1966). For a comprehensive account of the iconography of horns, see R. Mellinkoff, *The Horned Moses in Medieval Art and Thought* (Berkeley, CA, 1970).

70 For a discussion of the iconography of Garofalo's painting and its sources see P. Bensi and M. R. Montiani, 'L'iconografia della *croce vivente* in ambito emiliano e ferrarese', *Musei Ferraresi*, 13/14, 1983–4, 165.

71 C. Cieri Via, 'Il tempio come *locus iustitiae*: La pala Roverella di Cosimo Tura', in G. Papagno and A. Quondam, ed., *La corte e lo spazio: Ferrara Estense* (Rome, 1982), vol. II, 577. Drawing on Alberti's *De re aedificatoria*, Cieri Via sees the Temple as symbolic of *Iusticia*, which had been a predominant theme of Borso d'Este's personal imagery during the 1460s but which does not seem to have figured largely in Este iconography after his death. Moroever, the temple does not figure in the Borsian iconography of Justice.

72 The connection of the flame emblem on the Tablets of the Law with the Este was regarded sceptically by M. Davies; it does not resemble the Este emblem known as *il fogo* as it appears, for instance in Borso's illuminated Bible. See Davies, *The Earlier Italian Schools*, 513–16. As I have argued above, however, the motif need not be seen as a personal emblem, and may bear a meaning more directly relevant to the theological matter of the altarpiece. On Este emblems see V. Ferrari, *L'araldica estense nello sviluppo storico del dominio ferrarese* (Ferrara, 1989).

73 On Mary as Ark of the Covenant see Y. Hirn, *The Sacred Shrine: The Poetry and Art of the Catholic Church* (London, 1912), 458–9; for some late medieval instances of the Virgin as Tabernacle in art see C. Bynum, *Fragmentation and Redemption* (Cambridge, 1991), 101.

74 M. Davies, *Early Italian Schools*; C. Cieri Via, 'Il tempio', in Papagno and Quondam, ed., *La corte e lo spazio*.

75 'Entraremo con devotione ne la Santa Chiesa, et non piu ne la synagoga a far sacrificio, non piu de animali, ma di noi stessi, offerendo per vittima al signore la volontà nostra, et ivi dentro adoraremo dove stati sono i piedi dal signore, che sono le cerimonie, lequale si usano a consecrare la chiesa.' Bigo Pittorio, *I Salmi*, 340.

76 C. Roth, *The Jews in the Renaissance* (Philadelphia, 1959), 193–4, draws attention to an apparent peculiarity of the Hebrew inscription as it is rendered by Tura, in that the First Commandment follows the Hebrew form 'I am who...' instead of the Christian 'I am the Lord thy God who...'. 'Who was responsible?', asks Roth, 'Was it the painter? Or did some Jewish scholar, to whose assistance he had recourse for tracing the Hebrew letters, perform the pious fraud?' What follows shows that there is no fraud intended, and that the authentic observance of Jewish forms is central to the 'argument' of the altarpiece.

77 On Christian attitudes to the Second Commandment see H. Kessler, 'Pictures Fertile with Truth: How Christians Managed to

Make Images of God without Violating the Second Commandment', *Journal of the Walters Art Gallery*, 49/50, 1991/92, 53–65; M. Camille, *The Gothic Idol: Ideology and Image Making in Medieval Art* (Cambridge, 1989), 27. I have found one other almost contemporary example of attention being drawn to the Second Commandment in the representation of the Hebrew tablets. In the 'portrait' of Moses in the Montefeltro *studiolo* the patriarch points to this very text, an ironic gesture in which the very conditions for portraying him are wittily negated. The *studiolo* decorations coincide with the completion (1474) of a monumental altarpiece in Urbino which features anti-Jewish imagery, the Altarpiece of Corpus Domini in which the duke himself appears. For the altarpiece see M. A. Lavin, 'The Altarpiece of Corpus Domini in Urbino: Paolo Uccello, Joos van Ghent and Piero della Francesca', *Art Bulletin*, XLIX, 1967, 1–24, and G. Fioravanti, 'Gianozzo Manetti, l'*Adversus Judaeos et Gentes*, e l'altare del *Corpus Domini* a Urbino', in G. Chittolini *et al.*, *Federico da Montefeltro: Le arti* (Rome, 1986), 177–87.

78 For Nicholas' discussion of the Second Commandment see Baxandall, *The Limewood Sculptors of Renaissance Germany* (New Haven and London, 1980), 51–3. The anti-Judaic dimension to Nicholas' biblical scholarship is discussed at length in J. Cohen, *The Friars and the Jews* (Ithaca, NY, 1982).

79 Cited in H. Kessler, 'Medieval Art as Argument', in B. Cassidy, ed., *Iconography at the Crossroads* (Princeton, 1991), 60.

80 Cyril of Alexandria, 'Adoration in Spirit and in Truth', cited in Kessler, 'Medieval Art as Argument', 61. The topos was also applied by Cyril to the Jews in his commentary on Luke's Gospel: 'if you had been skilful in the law you would not have failed to recognise who he was. He was depicted to you by the shadowing of Moses. He was there in the lamb, in the arrangement of the Ark, of the Mercy Seat.' Quoted in R. L. Wilken, *Judaism and the Early Christian Mind: A Study of Cyril of Alexandria's Exegesis and Theology* (New Haven, 1971), 67.

81 Kessler, 'Medieval Art as Argument', 62.

82 Hebrews 10, 19–20: 'Habentes itaque, fratres, fiduciam in introitu Sanctorum in sanguine Christi/Quam initiavit nobis viam novam et viventem per velamen, id est, carnem suam.' The rich blue of the firmament beyond the throne might be seen as the heaven to which Christ is the doorway and to which the Roverella seek admittance. In the iconography of *Parousia* the cosmos is patterned after the Jewish tabernacle, with the blue veil of the sanctuary corresponding to the zone of the firmament, which separates heaven and earth. See Kessler, 'Gazing at the Future: The *Parousia* Miniature in the Vatican Cosmas', in D. Mouriki, ed., *Byzantine East and Latin*

West: Art Historical Studies in Honor of Kurt Weitzmann (Princeton, 1993).

83 'ed in questo luogo [San Clemente] massimanente si affolla il popolo per vederla, e adorarla.' G. Marangoni, *Istoria dell'antichissimo oratorio o cappella di San Lorenzo nel patriarcato Lateranese* (Rome, 1747), 122. See also the discussion in H. Belting, *Likeness and Presence: A History of the Image before the Era of Art*, trans. E. Jephcott (Chicago, 1994), 64–73, 121, 501. A Byzantine iconographic tradition which might be invoked here is that of the Mandylion, the veil bearing the miraculous image of Christ's face, which was associated both with the veil of the Temple and, when paired with its cermaic offset, the *keramion*, with the tables of the Law themselves. Following its transport to the Imperial chapel of Constantinople in 944, the Mandylion was kept in a chest called the Second Ark; this was placed in the Pharos Chapel which housed relics of Christ, the Virgin and, allegedly, the Tablets of the Law themselves. The paired icons depicting the miraculous images of Christ were hailed as the sacred tablets of the Christians. Not only did this signify the triumph of the image over the forces of Jewish and Christian iconoclasm, but also the victory of the living, visible embodiment of Christ over the abstract, moribund domain of writing, the laws of Moses obeserved by the Jews. On the Mandylion and its Roman rival, the Veronica, see Belting, ibid., 208–24, and K. Weitzmann, 'The Mandylion of Constantine Porphyrogennetos', *Studies in Classical and Byzantine Manuscript Illumination* (Chicago, 1971), 224–46.

84 Christ was circumcised, according to Thomas Aquinas, 'to take the burden of the Law upon himself, so as to liberate others from that burden'. *Summa Theologica*, III 9:39 art.1 resp.

85 On the Pope's veneration of the Torah see C. L. Stinger, *The Renaissance in Rome* (Bloomington, IN, 1985), 53–4.

86 This contrasts with the passive or even happily acquiescent demeanour of the Child in representations of the theme by Signorelli (London, National Gallery), Bartolomeo Veneto (Paris, Louvre), Giovanni Bellini (London, National Gallery), Michael Pacher (the St Wolfgang altarpiece, St Wolfgang in Salzkammergut, Austria), the Master of the Solomon Triptych (location unknown; for an illustration see L. C. Ragghianti, *Dipinti Fiamminghi in Italia 1420–1570* (Bologna, 1990), no. 358).

87 See A. Chiappini, 'Una biblioteca ed un *scriptorium* in Ferrara nel secolo XV: San Giorgio', *Analecta Pomposiana*, 6, 1981, 201–2, 214–17.

88 Sabbadini, ed., *Epistolario di Guarino Veronese* (Venice, 1915–19), vol. II, 473–4.

89 'Et estis in illo repleti, qui est caput omnis principatus et potestatis/in quo et circumcisi estis circumcisioni non manu facta in exspo-

liatione corporis carnis, sed in circumcisione Christi.' Colossians 2: 10–11. Paul then writes of the abolition of the Law through the Passion of Christ: 'Et vos cum mortui essetis in delictis, et praeputio carnis vestrae, cumvivificavit cum illo, donans vobis omnia delicta./ Delens quod adversus nos erat chirographum decreti [i.e. *handwriting* of ordinances] quod erat contrarium nobis, et ipsum tulit de medio, affigens illud cruci' (13–14).

90 II Corinthians 3; 5: 'Manifestati quod epistola estis Christi, ministrata a nobis, et scripta non atramento, sed spiritu Dei vivi: non in tabulis lapideis, sed in tabulis cordis carnalibus.'

91 *In Circumcisione Domini*, I: 'In omni siquidem contradicentium spiritui rebellione membrorum, solum illud usque adeo contumax invenitur, ut contra omnem voluntatis deliberationem ad inhonestos et illicitos motus assurgat.' For discussion of Bernard's sermons see Steinberg, *Sexuality of Christ*, 54–5.

92 For instance Antonio Campano, Biblioteca Apostolica Vaticana, Cod. Urb. Lat. 324, 111r: 'Tum quoque ut remissius libidine conflictarentur hebrei si in libidinis membro continentiae deferent castitasque memoriam et si quando incitaretur adeam voluptatem intemperantius . . .'

93 O'Malley, *Praise and Blame*, 84 (for Barzizza), 142, and Steinberg, *Sexuality of Christ*, 61–5.

94 See J. Cohen, *The Friars and the Jews*. The historical motivations for the mendicant campaigns against the Jews are still the subject of debate; see also Cohen's review of recent arguments, 'Recent Historiography on the Medieval Church and the Decline of Jewry', in J. R. Sweeney and S. Chodorow, ed., *Popes, Teachers and Canon Law in the Middle Ages* (Ithaca, NY, 1989), 251–62; also Cohen, 'Scholarship and Intolerance in the Medieval Academy: The Study and Evaluation of Judaism in European Christendom', *American Historical Review*, 91, 1986, 592–615, and in the same journal, D. Berger, 'Mission to the Jews and Jewish-Christian Contacts in the Polemical Literature of the High Middle Ages', 576–92. On the situation in Italy see the overview by G. Todeschini, 'Ebrei in Italia alla fine del medioevo: Studi recenti', *Studi medievali*, 30, 1989, 351–66.

95 'Nemini licet nunc contra vitia Judaeorum predicare . . . quia principes et magistratus pecuniis corrupti solent imponere silentium . . . Ipsi perfidi canes audent adire magistratus et mendatiis ita eos informare ut obtineant litteras execratorias et citatorias. Expertus sum ego. Nunc creditur magis Judaeorum nugis quam religiosorum veritati . . . Non curant ipsi magistratus predicatores a sermonibus deturbare.' Quoted in G. Fioravanti, 'Polemiche antigiudaiche nell'Italia del quattrocento: Un tentativo di interpretazione globale', in *Ebrei e cristiani nell'Italia medievale e moderna: Conversioni, scambi, contrasti* (Rome, 1988), 87.

96 'Hic est vere Israelita, in quo dolus non est.' Bucelino, *Rutiliae longe vetustissimae*, 73.

97 On Manetti's treatise see Fioravanti, 'L'apologetica antigiudaica di Gianozzo Manetti,' *Rinascimento*, n.s. 23, 1983, 3–32, and Fioravanti, 'L'altare del *Corpus Domini*'.

98 S. Simonsohn, *The Apostolic See and the Jews*, vol. II: *1394–1464* (Toronto, 1989), Document 705; Commission to the Franciscan Inquisitor Pons Feugeyron.

99 Abramo Pesaro, *Memorie storiche sulla communità israelitica ferrarese* (Ferrara, 1878; Bologna, 1986), 13.

100 Cohen, *The Friars and the Jews*, 146.

101 Cohen, ibid., 150.

102 Fioravanti, 'Polemiche antigiudaiche', 76.

103 A. Balletti, *Gli ebrei e gli Estensi* (Reggio Emilia, 1930), 27.

104 Quoted in D. Quaglioni, 'Propaganda antiebraiche e polemiche di Curia', in *Un pontificato ed una città*, 252. For the events at Trent see R. Po Chia-Hsia, *Trent 1475: Stories of a Ritual Murder Trial* (New Haven and London, 1992).

105 For some examples see G. Kaftal, *Iconography of the Saints in the Painting of North West Italy* (Florence, 1985), 594; *Iconography of the Saints in the Painting of North East Italy* (Florence, 1978), 942.

106 See K. Biddick, 'Genders, Bodies, Borders: Technologies of the Visible', in *Speculum*, 68, 1993, 389–418, a critique of Steinberg, *Sexuality of Christ*, and of Bynum, 'The Body of Christ in the Later Middle Ages: A Reply to Leo Steinberg', *Fragmentation and Redemption*, 79–119.

107   Melanconici tutti e saturnini,
  Retroganti, spietati e mal nassuti
  Non gallici, todeschi nè latini
  ma de giudaica setta son cernuti.
Full text in E. Levi, *Francesco da Vanozzo e la lirica nelle corte lombarde durante la seconda metà del secolo XIV* (Florence, 1908), 127–9.

108   che han posto all'alma l'elmo de giustizia
  di quegli ancor un car an de'nequizia
  e tutti asconde e scande in lingua ebraica.

109 Balletti, *Gli ebrei*, 43.

110 Zambotti, *Diario Ferrarese*, 92. Zambotti adds that 'Il Signore temè che non se fesse scandalo e che non fosse messo a saccomano il bancho, dove ge son le robbe de'citadini e zintilhomini, e anche de la Caxa Da Este.'

111 Modena, Archivio di Stato, Camera Ducale, Libri camerali diversi, *Conto Generale 1476*, pp. v, 22, 46, 54, 71, 89, 154, etc.

112 Simonsohn, *Apostolic See* II, doc. 771, July 1st 1448.

113 Balletti, *Gli Ebrei*, 46.

114 Simonsohn, *Apostolic See*, II, doc. 858: mandate to the Bishop of Spoleto and to the vicars of bishops in Bologna and Ferrara to curtail the activities of preachers following the complaints of certain Jews. The mandate reinforced the provisions of the bull 'Sicut Iudeis' first issued by Innocent III and reissued several times, a version appearing under Martin V in 1419; the bull protected the Jews from harassment and forced baptisms and allowed a discreet practice of Judaic ritual, but left space for other forms of discrimination such as Inquisitorial surveillance and the imposition of badges and earrings. For an overview of Papal pronouncements see E. Synan, *The Pope and the Jews in the Middle Ages* (New York, 1965), especially 97f. for 'Sicut Iudeis', and S. Dubnov, *History of the Jews: From the Late Middle Ages to the Renaissance* (New York, 1969).

115 Ibid., 689; a mandate was issued on 25 October 1432. For more on the social demarcation of Jews and its connection with the communal demands for sumptuary laws see D. Owen Hughes, 'Distinguishing Signs: Ear-Rings, Jews and Franciscan Rhetoric in the Italian Renaissance City', *Past and Present*, 112, 1986, 3–59, with many references to Ferrara.

116 Simonsohn, *Apostolic See*, III, doc. 990. A formula in II, doc. 830, is characteristic of the constant assertion of territorial claims of the Papacy aginst the Este: 'ac in dominiis dilectorum filiorum nobilium virorum ducis Mutine et Regii in civitate nostra Ferrarie pro nobis et Ecclesia Romana vicarii in temporalibus.'

117 On the foundation of the Monte di Pietà in Bologna see M. Maragi, 'Cenni storici del Monte di Bologna', in *Archivi storici delle Aziende di Credito*, 1, 1956, 616–20, and the many references and additional biography in Vittorio Meneghin, *Bernardino da Feltre e i Monti di Pietà* (Vicenza, 1974).

118 For a rather celebratory account of this figure see Meneghin, ibid. His connection with Filiasio Roverella is related in Litta, 'Roverella di Ferrara', *Famiglie celebre*, [unpaginated].

119 R. Segre, 'Gli ebrei a Ravenna nell'età veneziana', in Bolognesi, ed., *Ravenna in età veneziana*, 167.

120 See Gardner, *Dukes and Poets*, 153, and D. B. Ruderman, *The World of a Renaissance Jew; The Life and Thought of Abraham ben Mordecai Farissol* (Cincinnati, 1981), 21.

121 Balletti points to a number of instances of onerous fiscal dependency on the Jews by the *comune* of Reggio, including the commune's loan from the banker Zinatan of 100 gold florins to buy a wedding present for the duke. In 1463 certain citizens appealed to Borso to 'liberare questa povera citade de tanto divoramento quanto e questo di questo Zudio' (34).

122 See Camille, *The Gothic Idol*, 188.

123 See G. Griffiths, J. Hankins and D. Thompson, *The Humanism of Leonardo Bruni: Selected Texts* (Binghamton, NY, 1987), 334–5.

124 Balletti, *Gli Ebrei*, 33.

125 Catherine Turrill considers the figure of David (and Moses) as a type of Christ, but admits that 'a less Christ-like figure could scarcely be imagined'. *Ercole de' Roberti's Altarpieces for the Lateran Canons* (Ph.D. dissertation, University of Delaware, 1986), 87.

126 See the study by J. Perles, 'Ahron ben Gerson Aboulrabi', *Revue des études juives*, 20, 1890, 249–51.

127 Franceschini, *Artisti a Ferrara*, Part 1, nos 637, 638.

128 For documentation see Balletti, *Gli ebrei*, 55, n. 1.

129 Balletti, ibid., 54, n. 3.

130 As discussed by A. Funkenstein, 'Basic Types of Christian Anti-Jewish Polemics in the Middle Ages', *Viator*, 2, 1971, 373–82.

131 'Et per i meriti del tuo figliolo, il qual del seme di David piglio la forma di servo, non volere in tutto da giudei rimovere voltandogli le spalle la notitia de l'incarnato tuo verbo, ma degnati di fare che una volta almanco ne gli ultimi giorni le reliquie loro si salvino.'

132 Modena, Archivio di Stato, Camera Ducale, Libri camerali diversi, 27, 1458, fol. 109.

133 In 1435 the Pope ruled that the prior of Monte Oliveto in Pistoia should act as arbitrator in the disposal of the usury profits of Luca Ventura, a Jew who had converted to Christianity with his wife and children. The concession was apparently issued at Luca's request and the document suggests close contact between the family and the Olivetan congregation – one of Luca's sons took the name Benedetto. See Simonsohn, *Apostolic See*, II, document 736. On conversion see the study by A. Toaff, 'Conversioni al cristianesimo in Italia nel quattrocento: Movimenti e tendenze: il caso dell'Umbria', in M. Luzzati *et al.*, *Ebrei e cristiani nell'Italia medioevale e moderna* (Rome, 1988), esp. 109ff. Largely as a result of the founding of Monte di Pietà, the Jewish community of Umbria diminished by 40% between 1465 and 1485.

134 'il quale provò per raxone hebraiche che la fede nostra sè migliore che la hebraicha, che fu cosa notabile per la fede.' Zambotti, *Diario Ferrarese*, 12, 2 July 1476.

135 See Ruderman, 'The Italian Renaissance and Jewish Thought', in A. Rabil Jr., ed., *Renaissance Humanism: Foundations, Forms and Legacy* (Philadelphia, 1988), vol. II, 382–434.

136 On Moses as a figure of the Papacy see Stinger, *Renaissance in Rome*, 204–18.

137 Borso paid the lavish sum of 40 gold ducats to Vespasiano di Bisticci for a manuscript of Josephus' *De bello iudaico* and a Quintus Curtius *De gestis Alexandri* in 1469. Franceschini, *Artisti a Ferrara*, Part 1, Appendix 27p. Ercole acquired a *Josopho de antiquitate* in the translation of Battista Panetti; see G. Bertoni, *La Biblioteca Estense e la cultura ferrarese ai tempi del duca Ercole I (1471–1505)* (Turin, 1903), 49.

138 A. Luzio and A. Renier, 'I Filelfo e l'umanesimo alla corte dei Gonzaga', *Giornale storico della letteratura italianai*, 16, 1890, 153.

139 For the tapestry, see Franceschini, *Artisti a*

Ferrara, Part II, vol. I, no. 229dd. Pellegrino Prisciani, the humanist historian and astrologer who devised the programme for the Salone dei Mesi, interred his father Prisciano at San Domenico in a tomb ornamented with forms identical with the horned tablets in the Roverella altarpiece. R. Stemp, *Sculpture in Ferrara in the Fifteenth Century: Problems and Studies* (Ph.D. dissertation, Cambridge University, 1992), 27, reasonably proposes that Tura may have supplied designs for the tomb (now at the Carthusian monastery in Ferrara). The connotations of this form for Pellegrino might have been more as signifiers of 'antiquity' – which itself could be a play on the name 'Priscianus' – rather than as signs of Jewishness, but it is noteworthy that Pellegrino was himself interested in Jewish culture, knew Hebrew, and allowed a circumcision to be performed in his house in 1498; see Ruderman, *Abraham ben Mordecai Farissol*, 28; in 1449 Pellegrino acted as procurator for the Jew Abraham in a legal case concerning the deterioration of a Christian fresco in his house. See Franceschini, *Artisti a Ferrara*, Part I, no. 638.

140 On the Sforza wedding see P. Castelli, 'La *kermesse* degli Sforza pesaresi', *Mesura et arte del danzare: Guglielmo Ebreo da Pesaro e la danza nelle corti italiane del XV secolo* (Pesaro, 1987), 3–33.

141 Zambotti, *Diario Ferrarese*, 47. Ruderman, *Abraham ben Mordecai Farissol*, 57–71.

142 The predella of an altarpiece by Ercole de'Roberti showed a number of Old Testament subjects, among them a scene of the Israelites gathering manna which has been identified, through the writings of Pellegrino Prisciani, as also showing the Hebrew origins of theatre. See J. Manca, 'Renaissance Theater and Hebrew Ritual in Ercole de'Roberti's *Gathering of the Manna*', *Artibus et Historiae*, 17, 1988, 137–48.

143 As is noted by Stemp, *Sculpture in Ferrara*, 25–6.

144 Davies, *The Earlier Italian Schools*, 513–16.

145 'maestro Biasio da Parma, excellente mathematico e astrologo, fo singularmente trepevole. Havendo in presto un libro, dove trovava qualche notabele dicto, in luoco de mane, gli facea misser Santo Priapo, decendo che quel membro era piu noto che la mane, e meglio reduria a memoria tutti gli notabili.' A. E. K. Salza, *Facezie di Lodovico Carbone Ferrarese* (Livorno, 1900), 53.

146 C. Gilbert, 'The Archbishop on the Painters of Florence, 1450', *Art Bulletin*, 41, 1959, 75–87.

CHAPTER V

1 'unum organum bonum pulcrum decore ornatissimum et habens omnem perfectionem organi tam in pulcritudine quam in armonia vocis quantum dici possit . . .' The documents are discussed in E. Peverada, *Vita musicale nella chiesa ferrarese del quattrocento* (Ferrara, 1991), 40–46. See also the discussion by A. Cavicchi, 'L'organo della cattedrale nella tradizione musicale e organaria ferrarese', in J. Bentini, ed., *San Giorgio e la principessa di Cosmè Tura* (Bologna, 1985), 102ff.

2 '. . . cum suis fenestris fulcitis omnibus necessariis excepta pictura earum, quam picturam fieri facere debeat fabrica episcopatus Ferrarie suis expensis . . .' Peverada, ibid., 41.

3 The record was transcribed by Scalabrini in the eighteenth century: 'Et a die II zugno, L. cento undexe M. per lei facti boni a M. ro. Cosmè del Turra depintore per sua manufactura de haver depinto da tutti dui li lacti le porte de l'organo novo del vescoado daccordo cum lui in duc. quaranta octo da sol.55 d.6 l'uno, che pigliano deto precio et posto deto m. ro. Cosmè creditore in questo *c*.47: L.CXS.-d-.' From Peverada, ibid., 44.

4 'in la capella drieto el cuore sopra Yhesu Christo et li apostoli'. Peverada, ibid., 43.

5 Given its position in the major church of the city the painting may have been uniquely visible among the artist's works; it would have been the most likely to have been seen by foreign visitors, a fact to which Vasari's terse comments in his *Vite* of 1550 present certain testimony (see Vasari, *Le opere*, ed. G. Milanesi, 9 vols, Florence, 1906, vol. III, 92), while the walled mountain in Mantegna's Camera Picta frescoes and Leonardo's *Leda* stand as possible evidence of the attraction it may have held for other artists. It is not known when Leonardo would have visited Ferrara, but Mantegna visited the city in 1469 to wait upon the Emperor, who held court at Ferrara in October of that year.

6 On the condition of the painting at the restoration in 1948, when a substantial amount of eighteenth-century overpainting was removed, see C. Gnudi and A. Sorrentino, 'Restauro delle ante d'organo di Cosmè Tura nella cattedrale di Ferrara', *Bollettino d'arte*, III, 1948, 262–5; for a recent technical analysis see J. Bentini, ed., *San Giorgio e la principessa*, 17–20.

7 The most controversial and frequently discussed cases are Hieronymus Bosch and Giorgione, but it might be questioned as to whether these artists should dictate the terms of discussion of meaning for all artistic production in the period. For the case against the monolithic interpretation of Giorgione's *Tempest* and Bosch's *Garden of Earthly Delights* see respectively J. Elkins, 'On Monstrously Ambiguous Paintings', *History and Theory*, XXXII/3, 1993, 227–47, and M. De Certeau, *The Mystic Fable*, trans. M. B. Smith (Chicago, 1992), 49–72.

8 See R. Lightbown, *Mantegna* (Oxford, 1986), 90. Another example would be Pirro Ligorio's later insistence that grotesque ornaments should have a determinate meaning, like hieroglyphs or rebuses. N. Dacos, *La découverte de la Domus Aurea et la formation des grotesques à la Renaissance* (London and Leiden, 1969), 161–82. Vasari's decision to present Giorgione's figures on the *Fondaco dei Tedeschi* as instances of artistic ingenuity and fantasy, while he admits that their meaning eludes him, might be considered as a problematising of the separability of 'subject and non-subject' in the Renaissance.

9 For a still indispensable survey see Y. Hirn, *The Sacred Shrine: The Poetry and Art of the Catholic Church* (London, 1912).

10 De Certeau, *The Mystic Fable*, 52.

11 H. White, *Metahistory: The Historical Imagination in Nineteenth Century Europe* (Baltimore, 1973), 34. On catachresis and transumption in the Renaissance see L. Barkan, *Transuming Passion: Ganymede and the Erotics of Humanism* (Stanford, CA, 1991), 43.

12 De Certeau, *The Mystic Fable*, 70.

13 The badly cropped painting of the subject by Vitale da Bologna in the Pinacoteca, Bologna, features a princess who, although she turns away from the battle, maintains an impassive expression. For instances of the princess showing more faith than trepidation see the praying figure in Donatello's Orsanmichele relief and in Crivelli's *St George* (Boston, Isabella Stewart Gardner Museum), or her completely serene appearance in Uccello's versions of the scene in the National Gallery, London, or the Musée Jacquemart-André, Paris. In the choir books commissioned for the cathedral of Ferrara the kneeling princess confronts the saint's slaughter of the dragon; see Bentini, ed., *San Giorgio e la principessa*, 48–9.

14 G. Didi-Huberman, *Fra Angelico: Dissemblance and Figuration* (Chicago, 1995), 129.

15 For an account of the metaphorics of light in the iconography of the Incarnation, and its divergence from the tradition of auditory metaphor, see L. Steinberg, 'How Can This Be? Reflections on Filippo Lippi's *Annunciation* in London', *Artibus et Historiae*, 16, 1987, 38–41.

16 H. Friedmann, *A Bestiary for St Jerome* (Washington, DC, 1980), 119, identifies the squirrel as a symbol of 'seeking after divinity' on the basis of a text in the *Sequentiae* of Adam of St Victor which interpreted the nut as a symbol of Christ: 'the hard shell is the cross on which He was sacrificed, the green sheath is His flesh, His humanity, while the kernel within, from which nourishment may be derived, is His hidden divinity.' Yet Tura's squirrel is bound or restrained, which might signify instead a checking of the appetite or curiosity which seeks to pry too deeply into the mystery of Christ's hidden divinity, above all in its concealment by the mortal flesh of the Virgin. The bird above the angel resembles the *Tichodroma muraria* or wall creeper

which Friedmann convincingly identifies in Tura's London *St Jerome* (183), a bird believed to frequent graveyards and nest in human skulls – hence identifiable like the squirrel with the rapacity of time – yet whose popular Italian name is 'Madoneta' or 'osel della Madona'.

17 On the theme of the secret in the Western pictorial tradition of the *Annunciation* see L. Marin, *Opacité de la peinture: Essais sur le représentation au quattrocento* (Paris, 1989), 136–57. For an intriguing and persuasive account of the figuration of mystery in early Renaissance Annunciations, see Didi-Huberman, *Fra Angelico*.

18 See E. Guldan, 'Et verbum caro factum est: Die Darstellung der Inkarnation Christi im Verkündigungsbild', *Römische Quartalschrift für christliche Altertumskunde und Kirchengeschichte*, 63, 1968, 158. The formulation of *conceptio per aurem* is widely ascribed to Augustine by modern commentators, but without specific references: Hirn, *The Sacred Shrine*, 296 (no citation); E. Jones, 'The Madonna's Conception through the Ear', *Essays in Applied Psychoanalysis* (London, 1951), II, 269 (erroneous citation); H. van Campenhausen, *The Virgin Birth in the Theology of the Ancient Church* (Naperville, IL, 1964), 81 (no citation); Steinberg, 'How Can This Be?', 43n. (citation to Hirn).

19 Ennodius, quoted in Hirn, *The Sacred Shrine*, 296. More recent and more influential was St Bernard's formulation, 'missus est interim Gabriel angelus a Deo, ut verbum patris per aurem virginis in ventrem et mentem ipsius eructaret, ut eadem via intraret antidotum, qua venenum intraverat', *Sermo II in festo Pentecostes*. For images of the motif in the *Bible moralisée* and the Wurzburg *Marienkapelle* tympanum, see Guldan, 'Et verbum caro factum est'.

20 For example, the story of Salome the midwife, who received a withered arm for her disbelief in the Virgin Birth and for demanding empirical proof by examining the body of the Virgin. The analogy between the Virgin and the mystical container of the Jewish Law – the Ark of the Covenant – entailed a release of blinding or paralysing apotropaic energy against presumptuous or blasphemous hands. See the account of Mary's funeral in Jacopo da Voragine, *Legenda aurea*, CXIX, ed. T. Graesse (Osnabrück, 1890, 1969), 524; the story of Salome is in chapter VI (42).

21 On the homilectic development of the theme of Mary's enquiry and submission see M. Baxandall, *Painting and Experience in Fifteenth-Century Italy* (Oxford, 1972), 51.

22 The exegetical tradition of the occurrence of the Incarnation in the Jerusalem Temple is discussed by S. J. Edgerton Jr., 'Mensurare temporalia facit geometria spiritualis: Some fifteenth century notions about when and where the Annunciation happened', in I. Lavin and J. Plummer, ed., *Studies in Medieval and Renaissance Painting in Honor of Millard Meiss* (New York, 1978), vol. I, 115–30.

23 E. Guidoni and A. Marino, 'Cosmus Pictor: Il nuovo organo di Ferrara: Armonia, storia, e alchimia della creazione', *Storia dell'arte*, 1, 1968, 388–416.

24 Guidoni and Marino, ibid., 394.

25 M. Bertozzi, 'Il Signore della Serpe: Simbolismo ermetico e alchimia nel S. Giorgio e il drago di Cosmè Tura', in Bentini, ed., *San Giorgio e la principessa*, 55–65, and E. Domenicali, 'San Giorgio e gli Estensi', in R. Varese and L. Olivato, ed., *San Giorgio tra Ferrara e Praga*, exhibition catalogue (Ferrara, Castello Estense, 1991), 116–22.

26 Guidoni and Marino, ibid., 391–3. For the Borsian Addition see C. Rosenberg, 'Per il bene di . . . nostra cipta: Borso d'Este and the Certosa of Ferrara', *Renaissance Quarterly*, XXIX/3, 1976, 329–40.

27 Guidoni and Marino, ibid., 394.

28 Guidoni and Marino, ibid., 396.

29 The best-known example is Pisanello's *Virgin and Child with Sts George and Anthony Abbot* (London, National Gallery), in which St George closely resembles Pisanello's medallion portraits of Leonello d'Este. It is not known, however, whether this painting was deployed as a public self-image by the prince; the work may have been made for private or restricted viewing. Given the terms of friendship existing between Leonello and Pisanello, the image may reflect a personal initiative on the part of the painter, who sometimes provided the prince with works of art in the form of gifts rather than as formal commissions. Borso's identification with St George is far more discreet: a miniature in Borso's illuminated Bible (Modena, Biblioteca Estense) which shows his personal heraldic animal, the unicorn, neutralising a dragon's venom with its horn. This was pointed out by E. Domenicali, 'S. Giorgio e gli estensi', in Varese and Olivato, ed., *San Giorgio tra Ferrara e Praga*, 121.

30 The historical information on the cult of St George up to the fifteenth century recounted here is drawn from A. Samaritani, 'Il culto di San Giorgio a Ferrara', in Varese and Olivato, ed., *San Giorgio tra Ferrara e Praga*, 84–99.

31 On the choral books see P. T. Lombardi, 'I corali miniati del Duomo', in *La Cattedrale di Ferrara: Atti del Convegno dell'Accademia delle Scienze di Ferrara* (Ferrara, 1982), 353–411, and for the choir-screen G. Medri, *La scultura a Ferrara* (Rovigo, 1958), 48–50; R. Stemp, *Sculpture in Ferrara in the Fifteenth Century: Problems and Studies* (Ph.D. dissertation, University of Cambridge, 1992), 14f.

32 Samaritani, 'Il culto di San Giorgio', 99.

33 Voragine, *Legenda aurea*, LVIII, 262.

34 L. Célier, *Les dataires du XVe siècle et les origines de la Daterie Apostolique* (Paris, 1910), 35.

35 L. von Pastor, *The History of the Popes from the Close of the Middle Ages*, 5th edition (London, 1923), vol. IV, p. 81.

36 Pastor, ibid., 82–4.

37 'in communem Christianorum exercitum contra impiissimos hos canes Turchos comparandum contributuros, sicuti sepenumero Nobis polliciti sunt'; full text of the letter in E. Gardner, *Dukes and Poets in Ferrara* (London, 1904), 538. For Paul II and the Crusade see G. Valentini, 'La sospensione della crociata nei primi anni di Paolo II (1464–68)', *Archivium historiam pontificae*, 14, 1976, 71–103.

38 Lorenzo's contemporary reputation as a promoter of the crusade is reflected in the panegyric on the house of Roverella in Zambotti's *Diario Ferrarese*, ed. G. Pardi in *Rerum italicarum scriptores* (Bologna, 1928), vol. 24, Part 7, 77:

> O quotiens crucis ipse tenens vexilla furentes
> Agressus Turchos, perfida signa scidit.
> O quotiens primus per medios periturus in hostes
> Ipse ruens victos perdidit arce canes
> Hoc pastore fuit foelix Ferraria dictu
> Et peterent talem tempora nostra virum . . .

39 Pompeo Litta, *Famiglie celebri italiane* (Milan, 1819), vol. X, 'Roverella'; Pastor, *History of the Popes*, IV, 159.

40 Pastor, ibid., IV, 144; Célier, *Les dataires*, 36.

41 The Archivio di Stato in Modena houses his personal household accounts for 1473, which Thomas Tuohy kindly drew to my attention. Modena, Archivio di Stato, *Amministrazioni dei principi*, 22 1473: 'Zornale de entrata e uscita di Lorenzo Roverella.' The only artistic commissions referred to, however, are painted *stendardini* from the artist Gherardo da Vicenza, fol. 45v. The dioscesan archive in Ferrara has the incomplete record of a pastoral visit by Lorenzo conducted between May 1470 and June 1474, shown to me by Enrico Peverada. In January 1473 the diarist Ugo Caleffini records the donation of a valuable horse by Lorenzo to Ercole d'Este in the course of the duke's annual extortionate 'fortune seeking'. See Gardner, *Dukes and Poets*, 129.

42 Filiasio's membership of the chapter is recorded by Scalabrini, *Notizie istoriche del nobilissimo capitolo della s. chiesa di Ferrara*, Ferrara, Biblioteca Comunale Ariostaea, MS Cl. 1, 125. fol. 132v.

43 See Pastor, *History of the Popes*, IV, 24.

44 For instance by Pius II, in an oration before the Diet of Ratisbon: 'sunt enim angustiae freti per Bosforum Thraciae et per Hellspontum, quod Brachium Sancti Georgii nostri vocitant, in potestate Turcorum.' A. Pertusi, *Testi inediti e poco noti sulla caduta di Costantinopoli*, ed. A. Carile (Bologna, 1983), 184.

45 For an embassy at the Congress of Mantua on behalf of the patriarchs of Antioch, Alexandria and Jerusalem and 'numerous Christian princes of Asia' see Piccolomini (Pius II), *Commentaries*, Book IV, trans. F. A. Gragg, *Smith College Studies in History*, XXX, 1947, 320–21.

46 Pastor, *History of the Popes*, IV, 253 includes a transcription of a letter to Borso d'Este reporting the queen's arrival at the Papal court.

47 See H. Vast, *Le Cardinal Bessarion* (Paris, 1878; Geneva, 1977), 201–2; Pastor, ibid., 266.

48 'melius est Grecos tollerare sicut meretrices ecclesia tollerat propter maiora mala vitanda'; Pastor, ibid., 256n., my translation. Pastor provides substantial excerpts, including the following, where the position of those who oppose aid to the Greeks is summarised: 'Videtur quod Grecis non sit auxilium aliquod praestandum, hereticis et scismaticis et excommunicatis non est communicandum et multo minus auxilium praestandum, penis potius tormentis carcere coercendi sunt prout utriusque iuris leges et canones satis docent.' Notwithstanding this just theological classification, the author will argue that for the sake of the lawful Church, help should be proffered in this instance. The prejudices of Italians against Greeks during this period is discussed by J. Burckhardt, *The Civilization of the Renaissance in Italy* (New York, 1958), vol. I, 205, n.1. Another contemporary instance is the mistrust and resentment encountered by Bessarion from the Sacred College, as reported by Piccolomini (Pius II), *Commentaries*, I, 75.

49 See G. Bartazzi, in A. Mottola-Molfino and M. Natali, ed., *Le Muse e il Principe*, exhibition catalogue (Milan, Museo Poldi-Pezzoli, 1991), vol. II, 127–8 for citations.

50 'O Italia povera, o Italia dissoluta, teme dio, fa penitentia. Hai lo exempio de la povera Grecia, come la sta. O Constantinopoli, chi te ha mai posto ne la mane del Gran Turco? La pocha tua bontade, la luxuria, la infidelità tua.' Full text of the sermon delivered on July 1453 8 in Pertusi, *Testi inediti*, 295–6.

51 'La quale citade se perdé per la loro avaritia, però che non volseno mai asoldare zente alchune. Et foli una dona che li fuo trovato in zoglie et argenti e dinari e pagni el valore de 150 migliara de duchati, et uno huomo el valore de 80 migliara de duchati.' *Cronica di Bologna*, quoted in Pertusi, ibid., 26.

52 On Lorenzo's diocesan synods of 1465 and 1466 see D. Balboni, 'I sinodi diocesani di Ferrara', *Analecta Ferrariensia*, I, 1958, 120: 'Il 2 dicembre 1465 proibì ai "capellani," cioè agli ecclesiastici investiti di un beneficio con cura d'anime o richiedente la residenza personale, di avere un secondo beneficio gravato degli stessi oneri. L'anno seguente disciplinò il modo di vestire degli ecclesiastici proibendo di usare stoffe lussuose con colori indebiti e calzature eleganti.'

53 The Inquisitor Tommaso dai Liuti dedicated his *Il modo de ben governare* to Borso between 1452 and 1471, reminding him of his status as *vicario* of the *Sancta romana ecclesia*. See S. Macioce, 'Schifanoia e il ceremoniale', in R. Varese, ed. *Atlante di Schifanoia* (Modena, 1990), 72, and T. Kaeppeli, 'Tommaso dai Liuti di Ferrara e il suo *Declaratorio*', *Archivum fratrum praedicatorum*, 20, 1950, 195–206. For Savonarola see A. Samaritani, 'Michele Savonarola, riformatore cattolico nella Corte Estense a metà del sec. XV', *Atti e memorie della deputazione Ferrarese per la storia patria*, ser. 3, vol. XXII (1976), 44–64. On Fra Giovanni see chapter II above. Pius II's complaints to Borso regarding his failure to attend the council of Mantua and to abide by his ambassadors' promises, his diplomacy with Sigismondo Malatesta and other offences are in a letter of 1462. See Piccolomini, *Epistolae in pontificatu editae* (Milan, 1481), Epistola CXI, fol. 133. This letter ends with an exhortation to Borso to contemplate himself in his own statue in the marketplace of Ferrara, which if it could speak would make known the contempt and reproaches of the people. Paul II's upbraiding of Borso for *vanagloria* is known from Borso's reply, preserved with the diplomatic correspondence of Jacopo Trotti. Modena, Archivio di Stato, Fonte degli Ambasciatori: 'Jacopo Trotti, oratore residente preso il Papa.' Letter of Borso d'Este, 13 June 1468.

54 *Tractatus de Divina Providentia ad Borsium Ferrarie Dominum*, quoted in T. Ascari, 'Francesco Ariosto Peregrino', *Atti e memorie della Accademia di scienze, lettere ed arti di Modena*, ser. 5, XI, 1953, 108.

55 Modena, Biblioteca Estense, Cod. Est. Lat. 1906. I have followed the edition by G. Stendardo, 'L'*Iside* di Francesco Ariosto', *Archivum Romanicum* XX/1, 1936, 114–22, based on Modena, Biblioteca Estense, a.Q.7,32.

56 The title somewhat ambiguously refers to the 'religion of Isis', but at one point the connection with the ancient Egyptian cults which pervaded the Roman world is made explicit in a reference to Osiris and the phoenix: 'Isidis est oris dictus celebratus Osiris/Dicebant phoenix hac regione volat.'

57 Stendardo, '*Iside*', 119:

> Et docuit vanos velis operire capillos,
> Victa purpureas stringere sponte genas.
> Ornabant bullis gemmisque monilia frontem,
> Pro bulla et gemmis crux mihi sancta datur.
> Iussit acu pictas etiam deponere vestes
> Inque usus versa est aurea palla sacros.

58 > Vos moneo Nymphae vanus quas torquet amaror
> Vos moneo cruciet Christus amoenus amor.
> Linquite serpentis sinuata volumina castae,
> Et labyrinthos linquite sponte sinus . . .

59 > Cautus erat, quem multa dabat lascivia nobis,
> Aut amor, aut fervens vita petulca mihi.

60 The injunction to conversion was internalised by a number of aristocratic women and ladies of the court, most famously by Caterina Vegri (canonised in 1713) who forsook the court for the lay community of Corpus Domini in Ferrara in 1426. Her autobiographical account of her gradual mastery over worldly temptations, including the pressure to resume her life at court, is analogous to that of Ariosto's heroine.

61 The appearance of astrological schemes in a Christian context is not in itself unusual or controversial. Planetary gods or signs of the zodiac stand for the cosmos in both the Collegiata of San Gemignano and the Baptistery in Padua. The potential for controversy in Tura's painting arises from the explicit linkage of some form of celestial action with an event in sacred history.

62 Apollo, in turn, the nude male figure with the torch, is explained away as Mercury with a 'caduceus'. Guidoni and Marino, 393, rationalise these identifications by reference to the order of the planets in the Ptolemaic cosmos: Moon, Mercury, Venus, Sun, Mars, Jupiter, Saturn and the Fixed Stars. For the various possible planetary orders in ancient cosmology and astrology see J. Tester, *A History of Western Astrology* (Woodbridge, Suffolk, 1987), 167–8.

63 The doctrine of conjunctions, which related patterns and great events of human history to the various meetings of Jupiter with Saturn, and the fortunes of the world's religions to Jupiter's interactions with other planets, had considerable diffusion and influence in the universities and courts of Europe, in both Latin and vernacular literature. See E. Garin, *Astrology in the Renaissance: The Zodiac of Life* (London, 1983), 21–4; J. North, 'Astrology and the Fortunes of Churches', *Centaurus*, XXIV, 1980, 181–211; K. Pomian, 'Astrology as a Naturalistic Theology of History', in P. Zambelli, ed., '*Astrologi Hallucinati*': *Stars and the End of the World in Luther's Time* (Berlin and New York), 1986, 34–43. P. Zambelli, *The 'Speculum astronomiae' and its Enigma* (Dordrecht, Boston and London, 1992), 22, lists the variety of authors and genres in which the doctrine of conjunctions makes an appearance: 'the *Roman de la Rose*, the last avatar of the *Roman du Renard*, the *De mundi universitate* by Bernardus Silvester, the *Anticlaudianus* by Alain de Lille and the pseudo-Ovidian *De vetula* . . . Herman of Carinthia, the *Liber Hermetis de sex principiis*, the astrologer Guillaume de Reims, the theologian Caesarius von Heisterbach, Robert Grosseteste, Richard Fishacre, Roger Bacon and (Albertus Magnus).'

64 North, 'Astrology', 192. On Oresme's

polemics against astrology see L. Thorndike, *A History of Magic and Experimental Science* (New York, 1934), vol. III, 398–424; G. W. Coopland, *Nicole Oresme and the Astrologers: A Study of his 'Livre de Divinacions'* (Cambridge, MA, 1952); S. Caroti, 'Nicole Oresme's Polemic Against Astrology in His *Quodlibeta*', in P. Curry, ed., *Astrology, Science and Society: Historical Essays* (Woodbridge, Suffolk, 1987), 75–93.

65 Thorndike, *History of Magic*, IV, 104; Garin, *Astrology in the Renaissance* 22, 120; North, ibid., 200–201; Pomian, 'Astrology', in Zambelli, ed., '*Astrologi Hallucinati*', 39–43.

66 On Henry of Langenstein (Henry of Hesse) see Thorndike, ibid., III, 472–511; North, ibid., 199. On Pico see Thorndike, ibid., IV, 529–44; Garin, *Astrology in the Renaissance*, 77–99; Tester, *History of Western Astrology*, 204f. and the edition of Pico's *Disputationes adversus astrologiam divinatricem* by Garin (Valecchi, 1946–52).

67 On Cecco d'Ascoli see Tester, ibid., 193–6.

68 Quoted in Thorndike, *History of Magic*, IV, 241.

69 For a discussion of the correspondence see E. Zinner, *Regiomontanus: His Life and Work*, trans. E. Brown (Amsterdam, 1990), 79–82.

70 Bianchini's tables, which were presented to the Emperor through the sponsorship of Borso d'Este in 1452 were becoming the standard means of computing the relative positions of the planets on particular days. According to Zinner, *Regiomontanus*, 47, 62–9, Regiomontanus found fault with their accuracy (but see the different conclusions of Armin Gerl in an appendix to the same volume, 325–7). Bianchini was one of the chief astrologers of Ferrara and may have provided specialist advice, if any were needed, for the astrological theme of the cathedral paintings. However, as an official of the civic treasury he had been involved in long dispute with the cathedral chapter regarding the taxation of the clergy, which may not have inclined them to ask for his advice. See Scalabrini, *Notizie istoriche*, fol. 130v. On the presence of Regiomontanus in Ferrara in the mid-1460s see C. Vasoli, 'L'astrologia a Ferrara tra la metà del quattrocento e la metà del cinquecento', in *Il rinascimento nelle corti padane* (Bari, 1977), 473–4.

71 Guidoni and Marino, 'Cosmus Pictor', 394, seem unaware of the widespread discussion of the horoscope of religions, and believe that the apparent reference to a conjunction in the painting reflects the unrecorded pronouncements of a single contemporary astrologer, Giacomo da Novara. Their evidence comes from F. Gabotto, *Nuove ricerche e documenti sull'astrologia alla corte degli estensi e degli Sforza* (Milan and Turin, 1889), 394, the unreliability of whom in the case of this very question of Giacomo da Novara was

pointed out by Thorndike, *History of Magic*, IV, 544.

72 On Pellegrino Prisciani see A. Warburg, 'Italienische Kunst und internationale Astrologie im Palazzo Schifanoia zu Ferrara', *Die Erneurung der Heidnischen Antike* (Leipzig and Berlin, 1932), vol. II, 445–82 and the study by A. Rotondò, 'Pellegrino Prisciani 1435–1518', *Rinascimento*, IX (1960), 69–110; on Pietro d'Avogaro see the entry in *Dizionario biografico degli italiani*, vol. 4 (Rome, 1962); on Bianchini see n. 70 above. For recent research on astrology in Ferrara see Vasoli, ed. 'L'astrologia a Ferrara'.

73 For an account of this poem, dedicated to Borso in Latin and *materna lingua* versions in 1465, see Mottola-Molfino and Natali, ed., *Le Muse e il Principe*, I, 179–82.

74 'Ancho un numer dispar nel cielo è facto
 dico triplicitate, in cui congionto
 ogni mano Pianeta fa novo acto.
 E da questi l'astrologo tien conto
 di fè nascer fra noi diverse secte,
 che fà miracol chi nasce in quel ponto.
 Lassemo star di dir cose sospecte:
 io credo pur che Christo Vero Iddio
 fosse, si come la Scriptura el mette,
 e se in carne fu ben come son io,
 non credo che le stelle el fesser tale,
 ma 'l padre suo . . .

As cited in Guidoni and Marino, 'Cosmus Pictor', 394.

75 In the debate of 1463 on the veneration of relics of the Holy Blood, Lorenzo's associates included Fra Giacomo della Marca, Francesco della Rovere (the future Sixtus IV) and a theologian from the University of Paris named Guillaume de Varouillon. Piccolomini, *Commentaries*, trans. F. A. Gragg, *Smith College Studies in History*, XLIII, 1957, 704.

76 For Aquinas on natural astrology, *Summa Theologicae*, Part 1 Q. 115 Art. 4. On Bernardino see Garin, *Astrology in the Renaissance*, 31–2.

77 The standard study of the conspiracy is now R. J. Palermino, 'The Roman Academy, the Catacombs and the Conspiracy of 1468'. *Archivum storiam pontificae*, 18, 1980, 117–55. See also Pastor, *History of the Popes*, IV, 36–65, and P. Medioli Masotti, 'Callimaco, L'Accademia Romana, e la Congiura del 1468', in G. C. Garfagnani, ed., *Callimaco Esperiente Poeta e Politico del'400* (Florence, 1987), 169–79.

78 'et qui comenzò S.Sta. ad damnare molto questi *studi de humanita* dicendo che se Dio gli prestava vita, voleva providere ad due cose: l'una che non fosse licito studiare in queste vane historie et poesie perche sono piene de heresie et maledictione; l'altra che non fosse licito imparare ne exercire astrologia perche da essa nascono molti errori . . .'; Pastor, ibid., 491.

79 'Fo etiamdio recordato che como è prohibito alli preti de seguire le lege civile per le conditione differente che sono dal temporale al

spirituale cosi se po prohibire el studio de le poesie et astrologie perche da esso se cava mille heresie, etc.'; Pastor, *History of the Popes*, IV, 491.

80 It should be mentioned that while Paul's reported condemnation refers to *astrologia*, it is likely that that the Pope had particular kinds of astrology in mind about which he had good reason to complain. For Paul had to contend with the pronouncements of a number of divinatory astrologers, who prophesied not only his death but also the triumph of Islam. Such prophesies were an open affirmation of the success of any would-be insurgents. These included the *zanzatori* of the Campo di Fiore, mentioned in Bianchi's letter, and his old teacher George of Trebizond, who was duly imprisoned. See J. Monfasani, *George of Trebizond: A Biography and a Study of his Rhetoric and Logic* (Leiden, 1976), 184. A comet appearing in 1468 was also taken as a sign of Paul's impending death by the author of an anonymous treatise (see Thorndike, *History of Magic*, IV, 418), while death or danger to the Pope was predicted by the astrologers Laurens Hutz and Pierre de Lorraine and by Martin Ilkusz; Zinner, *Regiomontanus*, 94; Thorndike, ibid., 421–2, 425.

81 For a useful account of the Virgin Mary and celestial imagery see M. Warner, *Alone of All Her Sex: The Myth and Cult of the Virgin Mary* (London and New York, 1983), 255–69.

82 For discussion of the attribution and for the text and translation see Zambelli, *Speculum astronomiae*, passim.

83 Translation from Zambelli, ibid., 255, 257, of the following passage: 'Et ascendit in prima facie illius (scilicet Virginis) puella quam vocat Celchius Darostal; et est virgo pulchra et honesta et munda prolixi capilli, et pulchra facie, habens in manu sua duas spicas, et ipsa sedet super sedem stratam, et nutrit puerum dans ei comedendum ius in loco qui vocatur Abrie. Et vocat ipsum puerum quaedam gens Iesum, cuius interpretatio est arabice Eice' (254).

84 'non quia subiaceret stellarum motui aut earum iudicio natorum desideratissimus, qui creaverat ipsas stellas, sed quia cum extenderet caelum sicut pellem, formans librum universitatis, et dedignaretur opus facere incompletum, noluit litteris eius deesse, ex eis quae secundum providentiam suam in libro aeternitatis sunt scripta, etiam illud elongatissimum a natura quod de Virgine nasceretur, ut profecto per hoc innueretur homo naturalis et verus, qui non naturaliter nasceretur, non quod caeli figura esset causa quare nasceretur, sed potius significatio, immo ad vero verius, ipse erat causa quare modus admirandae suae nativitatis significaretur per caelum' (254, 256).

85 Pseudo-Ovid, *De vetula*, ed. D. Robathan (Amsterdam, 1968), Book III, 611–20:

Una quidem talis felice tempore nuper
Cesaris Augusti fuit, anno bis duodeno
A regni novitate sui, que significavit
Post annum sextum nasci debere
   prophetam
Absque maris coitu de virgine, cuius
   habetur
Typus, ubi plus Mercuriis vis
   multiplicatur,
Cuius erit concors complexio primo
   future
Secte; nam nusquam de signis sic
   dominatur
Mercurius, sicut in signo virginis; illic
Est eius domus . . .

86 Ibid., 773–5.

87 'Nec quia talis constellatio, aut talis coniunc-
tio Christum praecessit, ideo Christus fuit de
virgo nasciturus, aut legem daturus, sed
potius est contra; haec enim non erant causa
istorum sed signum, nec ideo Dominus stellarum et temporum ipsis subjicitur, sed haec
sibi.' Bradwardine, *De causa dei* (London,
1618), Book I, cap. 1 coroll. pars 35.

88 'In libello quoque de morte Aristotelis 9
refertur secundum sententiam Melonis dis-
cipuli Aristotelis, quam et Magister plurimum
commendavit, quod usque ad adventam Noe
homines aestimantes Solem et Lunam alias
quoque stellas ex seipsis moveri, quare et
esse primos motores simpliciter atque Deos,
ipsis tanquam diis secundaum varia idola
servierunt . . . Noe autem fuit primus qui
cognovit creatorem sphaerarum, et quod ipse
est principium cuiuslibet motionis; et ipse
habebat scientiam, et gradum altissimum
harum rerum.' Ibid., 75.

89 'Interpretatur quoque Mercurius sermo, et
dicitur medius currens, quod quid est aptius
figura quam verbum Dei, media persona, Dei
et hominum Mediator?' Ibid., 73. See also,
Augustine, *De civitate dei*, VII.14.

90 On Venus and witchcraft see Thorndike,
History of Magic, II, 225–6 (on the 'Books of
Venus' cited by Albertus Magnus and William
of Auvergne); see also Burckhardt, *Civilization*,
500–501, citing a letter of Pius II on the
teaching of witchcraft at a Mountain of
Venus.

91 The poem is referred to briefly, and belit-
tlingly, by Burckhardt, *Civilization*, 262. The
present text is from *Fastorum libri duodecim*
(Strasbourg, 1518), Book III:

Cum Deus extremi vellet primordia secli
texere, progeniem divinae mentis
   alumnam
misit, et humanae vestivit imagine
   formae
Propterea missus summo legatus Olympo,
Coelica qui matri ferret mandata futurae
Haec foetura recens Coelo mirabilis,
   Orco
Terribilis, quia Dijs priscis fatale ferebat
Exilium, traxit Phoebo primordia ab isto.

Mercurius qui tunc casu veniebat ab
   Orco
vidit ut ex summo Carmeli vertice
   sanctum
Gabriel allabi versus florentia rura
Nazaret, insidias metuens post illius ivit
Virginis ad thalamos celeri vestigia gressu
liminesque in primo residens audivit
   eorum
coloquium, nec cuncta tamen verba
   auribus hausit,
sed quia versutus, quiddam deprehendit
   in illis
arcani, quod se, divos quot tangeret
   omnes.
Tum se proripiens Romam prope
   Leuctra deorum
repperit ingentem cunctum, quibus
   omnina fatus.
Illi autem magno inter se trepidare
   tumultu
Incepere, Venus flevit, Saturnia Juno
flevit, et abiecta Pallas contabuit hasta.
Moxque ait, O comites quodcumque
   evenerit aequo
ferte animo, regno quod tempestate
   tenemus
iam longa (fari inter nos licet omnia)
   furtum est.
Nos quoad ille sinet cuius sunt regna
   fruamur
imperijs, cum nos regno spoliabimur isto
ad fraudes alias, alias vertemur ad artes,
Nec sine lucro erimus, per vaframenta
   dolosque
dedecore, et damno Christi afficiemus
   alumnos:
Tunc princeps signorum Aries tria sydera
   portans
Vertice, Delta vocant, prima surgebat ab
   ortu
Cum Titane, suos cum iam Philomela
   pararet
Aedere per villas, et per viridaria cantus,
Exonerata gelu tellus gaudebat, et omnes
Floribus, et tenero vernabant gramine
   campi.
Haec igitur praeclara dies vigesima
   quinta
mensis apud veteres primi damnata
   fugavit
secula, et aetati fecit primordia sanctae.
Propterea non immerito sibi vendicat
   anni
Principium penes Etruscos, et digna
   videtur
his titulis, viditque Deum descendere ab
   astris
ante alias, et prima fores aperire saluti
digna fuit, commune bonum prior ipsa
   recepit
et commune decus longis sperata diebus
dona Dei lux ista dedit, laudabilis ergo
gloria, quam misit lucem Tyrrhenia in
   istam.

Tunc Deus aeternis coepit mortalia
   vinculo
iungere perpetuo faciens hominemque
   Deumque
personam coitu miro concurrere in
   unam.
Tum superi coepere homines reverentes
   habere
Maioremque operam nostris impendere
   rebus,
tum foetura recens timidas ingressu per
   aures
crevit in ignara coitus, et feminis alvo.
Nazaret exulta Libano contermina tellus
carmelo vicina iugo, Phoenica versus
littora qua Tyrus, et Sidon florere
   solebant
haec arcana tui quondam videre penates.
Iubila, et exulta fortunatissima tanti
Fama operis tellus, regio to praedicat
   omnis
Nulla aetas sine laude tua descendit as
   astris.
Ipse tibi decus hoc tantum coelestis
   Olympus
invidet, et sibi deberi hunc testatur
   honorem.
O rerum seriem aeternam quae pendet
   ab alto,
O magnas, mirasque vices, quas sydera
   voluunt
quas Deus importat, seclorum immobilis
   ordo est,
Ponite mortales curas, facit omnia
   Coelum,
Coelo agimur, sicut naves spirantibus
   euris.
Sancta parens cui luce Deus communicat
   ista
splendorem, regnumque suum, cui
   subijcit orbem
terrarum, mundique polos, dignare
   tuorum
exaudire preces, et nostra piacula solve,
nec sine nos Stygiis ludibria manibus
   esse,
Quae nostrum interitum sicut Tritonia
   dixit
Qui tua, quique tui quaerunt opprobria
   nati.

92 Voragine, *Legenda aurea*, VI, 43. See George of
Trebizond, 'On the Eternal Glory of the
Autocrat and his World Dominion', in J.
Monfasani, ed., *Collectanea Trapezuntiana*
(Binghamton, NY, 1984), 516, 521.

93 M. Camille, *The Gothic Idol: Ideology and Image
Making in Medieval Art* (Cambridge, 1989),
219.

94 Camille, ibid., 345.

95 Pius II's famous attack on the Tempio Malatestiano is in [Piccolomini], *Commentaries*,
trans. F. A. Gragg, *Smith College Studies in
History*, XXV, 1939–40, 167. George of Trebizond attributed Sigismondo's final illness to
the interment in the Tempio of the bones of

Gemisthos Pletho; See Monfasani, *George of Trebizond*, 214.

96 Johannes Ferrariensis, 'Excerpta ex Annalium Libris illustris Familiae Marchionum Estensium, 1409–1454', in *Rerum italicarum scriptores*, 20, vol. 2 (Bologna, 1936), 44.

97 Guarino, according to Lodovico Carbone's funeral panegyric, would frequently interrupt a lecture 'to refute the foolish ideas of the ancients about the immortal gods'. See I. Thomson, *Humanist Pietas: The Panegyric of Ianus Pannonius on Guarinus Veronensis* (Bloomington, IN, 1988), 82, n. 65. A modern scholar of Guarino has noted an annotation by him on a Strabo codex formerly belonging to Ciriaco of Ancona. Where Ciriaco had written 'thauma theou Pythiou' ('wonder of the Pythian god') Guarino added 'mallon de ton daimonon' ('but rather of the demons'). Thomson, ibid., 84, n. 71.

98 Dacos, *La découverte de la Domus Aurea*, 69–72.

99 'Res omnis quae loco movetur, septem habet movendi itinera, nam aut sursum versus aut deorsum aut in dexteram aut in sinistram aut illuc longe recedendo aut contra nos redeundo. Septinus vero movendi modus est is qui in Girum ambiendo vehitur. Hos igitur omnes motus cupio esse in pictura. Adsint corpora nonnulla quae sese ad nos porrigant, alia abeant horsum, dextrorsum et sinistrorsum. Tum ex ipsis corporibus nonnullae partes adversus conspectantes ostententur, aliquae retrocedant, aliae sursum tollantur, aliquae in infimum tendantur.' Alberti, *On Painting and On Sculpture*, trans. C. Grayson (London 1972), 82–3.

100 'Capitis vero motus animadverti vix unquam ullam in partem esse tales, ut non semper aliquas reliqui corporis partes sub se positas habeat, quo immane pondus regatur, aut certe in adversam partem tamquam alteram lancem aliquod membrum protendit quod ponderi correspondeat.' Alberti, ibid., 82, 84.

101 'Tum spectavi, si quam in altum protendamus manum, eum motum caeteras omnes eius lateris partes ad pedem usque subsequi, ut etiam ipsius pedis calcaneus eiusdem bracchii motu a pavimento levetur.' Alberti, ibid., 84.

102 'Sed hi, quo audiunt eas imagines maxime vivas videri, quae plurimum membra agitent, eo histrionum motus, spreta omni picturae dignitate, imitantur. Ex quo non modo gratia et lepore eorum opera nuda sunt, sed etiam artificis nimis fervens ingenium exprimunt. Suaves enim et gratos atque ad rem de qua agitur condecentes habere pictura motus debet.' Alberti, ibid., 84.

103 For a discussion of Alberti's distinction in *De pictura* between the orator and the actor and its social implications, see S. Fermor, *Studies in the Depiction of the Moving Figure in Italian Renaissance Art, Art Criticism and Dance Theory* (Ph.D. dissertation, University of London, 1990), 79–82. For a survey of Alberti's references to masks and actors throughout his

moral and aesthetic writings see L. Cesarini Martinelli, 'Metafori teatrali in Leon Battista Alberti', *Rinascimento*, 29, 1989, 3–53. In *De Iciarchia* the same oratorical norms derived from Cicero and Quintilian are used to criticise those who comport themselves extravagantly in public: 'ogni lor moto par fatto con arte di schermidore o di danzare a molto ostentazione.'

104 Augustine, *De civitate dei*, II.13. The passage and its impact on the theme of idolatry in art is discussed by Camille, *The Gothic Idol*, 268.

105 On the astrological doctrine of the *imagines* and *simulacra* see Garin, *Astrology in the Renaissance*, 40, 46, 75.

106 Alberti, *On the Art of Building in Ten Books*, trans. J. Rykwert, N. Leach and R. Tavernor (Cambridge, MA, 1988). 'Horum quisque deorum heroum habitu et gestu suam, quoad per artificem id possis, vitam et mores exprimat exposco. Nolo, quoad pulchrum illi ducunt, *pugilem aut ludionem scaenicum gestiat*; sed ex vultu totaque corporis facie gratiam et maiestatem deo dignam praebere de se velim adventibus, ut quasi nutu et manu benignissime excipere atque supplicantibus gratificari ultor velle videatur.' Alberti, *De re aedificatoria*, ed. G. Orlandi (Milan, 1966), vol. II, 663.

107 Alberti, *On the Art of Building*, 243: 'Et fortassis barba et supercilio severiores maximorum deorum facies cum molliori virginam effigie non belle condicunt.' *De re aedificatoria*, 663.

108 Both Petrarch and Coluccio Salutati draw upon the Hermetic passages on idols in *De civitate dei* and in a vein consistent with Augustine's interpretation of them. On Petrarch, see C. Trinkaus, *In Our Image and Likeness* (London, 1970), 33–4; for Salutati, see his *De laboribus Herculis*, ed. B. Ullman (Zurich, 1951), II.vi, 78.

109 On Hermes and magic and astrology see Thorndike, *History of Magic*, II, 214–28. On the tradition of the Hermetic *corpus* and other texts ascribed to Hermes see F. Yates, *Giordano Bruno and the Hermetic Tradition* (Chicago, 1964), esp. 1–61; D. P. Walker, *Spiritual and Demonic Magic from Ficino to Campanella* (London, 1958); A. J. Festugière, *La revelation d'Hermès Trismegiste* (Paris, 1950–54); G. Fowden, *The Egyptian Hermes: A Historical Approach to the Late Pagan Mind* (Cambridge, 1986); B. P. Copenhaver, *Hermetica* (translation of the Greek *Corpus Hermeticum* and the Latin *Asclepius*) (Cambridge, 1992); P. Dronke, *Hermes and the Sibyls: Continuity and Creation* (Cambridge, 1990).

110 For such a repudiation of Hermetic magic see Albertus Magnus in Zambelli, *Speculum Astronomiae*, 240–47.

111 Lactantius, *The Divine Institutes*, VI.25, trans. Mary Francis McDonald (Washington, DC, 1964), 468.

112 Lactantius, ibid., VII.18, trans., 520.

113 Ibid, VII.4, trans., 481.

114 Lactantius, ibid., trans., 255–6.

115 Trinkaus, *In Our Image and Likeness*, II, 184. For further discussion on Lactantius in the fifteenth century see B. Vickers, 'Valla's Ambivalent Praise of Pleasure: Rhetoric in the Service of Christianity', *Viator*, 17, 1986, 271–321.

116 Both now in Ferrara, Biblioteca Comunale Ariostaea, MS Cl. 2 167 (Augustine) and S.11.5.8 (Lactantius).

117 *De civitate dei*, VIII.23; trans. Marcus Dods (New York, 1950), 270.

118 The image has never been satisfactorily explained. As I understand it, the youthful Herculean nudity of Hermes' disciple designates him as a model for the idol and evokes the celebration of the human body in *Asclepius*, 23; for humanity, according to Hermes, is superior to the gods in possessing a body, and thus men make gods patterned after the human body.

119 Ibid., VIII.23, trans., 272.

120 St Paul, I Corinthians 10: 19–20.

121 Images, according to Fulgentius, were first created to commemorate the dead, but since 'forgetting is the true healer of distress', they only added to the sorrow of the living, and hence are called *idos dolu*, 'appearance of grief'. See L. G. Whitbread, *Fulgentius the Mythographer* (Columbus, OH, 1971), 48. For agitated and mourning idols see Camille, ibid., 120–22. Such images occur characteristically in illustrations of the *Legenda aurea* and the lives of saints.

122 'Nor are there now any more idols to be overturned, but everywhere they have been overturned and broken, and as though dead souls depart from bodies, so through faith the impious and evil-doing spirits have departed from the idols.' Cited in Trinkaus, *In Our Image and Likeness*, 33–4.

123 *De civitate dei*, VIII.26, trans., 278.

124 *Legenda aurea*, LVIII, 262.

125 Pliny the Elder, *Natural History*, XXXVI.17.

126 Quoted from the translation of *Asclepius* in Copenhaver, *Hermetica*, 81.

127 Bradwardine, *De causa dei*, I.i, 75. On the origins of the triple Hermes in the twelfth century *Liber Hermetis Mercurii Triplicis de Vi rerum principiis* see Yates, *Giordano Bruno and the Hermetic Tradition*, 48–9.

128 'Hic enim post diluvium cum summa aequitate regnum Aegypti tenuit, & in liberalibus & in mechanicis artibus praevaluit, & Astronomiam prius elucidavit, virgam auream, librum latitudinis, & longitudinis, librum electionis & Erich. super aequationem planetarum, & super Astrolabium, & alia multa opere luculento complevit.' On the legend of the three Hermes and its origins with Abumasar see also C. S. F. Burnett, 'The Legend of the Three Hermes and Abu Ma'shar's *Kitab al-Uluf* in the Latin Middle

Ages,' *Journal of the Warburg and Courtauld Institutes*, 39, 1976, 231–4.–

129 Zinner, *Regiomontanus*, 70.

130 Polydore Vergil, writing at the end of the fifteenth century, made Hermes the inventor of the calendar; see J. Seznec, *The Survival of the Pagan Gods* (Princeton and New York, 1953, 1972), 22.

131 Lactantius, *Divine Institutes*, I.vi.

132 In *The Divine Institutes*, I, 6, he cites Cicero, *De natura deorum*, III.22, to the effect that the fifth Mercury was the slayer of Argus who took refuge in Egypt and dispensed 'laws and letters' to the Egyptians. Later, in Book VII.13, he raises the question of the kind of authority represented by Hermes Trismegistus: 'But perhaps someone may reckon this one [i.e. Hermes] in the number of philosophers (although carried back among the gods he is honored by the Egyptians with the name of Mercury) and not attribute any more honor to him than to Plato or Pythagoras.' Lactantius, trans. McDonald, 507.

133 *Asclepius*, 35, in Copenhaver, *Hermetica*, 89.

134 'Censet Trismegistus vetustissimus scriptor una cum religione sculpturam et picturam exortam. sic enim inquit ad Asclepium: humanitas memor naturae et originis suae deos ex sui vultus similitudine figuravit.' Alberti, *On Painting*, 64.

135 English citations from Copenhaver, *Hermetica*, 69, 81.

136 M. J. Powers, 'Discourses of Representation in Tenth- and Eleventh-Century China', in S. C. Scott, ed., *The Art of Interpreting: Papers in Art History from the Pennsylvania State University*, vol. IX, 1996, 107. For other considerations of irony in Chinese painting see A. Plaks, 'The Aesthetics of irony in Late Ming Literature and Painting', in A. Murck and W. C. Fong, ed., *Words and Images: Chinese Poetry, Calligraphy and Painting* (New York, 1991), 487–500.

137 From the *Life of Alberti*, trans. in J. B. Ross and M. M. McLaughlin, *The Portable Renaissance Reader* (New York 1953, 1981), 484.

138 For J. L. Koerner, it is Albrecht Dürer around 1500 who confidently claims to have closed the gap between the divinely authorised

image and human artifice. See Koerner, *Albrecht Dürer: The Moment of Self-Portraiture in German Renaissance Art* (New York, 1992).

139 Francesco Ariosto Peregrino, *De novi intra Ducalem Regiam Ferrariensem delubri in gloriossime Virginis honorem et reverentiam dicati origine, situ ac veneratione, et admirabilis simulacri translatione*. Modena, Biblioteca Estense, cod. lat. 309, Alpha W4, 4. For a brief account see G. Zarri, 'Pietà e profezia alle corti padane,' 219–20, and Brown, *Politics of Magnificence*, 389–92.

140 See the 'Presentazione' by Nanni Balestrini in Leon Battista Alberti, *Momo o del principe*, ed. and trans. Rino Consolo (Genoa, 1986), v.

141 Leon Battista Alberti, *Dinner Pieces: A Translation of the Intercenales*, trans. D. Marsh (Binghamton, NY, 1987), 54–7, 175–6.

142 Lucian represents dance as a mimetic art, like that of the rhetorician, and asserts that the dancer should have knowledge of poetry. He attacks inappropriate extremes of music, superfluous gestures, exaggeration and 'performing for the rabble'.

BIBLIOGRAPHY

MANUSCRIPT SOURCES

Ferrara, Archivio di Stato: Archivio Notarile di Ferrara.

Ferrara, Archivio Diocesano.

Modena, Archivio di Stato: Camera Ducale.

Vatican, Archivio Segreto Vaticano.

Caleffini, Ugo. *Croniche facte et scripte per me Ugo Caleffini notaio Ferrarese.* Biblioteca Apostolica Vaticana, MS Vat. Chig. I, I, 4 and transcription by Giulio Mosti, 1581. British Museum, Add. MS 22, 324.

Pius II. *Epistolae Pontificales.* Biblioteca Apostolica Vaticana, Cod. Urb. Lat. 404.

Scalabrini, Giuseppe Antenore. *Notizie istoriche del nobilissimo capitolo della s. chiesa di Ferrara.* Ferrara, Biblioteca Comunale Ariostaea, MS Cl. I, 125.

Zambotti, Bernardino. *Silva chronicarum.* Ferrara, Biblioteca Comunale Ariostaea, MS Cl. I, 16.

PUBLISHED WORKS

Note: Exhibition catalogues are entered in this bibliography under the name of their editor(s) if cited on the title-page; otherwise under the name of the city in which the exhibition was held. Individual essays within exhibition catalogues are entered under the name of the author. Similarly, conference proceedings are designated by location and individual papers by author.

Agnelli, G. 'I monumenti di Niccolò III e Borso d'Este in Ferrara', *Atti e memorie della deputazione ferrarese di storia patria,* 23, 1919, 1–32.

Alberti, Leon Battista. *On the Art of Building in Ten Books.* Translation of *De re aedificatoria* by Joseph Rykwert, Neil Leach and Robert Tavernor. Cambridge, MA: 1988.

Alberti, Leon Battista. *Dinner Pieces: A Translation of the Intercenales.* Translated by David Marsh. Binghamton, NY: 1987.

Alberti, Leon Battista. *Momus/Momo o del principe.* Latin edition and translation by Rino Consolo. Genoa: 1986.

Alberti, Leon Battista. *On Painting and On Sculpture; The Latin Texts of De Pictura and De Statua.* Edited and translated by Cecil Grayson. London: 1972.

Alberti, Leon Battista. *De re aedificatoria.* Edited by Giovanni Orlandi. 2 vols. Milan: 1966.

Alberti, Leon Battista. *Opera inedita.* Edited by G. Mancini. Florence: 1890.

Anderson, Jaynie. 'The Rediscovery of Ferrarese Renaissance Painting in the Risorgimento', *Burlington Magazine,* CXXXV, 1993, 539–51.

Apfelstadt, Eric. *The Later Sculpture of Antonio Rossellino.* Ph.D dissertation, Princeton University: 1987.

Ascari, Tiziano. 'Francesco Ariosto Peregrino', *Atti e memorie della Accademia di scienze, lettere ed arti di Modena,* ser. 5, XI, 1953, 94–116.

Augustine. *De civitate dei. Corpus Christianorum. Series latina.* Turnholt: 1955.

Augustine. *City of God.* Translated by Marcus Dods. New York: 1950.

Augustine. *Expositions on the Book of Psalms* ('Ennarationes in Psalmos'). Translated by A. Cleveland Coxe. Edinburgh: 1888; Grand Rapids, MI: 1989.

Bacchi, Andrea. *Dipinti ferraresi dalla collezione Vittorio Cini.* Vicenza: 1990.

Balboni, Dante. 'I sinodi diocesani di Ferrara', *Analecta Ferrariensia,* I, 1958, 113–26.

Balletti, Adamo. *Gli ebrei e gli Estensi.* Reggio Emilia: 1930.

Barasch, Moshe. 'Some Oriental Pseudo-Inscriptions in Renaissance Art', *Visible Language,* 23, 1989, 171–87.

Barbaro, Ermolao the Elder. *Orationes contra poetas.* Edited by Giorgio Ronconi. Florence: 1972.

Bargellesi, G. 'Tura o Aleotti ad Argenta?', *Atti e memorie della deputazione provinciale Ferrarese di storia patria,* ser. III, II, 1972.

Barkan, Leonard. *Transuming Passion: Ganymede and the Erotics of Humanism.* Stanford, CA: 1991.

Baron, Hans. *The Crisis of the Early Italian Renaissance.* Princeton: 1955.

Barotti, C. *Pitture e scolture che si trovano nelle chiese, luoghi pubblici, e sobborghi della città di Ferrara.* Ferrara: 1770.

Barotti, Luciano. *Serie di vescovi ed arcivescovi di Ferrara.* Ferrara: 1781.

Baruffaldi, Girolamo. *Vite de' pittori e scultori ferraresi.* 2 vols. Ferrara: 1844–6 [written after 1722].

Baruffaldi, Girolamo. *Vita di Cosimo Tura.* Bologna: 1836 [1706].

Baruffaldi, Girolamo. *Rime scelti de poeti ferraresi, antichi e moderni.* Ferrara: 1713.

Baruffaldi, Girolamo. *Vita della Beata Caterina da Bologna.* Ferrara: 1708.

Basil, Saint. *The Letters.* Translated by R. J. Deferrari and M. R. P. Maguire. Cambridge, MA: 1934.

Battisti, Eugenio. *L'Antirinascimento.* Milan: 1962, 1989.

Baxandall, Michael. *Painting and Experience in Fifteenth-Century Italy.* 2nd edition. Oxford: 1988.

Baxandall, Michael. *The Limewood Sculptors of Renaissance Germany.* New Haven and

London: 1980.

Baxandall, Michael. *Giotto and the Orators.* Oxford: 1971.

Baxandall, Michael. 'Guarino, Pisanello and Manuel Chrysoloras', *Journal of the Warburg and Courtauld Institutes*, 28, 1965, 183–205.

Baxandall, Michael. 'A Dialogue on Art from the Court of Leonello d'Este: Angelo Decembrio's *De politia litteraria* Pars LXVII', *Journal of the Warburg and Courtauld Institutes*, 26, 1963, 304–26.

Beccadelli, Antonio, 'Panormita', *Antonii Panormitae Hermaphroditus*. Edited by C. F. Forberg. Leipzig: 1908.

Beck, James. *Jacopo della Quercia.* 2 vols. New York: 1992.

Belting, Hans. *Likeness and Presence: A History of the Image before the Era of Art.* Translated by E. Jephcott. Chicago: 1994.

Bensi, Paolo, and Maria Rosa Montiani. 'L'iconografia della *croce vivente* in ambito emiliano e ferrarese', *Musei Ferraresi*, 13/14, 1983–4, 161–83.

Bentini, Jadranka, ed. *San Giorgio e la principessa di Cosmè Tura: Dipinti restaurati per l'officina ferrarese.* Bologna: 1985.

Berenson, Bernard. *The North Italian Painters of the Renaissance.* New York: 1952.

Berenson, Bernard. *Italian Pictures of the Renaissance.* Oxford: 1932.

Berger, David. 'Mission to the Jews and Jewish-Christian Contacts in the Polemical Literature of the High Middle Ages', *American Historical Review*, 91, 1986, 576–92.

Bertoni, Giulio. *Guarino da Verona fra letterati e cortigiani a Ferrara.* Geneva: 1921.

Bertoni, Giulio. 'Notizie sugli amanuensi degli Estensi nel quattrocento', *Archivium Romanicum*, II, 1918, 29–57.

Bertoni, Giulio. *La Biblioteca Estense e la cultura ferrarese ai tempi del duca Ercole I (1471–1505).* Turin: 1903.

Bigo Pittorio, Lodovico. *I Salmi di David per Lodovico Pittorio da Ferrara moralmente in forma di Omelario col latino all'incontro dechiarati, e di sententia in sentitia volgarizzati.* Venice: n.p. 1547.

Bigo Pittorio, Lodovico. *Tumultuaria Carmina.* Modena: Domenicus Rocociolus, 1492 [unpaginated].

Blumenkranz, Bernard. *Le juif médieval au miroir de l'art chrétien.* Paris: 1966.

Boccaccio, Giovanni. *De genealogia deorum.* Venice: Octavius Scotus, 1494; New York: 1976.

Bolognesi, Dante, ed. *Ravenna in età Veneziana.* Ravenna: 1983.

Boskovits, Miklos. 'Ferrarese Painting around 1450: Some Recent Arguments', *Burlington Magazine*, 120, 1978, 370–85.

Bradwardine, Thomas. *De causa dei.* London: Ioannes Billius, 1618.

Bridgeman, Jane. '*Belle considerazioni.* Dress in the Works of Piero della Francesca', *Apollo*, 136, October 1992, 218–25.

Brisighella, Carlo. *Descrizione delle pitture e sculture della cità di Ferrara.* Edited by M. A. Novelli. Ferrara: 1991

Brown, A. M., and A. C. de la Mare. 'Bartolomeo Scala's Dealings with Booksellers, Scribes and Illuminators, 1459–63', *Journal of the Warburg and Courtauld Institutes*, 39, 1976, 237–46.

Brown, Peter. *The Body and Society: Men, Women and Sexual Renunciation in Early Christianity.* New York: 1988.

Brown, Richard Gordon. *The Politics of Magnificence in Ferrara, 1450–1505: A Study in the Socio-Political Implications of Renaissance Spectacle.* D.Phil. University of Edinburgh: 1982.

Bucelino, Gabriele. *Rutiliae longe vetustissimae et illustrissimae inter Romanae urbis principis familiae.* Veldkirch, n.p.: 1677.

Bühler, Carl. *The Fifteenth Century Book.* Philadephia: 1960.

Burckhardt, Jacob. *The Civilization of the Renaissance in Italy.* Translated by S. G. C. Middlemore. 2 vols. New York: 1958.

Burnett, Charles S. F. 'The Legend of the Three Hermes and Abu Ma'shar's *Kitab al-Uluf* in the Latin Middle Ages', *Journal of the Warburg and Courtauld Institutes*, 39, 1976, 231–4.

Busi, G. 'Officina ebraica ferrarese', *Vita e cultura ebraica nello Stato Estense. Archivio storico nonantolano*, 2, 1993, 188–211.

Bynum, Caroline Walker. *The Resurrection of the Body in Western Christianity, 200–1336.* New York: 1995.

Bynum, Caroline Walker. *Fragmentation and Redemption: Essays on Gender and the Human Body in Medieval Religion.* New York: 1991.

Bynum, Caroline Walker. *Holy Feast and Holy Fast.* Berkeley: 1987.

Caleffini, Ugo. *Diario di Ugo Caleffini.* Edited by Giuseppe Pardi. Deputazione di Storia patria per l'Emilia e la Romagna; Sezione di Ferrara. Serie: Monumenti, I/I, 1938.

Camille, Michael. *Image on the Edge.* London: 1992.

Camille, Michael. *The Gothic Idol: Ideology and Image Making in Medieval Art.* Cambridge: 1989.

Campbell, Stephen J. Review of Tuohy, *Her-*

culean Ferrara, *Journal of the Society of Architectural Historians*, LVI/3, 1997, 354–6.

Campbell, Stephen J. '*Pictura and Scriptura*: Cosmè Tura and Style as Courtly Performance', *Art History*, 19, 1996, 267–95.

Campbell, Stephen J. '*Sic in amore furens*: Painting as Poetic Theory in the Early Renaissance', *I Tatti Studies*, 6, 1995, 145–69.

Campbell, Stephen J. 'The Traffic in Muses: Painting and Poetry in Ferrara around 1450', J. Hairston, S. Ross and L. Benedetti, ed. *Gendered Contexts: New Dimensions in Italian Cultural Studies.* New York: 1995, 49–68.

Campbell, Stephen J. Review of Manca, *The Art of Ercole de' Roberti, Burlington Magazine*, CXXXV, 1993, 766–7.

Campenhausen, Hans van. The *Virgin Birth in the Theology of the Ancient Church.* Naperville, IL: 1964.

Camporesi, Piero. *The Incorruptible Flesh: Bodily Mutation in Religion and Folklore.* Translated by T. Croft-Murray. Cambridge: 1988.

Campori, Giuseppe. 'I pittori Estensi del sec. XV', *Atti della deputazione di storia patria modenese*, ser. III, iii.2, 1886, 525–604.

Campori, Giuseppe. *Artisti degli Estensi: I pittori.* Modena: 1875.

Campori, Giuseppe. *Raccolta dei cataloghi ed inventarii inediti.* Modena: 1870.

Canova, Giordana Mariani. *Ferrara 1474: Miniatura, tipografia, committenza. Il 'Decretum Gratiani' Roverella.* Florence: 1988.

Cappelli, Antonio. 'La congiura contro il Duca Borso d'Este scritta da Carlo da San Giorgio', *Atti e memorie delle RR. deputazioni di storia patria per le provincie Modenesi e Parmensi*, II, 1864, 367–416.

Capra, Luciano. 'Gli epitafi per Nicolò III d'Este', *Italia medioevale e umanistica*, 16, 1973, 197–226.

Capra, Luciano, and Camillo Colombo. 'Giunte all'epistolario di Guarino Veronese', *Italia medioevale e umanistica*, 10, 1967, 165–259.

Capra, Luciano. 'Tura inventato', *Biblioteca Communale Ariostea: Recenti ingressi*, 5, 1961, 13–16.

Carruthers, Mary. *The Book of Memory: A Study of Memory in Medieval Culture.* Cambridge: 1990.

Castelli, Patrizia, ed. *Il Rinascimento del sapere: Libri e maestri dello studio ferrarese.* Venice: 1991.

Castelli, Patrizia, ed. *Mesura et arte del danzare: Guglielmo Ebreo da Pesaro e la danza nelle corti italiane del XV secolo.* Pesaro: 1987.

Castelnuovo, Enrico and Carlo Ginzburg, 'Centre and Periphery', *History of Italian Art*. Translated by E. Bianchini and C. Dorey. Cambridge: 1994, vol. I, 29–113.

Célier, Léonce. *Les dataires du XVe siècle et les origines de la Daterie Apostolique*. Paris: 1910.

Cennini, Cennino. *Il libro dell'arte*. Edited by Franco Brunello. Vicenza: 1971.

Chodorow, Stanley, and James Ross Sweeney, eds. *Popes, Teachers and Canon Law in the Middle Ages*. Ithaca, NY: 1989.

Christiansen, K., L. Kanter and C. Strehlke. *Painting in Renaissance Siena, 1420–1500*. New York: The Metropolitan Museum, 1988.

Christiansen, Keith. 'Lorenzo Lotto and the Tradition of Epithalamic Paintings', *Apollo*, September 1986, 166–73.

Cipolla, C. M. *Studi di storia della moneta, i movimenti dei cambii in Italia dal secolo XIII al XV*. Pavia: 1948.

Cittadella, Cesare. *Catalogo istorico de'pittori e scultori ferraresi*, 4 vols. Ferrara: 1782–3 [vol. I for Tura].

Cittadella, Luigi Napoleone. *Ricordi e documenti intorno alla vita di Cosimo Tura, detto Cosmè*. Ferrara: 1866.

Cittadella, Luigi Napoleone. *Notizie amministrative, storiche ed artistiche relative a Ferrara*. Ferrara: 1864.

Cohen, Jeremy. 'Scholarship and Intolerance in the Medieval Academy: The Study and Evaluation of Judaism in European Christendom', *American Historical Review*, 91, 1986, 592–615.

Cohen, Jeremy. *The Friars and the Jews*. Ithaca, NY: 1982.

Colantuono, Anthony. '*Dies Alcyoniae*: The Invention of Bellini's *Feast of the Gods*', *Art Bulletin*, LXXIII/2, 1991, 237–56.

Cole, Alison. *Art of the Italian Renaissance Courts: Virtue and Magnificence*. London, 1995.

Colvin, Sidney. *A Florentine Picture Chronicle*. London: 1898.

Coopland, G. W. *Nicole Oresme and the Astrologers: A Study of his 'Livre de Divinacions'*. Cambridge, MA: 1952.

Copenhaver, Brian P. *Hermetica* (translation of the Greek *Corpus Hermeticum* and the Latin *Asclepius*). Cambridge: 1992.

Cossart, Michael de. *Antonio Beccadelli and the Hermaphrodite*. Liverpool: 1984.

Craven, W. G. 'Coluccio Salutati's Defence of Poetry', *Renaissance Studies*, X/1, 1996, 1–30.

Cropper, Elizabeth. 'The Place of Beauty in the High Renaissance and its Displacement in the History of Art', A. Vos, ed., *Place and Displacement in the Renaissance*. Binghamton, NY: 1994, 159–205.

Cropper, Elizabeth. 'The Beauty of Women: Problems in the Rhetoric of Renaissance Portraiture', in M. Ferguson, M. Quilligan and N. Vickers, ed. *Rewriting the Renaissance: The Discourses of Sexual Differences in Early Modern Europe*. Chicago: 1986, 175–90.

Curry, Patrick, ed. *Astrology, Science and Society: Historical Essays*. Woodbridge, Suffolk: 1987.

Curtius, Ernst Robert. *European Literature in the Latin Middle Ages*. Princeton and New York: 1953, 1990.

Curtze, Maximilian. 'Der Briefwechsel Regiomontans mit Giovanni Bianchini, Jacob von Speier und Christian Roder', *Abhandlungen zur Geschicte der mathematischen Wissenschaften*, XII, 1902, 292–323.

Dacos, Nicole. *La découverte de la Domus Aurea e la formation des grotesques à la Renaissance*. London and Leiden: 1969.

Davies, Martin. *National Gallery Catalogues: The Earlier Italian Schools*. London: The National Gallery, 1951.

Davis, Natalie Zemon. 'Boundaries and the Sense of Self in Sixteenth Century France', in Thomas Heller *et al.* ed. *Reconstructing Individualism: Autonomy, Individuality and the Self in Western Thought*. Stanford, CA: 1986, 53–63.

Dean, Trevor. 'The Courts', *The Origin of the State in Italy, 1300–1600*. Supplement to *Journal of Modern History*, 67, 1995, 136–52.

Dean, Trevor. 'Commune and Despot: The Commune of Ferrara under Este Rule, 1300–1450', in *City and Countryside in Late Medieval and Renaissance Italy. Essays Presented to Philip Jones*. Edited by T. Dean. London, 1990, 183–97.

Dean, Trevor. 'Notes on the Ferrarese Court in the Later Middle Ages', *Renaissance Studies*, III/4, 1989, 357–69.

Dean, Trevor. *Land and Power in Late Medieval Ferrara*. Cambridge: 1988.

Decembrio, Angelo. *De politia litteraria*. Augusta: Heinrich Steiner, 1540.

De Certeau, Michel. *The Mystic Fable*. Translated by M. B. Smith. Chicago: 1992.

Della Guardia, Anita. *Tito Vespasiano Strozzi: Poesie latine tratte dall'Aldina e confrontate coi Codici*. Modena: 1916.

Della Guardia, Anita. *La 'Politia Litteraria' di Angelo e l'umanesimo a Ferrara nella prima metà del secolo XV*. Modena: 1910.

Dempsey, Charles. *The Portrayal of Love: Botticelli's 'Primavera' and Humanist Culture at the Time of Lorenzo the Magnificent*. Princeton: 1992.

Denieul-Cormier, A. 'La très ancienne physiognomonie et Michel Savonarole', *Biologie médicale*, 55, 1956, i–cvii.

Derrida, Jacques. *The Truth in Painting*. Translated by Geoff Bennington and Ian McLeod. Chicago: 1987.

Diario Ferrarese dall'anno 1409 sino al 1502 di autori incerti. Edited by Giuseppe Pardi in *Rerum italicarum scriptores*, 24, Part 7, no. 1. Bologna: 1928.

Didi-Hubermann, Georges. *Fra Angelico: Dissemblance and Figuration*. Chicago: 1995.

Dominici, Giovanni. *Lucula Noctis*. Edited by Edmund Hunt. South Bend, IN: 1940.

Donati, Claudio. *L'idea di nobiltà in Italia, secoli XIV–XVIII*. Bari: 1988.

Dorigato, A., ed. *Carpaccio, Bellini, Tura, Antonello e altri restauri quattrocenteschi della Pinacoteca del Museo Correr*. Milan: 1993.

Dronke, Peter. *Hermes and the Sibyls: Continuity and Creation*. Cambridge: 1990.

Drysdall, D. L. 'Filippo Fasanini and his *Explanation of Sacred Writing*', *Journal of Medieval and Renaissance Studies*, 13/1, 1983, 127–55.

Dubnov, Simon. *History of the Jews: From the Late Middle Ages to the Renaissance*. New York: 1969.

Duby, Georges, and Philippe Ariès, eds. *A History of Private Life II: Reflections of the Medieval World*. Translated by Arthur Goldhammer. Cambridge, MA, and London: 1988.

Dufner, Georg. 'Il Beato Giovanni Tavelli vescovo gesuato', in *Il Beato Giovanni Tavelli di Ferrara nel VI centenario della nascita (1386–1446)*. Ferrara: 1987.

Dunkerton, Jill. 'Cosimo Tura as Painter and Draughtsman: The Cleaning and Examination of his *Saint Jerome*,' *National Gallery Technical Bulletin*, 15, 1994, 42–54.

Dunkerton, Jill. 'La *Vergine Annunciata* di Cosmè Tura', *OPD Restauro*, 5, 1993, 16–22.

Dunkerton, Jill, Ashok Roy and Alistair Smith. 'The Unmasking of Tura's *Allegorical Figure*: A Painting and its Concealed Image', *National Gallery Technical Bulletin*, 11, 1987, 5–35.

Edgerton, Samuel, J., Jr. 'Mensurare temporalia facit geometria spiritualis: Some fifteenth century notions about when and where the Annunciation happened', in I. Lavin and J. Plummer, ed. *Studies in Medieval and Renaissance Painting in Honor of Millard Meiss*. New York: 1978, vol. I, 115–30.

Eisler, Colin. *The Genius of Jacopo Bellini*. New York: 1989.

Elias, Norbert. *The Court Society*. Translated by E. Jephcott. New York: 1983.

Elias, Norbert. *Power and Civility*. Vol. II of *The Civilizing Process*. Translated by E. Jephcott. New York: 1982.

Elkins, James. 'On Monstrously Ambiguous Paintings', *History and Theory*, XXXII/3, 1993, 227–47.

Eörsi, Anna. 'Lo studiolo di Leonello d'Este e il programma di Guarino da Verona', *Acta Historiae Artium Accademicae Scientarum Hungaricae*, 21, 1975, 15–52.

Farquhar, James Douglas. 'Identity in an Anonymous Age: Bruges Manuscript Illuminators and their Signs', *Viator*, II, 1980, 371–85.

Fava, Domenico. *La Biblioteca Estense nel suo sviluppo storico*. Modena: 1925.

Fermor, Sharon. *Studies in the Depiction of the Moving Figure in Italian Renaissance Art, Art Criticism and Dance Theory*. Ph.D. dissertation, University of London, Warburg Institute: 1990.

Ferrara, 1982. *La Cattedrale di Ferrara: Atti del convegno dell'Accademia delle scienze di Ferrara*. Ferrara: 1982.

Ferraresi, Guerrino. *Il Beato Giovanni Tavelli da Tossignano e la riforma di Ferrara nel quattrocento*. 4 vols. Brescia: 1969.

Ferrari, Virgilio. *L'araldica estense nello sviluppo storico del dominio ferrarese*. Ferrara: 1989.

Ferri, Ferruccio. *La giovinezza di un poeta: Basinii Parmensi Carmina*. Rimini: 1914.

Festugière, A. J. *La révélation d'Hermès Trismegiste*. Paris: 1950–54.

Filarete. *Trattato di architettura*. Edited by Anna Maria Finoli and Lilianna Grassi. 2 vols. Milan: 1972.

Filarete. *Treatise on Architecture*. Translated by John Spencer. 2 vols. London and New Haven: 1965.

Fioravanti, Gianfranco. 'Polemiche antigiudaiche nell'Italia del quattrocento: Un tentativo di interpretazione globale', in *Ebrei e cristiani nell'Italia medievale e moderna: Conversioni, scambi, contrasti* (Atti del VI convegno internazionale dell'Associazione Internazionale per Studi Giudaichi). Rome: 1988, 75–91.

Fioravanti, Gianfranco. 'Gianozzo Manetti, l'*Adversus Judaeos et Gentes*, e l'altare del *Corpus Domini* a Urbino', in G. Chittolini *et al. Federico da Montefeltro: Le arti*. Rome: 1986, 177–87.

Fioravanti, Gianfranco. 'L'apologetica antigiu-

daica di Gianozzo Manetti', *Rinascimento*, n.s. 23, 1983, 3–32.

Fisher, Alan. 'Three Meditations on the Destruction of Virgil's Statue: The Early Humanist Theory of Poetry', *Renaissance Quarterly*, XL/4, 1987, 607–36.

Florence, 1720. *Carmina illustrium poetarum italorum*. 8 vols. Florence, Johannes Cajetanus, 1720.

Fowden, Garth. *The Egyptian Hermes: A Historical Approach to the Late Pagan Mind*. Cambridge: 1986.

Franceschini, Adriano. *Artisti a Ferrara in età umanistica e rinascimentale: Testimonianze archivistiche*, Part I: *dal 1341 al 1471*; Part II, vol. I: *dal 1472 al 1492*, Ferrara, 1995.

Franceschini, Adriano. 'Associazioni laiche ferraresi di gravitazione francescana nei secoli XIII–XV', *Analecta Pomposiana*, VII, 1982, 185–248.

Franceschini, Adriano. 'Confraternite di disciplinati a Ferrara avanti il Concilio Tridentino', *Atti e memorie della deputazione provinciale Ferrarese di storia patria*, ser. iii, 19, 1975.

Freud, Sigmund. 'Medusa's Head', in J. Strachey, ed. *Standard Edition of the Works of Sigmund Freud*. London: 1953, vol. 18, 273–4.

Friedmann, Herbert. *A Bestiary for St. Jerome*. Washington, D.C.: 1980.

Frizzi, Antonio. *Memorie per la storia di Ferrara*. 5 vols. Ferrara: 1847–8.

Fulgentius. *The Mythologies*, in Leslie George Whitbread, *Fulgentius the Mythographer*. Colombus, OH: 1971.

Funkenstein, Amos. 'Basic Types of Christian Anti-Jewish Polemics in the Middle Ages', *Viator*, 2, 1971, 373–82.

Gardner, Edmund. *Dukes and Poets in Ferrara*. London: 1904.

Garin, Eugenio. *Astrology in the Renaissance. The Zodiac of Life*. Translated by Carolyn Jackson and June Allen. London: 1983.

Garin, Eugenio. *Il pensiero pedagogico dello umanesimo*. Florence: 1958.

Gilbert, Creighton. 'Cosimo di Domenico di Bonaventura (Cosmè Tura)'. *Dizionario biografico degli italiani*, vol. 30. Rome: 1984, 25–30.

Gilbert, Creighton. *Italian Art 1400–1500: Sources and Documents*. Englewood Cliffs, NJ: 1980.

Gino, P. and M. Zanotti. *La Basilica di San Francesco di Ferrara*. Genoa: 1958.

Giovanni da Ferrara, Fra. 'Excerpta ex Annalium Libris illustris Familiae Marchionum

Estensium, 1409–1454', *Rerum Italicarum Scriptores*, XX, ii. Bologna: 1936.

Glasser, Hannelore. *Artists' Contracts of the Early Renaissance*. Ph.D. dissertation, Columbia University, New York, 1965.

Gnudi, Cesare, with Antonio Sorrentino. 'Restauro delle ante d'organo di Cosmè Tura nella cattedrale di Ferrara', *Bollettino d'arte*, III, 1948, 262–5.

Goldberg, Jonathan. *Writing Matter from the Hands of the English Renaissance*. Stanford, CA: 1990.

Goldberg, Jonathan. *James I and the Politics of Literature*. Stanford, CA: 1989.

Grafton, Anthony. *Defenders of the Text: Traditions of Scholarship in an Age of Science, 1450–1800*. Cambridge, MA, and London: 1991.

Grafton, Anthony, and Lisa Jardine. *From Humanism to the Humanities: Education and the Liberal Arts in Fifteenth and Sixteenth Century Europe*. London: 1984.

Grafton, Anthony, and Lisa Jardine. 'Humanism and the School of Guarino: A Problem of Evaluation', *Past and Present*, 96, 1982, 51–80.

Grammaccini, Norberto. 'Wie Jacopo Bellini Pisanello Besiegte: Der Ferrareser Wettbewerb von 1441', *Idea: Jahrbuch der Hamburger Kunsthalle*, I, 1982, 27–53.

Grassi, Ernesto. *Renaissance Humanism: Studies in Philosophy and Poetics*. Binghamton, NY: 1988.

Grayson, Cecil. 'The *construzzione leggitima* of Leon Battista Alberti', *Italian Studies*, 19, 1964, 1–27.

Grayson, Cecil. 'Studi su Leon Battista Alberti', *Rinascimento*, IV, 1953, 45–62.

Greenblatt, Stephen. 'Resonance and Wonder', in P. Collier and H. Geyer-Ryan, *Literary Theory Today*. Cambridge: 1990, 74–90.

Greenblatt, Stephen. *Renaissance Self-Fashioning: From More to Shakespeare*. Chicago: 1980.

Greene, Thomas. *The Light in Troy: Imitation and Discovery in Renaissance Poetry*. New Haven: 1983.

Gruyer, Gustave. *L'art ferrarais à l'époque des princes d'Este*. 2 vols. Paris: 1897.

Guidoni, Enrico, and Angela Marino. 'Cosmus Pictor: Il nuovo organo di Ferrara: Armonia, storia, e alchimia della creazione', *Storia dell'arte*, I, 1968, 388–416.

Gundersheimer, Werner. *Ferrara: The Style of a Renaissance Despotism*. Princeton: 1973.

Hankins, James. 'A Manuscript of Plato's Republic in the Translation of Chrysoloras and Uberto Decembrio with Annotations of Guarino Veronese', in Hankins, John Monfasani and Frederick Purnell Jr., ed., *Supplementum Festivum: Studies in Honor of Paul Oskar Kristeller*. Binghamton, NY: 1987, 149–84.

Hanson, Anne Coffin. *Jacopo della Quercia's Fonte Gaia*. Oxford: 1965.

Hay, Denis. *The Church in Italy in the Fifteenth Century*. Cambridge: 1977.

Heninger, S. K., Jr. *Touches of Sweet Harmony: Pythagorean Cosmology and Renaissance Poetics*. San Marino, CA: 1974.

Hermann, H. J. 'Zur Geschichte der Miniaturmalerei zum Hofe der Este in Ferrara', *Jahrbuch der kunsthistorischen Sammlungen des allerhöchsten Kaiserhauses*, XXI, 1900, 114–271.

Hill, G. F. *A Corpus of Italian Medals of the Renaissance before Cellini*. 2 vols. London: 1930.

Hirn, Yrjö. *The Sacred Shrine: The Poetry and Art of the Catholic Church*. London: 1912.

Hughes, Diana Owen. 'Distinguishing Signs: Ear-Rings, Jews and Franciscan Rhetoric in the Italian Renaissance City', *Past and Present*, 112, 1986, 3–59.

Jacobsen, Michael A., and Vivian Jean Rogers-Price. 'The Dolphin in Renaissance Art', *Studies in Iconography*, 9, 1983, 31–56.

Jacobus, Mary. 'Judith, Holofernes and the Phallic Woman', in *Reading Women: Essays in Feminist Criticism*. New York: 1986, 110–36.

Janus Pannonius. *Jani Pannonii Carmina Selectiora*. Edited by Tibor Kardos. Budapest: 1973.

Jarzombek, Mark. *Leon Battista Alberti: Literary and Aesthetic Theories*. Cambridge: 1989.

Jed, Stephanie H. *Chaste Thinking: The Rape of Lucretia and the Birth of Humanism*. Bloomington, IN: 1989.

Johannes Ferrariensis. 'Excerpta ex annalium libris illustris familiae marchionum Estensium', *Rerum Italicarum Scriptores*, 20, Part ii. Bologna: 1936.

John Climacus. *The Ladder of Divine Ascent*. Translated by C. Luibheid and N. Russell. New York: 1982.

Kaeppeli, Tommaso. 'Tommaso dai Liuti di Ferrara e il suo *Declaratorio*', *Archivum fratrum praedicatorum*, 20, 1950, 195–206.

Kaftal, George. *Iconography of the Saints in the Painting of North West Italy*. Florence: 1985.

Kaftal, George. *Iconography of the Saints in the Painting of North East Italy*. Florence: 1978.

Kaftal, George. *Iconography of the Saints in Central Italy*. Florence: 1965.

Kantorowicz, Ernst. 'The Este Portrait by Rogier van der Weyden', *Journal of the Warburg and Courtauld Institutes*, 3, 1939–40, 165–80.

Kemp, Martin, ed. *Leonardo On Painting*. New Haven and London: 1989.

Kemp, Martin. 'Equal Excellences: Lomazzo and the Explanation of Individual Style in the Visual Arts', *Renaissance Studies*, I/1, 1988, 1–27.

Kessler, Herbert. 'Pictures Fertile with Truth: How Christians Managed to Make Images of God without Violating the Second Commandment', *Journal of the Walters Art Gallery*, 49/50, 1991/2, 53–65.

Kessler, Herbert. 'Medieval Art as Argument', in Brendan Cassidy, ed. *Iconography at the Crossroads*. Princeton: 1991, 59–75.

Kieckhefer, Richard. 'Holiness and the Culture of Devotion: Remarks on some Late Medieval Male Saints', in R. Blumenfeld-Kosinski and T. Szell, eds. *Images of Sainthood in Medieval Europe*. Ithaca, NY: 1991, 288–306.

Kieckhefer, Richard. *Unquiet Souls: Fourteenth Century Saints and their Religious Milieu*. Chicago: 1984.

Kristeller, Paul Otto. 'The Modern System of the Arts', in Kristeller, *Renaissance Thought II: Papers on Humanism and the Arts*. New York: 1965, 163–228.

Lactantius, Caius Firmianus. *The Divine Institutes*. Translated by Mary Francis McDonald. Washington, DC: 1964.

Ladner, Gerhart B. 'Aspects of Patristic Anti-Judaism', *Viator*, 2, 1971, 355–63.

Lavin, Marilyn A. 'The Altarpiece of Corpus Domini in Urbino: Paolo Uccello, Joos van Ghent and Piero della Francesca', *Art Bulletin*, XLIX, 1967, 1–24.

Lazzari, Alfonso. 'Il *Barco* di Ludovico Carbone', *Atti e Memorie della deputazione Ferrarese di storia patria*, XXIV/1, 1919, 5–44.

Levi, Ezio. *Francesco da Vanozzo e la lirica nelle corte lombarde durante la seconda metà del secolo XIV*. Florence: 1908.

Lichtenstein, Jacqueline. 'Making up Representation: The Risks of Femininity', *Representations*, 20, 1987, 77–87.

Liebenwein, Wolfgang. *Studiolo: Storia e tipologia di uno spazio culturale*. Translated by C. Cieri Via. Modena: 1988.

Lightbown, Ronald. *Mantegna*. Oxford: 1986.

Lincoln, Evelyn. 'Mantegna's Culture of Line', *Art History*, 16/1, 1993, 33–57.

Lippincott, Kristen. 'Tura, Cosimo', in Jane

Turner, ed. *The Dictionary of Art*. London: 1996, vol. 31, 428–33.

Lippincott, Kristen. 'Mantegna and the *Scientia* of Painting', in F. Ames-Lewis and A. Bednarek, *Mantegna and Fifteenth-Century Court Culture*. London: 1993, 45–56.

Lippincott, Kristen. 'The Genesis and Significance of the Fifteenth Century Italian *Impresa*', in Sydney Angelo, ed. *Chivalry in the Renaissance*. Woodbridge, Suffolk: 1991.

Lippincott, Kristen. 'The Neo-Latin Epics of the North Italian Courts', *Renaissance Studies*, III/4, 1990, 422–5.

Lippincott, Kristen. *The Frescoes of the Salone dei Mesi in the Palazzo Schifanoia in Ferrara: Style, Iconography and Cultural Context*. Ph.D. dissertation, University of Chicago: 1987.

Litta, Pompeo. *Famiglie celebri italiane*. 11 vols. Milan: 1819/1856–85 [unpaginated].

Lockwood, Lewis. *Music in Renaissance Ferrara, 1400–1505*. Cambridge, MA: 1984.

Lombardi, P. Teodosio. 'I corali miniati del Duomo', in *La Cattedrale di Ferrara: Atti del Convegno dell'Accademia delle Scienze di Ferrara*. Ferrara: 1982, 353–411.

Lombardi, P. Teodosio. 'Le corporazioni di arti e mestieri a Ferrara dal 1173 al 1796', *La Pianura*, 4, 1976, 3–20.

Lombardi, P. Teodosio. *I Francescani a Ferrara*. 4 vols. Bologna: 1974–5.

London, 1984. *From Borso to Cesare d'Este: The School of Ferrara 1450–1628*. Exhibition catalogue, London, Matthiesen Fine Art Ltd, 1984.

Longhi, Roberto. *Officina Ferrarese*. Rome: 1934; with *Ampliamenti*, Florence: 1956.

Lorch, Maristella de Panizza. *Il teatro italiano del rinascimento*. Milan: 1980.

Ludwig, Walther. 'The Origin and Development of the Catullan Style in Neo-Latin Poetry', In Peter Godman and Oswyn Murray, ed. *Latin Poetry and the Classical Tradition: Essays in Medieval and Renaissance Literature*. Oxford: 1990.

Ludwig, Walther. *Die Borsias des Tito Strozzi*. Munich: 1977.

Lugano, Placido. *Memorie dei piu antichi miniatori e calligrafi olivetani*. Florence: 1903.

MacLean, Ian. *The Renaissance Notion of Women*. Cambridge: 1980.

McLaughlin, Mary Martin. 'Creating and Recreating Communities of Women: The Case of Corpus Domini, Ferrara, 1406–1452', *Signs*, 14/2, 1989, 261–88.

McMenamon, John J. *Funeral Oratory and the Cultural Ideals of Italian Humanism*. Chapel Hill, NC: 1989.

Macioce, Stefania. 'Il *San Girolamo* di Cosmè Tura e le disputi ereticali del secondo quattrocento', *Musei Ferraresi*, 15, 1985–7, 28–38.

Manca, Joseph. *The Art of Ercole de' Roberti*. Cambridge: 1992.

Manca, Joseph. 'A Note on Cosmè Tura as Portraitist', *Antichità viva*, XXX/3, 1991, 17–20.

Manca, Joseph. 'A Ferrarese Painter of the Quattrocento', *Gazette des beaux-arts*, CXVI, November 1990, 157–72.

Manca, Joseph. 'Renaissance Theater and Hebrew Ritual in Ercole de'Roberti's *Gattering of the Manna*', *Artibus et historiae*, 17, 1988, 137–48.

Mantuan (Mantuanus), Baptista (Battista Spagnoli). *Fastorum libri duodecim*. Strasbourg: Schurer, 1518.

Marin, Louis. *Opacité de la peinture: Essais sur le représentation au quattrocento*. Paris: 1989.

Martineau, Jane, ed. *Andrea Mantegna*. Exhibition catalogue, London, Royal Academy, and New York, Metropolitan: 1992.

Martinelli, Lucia Cesarini. 'Metafori teatrali in Leon Battista Alberti', *Rinascimento*, 29, 1989, 3–53.

Medri, Gualtiero. *La scultura a Ferrara*. Rovigo: 1958.

Meinhoff, Werner. 'Leonardos *Hieronymus*', *Repertorium für Kunstwissenschaft*, 52, 1931, 101–25.

Mellinkoff, Ruth. *The Horned Moses in Medieval Art and Thought*. Berkeley: 1970.

Meneghin, Vittorio. *Bernardino da Feltre e i Monti di Pietà*. Vicenza: 1974.

Meyer-Baer, Kathi. *Music of the Spheres and the Dance of Death: Studies in Musical Iconology*. Princeton: 1970.

Miner, V., P. Carlson and P. W. Filby. *Two Thousand Years of Calligraphy*. Baltimore: Walters Art Gallery, 1965.

Mitchell, Charles. 'Felice Feliciano Antiquarius', *Proceedings of the British Academy*, XLVII, 1961, 197–223.

Molajoli, Rosemarie. *L'opera completa di Cosmè Tura e i grandi pittori ferraresi del suo tempo*. Milan: 1974.

Monfasani, John, ed. *Collectanea Trapezuntiana*. Binghamton, NY: 1984.

Monfasani, John. *George of Trebizond: A Biography and a Study of his Rhetoric and Logic*. Leiden: 1976.

Moroni, Gaetano. *Dizionario di erudizione storico-ecclesiastica*. 103 vols., Venice: 1840–61.

Mottola-Molfino, Alessandra and Mauro Natali, ed. *Le Muse e il Principe: Arte di corte nel rinascimento padano*. Exhibition catalogue, 2 vols., Milan, Museo Poldi-Pezzoli, 1991.

Nicolson, Benedict. *The Painters of Ferrara*. London: 1950.

Norris, Andrea S. 'The Sforza of Milan', *Schifanoia*, 10, 1990, 19–22.

North, John. 'Celestial Influence. The Major Premiss of Astrology', in Zambelli, 1986, 45–100.

North, John. 'Astrology and the Fortunes of Churches', *Centaurus*, XXIV, 1980, 181–211.

O'Malley, John J. *Praise and Blame in Renaissance Rome*. Durham, NC: 1979.

Origo, Iris. *The World of San Bernardino*. New York: 1962.

Ortolani, Sergio. *Cosimo Tura, Francesco del Cossa, Ercole de' Roberti*. Milan: 1941.

Osgood, Charles G. *Boccaccio on Poetry: Being the Preface and the Fourteenth and Fifteenth Books of Boccaccio's Genealogia Deorum Gentilium*. Indianapolis and New York: 1956.

Osley, A. S. *Scribes and Sources*. Boston: 1980.

Ost, Hans. *Leonardo Studien*. Berlin: 1975.

(Pseudo) Ovid. *De vetula*. Edited by Dorothy Robathan. Amsterdam: 1968.

Padovani, Corrado. *La critica d'arte e la pittura Ferrarese*. Rovigo: 1954.

Palermino, R. J. 'The Roman Academy, the Catacombs and the Conspiracy of 1468', *Archivum storiam pontificae*, 18, 1980, 117–55.

Panizza, Laetitia. 'Italian Humanists and Boethius: Was Philosophy For or Against Poetry?', in John Henry and Sarah Hutton, ed. *New Perspectives on Renaissance Thought: Essays in the History of Science, Rhetoric and Philosophy*. London: 1990, 48–67.

Papagno, Giovanni, and Amadeo Quondam, ed. *La corte e lo spazio: Ferrara estense*. 3 vols. Rome: 1982.

Pardi, Giuseppe. *Leonello d'Este*. Bologna: 1904.

Park, Katherine. 'The Criminal and the Saintly Body', *Renaissance Quarterly*, XLVII/1, 1994, 1–33.

Park, Katherine. 'The Organic Soul', in C. B. Schmitt, ed. *The Cambridge History of Renaissance Philosophy*. Cambridge: 1987.

Parker, W. H. *Priapea: Songs for a Phallic God*. London: 1988.

Partner, Peter. 'Francesco dal Legname: A Curial Bishop in Disgrace', in P. Denley and C. Elam, ed., *Florence and Italy: Renaissance Studies in Honour of Nicolai Rubinstein*. London: 1988, 395–404.

Pasini Frassoni, Ferruccio. *Dizionario storico-araldico del antico ducato di Ferrara*. Rome: 1904.

Pasquazi, Silvio. *Poeti estensi del rinascimento*. Florence: 1966.

Pastor, Ludwig von. *The History of the Popes from the Close of the Middle Ages*. 5th edition. 40 vols., London: 1923.

Perles, J. 'Ahron ben Gerson Aboulrabi', *Revue des études juives*, 20, 1890, 246–69.

Perry, Jon Pearson. 'Practical and Ceremonial Uses of Plant Materials as "Literary Refinements" in the Libraries of Leonello d'Este and his Courtly Circle', *La bibliofilia*, XCI, 1989, II, 121–73.

Perry, Jon Pearson. 'A Fifteenth Century Dialogue on Literary Taste: Angelo Decembrio's Account of Playwright Ugolino Pisano at the Court of Leonello d'Este', *Renaissance Quarterly*, XXXIX/4, 1986, 613–43.

Pesaro, Abramo. *Memoire storiche sulla communità israelitica ferrarese*. Ferrara: 1878; Bologna: 1986.

Peverada, Enrico. 'Un organo per Leonello d'Este', *L'Organo*, XXVIII, 1993–4, 1–30.

Peverada, Enrico. *Vita musicale nella chiesa ferrarese del quattrocento*. Ferrara: 1991.

Peverada, Enrico. 'Attestati di santità nel quattrocento per il vescovo di Ferrara Giovanni Tavelli', *Analecta Pomposiana*, 14, 1989, 63–108.

Peverada, Enrico. 'La tonsura clericale di Cosimo Tura', *Analecta Pomposiana*, 10, 1985, 159–68.

Peverada, Enrico. *La visita pastorale del vescovo Francesco dal Legname a Ferrara (1447–1450)*. Ferrara: 1982.

Piacentini, Paola Scarcia. 'Angelo Decembrio e la sua scrittura', *Scrittura e civiltà*, IV, 1980, 247–77.

Piccolomini, Aeneas Silvius. *The Commentaries*. Translated by Florence Alden Gragg with Leona Christine Gebel. *Smith College Studies in History*, XXII/1–2, 1936–7; XXV/1–4, 1939–40; XXX, 1947; XXXV, 1951; XLIII, 1957.

Piccolomini, Aeneas Silvius (Pius II). *Epistolae in pontificatu editae*. Milan: Antonius Zarothus, 1481.

Pliny the Elder. *Natural History*. Edited and translated by H. Rackham, Loeb Classical Library. Cambridge, MA: 1952.

Po-Chia Hsia, R. *Trent 1475: Studies of a Ritual Murder Trial*. New Haven and London: 1992.

Ponsi, D. *Vita della Beata Lucia Vergine di Narni*. Rome: 1709.

Pontano, Giovanni Gioviano. *Poesie latine*. Edited by Liliana Monti Babia. 2 vols. Turin: 1977.

Pontano, Giovanni Gioviano. *Carmina*. Edited by B. Soldati. 2 vols. Florence: 1902.

Pouchelle, M. C. 'Représentations du corps dans la *Légende dorée*', *Ethnologie française*, 6, 1976, 293–308.

Prete, Sesto. *Studies in Latin Poets of the Quattrocento*. Lawrence, KS: 1978.

Prosperi, Adriano. 'Le istituzioni ecclesiastiche e le idee religiose', in *Il rinascimento nelle corti padane: Società e cultura*. Bari: 1977, 125–63.

Ragghianti, Licia Collobi. *Dipinti Fiamminghi in Italia 1420–1570*. Bologna: 1990.

Rajna, Pio. 'Ricordi di codici francesi posseduti dagli Estensi nel sec. xv', *Romania*, II, 1873, 49–58.

Rice, Eugene F. *St. Jerome in the Renaissance*. Baltimore: 1985.

Righini, G. 'Cosimo Tura a San Giorgio', *Atti e memorie dell deputazione provinciale Ferrarese per la storia patria*, IV, 1953, 93–110.

Robey, David. 'Humanist Views on the Study of Poetry in the Early Renaissance', *History of Education*, 13, 1984, 7–25.

Rome, 1986. *Un pontificato ed una città: Sisto IV*. Rome: Associazione Roma nel Rinascimento, 1986.

Rosalind-Jones, Ann, and Peter Stallybrass. 'Fetishizing Gender: Constructing the Hermaphrodite in Renaissance Europe', in Julia Epstein and Kristina Straub, ed. *Bodyguards: The Cultural Politics of Gender Ambiguity*. New York: 1991, 80–111.

Rosenberg, Charles. 'The Iconography of the Sala degli Stucchi in the Palazzo Schifanoia in Ferrara', *Art Bulletin*, 61, 1979, 377–84.

Rosenberg, Charles. 'Per il bene di . . . nostra cipta: Borso d'Este and the Certosa of Ferrara', *Renaissance Quarterly*, XXIX/3, 1976, 329–40.

Rosenberg, Charles. 'Francesco Cossa's Letter Reconsidered', *Musei Ferraresi*, 5/6, 1975–6, 11–16.

Rosenberg, Charles. *Art in Ferrara during the Reign of Borso d'Este (1450–1471): A Study in Court Patronage*. Ph.D. dissertation, University of Michigan: 1974.

Roth, Cecil. *The Jews in the Renaissance*. Philadelphia: 1959.

Rotondò, Antonio. 'Pellegrino Prisciani, 1435–1518', *Rinascimento*, IX, 1960, 69–110.

Rubin, Gayle. 'The Traffic in Women: Notes on the "Political Economy" of Sex', in Rayna Reiter, ed. *Toward an Anthropology of Women*. New York: 1975.

Ruderman, David B. 'The Italian Renaissance and Jewish Thought', in Albert Rabil Jr., ed.

Renaissance Humanism: Foundations, Forms and Legacy. Philadelphia: 1988, vol. II, 382–434.

Ruderman, David B. *The World of a Renaissance Jew: The Life and Thought of Abraham ben Mordecai Farissol*. Cincinnati: 1981.

Ruhmer, Eberhard. *Cosimo Tura: Paintings and Drawings*. London: 1958.

Sabbadini, Remigio. *Classicisti e umanisti negli codici Ambrosiani*. Florence: 1933.

Sabbadini, Remigio, ed. *Epistolario di Guarino Veronese*. 3 vols. Venice, 1915–19.

Sabbadini, Remigio. *La scuola e gli studi di Guarino Guarini Veronese*. Catania: 1896.

Sabbadini, Remigio. *L'Angineletum di Giovanni Marrasio*. Verona: 1892.

Sabbadini, Remigio. *Biografia documentata di Giovanni Aurispa*. Noto: 1890.

Sabbadini, Remigio. 'Se Guarino abbia fatto una recensione di Catullo', *Studi Vergiliani*, 1885, 27–30.

Salutati, Coluccio. *De laboribus Herculis*. Edited by Berthold Ullman. Zurich: 1951.

Salza, A. E. Kader, ed. *Facezie di Lodovico Carbone Ferrarese*. Livorno: 1900.

Salmi, Mario. *Cosmè Tura*. Milan: 1957.

Samaritani, Antonio. 'Gli Olivetani nella società ferrarese del'400: Tra Estensi e movimenti di riforma', *Analecta Pomposiana*, 6: *Studi Monastici*, 1981, 75–145.

Samaritani, Antonio. 'Michele Savonarola, riformatore cattolico nella Corte Estense a metà del sec. xv', *Atti e memorie della deputazione provinciale Ferrarese di storia patria*, ser. 3, XXII, 1976, 44–64.

Samaritani, Antonio. 'Ailisia de Baldo e le correnti reformatrici femminili de Ferrara nella prima meta del sec. xv', *Atti e memorie della deputazione provinciale Ferrarese di storia patria*, ser. 3, XIII, 1973, 91–157.

Scaglione, Aldo. *Knights at Court: Courtly Chivalry and Courtesy from Ottonian Germany to the Italian Renaissance*. Berkeley and Los Angeles: 1991.

Scalabrini, Giuseppe Antenore. *Memorie istoriche delle chiese di Ferrara e di suoi borghi*. Ferrara: 1773.

Sedgwick, Eve Kosofsky. *Between Men: English Literature and Male Homosocial Desire*. New York: 1986.

Seymour, Charles. *Jacopo della Quercia, Sculptor*. New Haven and London: 1973.

Seznec, Jean. *The Survival of the Pagan Gods: The Mythological Tradition and its Place in Renaissance Humanism and Art*. Princeton and New York: 1953, 1972.

Sgarbi, Vittorio. *Antonio del Crevalcore e la*

pittura ferrarese del quattrocento a Bologna. Milan: 1985.

Shearman, John. 'Maniera as an Aesthetic Ideal', in Creighton Gilbert, ed. *Renaissance Art*. New York: 1970.

Simonsohn, Schlomo. *The Apostolic See and the Jews*. Vol. II, *1394–1464*. Toronto: 1989; Vol. III: *1464–1521*. Toronto: 1990.

Sitta, Pietro. 'Le Università delle Arti a Ferrara dal secolo XII al secolo XVIII', *Atti e memorie della deputazione Ferrarese di storia patria*, VIII, 1896, 5–204.

Spezzani, Paolo. *Riflettoscopia e Indagini non distruttive*, Milan, 1992.

Springarn, J. E. *A History of Literary Criticism in the Renaissance*. New York: 1899, 1924.

Starn, Randolph, and Loren Partridge. *Arts of Power: Three Halls of State in Renaissance Italy*. Berkeley: 1992.

Starn, Randolph. 'Seeing Culture in a Room for a Renaissance Prince', in L. Hunt, ed. *The New Cultural History*, Berkeley: 1989.

Steinberg, Leo. 'How Shall This Be? Reflections on Filippo Lippi's *Annunciation* in London', *Artibus et Historiae*, 16, 1987, 25–45.

Steinberg, Leo. *The Sexuality of Christ in Renaissance Art and Modern Oblivion*. New York: 1983.

Steinberg, S. H. 'Medieval Writing Masters', *The Library*, 4th ser., 22, 1941–2.

Stemp, Richard. *Sculpture in Ferrara in the Fifteenth Century: Problems and Studies*. Ph.D. dissertation, University of Cambridge: 1992.

Stemp, Richard. 'Cosimo Tura and the Sacrati Chapels in Ferrara', *Musei Ferraresi*, 17, 1990–91, 61–70.

Stendardo, Guido. 'L'*Iside* di Francesco Ariosto', *Archivum Romanicum*, XX/1, 1936, 114–22.

Stinger, Charles L. *The Renaissance in Rome*. Bloomington, IN: 1985.

Suida, W. *Leonardo und sein Kreis*. Munich: 1929.

Summers, David. *The Judgement of Sense: Renaissance Naturalism and the Rise of Aesthetics*. Cambridge: 1986.

Synan, Edward. *The Pope and the Jews in the Middle Ages*. New York: 1965.

Tagliabue, M. 'L'anonima *Vita* latina di san Maurelio martire vescovo di Ferrara e il *De inventione* di Matteo Ronto', *Analecta Pomposiana*, 6: *Studi Monastici*, 1981, 221–63.

Tagliati, Gilberto. 'Relazione tra al famiglia Romei e la corte estense nel secolo XV', *Il rinascimento nelle corti padane: Società e cultura*. Bari: 1977, 61–77.

Tanaka, Hidemichi. 'Oriental Scripts in the Painting of Giotto's Period', *Gazette des beaux-arts*, CXII, 1989, 214–21.

Tester, James. *A History of Western Astrology*. Woodbridge, Suffolk: 1987.

Thomson, Ian. *Humanist Pietas: The Panegyric of Ianus Pannonius on Guarinus Veronensis*. Bloomington, IN: 1988.

Thorndike, Lynn. *A History of Magic and Experimental Science*. 8 vols. New York: 1934.

Toaff, Ariel. 'Conversioni al cristianesimo in Italia nel quattrocento: Movimenti e tendenze: il caso dell'Umbria', in M. Luzzati *et al. Ebrei e cristiani nell'Italia medioevale e moderna*. Rome: 1988.

Todeschini, Giacomo. 'Ebrei in Italia alla fine del medioevo: Studi recenti', *Studi medievali*, 30, 1989, 351–66.

Trachtenberg, Joshua. *The Devil and the Jews: The Medieval Conception of the Jew and its Relation to Modern Antisemitism*. 2nd edition. Philadelphia: 1983.

Trexler, Richard C., ed. *Persons in Groups: Social Behaviour as Identity Formation in Medieval and Renaissance Europe*. Binghamton, NY: 1985.

Trexler, Richard C. *Public Life in Renaissance Florence*. Ithaca, NY: 1980.

Trexler, Richard C. 'Florentine Religious Experience: The Sacred Image', *Studies in the Renaissance*, XIX, 1972, 7–41.

Trinkaus, Charles. *In Our Image and Likeness: Humanity and Divinity in Italian Humanist Thought*. London: 1970.

Tristano, Richard C. 'Vassals, Fiefs and Social Mobility in Ferrara in the Middle Ages and Renaissance'. *Medievalia et humanistica*, 15, 1987, 43–64.

Tristano, Richard C. *Ferrara in the Fifteenth Century: Borso d'Este and the Development of a New Nobility*. Ph.D. dissertation, New York University: 1983.

Trithemius, Johannes. *De laude scriptorum*. Edited by Klaus Arnold. Lawrence, KS: 1974.

Tuohy, Thomas. *Herculean Ferrara: Ercole d'Este, 1471–1505, and the Invention of a Ducal Capital*. Cambridge: 1996.

Tuohy, Thomas. Review of *Le Muse e il Principe*. *Apollo*, 134, December 1991, 425–7.

Tuohy, Thomas. *Studies in Domestic Expenditure at the Court of Ferrara, 1451–1505*. Ph.D. dissertation, University of London: 1982.

Turrill, Catherine. *Ercole de' Roberti's Altarpieces for the Lateran Canons*. Ph.D dissertation, University of Delaware: 1986.

Ullman, Berthold. *The Origin and Development of Humanist Script*. Rome: 1960.

Valentini, Giuseppe. 'La sospensione della crociata nei primi anni di Paolo II (1464–68)', *Archivium historiam pontificae*, 14, 1976, 71–103.

Van de Waal, Hans. 'The Linea Summae Tenuitatis of Apelles: Pliny's Phrase and its Interpreters', *Zeitschrift für Aesthetik und Allgemeine Kunstwissenschaft*, XII/1, 1967, 5–32.

Van Marle, Raimond. *Iconographie de l'art profane au Moyen-Age et à la Renaissance*. The Hague: 1932.

Van Os, Hendrick. 'Vecchietta and the Persona of the Renaissance Artist', in I. Lavin and J. Plummer, ed. *Studies in Late Medieval and Renaissance Painting in Honor of Millard Meiss*. New York: 1977, 445–53.

Varese, Rainieri, and Luciano Olivato, eds. *San Giorgio tra Ferrara e Praga*. Exhibition catalogue, Ferrara, Castello Estense: 1991.

Varese, Rainieri, ed. *Atlante di Schifanoia*. Modena: 1990.

Vasari, Giorgio. *Le opere di Giorgio Vasari*. Edited by Gaetano Milanesi. 9 vols. Florence, 1906.

Vasoli, Cesare. 'L'astrologia a Ferrara tra la metà del quattrocento e la metà del cinquecento', in *Il rinascimento nelle corti padane: Società e cultura*. Bari: 1977, 469–95.

Vast, Henri. *Le Cardinal Bessarion*. Paris: 1878; Geneva: 1977.

Vauchez, André. *La sainteté en occident aux derniers siècles du moyen age*. Rome: 1988.

Vegri, Caterina. *Le armi necessarie alla battaglia spirituale*. Bologna: 1614.

Venturi, Adolfo. 'Documento per la determinazione approssimativa della data della nascita di Cosmè Tura', *Archivio storico dell'arte*, 2, 1894, 52–3.

Venturi, Adolfo. 'L'arte a Ferrara nel periodo di Ercole d'Este', *Atti e memorie della R. deputazione di storia patria per le provincie di Romagna*, 6, 1888, 91–119 and 350–422, and 7, 1889, 368–412.

Venturi, Adolfo. 'Cosma Tura genannt Cosmè, 1432 bis 1495', *Jahrbuch der Königlich preussischen Kunstsammlungen*, 8, 1887, 3–33.

Venturi, Adolfo. 'L'arte a Ferrara nel periodo di Borso d'Este', *Rivista storica italiana*, II, 1885, 689–749.

Venturi, Adolfo. 'I primordi del rinascimento artistico ferrarese', *Rivista storica italiana*, I, 1884, 591–631.

Vespasiano da Bisticci. *Renaissance Princes, Popes and Prelates*. Translation of the *Vite di uomini illustri del secolo XV* by William George and Emily Waters. New York: 1963.

Vickers, Brian. 'Valla's Ambivalent Praise of Pleasure: Rhetoric in the Service of Christianity', *Viator*, 17, 1986, 271–321.

Voragine, Jacopo da. *Legenda aurea*. 13th century. Edited by T. Graesse. 2nd edition, Osnabrück: 1969.

Voraginus Jacobus de. *The Golden Legend*. Translated by William Granger Ryan. Princeton, 1993.

Walker, D. P. *Spiritual and Demonic Magic from Ficino to Campanella*. London: 1958.

Warburg, Aby. 'Italienische Kunst und internationale Astrologie im Palazzo Schifanoia zu Ferrara', *Die Erneurung der Heidnischen Antike*. Leipzig and Berlin: 1932, II, 445–82.

Warner, Marina. *Alone of All Her Sex: The Myth and Cult of the Virgin Mary*. London and New York: 1983.

Warnke, Martin. *The Court Artist: On the Ancestry of the Modern Artist*. Translated by D. McLintock. Cambridge: 1993.

Warnke, Martin. 'Praxisfelder der Kunsttheorie: Über die Geburtswehen des Individualstils', *Idea: Jahrbuch der Hamburger Kunsthalle*, I, 1982, 54–71.

Weinstein, Donald, and Rudolph M. Bell. *Saints and Society. The Two Worlds of Western Christendom, 1000–1700*. Chicago: 1982.

Weitzmann, Kurt. 'The Mandylion of Constantine Porphyrogennetos', *Studies in Classical and Byzantine Manuscript Illumination*. Chicago: 1971, 224–46.

Welch, Evelyn Samuels. *Art and Authority in Renaissance Milan*. New Haven and London: 1995.

Wilken, Robert L. *Judaism and the Early Christian Mind: A Study of Cyril of Alexandria's Exegesis and Theology*. New Haven: 1971.

Willard, Charity Cannon. 'The Concept of True Nobility at the Burgundian Court', *Studies in the Renaissance*, 14, 1967, 33–48.

Williams, Raymond. *Keywords: A Vocabulary of Culture and Society*. London: 1976, 1983.

Wilson, Nigel. *From Byzantium to Italy: Greek Studies in the Italian Renaissance*. Baltimore: 1992.

Wischnitzer, Rachel. *The Architecture of the European Synagogue*. Philadelphia: 1964.

Witt, Ronald G. 'Coluccio Salutati and the Conception of the *Poeta Theologus* in the Renaissance', *Renaissance Quarterly*, XXX/4, 1977, 53–70.

Woods-Marsden, Joanna. *The Gonzaga of*

Mantua and Pisanello's Arthurian Frescoes. Princeton: 1988.

Yates, Frances. *Giordano Bruno and the Hermetic Tradition.* Chicago: 1964.

Zambelli, Paola. *The 'speculum astronomiae' and its Enigma: Astrology, Theology and Science in Albertus Magnus and his Contemporaries.* Dordrecht, Boston and London: 1992.

Zambelli, Paola, ed. *'Astrologi hallucinati': Stars and the End of the World in Luther's Time.* Berlin and New York: 1986.

Zamboni, Silla. *Pittori di Ercole I d'Este: Giovan Francesco Mainieri, Lazzaro Grimaldi, Domenico Panetti, Michele Coltellini.* Milan: 1975.

Zambotti, Bernardino. *Diario Ferrarese dal anno 1476 sino al 1504.* Edited by G. Pardi. In *Rerum italicarum scriptores,* 24, Part 7, no. 2. Bologna: 1928.

Zeri, Federico. 'Renaissance and Pseudo-Renaissance'. Translated by C. Dorey in *History of Italian Art.* Cambridge: 1994, vol. II, 326–72.

Zinner, Ernst. *Regiomontanus: His Life and Work.* Translated by Ezra Brown. Amsterdam: 1990.

Zippel, Giuseppe. 'Artisti alla corte Estense nel'400', *L'arte,* 5, 1902, 405–7.

INDEX

PHOTOGRAPH CREDITS